Persuasion:
a means of social influence

Persuasion:
a means of social influence

SECOND EDITION

Winston L. Brembeck
University of Wisconsin

William S. Howell
University of Minnesota

Prentice-Hall, Inc., Englewood Cliffs, New Jersey

Library of Congress Cataloging in Publication Data

BREMBECK, WINSTON LAMONT.
    Persuasion, a means of social influence.

    Includes bibliographical references and index.
    1. Persuasion (Psychology) I. Howell, William
Smiley, joint author.   II. Title.
BF637.P4B65 1976   153.8'52   75-14435
ISBN   0-13-661090-0

To Neva and Jessie

©1976, 1952 by Prentice-Hall, Inc.
Englewood Cliffs, New Jersey

10 9 8 7 6 5 4 3 2 1

Printed in the United States of America

Prentice-Hall International, Inc., *London*
Prentice-Hall of Australia, Pty. Ltd., *Sydney*
Prentice-Hall of Canada, Ltd., *Toronto*
Prentice-Hall of India Private Limited, *New Delhi*
Prentice-Hall of Japan, Inc., *Tokyo*
Prentice-Hall of Southeast Asia (Pte.) Ltd., *Singapore*

Contents

Preface

Persuade or perish is becoming an alarmingly real disjunction as increasing numbers of people everywhere are forsaking free trade in ideas and are resorting to violence, threats of violence, and authoritarianism in attempts to gain their goals. Substituting force for more civilized forms of influence threatens our progress toward the reasoned settlement of differences among people. It must be clear to all astute observers that now more than ever before, our people in general and our students in particular must be aware of the principles and methods of persuasion if a free society is to remain free.

Since the first edition of this book was published, those who work with people rather than things have become a majority in the United States. The mass media, increased education, and modern means of transportation have brought together the ideas and problems of many people. Whereas some observers predicted that this condition would result in greater understanding, greater clash has often ensued. Social problems have acquired demonstrative and violent protagonists. Industry and labor find themselves in much more competitive practices. Political leaders and government have found themselves confronted by vocal and dissident groups. The churches have become more overtly active in the social scene, and education is finding itself on the defensive. In sum, we are not only living in the greatest persuasion density of all time, but in a society that is becoming restless as a result of its increased awareness of many conflicting interests.

Also, since the first edition of this book was written, a number of new insights into the nature of persuasion have been achieved. Theorists, experimentalists, and practitioners have provided additional knowledge with which the student of modern persuasion must be acquainted. This body of new knowledge comes primarily from scholars in public address, communications, psychology, social-psychology, sociology, anthropology, journalism, commerce and marketing, and, to a lesser extent, from traditional rhetoric. The authors believe that those new materials are of sufficient quality and quantity to necessitate this second and virtually entirely new edition of the original book. Because scholars in these various fields work from their own frames of reference and develop their own jargon, there has been a regrettable lack of synthesis of those materials into meaningful and useful forms for the person interested in persuasion as a theoretical as well as a practical study. This book attempts to provide this synthesis in as thorough and useful a manner as a single volume will permit. In our judgment, a textbook should be something more than a compilation of carefully footnoted research studies organized loosely around topics that lack a cementing principle. In short, we think a textbook should attempt to synthesize and interpret theoretical and practical materials to lead the reader toward the development of a meaningful approach to the study and practice of suasive discourse.

Finally, we have attempted to retain those qualities that users of the first edition have stated made of it a very readable and teachable textbook. The authors have been grateful for the wide reception the first edition of this book received. We trust this new edition may earn similar approval.

Persuasion:
a means of social influence

I

Introduction

Persuasion has been and will continue to be the chief instrument in the conduct of human affairs. Today our society—as well as the world in general—faces the greatest density and intensity of competing persuasions in man's history. To live effectively in such an environment the study of persuasion is not only necessary for those specializing in promotional activities, but requisite for all who produce and use persuasion in daily life.

The chapters of part 1 provide a modern approach to the study of persuasion by discussing the significance, characteristics, problems, and vehicles of persuasive communication. These chapters should help to orient the reader for the material presented in succeeding chapters.

1

The study of persuasion

The significance of the study of persuasion in contemporary education

The United States is now in the midst of a revolution: customs, values, and institutions are in a state of flux. To respond favorably to this new reality is difficult, but because this season of unrest and re-examination will surely be with us for the remainder of this century, we must acknowledge both its challenges and its distresses. Since change in a free society relies primarily on persuasion, let us begin our study of this mode of influence by reviewing briefly some of the characteristics of our society's conditions.

Today our newspapers, news magazines, television, radio, and many private and public speeches report that an ever-increasing number of our citizens are abandoning the traditional methods of a free and orderly society—persuasion by the written and spoken word—and are reverting to the more primitive methods of violence, threats of violence, and other kinds of planned unrest and revolt to achieve their goals. Riots, demonstrations, civil disobedience, wanton disregard for peaceful assembly, and general disruption of the normal processes of civil life often characterize the behavior of those with grievances, who desire social change. This is a time when the life of a president, a presidential candidate, or a noted civil rights leader is not safe from the assassin's bullet, when campus hecklers interrupt speakers with unpopular topics, when extremists suggest that minorities should get their rights "by any means," and when some even advocate open rebellion. This is a day when dissent is becoming conformity and when the defense of prevailing customs often requires more courage than attacking them. Our nation was born in dissent, and this right has been protected as indeed it should be. However, all too often the spirit of dissent has been followed by repressive actions that do not keep men free.

This disregard of the methods of oral and written persuasion is not confined to those who are involved in the civil rights movement, the question of American military intervention abroad, or student rights; it is increasingly apparent—perhaps less spectacularly—in the actions of other groups. Farm organizations, attempting to drive prices up, have used violence in their attempts to keep farmers from delivering their milk and livestock to market. Labor grievances have erupted into violence periodically for many years, and recently even religious leaders have argued in favor of violence to solve problems of poverty and civil rights. Still other examples of the abandonment of persuasion and reversion to the methods of violence could be cited, but these are enough to suggest a sobering trend away from the more peaceful methods of social influence.

The harsh realization of man's predilection to use violence, or non-symbolic means—rather than persuasion, or symbolic means—to settle his differences may be softened by recalling briefly his biological heritage.[1] Man's primitive impulses have been exercised for millions of years while his so-called higher impulses or civilized modes of behavior have developed relatively recently. For man to abandon completely his accumulated genetic legacy may be expecting the biologically impossible.

The behavior pattern called speech—which certainly must have evolved out of a need for the exchange of information—permitted man to begin to live symbolically, to develop many complex forms of response, and to live on what we call a more humane level. Nevertheless, the values and satisfactions gained by such living have not prevented reversions in times of stress and frustration to his more primitive aggressive actions. The development of a vast industrialized society brought desired comforts, as well as the growth of many impersonal contacts, overcrowded conditions, and numerous complex interrelationships. In turn, social stresses and tensions have mounted. The resulting situation is charged with potential emotional explosions that might cause reversions to various forms of violence.

The study of persuasion and its values should be encouraged not only because many seem to distrust its worth, but also because our delicately balanced society, with its numerous interrelationships, can profit from a general awareness, and skilled use, of persuasion as a mode of social influence. The marketplace of opinion is crowded by those attempting to sell their ideas and products. White-collar workers who work with people rather than things are now in the majority among the workers in the United States. People in virtually all areas are therefore seeking to know more about the nature and skills of persuasive communication—the cementing principle of a free society.

It should thus be clear that a free society must either use persuasion or risk its freedom; violent dissent is not rational disagreement, it is a formless, unintellectualized, and unproductive procedure. Justice Holmes, in a 1919 decision, summed up the point well when he said:

> When men have realized that time has upset many fighting faiths, they may come to believe even more than they believe the very foundations of their own conduct that the ultimate good desired is better reached by free trade in ideas—that the best test of truth is the power

[1] Desmond Morris, *The Naked Ape* (New York: McGraw-Hill, 1968).

of the thought to get itself accepted in the competition of the market, and that truth is the only ground upon which their wishes safely can be carried out. That at any rate is the theory of our constitution. It is an experiment, as all life is an experiment.[2]

This book is written on the premise that the careful study of the theories, principles, and methods of persuasion—considered from the point of view of the theorist, producer, consumer, and critic—should be a vital area of concern in contemporary education. Here is a discipline that should challenge all who wish to grapple with a subject matter that has great depth, breadth, and relevance, one that enables student and teacher alike to understand much of the character and dynamism of a free society.

Problems related to the study of persuasion

As we attempt to delineate those concepts central to a theory of persuasion and to suggest a meaningful approach to the study of the field, it should be useful to consider first several general obstacles that make the achievement of a coherent theory difficult. These difficulties arise because persuasion as a study is intrinsically multidisciplinary.

The varied workmen in the field of persuasion

Many differing types of scholars work in the fields of persuasive discourse and human motivation, and each person operates within those frames of reference common to his discipline. Characteristically the scholar in traditional rhetoric is concerned with language, the invention and arrangement of lines of argument, style, presentational modes, and criticism. His orientation is essentially historical, theoretical, descriptive, and empirical. The modern student of communication theory stresses the nature, models, and problems involved in the process of communicating, and he follows carefully the message development and progress from a source and/or encoder via some channel to the receiver and/or decoder. His interests focus primarily on the mechanics, methods, and barriers to efficient communication, and he does not concentrate intensively on the complex psychological aspects involved. Communication theorists have brought scientific procedures into their field of study, resulting in some very useful quantitative and experimental research.

In the fields of psychology and social psychology the natives have been

---

[2] *Abrams* v. *U.S.*, 250 U.S. 616, at 630 (1919).

unusually restless. They have splintered into a number of smaller interest groups clustered around particular aspects of the broad field of motivation, and their areas of agreement are still limited. Their method has been essentially experimental with little attempt to link their studies with earlier research.

As a result, a unified continuum of knowledge does not readily present itself, and an orderly theory of motivation is difficult to formulate. Nonetheless one can discern three broad, representative, and not greatly different approaches to the study of motivation: (1) behavior theory, (2) the theory of unconscious motivation, and (3) cognitive theory. Behavior theory begins with the need-drive-incentive approach and utilizes learning as a central concept:

> It uses the derived motivation interpretation and attempts to apply it specifically to human behavior. The theory of unconscious motivation was brought forward by Freud in the interpretation of irrational, neurotic behavior, and then extended to account for much ordinary socially acceptable behavior. The main point is that motives are not clear to the person who is expressing them, and actual behavior often must be understood as some form of conversion or symbolic representation of a hidden or unconscious motive. Finally, the cognitive theory places more attention upon man's awareness of what is going on, his deliberate tendency to anticipate the future, to plan, to take risks.[3]

Within these three broad approaches there are many smaller and differing areas of study. The theoretical psychologist is usually concerned with all or most of the determinants of behavior. In applied psychology, motivation is essentially not analyzed, and the theorists and researchers deal with the more practical problems of discovering the correlates of certain kinds of behavior. The industrial psychologist is interested in effective labor-management relations, and the educational psychologist wishes to know more of the processes and procedures in making Johnny study more effectively. Other professional psychologists attempt to unravel the tangle of motives and to find causations in their concern for solving individual problems. The physiological psychologist is interested in accounting for the underlying bodily processes that arouse, sustain, and regulate behavior. Social psychologists, as well as sociologists and anthropologists, contend that human behavior to a very large extent is determined by our social and cultural environment and that to understand motivation one must focus on these factors.

---

[3] Ernest R. Hilgard and Richard C. Atkinson, *Introduction to Psychology*, 4th ed. (New York: Harcourt, Brace and World, 1967), pp. 142–43.

Those in public relations are also interested in motivation, and they emphasize the theories and means of creating favorable public images for an institution, industry, profession, or individual. People working in sales promotion and marketing are interested in applying methods of arousing or triggering selected motivations.

This cursory review of the chief workmen in the broad area of human motivation should be sufficient to make the point. The varied approaches and points of emphasis produce a varied literature, and it is no small task to distill from it those items useful to the teacher, student, and practitioner in persuasive discourse. In chapters 3 through 7 we will deal in some detail with theories and approaches only suggested here.

Differing terminologies among theorists and researchers

A second problem encountered in striving for some coherence in persuasion theory arises out of the first. Increasingly the scholars working in the various approaches to persuasion and motivation have become less able to communicate with each other. Predilection for one's own jargon and the scientific vocabularies linked with specialization—which to some degree may be necessary—have provided little opportunity for mutual understanding. The classical rhetorician and the modern experimentalist in communication and behavioral science work in quite different worlds and can hardly understand each other. The differing schools of psychology develop their own special terminologies. And instead of being alarmed at this inability to communicate—and thus to understand and profit from the knowledge each has to contribute to the other—there is often indifference and even pride in the exclusiveness of the language and the consequent separation from colleagues who are working on the same general problem but from another point of view.

Problems related to the research in persuasion

The third general problem that faces the person attempting to draw the materials of this vast and complex field into some meaningful framework lies in the nature of the researches with which he must work. Some researchers are interested only in pure research, others in applied research. Some work in experimental or in quantitative, and still others in historic and descriptive research. Some of the studies are carefully executed; others are of questionable methodology. Some researchers seem devoted to finding answers to truly significant questions; others belabor the inconsequential. Some researches are given birth not because they complete a vital link in a larger body of useful evidence, but because they fit a given prerequisite for obtaining a governmental or private grant. As a result, the body of research literature unfortunately lacks as much organization and direction as might be desired. These points are mentioned to indicate the problem a student of persuasion will find and not to suggest that the literature lacks important research. The field contains many excellent examples of productive research, and the authors of this book have attempted to use these and to credit those who have performed them.

A modern approach to the study of persuasion

An eclectic, pluralistic, integrative approach

It should be clear from our brief consideration of these three general obstacles to a coherent theory of persuasion that it can indeed be a fatiguing and sometimes frustrating job to distill from the various approaches, terminologies, and researches those materials that are most relevant, reliable, and appropriate for the student of persuasive discourse. This is compounded by the necessity to attempt to satisfy in a measure the zealous scholar, the student relatively unsophisticated in the field, and the person primarily interested in the use or practice of persuasion. Nonetheless, if we are to make use of the best knowledge available and to satisfy more than only those with a special interest in some aspect of persuasion, we must try to meet a variety of needs. One is tempted to avoid the disorganization of the field of human motivation by restricting one's view to a single theory, a given set of compatible writers, or a given area of research. We have attempted to avoid any particular bias that might dispose us to posit a narrow theory of persuasion or to explain all the elements of the total process of persuasion by strict adherence, for instance, to the canons of classical rhetoric, to a given communications model, or to a given behavioral school of thought. To strive for anything less than some coherence and unity among the contributions made by various differing excursions into the field would be to settle for a relatively inadequate and distorted view of the knowledge available. For the student to be mildly and temporarily distressed at the lack of a neat, orderly, *established* theory is to be preferred to barricading his mind within the more comfortable confines of a single, incomplete view of persuasive discourse or of rhetoric. Our approach, then, must be eclectic, pluralistic, and, we trust, integrative.

In the present volume we have drawn from those various fields that seem to have significant knowledge useful in understanding and using persuasive communication. This approach suggests that persuasive speaking cannot be taught simply in a "speech-centered" or "rhetorical" manner as has been done traditionally. To grasp the full nature of any attempt at persuasion, the student must draw on materials in such fields as rhetoric, communications, psychology, sociology, social psychology, commerce and marketing, journalism, and logic.

Finally, as the reader progresses in this book he should keep in mind that our knowledge of human persuasion and motivation can never be complete nor precisely unified, for the infinitely varied, complex, and fascinating subject of human behavior will continue to be a field for further research and theorizing as long as man and his cultures continue to develop.

Characteristics of the field of persuasion

PERSUASION—A FORM OF COMMUNICATION. We have suggested thus far that persuasion is a complex social act, that it operates by manipulating symbols (mainly visual and auditory), and that it assumes interaction between persuader and persuadee. Thus persuasion is basically a form of communication and must share the attributes of effective communication: it has a clearly specified purpose, it makes use of effective symbolization in the oral, written, or other visual language it employs, and it provides for a reciprocal process of interstimulation between the source or encoder and the receiver or decoder of a message. Therefore, we will be concerned throughout our treatment of persuasion with the basic elements of communication.

Since we are dealing in the use of all verbal and nonverbal symbols, we exclude all nonsymbolic modes of influence from the province of persuasion, that is, the forms of physical violence. The reader will also be aware that people are sometimes influenced by a persuasive message they were not intended to receive. These incidents we exclude from persuasion per se as examples of *accidental influence*. Your speech to the Rotarians in your home town may by chance have been read later by a person in another locale and the person's behavior modified by it. All of us are quite aware that certain effects of persuasion may occur that were not intended, not predetermined, and which may or may not be useful to the initiator of the message. However, in the interests of providing research controls, pedagogical usefulness, and as an aid to criticism, it seems justified to evaluate persuasive messages in terms of purposeful goals.

THE PURPOSES OF PERSUASION. Persuasion is that form of discourse that attempts to modify the intended receiver's attitudes or behavior in some predetermined manner. The specific nature of attitudes and their relation to overt behavior are discussed in chapter 6. Our concern here is simply to stress the importance of a clearly delineated purpose and to classify the kinds of purposes characteristic of persuasive messages.

Several excellent reasons why a persuader should word his purpose with some precision before he begins to prepare his message are:

1. Unity, coherence, and emphasis—those imperatives of good composition—are possible only when they advance a specific proposition. The persuader's purpose must be carefully worded in his mind, regardless of any intention to delay revealing his purpose to a receiver or to conceal it.

2. A specific objective reassures the persuader of the need for his communication; it can motivate him.

3. A concrete, specified purpose enables the persuader to select with greater precision only those materials that are relevant and necessary to his message.

4. A clear purpose enables the persuader to adjust continuously to the feedback cues of his audience. Feedback can be interpreted meaningfully only when compared to *desired* responses, a function of purpose.

5. The receiver is helped by a clear purpose. The thoughtful consumer of a message can proceed in his analysis and criticism when guided by an accurate perception of the persuader's purpose. Misperceptions due to a vague purpose lead to correspondingly nebulous evaluations. Of course, intentional vagueness is used by some persuaders to prevent precise, analytical, and critical responses.

Careful formulation of purpose in context is thus a high-priority characteristic of effective persuasion. To encapsulate the importance of purpose in a specific instance of persuasion, we suggest the following rather sweeping generalization: *it is impossible to predict or assess the effectiveness of a unit of persuasion without knowledge of a definite purpose and information about a specific audience.*

We can distinguish four kinds of purposes that concern the persuader: *immediate* and *delayed* purposes, and purposes that are oriented to *belief* and to *action.*

When a persuader's objective is to attain the desired goal during or at the completion of the message, we classify the purpose as *immediate.* If the message is designed to build a foundation for later behavioral change, we classify the purpose as *delayed.* Some persuasive purposes are predominantly one or the other, but persuasive messages often seek both goals. Thus one may conceptualize immediate or delayed purposes as a continuum rather than a dichotomy. Using the terms *consummatory* and *instrumental* instead of immediate and delayed, Fotheringham suggests that the ratio of consummatory to instrumental value placed on message effects by various communicators could be depicted as follows:[4]

Mostly consummatory	More consummatory than instrumental	Equally consummatory and instrumental	More instrumental than consummatory	Mostly instrumental

The door-to-door salesman in a one-shot sweep through a suburb to sell Little Jiffy Dandy can openers has a predominantly consummatory, immediate purpose, as does the neighbor lady collecting for the Heart Fund on a Sunday afternoon. The broadcasting of Radio Moscow's North American Service would be mostly instrumental, or delayed, since there is little chance that the United States citizen, listening to a single broadcast, would decide to switch his allegiance to the USSR. International broadcast persuasion has long-term objectives and is in fact a form of campaign, planned over months and years to bring the purposes of the listeners closer to the purposes of the broadcasters.

"Equally consummatory and instrumental" might refer to the purpose of a professional organizer attempting to persuade the membership of a union to go on strike. When the vote is tallied his immediate goal will or will not have been achieved. But arousing enthusiasm and increasing dedication necessary to sustain the union bargaining effort in the weeks and months ahead amount to an equally important delayed purpose, to be served by the same units of persuasion.

The persuader is well advised to classify his immediate and delayed purposes, note their interrelationships, and decide how best to advance them, both individually and collectively.

Behavioral change (action) generally involves modification of *attitudes* (beliefs, feelings) as well as overt physical *activity*. It is difficult to separate them. If we exclude whimsical and random actions, we are probably justified in generalizing that a person will not be persuaded to perform some action without first being persuaded to a change in one or more attitudes. However, persuasion is usually directed toward either a change in attitude or a change in behavior as its central objective. Occasionally, belief and action as goals may be equally emphasized. Frequently, belief or attitude-oriented persuasion is instrumental or delayed, and action-oriented persuasion tends to be immediate or consummatory.

[4] Wallace Fotheringham, *Perspectives on Persuasion* (Boston: Allyn and Bacon, 1966), p. 25.

In those persuasive messages where attitude change is the chief objective, the change may be a change in *position* on an acceptance-rejection scale or a change in *intensity*, that is, the firmness with which the position is held. Thus the persuader who is primarily interested in attitude change or formation has three purposes available: (1) the intensification of an established attitude without modifying its position on the belief or attitude scale, (2) the actual changing of the attitude or belief position, such as a change from moderate acceptance to total acceptance, from total rejection to neutrality, from total rejection through neutrality to acceptance, and (3) the creation of a new attitude, rather than the modification of an existing one. A new attitude may be established when the persuader introduces a recommendation that has not been entertained before by the audience. In this situation the persuader has a great opportunity to shape fresh opinions. Here, too, he has perhaps the best opportunity to gain a more uniform response in the form of similar beliefs than under any other circumstance.

In action-oriented purposes the goal is to precipitate a behavioral change whether the action be immediate (as is frequently the case) or delayed. The action-outcome intended by the persuader may be clearly specified, or it may be vague enough to encourage widely ranging responses. A recommendation to "drink milk every day" is quite specific; to "buy a Buick" with the model and time unspecified is somewhat less specific, and to "continue your education" is quite general and can lead to many diverse activities which can serve as a response to the request. In general, persuasion designed to produce physical action is usually more concrete than persuasion intended primarily to change attitudes. Vagueness of purpose increases the variability of response which, in turn, contributes to ineffectiveness of persuasion. Indirectly suggesting an action-purpose is risky business, indeed.

We reiterate that action and attitude change as goals of persuasion are interwoven. They are interdependent, yet persuasion often has as its immediate or primary objective changing one or the other.

PERSUASION INVOLVES FREEDOM OF CHOICE. Another attribute of persuasion is that the receiver of the message has freedom of choice; he can accept or reject the persuader's recommendation. A free society attempts to assure this freedom by laws and social custom. Anti-monopoly laws are designed to provide the buyer with an adequate choice of products and services, the voter is given a choice of candidates, and opportunities for rejoinders in public meetings are usually provided. When this freedom is absent, coercion, not persuasion, is attempted.

History is dotted with the exploits of dictators and demagogues who have sought to establish power and govern through physical force. Ultimately the Hitlers and Mussolinis of the past and present allow no freedom of choice. To them persuasion is a questionable tool, and one that places an undeserved trust in the masses.

PERSUASION INVOLVES ALL THE MODES OF INTENTIONAL SYMBOLIC INFLUENCE. Reflecting the perseverating influence of early faculty psychology, some scholars in the field of public address have divided persuasion and argumentation, contending that discourse which relies primarily on the nonlogical methods of influence is *persuasion* and that which relies primarily on reasoned discourse with its foundations essentially in logic is *argumentation*. The differences aroused over this distinction traditionally have been called the "conviction-persuasion duality debate."[5] We can see no defensible case for excluding what has been called "logical proof" from the province of persuasion. This encoder- and message-oriented approach does not consider sufficiently the importance of the decoder or receiver of a message, nor does it recognize the virtually inextricable nature of nonlogical and logical materials as they operate in discourse. What is logical to one receiver may not be so considered by another. Research indicates that even a panel of expert critics cannot agree when asked to categorize the appeals in a given speech. Also, from the point of view of a complete rhetoric, argumentation and debate are justifiably included as forms of persuasion.

PERSUASION IS RECEIVER- OR AUDIENCE-CENTERED. The student of persuasion should always keep in mind that persuasion is receiver- or audience-centered. The speaker may be message-oriented, but this concern for preparing and presenting a message must be anchored in a thorough analysis of the intended receiver. What a speaker thinks about his subject is important, of course; but what the *receiver* thinks of it is more important. The old notion that the content of a message is mostly words that can be understood in isolation has been abandoned. We must remember that the meaning of a word or gesture lies not in the symbol, but in the person hearing or seeing it. The speaker who thinks that he can arbitrarily prepare a logical message cannot be certain of the receiver's interpretation of that message. Thus we are hinting that a complete grasp of this receiver-centered approach to persuasive speaking means that the usual sketchy, hasty audience analyses made prior to casual or formal speech situations are not generally sufficient. We must remember that the receiver of a message runs it through his elaborate filter system made up of his experiences, perceptions, attitudes, motives, biases, and prejudices, and makes

[5] Edward Z. Rowell, "Prolegomena to Argumentation," *The Quarterly Journal of Speech* 18 (February, April, June, November, 1932): 1–13, 224–48, 381–405, 585–606.

of the original message only that which his own interpretations permit. In this sense, and please do not misunderstand the point, *if* the receiver is persuaded, he is persuaded by his *own* message and not necessarily by that planned by the speaker. Ideally, of course, *that message structured by the receiver is an approximation or duplication of that intended by the speaker.*

PERSUASION AS PROCESS. Because persuasion can best be understood as a process, let us consider first what the concept of process means and how it relates to communication.

When events are viewed as process one comes to realize that starting and stopping points are arbitrary and that they actually can be pursued to infinity, that change in any one of the constellation of factors involved in the event is reflected in change in one or more of the other factors involved. The concept of process grasps the continuum of many interrelationships that make up the dynamic nature of an event. Thus a process view of one's universe means that events are not fixed, static conditions, but are composed of an ever-changing set of variables operative in time and space.

To apply the idea of process to human communication suggests that a given act of persuasion is not a fixed exercise where a few variables (auditory and visual) occur independent of each other and of what has happened prior to the speech and after the speech. Rather, a speech must be viewed as a small clip of time within which certain variables are operating dependently and linked causally to many other variables. The culture, the value systems, the mores, attitudes, and motives of the audience members and the speaker usually have been long established. Likewise, the speaker's reputation and other influence factors usually have been operative some time before he utters the first word in a speech. These many variables operate prior to the speech, play significant roles during the speech, and will persist after the speech. Thus the process view of a persuasive message enables one to grasp attempts at persuasion more completely and without some of the arbitrary oversimplifications of earlier rhetorical criticism. It sensitizes the theorist, practitioner, and critic to the many variables in a persuasive situation; it keeps them ever mindful of the antecedent and consequent variables that can play a significant role.

The concept of process could be expanded, but surely it is clear that a persuasive speech, in the usual sense, is merely a brief oral and visual segment out of a continuing influence chain of variables upon which a speaker concentrates for a given number of minutes in his efforts to usher his audience toward a predetermined goal.

Let us turn now to a model that depicts schematically the interaction process between speaker and audience and suggests what any speaker must understand and utilize.[6] (See figure 1–1.) Much of this book is devoted to developing in detail materials suited to this model.

In looking at this model we start with the tasks the source of the message or the speaker has to perform. First (block *A*) the speaker must formulate in his mind the specific goal he wishes to achieve or recommendation he wishes to make. Any speech must seek a clearly formulated goal—the speech that aims at nothing usually accomplishes nothing. Next (block *B*), the persuader must perform a comprehensive analysis of the intended receivers, for only by so doing can he know how to prepare his message. Then he is ready to prepare the message (block *C*). Next the persuader must select a channel or vehicle to carry the message to the receiver (block *D*). In the case of the public speech, that form becomes the vehicle, whether it be a very formal speech, a debate, a sermon, or a sit-in, which is a nonverbal type of public speech. On occasion, of

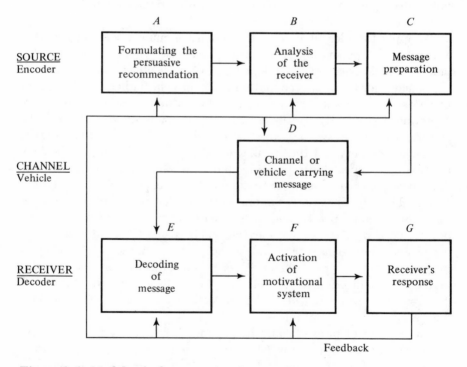

Figure 1–1. Model of the process of persuasive communication—"source-oriented, receiver-centered."

---

[6] Succeeding chapters discuss in detail those topics only schematized and briefly discussed here.

course, the vehicle may be television, radio, an editorial, a billboard poster, or other vehicle as discussed in chapter 2.

Next, the receiver of the message plays his roles in the process. He decodes or interprets the original message (block *E*) in terms of his experiences, attitudes, values, motives, and prejudices. The message may arouse his desire systems (block *F*) which may be useful to the speaker's purposes. And, finally, the receiver responds covertly and overtly to what he is hearing and seeing (block *G*). Those responses that can be observed are in turn relayed as feedback messages to the original source or speaker, letting him know how accurate he has been in his audience analysis, how well or ill his purpose is being considered, how interesting or boring he is. The speaker must be able to interpret and make adjustments—as necessary—to what the feedback messages are telling him.

Finally, as a result of continuous feedback and revision, an incident of persuasion typically involves several—or many—cycles of this model.

The process of persuasion involves five basic *psychological steps* or stages that must be accomplished by rhetorical means. These steps are often telescoped and interrelated. We will mention these steps briefly here, and succeeding chapters will develop them in some detail.

1. Gain and maintain attention. Without attention persuasion cannot take place. Attention must be maintained until the communication situation ceases.

2. Provide visual and/or auditory symbols to facilitate the predictable perception of the materials within the message. Useful meanings can be aroused by a message only if the materials are perceived by the audience in a way similar to the understanding of the speaker. Usually the receiver's experiences are unlike those of the speaker, and therefore the receiver is likely to perceive the message quite differently. The study of perception is vital to effective and accurate communication.

3. Appropriate and create desires useful in directing motivations helpful to your purposes. The persuasive message must arouse those desires which propel the persuadee toward the goal being sought. This requires the persuader to know the bases of human desire systems and the methods of appropriating them for predetermined ends.

4. Demonstrate how these desires can best be satisfied by acceptance of the persuader's proposition. If desires are to supply the impelling power to persuasion, the persuader must be able to demonstrate that what he proposes can satisfy those desires and satisfy them better than competing ideas or products. This presents at once a task of considerable magnitude, for our desires are woven into an intricate psychological fabric that often seems to defy analysis. To present a proposition satisfying some basic need or want without at the same time conflicting with others requires careful audience analysis and message preparation.

5. Produce the desired response. As we suggested earlier, successful persuasion begins with and perseveres in its attempt to gain a clearly formulated goal. A specific type of response is sought. All the steps given above seek to usher the receiver of the message in the direction of this goal. It may be that these earlier steps were sufficiently strong that the receiver proceeds immediately to the desired response. Nonetheless, on many occasions the specific response cannot be achieved without some specific directions and perhaps additional persuasive appeals. The receiver may need to sign appropriate papers for the new Ford or Chevrolet in working out the payments, he may need to be specifically informed and directed regarding the place and procedures in giving blood to the blood bank. Specific and impelling directions can be very important in consummating a given persuasive message. Much persuasion fails because this step has not been carefully worked out.

In summing up the process view of persuasive discourse, we hope it is clearly suggested that the theorist, the practitioner, and the critic must be sensitive to the total continuum of factors or variables that may be germane to the influence situation and that a very complete analysis of the receiver or audience involved is necessary. Without an astute analysis of the receiver, the speaker cannot know if his message will be perceived with fidelity, or whether the materials of the message will be perceived as either logical or nonlogical. As Krech and Crutchfield have pointed out, "There are no impartial facts. Data do not have a logic of their own that results in the same perceptions and cognition for all people. Data are perceived and interpreted in terms of the individual perceiver's own needs, own emotions, own personality, own previously formed cognitive patterns."[7]

This view suggests, too, that an audience contains many attitudinal variables and that the individuals within the audience often will fall at different places on an attitude scale ranging from extreme favorableness to extreme opposition toward some proposition. The persuader's message must take these variables into account and appropriate the available means of persuasion for each as far as possible. It also means that one must be very careful in labeling a persuasive attempt as "success" or as "failure." What is apparently a successful persuasive speech may simply have had the good fortune of having an audience near the favorable end of the attitude scale, and what is sometimes called a failure actually may

[7] David Krech and Richard S. Crutchfield, *Theory and Problems of Social Psychology* (New York: McGraw-Hill, 1948), p. 94.

have moved the audience farther along the scale toward acceptance but, because the audience's prior position may have been more unfavorable, the speaker's final goal was not reached. In this connection we should keep in mind that in situations where basic, unfavorable attitudes are involved, one speech usually does not change such attitudes significantly. Time and the frequency of exposure to an idea are important to persuasion on topics of significant concern to people.

A DEFINITION OF PERSUASION. We are now ready to distill from the various attributes we have assigned to persuasion a definition that accounts for these characteristics. We are aware that a definition need not provide a complete account of what it attempts to define. Efforts to make an all-encompassing definition can on occasion delay deeper understanding. Nonetheless, we believe a definition should account for the salient features of the thing to be defined in as brief and simple a manner as possible. We define persuasion as *communication intended to influence choice*. The word *communication* denotes that this phenomenon is symbolic and interactive, the word *intended* suggests that the persuasive attempt has a predetermined goal, the word *influence* suggests that behavioral change of some sort is sought, and the word *choice* reflects the view that the receiver has options available to him.

The reader will note also that argumentation is included in this definition and may be defined as *that form of persuasion that employs essentially reasoned discourse while using nonlogical appeals as supplementary means of influence.*

Propaganda, too, is considered a form of persuasion. It may be said to be *a type of persuasive campaign designed to influence large numbers of people, usually in non-face-to-face situations, with its purpose either revealed or concealed, and employing such vehicles as organization, radio, television, the stage, newspapers, news magazines, books, and billboards to carry its messages.*

It may be deduced from examining these definitions that a distinction may be made between *persuading* and *informing*. As long as instruction in the classroom presents materials in a strictly expository manner with the concern being only with understanding a theory, a research method or project, or a book of historic information, without an attempt to influence the use made of learned materials, informing takes place. However, when the instructor proceeds to bring in materials in such a way as to predetermine a choice among options, then he is engaging in persuasion. It should be clear from this that persuasion is frequently a part of education.

SOME PROBLEMS AND LIMITATIONS OF PERSUASION. As a method of influence persuasion is not without its problems and limitations. Below we enumerate a few of the chief ones.

1. Because persuasion allows free trade in ideas, not all suggestions for behavioral change can be expected to meet with approval. As a result of some ethically questionable practices in persuasion, some naive moralists are beginning to condemn all persuasion as of dubious value, forgetting that a free society cannot survive by condemning the free exchange of ideas, however distasteful some of those ideas may be. Our methods frequently need refinement, and our ethical codes need to be sharpened; but let us not discard the system.

2. Attitudes and behavioral patterns change slowly, and thus persuasion may not provide as rapid a change as might be desired. People may become impatient with the sometimes slow, even tedious, processes of a free society and be inclined to revert to violence or to authoritative procedures. We now see many sobering evidences of this attitude.

3. Within a freedom-of-speech framework, competing persuasions are seldom championed by persuaders of equal competence. It can thus be argued that *truth* may be lost as a result of unequal persuasive skills.

4. In the great density and intensity of contemporary persuasion, people may learn not to listen, or to listen and disbelieve.

5. Attitude and behavioral change are not final, not eternally fixed. Persuasion as a method of influence has to be continuous. Studies of attitude change demonstrate that definite retrogression toward original position tends to take place.

6. There is the danger that the spurious, the insincere, and the insignificant may crowd out the meaningful, the sincere, and the significant.

7. The channels of mass communication, which carry much of today's persuasion, may, because of the costs involved, become available only to the few.

8. What happens to our so-called grass-roots democracy when candidates and government become merchandized much like toothpaste, a bar of soap, or a 24-hour deodorant? This question gives pause not only to the political scientist, the communication teacher, and governmental philosophers, but to every thoughtful citizen.

9. Finally, some fear that, in a day when craftsmen in persuasion are becoming increasingly effective, the consumer of persuasive messages may become a helpless victim, and that the gap between the skills of the persuader and the level of critical evaluation of the consumer may be becoming dangerously great. This is, indeed, a matter for our concern, but the available evidence is neither clear nor adequate. Certainly we know that the pace of the race has quickened, but who has gained on whom is not established.

The inductive approach to the study of persuasion

At the beginning of this chapter we discussed the significance of the study of persuasion in contemporary education. We also said that the study of human motivation is by no means complete, and we implied that the reader should be alert to new insights into the ever-intriguing nature of human behavior. The student must not confine his attempt to learn about human persuasion solely from *reading about it* or from performing class exercises in a very prescribed manner before a captive audience. His learning must be supplemented by astute observations and participations outside the classroom. The authors' experiences indicate that the collection, careful evaluation, and reporting of ongoing systems of persuasion in community, state, national, and international situations should be a bona fide part of any course in persuasion. As such experiences become more sophisticated, the student will establish bases from which more meaningful and perhaps new interpretations and principles of human behavior may be derived.

Finally, it should be clear that our quest for a modern theory of persuasion is based on the premise that a theory should be *descriptive* of the phenomena for which it seeks to account, rather than *prescriptive*, which would lead to the study of a desired or ideal, not realistic, practice of human persuasion.

The right to persuade

What then is the philosophical base that underlies our acceptance of the process of persuasion? The reader is quite correct if he concludes that the importance assigned to persuasion in this book, and our contention that competing persuasions are essential to a free society, imply a belief that persuasion per se is a constructive, desirable activity.

Although we have examined the socially desirable consequences of unrestricted persuasion, we have not yet dealt with the matter of individual freedom and the charge that persuasion is an invasion of personal privacy. The question we wish to confront is: By what right does one human being persuade another? A related question arises: Is yielding to persuasion permitting another to make your decisions, hence an abdication of free will?

One major right, or obligation, to persuade is the necessity to safeguard the welfare of the individual and the group with whom he is involved. For example, when a leader in an urban ghetto plans widespread violence and destruction, it may be both a right and an obligation for his friend to dissuade him. When a needed social reform, perhaps a local gun control law, is threatened with defeat in an apathetic community, it may well be the right of the informed citizen to interfere with the lives of his neighbors to the extent of diverting some of their time and energy to supporting, or at least voting for, the needed legislation. Collective gains can come only from changes in individuals. Concerted, spontaneous support of reform is rare. Usually people must be guided, cajoled, reasoned with, even pressured, before a worthwhile new idea takes root.

A little understood phenomenon of group living argues for the right to persuade. In order to live together successfully, people must cooperate. Cooperation comes only through voluntary limitation of personal freedom, which in turn is achieved only through directive communication. People can be influenced to "go along with their group" in only two ways, by threat or by persuasion. Since persuasion preserves choice and threat destroys it, persuasion is the preferred means of influencing people to cooperate.

Individual freedom results from a balance between forces of order and forces of anarchy. Without coordinating controls, anarchy reduces individual freedom. The people living in a riot-torn, devastated urban area where police have been driven out have very little freedom. No laws restrict them, but few choices remain. Ideally, we strive for that minimum of social control that will maximize freedom. We want to supply enough direction so that one person implementing his freedom does not reduce the freedom of another. The need to supply essential guidelines—social control—in a democratic society is the philosophical foundation of our "right" to persuade.

We turn now to the related suggestion that in yielding to persuasion, a person abdicates his free will. The reader will remember that persuasion was defined as "communication intended to influence choice." The safeguard of free will is in the word *influence*. Persuasion is a process of attempting to build a preference for an option, not controlling or dictating or forcing the abandonment of other possibilities. Consequently, the individual making the decision has the last word. If he "yields" to persuasion, it is voluntary; his free will remains in control. If his judgment tells him to reject the recommendation, he is equally free to decide in favor of a contrary course of action. Only when a person refuses to listen to available differing persuasions can he be said to be "abdicating his free will."

In our view, the individual who benefits most by the exercise of free will never purposefully keeps himself uninformed. He receives contrary persuasions thoughtfully, extracting from each what is meaningful to him. He reaches a decision when his good judgment tells him the time for decision has come, and he makes his decision according to explicit criteria formulated in part by the persuasion received. When citizens function in this fashion as persuadees, persuasion plays a truly constructive role in human affairs.

Conclusion

We have attempted to delineate in as succinct a manner as possible the significance of, the problems in, an approach to, and a philosophical base for the study of persuasion. We trust that the reader now has a meaningful foundation which may serve him well as he proceeds into a study of the specific theories, principles, and methods of persuasion.

2

The vehicles of persuasion

I. The role of the media
  A. The importance of carriers of persuasive messages
  B. The credibility factor and the vehicles of persuasion
  C. Reaching the intended receiver
II. Speech
  A. Speech in direct speaker-receiver situations
    1. Public speeches
    2. Group and public discussions
    3. Public debates
    4. Public readings
    5. The stage
    6. The interview
    7. Role-playing
    8. Rumor—the whispering campaign
  B. Speech with electronic aids
    1. The public address system
    2. Radio
    3. Television
    4. The film
III. Printed media
  A. Books
  B. Newspapers
  C. Magazines
  D. Pamphlets, leaflets, and handbills
  E. Photographs, drawings, cartoons, and comic strips
  F. Billboards, posters, banners, and mottos
IV. Mass nonverbal vehicles
  A. Parades and marches
  B. Sit-ins and kneel-ins
V. Conclusion

The role of the media

The importance of carriers of persuasive messages

How can I get my message to the fellow I want to receive it? Will he come to a public speech? Will he be in church on Sunday? Will he get it by radio? Television? Does he read the newspaper in which I plan to place my advertisement? How will he react to a sit-in or other mass demonstration? Will he resent the vehicle I plan to use to carry my message to him? These are the types of questions a persuader must constantly ask himself, for if he doesn't reach the person he is after, the best prepared message will come to naught. Thus an understanding of the types, values, limitations, and criteria of selection of the available vehicles for carrying messages, as well as alertness to the creation of new ones, are matters of primary concern to the persuader. Although this chapter is concerned chiefly with the speech vehicles or media, other vehicles are also considered so that the reader may get a more complete picture of the chief implements for carrying messages designed to influence.

The credibility factor
and the vehicles of persuasion

"I agreed with the point of his dissent, but I didn't agree with his method." Such statements have been heard many times on campuses in recent years, referring to student requests via class strikes, marches, sit-ins, and violence in attempts to influence administrators to change certain regulations or policies. "I agree that religious commitment is important, but why does that preacher use that old-fashioned evangelistic method in trying to persuade me? It turns me off." "That insurance policy must be put out by a reputable company because I saw it advertised in *Time*." "I heard it on television, so it must be true." These statements point to a fundamental fact in the process of persuasion: the persuader finds it difficult to separate the message from its carrier. The matter of credibility seems to operate not only in relation to the speaker and his message, but also in relation to the vehicle carrying the message. Although we do not wish here to enter the debate over whether such a vehicle as television does, in fact, *become* the message, it seems possible that the carrier is a more significant part of the message than was traditionally thought. A vehicle or medium influences the message itself, and our point is that considerable care must therefore be exercised in selecting the vehicle to carry a message. Many persuasive attempts fail because the acceptance of the message means the approval of an unacceptable vehicle carrying the message.[1]

Reaching the intended receiver

The basic question to be answered in the selection of a message carrier is: Will the vehicle reach the person (or persons) I want to receive my message? Specific questions might be: Will those I wish to persuade come to a political rally? Will a sales talk in the customer's home be best received? Will a public debate draw the group I wish to influence? Will a radio or television presentation reach most of my intended receivers, and at what hour? Will a letter, leaflet, or pamphlet reach the right hands? In short, the originator of a persuasive message must first make certain he has chosen a vehicle or carrier that will assure reception by those he seeks to influence.

Limited research has been performed regarding people's preferences for such speech forms as the single public speech, debate, and discussion. The continuing rather widespread use of such forms—the political address, the sermon, and the political debate—suggests a preference for them. But habit and cultural inertia also probably play a large part in their continued use, and the available research suggests a decreasing interest in these speech forms.

We have more evidence regarding the habits and preferences of people in regard to the mass media (radio, television, and newspapers). Although the electronic media cannot determine precisely how many people are watching a certain television program or listening to a certain radio broadcast, research organizations such as Daniel Starch, Alfred Politz, A. C. Nielsen, and Gallup and Robinson have gathered useful data. Advertisers wishing to evaluate the printed media can examine the circulation coverage of the newspapers and news magazines they wish to use. They can prepare specific units of persuasion for the readers of *Commentary*, *Ebony*, or *Christian Century*. Promotion experts in sales work have information on the effectiveness of direct-mail advertising and door-to-door sales.

The researches on the marketing of ideas and products represent a lengthy study in themselves. Our purpose here is to alert the reader to the need for evaluating the effect of the various vehicles of persuasive messages on an intended receiver. The persuader must select his method wisely.

---

[1] For further discussion of this point, refer to chapter 11.

Speech

Man is a communicating creature. In his gradual and sometimes erratic ascent toward a more humane and rational existence he has learned to live on a relatively symbolic level. Thus speech has provided him with an ever increasing means of social control, until today the various speech forms that have been developed have achieved some status as effective media of persuasion. The rise of popular governments and guarantees of freedom of speech in many nations have made those who wish to influence others conscious of the need for training in the uses of speech. We shall now examine briefly some of the chief speech forms as carriers of persuasive messages.

Speech in direct speaker-receiver situations

PUBLIC SPEECHES.   If we could re-create the past and watch the greater and lesser public figures of history as they uttered their most significant speeches, we would see quite vividly the influence role public speeches have played in the course of human history. We would see Socrates pleading his own defense, Christ preaching a nobler life to groups in the synagogues and along the shores of Galilee, Demosthenes attempting to win back his possessions, Edmund Burke pleading for conciliation with the American colonies, Henry Ward Beecher decrying slavery from platform and pulpit, William Jennings Bryan championing free silver, Abraham Lincoln defending the Union, Susan B. Anthony pleading the cause of woman suffrage, Winston Churchill holding an empire together in its darkest hour, Franklin D. Roosevelt promoting his New Deal, Adolf Hitler defaming the Jews and the Treaty of Versailles, John F. Kennedy admonishing Russia to withdraw her missiles from Cuba, Martin Luther King, Jr., describing his dream for his people, Pope Paul VI addressing the United Nations, and Gerald Ford defending his plan to cope with the problems of inflation and recession.

The complete roster would include an almost endless list of public speeches on a nearly infinite variety of topics. Thousands of public speeches are woven into the fabric of one American presidential campaign. Outside of political campaigns, direct public speaking plays a vital role as a vehicle of persuasion in such fields as business and industry, labor, education, agriculture, and religion. It should be pointed out, however, that the public speech is declining in usage as a result of television. The sermon, once a virtually sacred form in the services of most churches, has come to be less preferred as a carrier of religious messages. Often the political campaigner can get much more coverage from a televised or newspaper-reported news conference than he can by setting up a public speech situation. Nonetheless, it seems safe to say that the direct public speech remains a significant vehicle for many who would influence the minds of others.

GROUP AND PUBLIC DISCUSSIONS. Beginning with the Mayflower Compact and continuing through the many discussions in the early New England town meetings, the Lyceum and Chautauqua movements begun in 1826 and 1874, the Federal Forum Project established in 1937, and many other discussion formats down to the most recent public hearing in your home town, the method of "thinking independently together" has been useful. Generally group and public discussions are established to investigate a problem. When the group is small, all members may participate in the exchange of ideas. When the group is too large for all to participate in a private or group discussion, some audience form of public discussion—such as a panel or symposium—is used. But whatever the form, participants often use discussion not only to investigate a problem but also to promote ideas. The informal, democratic nature of group discussion can make it a very effective vehicle of the persuader, because the persuader's ideas are open to the immediate criticism of others, the discussion provides persuadees with additional information for evaluating those ideas.

PUBLIC DEBATES. Like discussion, debate has been a traditional democratic tool in American life. From the time of the Constitutional Debates on through such notable contests as the Webster-Hayne, Lincoln-Douglas, and Kennedy-Nixon debates, the many congressional and judicial debates, and the numerous lesser known forensic battles, this tool of the persuader has had a long and remarkable history in the United States.

Debate is used to test possible solutions by providing the pros and cons of specific problems. Each side of the controversy employs the tools of advocacy and presses for decision. As a vehicle of the persuader, debate provides a rigorous test of his persuasion. It must withstand critical evaluation made in immediate refutation. The persuader who is willing to enter his persuasion into the crucible of debate and whose case is strong enough to survive the contest scores a signal victory indeed. Debate is not a suitable vehicle for that type of persuader who wishes to have only his side of the argument presented. From the listener's point of view, debate can provide a more intelligent base for decision because it compels the participants to use rational elements of persuasion. It is regrettable that those aspiring to political office, as well as others who seek places of influence, are often not willing to engage in debate. It is equally regrettable that we, as citizens, do not insist that more of the vital issues of the day be tested in this manner.

PUBLIC READINGS.   Oral interpretation is generally considered an art form whose chief purposes are to help others appreciate literature and to entertain them. The interpreter tries to capture for the audience the rich and varied meanings in a selection of great prose or poetry. To this end, the interpreter is taught to seek out the central theme of the writer, to grasp fully the nuances of meaning, to demonstrate the stylistic devices of the writer, and to display all this through the expert uses of voice and body.

We agree that these aims are quite worthy and provide a significant area for speech training. Our concern, here, however, is with the use of this speech form as a persuasive tool. Some selections of prose or poetry have persuasive goals relative to specific changes in personal or group living and, when read in public, constitute a form of social control. When this occurs, the artistry of a public reading can be a very effective and sometimes subtle means for carrying persuasive messages.

Whether it be a reading of William Allen White's Pulitzer prize editorial in his 1922 *Emporia Gazette* on "Freedom of Utterance," Alice Duer Miller's poem "White Cliffs of Dover," written prior to the U.S. entry into World War II, a portion of John Steinbeck's *Grapes of Wrath*, Robert Frost's "Mending Wall," or a selection from John Hersey's *Hiroshima*, oral interpretation to either a small or large audience provides a means of formulating or changing attitudes and of encouraging modifications in behavior. The interpreter often has high credibility as a reader, the situation in which such performances take place is usually disarming, and the artistry commands a certain appreciation. These factors can make of the oral reading a very sophisticated tool of persuasion, often opening the minds of people who would not give fair hearing or even presence to a public speech, debate, or discussion.

THE STAGE.   The stage has traditionally been used not only as a means of entertainment and cultural enlightenment, but also as a vehicle to carry persuasive messages. It has afforded playwrights, producers, and organizations a means to be missionary to the minds of men. The stage has taken sides on problems involving peace and war, marriage, religion, race, politics, economics, education, temperance, and sex. Our churches have used the play as a medium of persuasion for many years; education, too, has used the stage to create favorable attitudes towards its goal; farm groups have employed this means to bring about reforms; for many years the temperance movement used the stage to depict the evils of drink; and civic organizations frequently employ the play to foster desired attitudes toward civic improvements. The Soviet Union has used touring dramatic groups to entertain and to propagandize those who live in the more isolated areas of the country.

The play can be adapted to smaller, more specialized audiences and therefore can employ more selective appeals than the motion picture, which generally needs to reach a large mass of people to justify its cost. The sight and sound of real people on the stage appeals in a way that the electronically aided screen cannot. But the stage is not a cheap and readily available tool for the persuader. It demands time in preparation, effective talent, and adequate lighting and scenery skills and equipment. A well-written play with a well-motivated plot and skillful acting and staging can make of the stage a tool of high attention value and general social impact. Regrettably, few in the theatre are interested in conducting research specifically designed to assess the stage as a vehicle of persuasion.

THE INTERVIEW.   Heretofore we have been considering those vehicles operating in audience situations. We turn now to those many situations involving a persuader and a single persuadee. These are called broadly *interviews* and include such situations as applications for jobs, sales talks by clerks in retail stores, house-to-house sales work, pastoral calls, street corner persuasion, and many other person-to-person instances of persuasion.

As vehicles of persuasion, the various forms of the interview are used in many situations to promote goods, services, and ideas. Persuasion at the mass level may be regarded as more glamorous and newsworthy, but throughout history the individual type of persuasion has been a very useful promotional tool. The personal missionary work of the clergyman, the person-to-person persuasion in the smoke-filled rooms of the political convention, the direct manager-laborer contest, the direct social-worker-to-case approach, and many other such direct, personal situations have established the interview as a vital vehicle of persuasion in human affairs. Let us suggest a few of the points to be considered in this regard.

Although the face-to-face persuader does not have the advantage of group psychology that operates in audiences, neither does he have the job of analyzing a vast audience. He can explore his customer's behavior more meticulously. He can learn about the potential persuadee's family and educational background, his likes, dislikes, biases, hobbies, ambitions, economic status, and political and religious preferences. A complete plan of persuasion based upon his specific consumer analysis can be worked out in advance in many cases. Another advantage is that in many situations the persuadee wants special attention or personal service, much like the lady who will deal with only one butcher when she buys her meat or the client who wishes the personal counsel of his lawyer, clergy, or insurance agent. The individual wants a persuader he can rely upon, with whom he can relate in a satisfying manner.

Business concerns generally use personal selling in situations where the size, complexity, and cost of the product are substantial and where there may be many questions that only a respected, knowledgeable salesman can handle. In retail selling in markets and department stores, the salesperson is still essential, although self-service stores are becoming more numerous. Of course, the salesperson is often aided by advertising campaigns that run concurrently with the personal selling attempt.

Face-to-face persuasion has some limitations, however, that cannot be ignored. A major obstacle is the relatively low prestige that is assigned to the salesperson. John L. Mason, in the *Journal of Marketing*, states that:

> . . . *absence of formalized educational and training requirements* and lack of authority are the major reasons for the relatively low occupational prestige of salesmen, as compared with the prestige of other white-collar occupations in our society. . . . When and if a formalized curriculum is devised which enables the salesman to improve his performance substantially, he will be widely in demand by employers.
> . . . The second of the adverse prestige elements—lack of authority and responsibility for controlling behavior without authority—is inherent in the occupation's role in our society. About the only possibility for prestige improvement here would be a concerted effort to answer more palatably the implicit question, "How do salesmen persuade others to buy?" After all, personal selling is not some fearsome or mystical activity; but this does not change the basic facts of lack of authority and responsibility for controlling behavior without authority.[2]

One must remember, too, that person-to-person persuasion can take considerable time. The political zealot may start out to talk with, and shake the hand of, every voter in his district, only to conclude after a week of interviews that he'll never make it by election day. In situations where great masses are to be reached, the interview may be a realistic tool only in reaching the opinion leaders of the populace.

ROLE-PLAYING. In recent years the technique of role-playing has been used to achieve attitude and behavioral changes through participation in simulation exercises. Persuasive strategy assumes that by having a subject assume the role of another person or espouse an idea contrary to his own, the subject's understanding will increase and his

[2] John L. Mason, "The Low Prestige of Personal Selling," *Journal of Marketing* (October, 1965): 10.

attitudes and behavior may be modified. Out of illusion or fantasy, a person is to come closer to reality. Though the evidence regarding the persuasive capacity of role-playing is still limited, we feel that it is adequate to be included in a survey of the vehicles of persuasion.

In a study prepared for the office of the Chief of Research and Development, Department of the Army, Stewart, Danielian, and Foster conducted research in simulating intercultural communication through role-playing. The purpose of the training sessions was "to increase cultural sensitivity and awareness and thereby increase the behavioral adaptability and communicative skills of the overseas advisor."[3] The authors indicated that "changes in the attitudinal factors that underlie interpersonal behavior are seldom accomplished by traditional lecture-type training." Because they believed it desirable to use a method that produced more personal involvement they developed a series of intercultural simulation exercises. (Their topic was plausible overseas advisory situations.) The data gathered in this interesting experiment suggest that positive results in terms of attitudinal and behavior changes can be produced by this technique. The authors state cautiously, however, that "while the reliability data are favorable, the scales must continue to be regarded as in the development stage."

Role-playing has been used in several studies using an emotion-laden scene in a doctor's office between a doctor and patient (the subject) whose smoking is assumed to have resulted in lung cancer. Janis and Mann[4] used such a technique and their results indicated that the role-playing did modify the attitudes and behaviors of the participants more than those of the control subjects who only listened to the information contained in a tape of a role-playing session. The authors reported in follow-up studies that the changes in smoking behavior tended to persist.[5]

If role-playing is an effective persuasive strategy, why is this true? Mann[6] sought to answer this question by comparing the results of three role-playing events using the doctor-patient simulation. In one situation

[3] E. C. Stewart, J. Danielian, and R. J. Foster, Simulating Intercultural Communication Through Role-Playing (Alexandria, Va.: George Washington University—Human Resources Research Office, May, 1967).

[4] I. L. Janis and L. Mann, "Effectiveness of Emotional Role-playing in Modifying Smoking Habits and Attitudes," Journal of Experimental Research in Personality 1 (1965): 84–90.

[5] L. Mann and I. L. Janis, "A Follow-up Study on the Long Term Effects of Emotional Role Playing," Journal of Personality and Social Psychology 8 (1968): 339–42.

[6] L. Mann, "The Effects of Emotional Role Playing on Desire to Modify Smoking Habits," Journal of Experimental Social Psychology 3 (1967): 334–48.

fear was used (smoking is harmful to health); in a second situation the shame appeal was used (smokers show lack of self-control and set a bad example for others); and the third situation used a cognitive appeal (the participant is a debater and must argue a case on why people should stop smoking). In general, the results demonstrated that the fear approach produced greater change in attitudes toward smoking than did the cognitive role-playing situation. The fear and shame events produced results that did not differ significantly. The men who became highly involved (as indicated by a high level of verbalization) showed greater attitude change in the fear and shame situations than did the low-verbalization level males. Interestingly, however, the highly verbal females resented the shame appeal so much as to become more fixed regarding their smoking habits.

The evidence regarding the persuasiveness of role-play as a technique is not all affirmative. In a study by Keutzer, Lichtenstein, and Himes,[7] using the same subject matter area, no persuasive effect was found. The authors pointed out that their female subjects may have been more aware of the hazards of smoking before the study because the Surgeon General's report had been released prior to their study.

Role-playing is used not only in the hope of changing a person's attitudes and behavior toward some external object, idea, or practice, but also in attempts to change attitudes toward oneself; the *psychodrama* is employed by some therapists in working with a patient. Introduced by J. L. Moreno, the psychodramatic session is said by its author to be "like life in its highest potential. Life, as you are living it, with the one difference that all the inner forces that you have are coming out. The psychodrama is, therefore, a vehicle by means of which life itself is lived under the most favorable and most intensive kind of circumstances."[8]

Role-playing by groups, such as in group therapy and encounter groups, is also used to change self-attitudes and to bring the participant's attitudes and behaviors into greater balance or consonance. Observations on the successful uses of such group techniques have been made by Forer[9] and Polster.[10]

---

[7] C. S. Keutzer, E. Lichtenstein, and K. H. Himes, " 'Emotional' Role Playing and Changes in Smoking Attitudes and Behavior," *Proceedings*, 77th Annual Convention, APA (1969): 373–74.

[8] J. L. Moreno, "The Psychodrama" in J. E. Fairchild, ed., *Personal Problems and Psychological Frontiers* (New York: Sheridan House, 1957), p. 281.

[9] B. R. Forer, "Therapeutic Relationships in Groups" in A. Burton, ed., *Encounter* (San Francisco: Jossey-Bass, 1969), pp. 27–41.

[10] E. Polster, "Encounter in Community" in A. Burton, ed., *Encounter* (San Francisco: Jossey-Bass, 1969), pp. 138–61.

As the subject matter areas and the situational settings become more varied in future research and the methods and results more carefully controlled, we should expect the technique of role-playing to come into greater use by persuaders of many kinds. From a methodological point of view, this technique has the advantage of providing considerable personal involvement on the part of the participants; it has the capacity to help subjects introject themselves into potential reality. Such a technique certainly has a good chance of changing attitudes and behaviors.[11]

RUMOR—THE WHISPERING CAMPAIGN. Rumor is one of the more informal and less predictable vehicles of communication and persuasion and, contrary to the popular notion, rumor is not always mere "idle gossip." In their usual connotation, rumors are propositions for belief that are communicated informally from person to person (usually orally), and they lack secure standards of verification or official support. They tend to develop out of disaster situations or social disturbances where the experiencing individuals do not have the information to cope with the situations. The diffusion of information by rumor is difficult to trace and to study because the process is very informal.

Another type of rumor, however, is more structured and purposeful and is planned to achieve a specified goal. This more diabolical use of rumor is called the *whispering campaign*. The distressed people of Rome spread the rumor that Nero had set fire to the city and thereupon proceeded to "fiddle" while it burned. In self-defense, Nero is said to have started a counter rumor (or whispering campaign) that the Christians started the fire, a rumor that proved quite useful from Nero's point of view. No little responsibility for the death of Socrates can be attributed to the purposeful rumors spread claiming that he perverted the youth of Athens and incited them to rebellion. In 1932, historian James Truslow Adams reported a study of the whispering campaigns used against American presidents. He concluded:

> The whispering campaign, disgusting as it is, would appear to be a
> permanent campaign method with us. So long, at least, as our politics are
> primarily concerned with men rather than with measures, it will be
> the men who will be attacked; characters, not ideas. The attack will
> be planned without reference to the real characters of the men
> themselves; for almost every charge ever made has been abominably
> false, not with reference to the dominant prejudices or standards of the
> voters to be influenced. If these prejudices or standards should
> change, the slanderers of the politicians would change. . . . The

[11] G. R. Miller and M. Burgoon, *New Techniques of Persuasion* (New York: Harper and Row, 1973), pp. 45–58.

whispering campaign is a cruel and cowardly weapon but it will probably be used as long as it is accepted by the people themselves. It would not be employed in a decent and a civilized electorate, but, however decent and civilized we may be as individuals, we are neither when it comes to political campaigns.[12]

As early as 1936, Littell and McCarthy reported that organizations existed whose services are for hire in the spreading of rumors on behalf of a client. These organizations were said to have engaged in such activities as planting false stories regarding a disease allegedly carried by the workers in a competitor's factory, placing actors in conspicuous public places as their conversations praised a given product, and sending women to stores to ask for gloves manufactured by their sponsor and to put on an act of great disgust and disappointment when the gloves were not sold by a particular merchant. The method of breaking labor strikes by rumor was also reported.[13] Since these early studies of rumor, there have been sporadic attempts to assess its basic nature and its more recent practices. The reader is encouraged to pursue this subject by first studying the work of Allport and Postman.[14]

How many "word-of-mouth advertisers" exist is impossible to determine. Available evidence does suggest that the whispering campaign has been used by both large and small organizations and in many personal situations. It is psychologically effective because it is linked with the satisfaction of human motives, and the person planting the rumor is generally not suspected of any ulterior motive.

Speech with electronic aids

Throughout the early history of public address the limitations of the human voice were decried by speakers and listeners alike. Political stump orators and preachers strained their voices, often to injurious limits. How Lincoln and Douglas would have welcomed an aid that could bring their arguments to those standing on the periphery of their crowds, who could only see the speakers and catch an occasional word if the wind were just right! How speakers of the past have wished for some means to bring their message to latecomers who could not get in a

[12] J. T. Adams, "Our Whispering Campaigns," *Harper's* (September, 1932): 449–50.

[13] R. Littell and J. J. McCarthy, "Whispers for Sale," *Harper's* (February, 1936): 364–72.

[14] G. W. Allport and L. Postman, *The Psychology of Rumor* (New York: Henry Holt and Company, 1947).

limited auditorium and could only linger impatiently on the outside! The constant demand to be heard caused speakers to develop a style characterized by a strained vocal quality, great intensity, and loud sonorous tones—a style now criticized as lacking the genuine directness and adaptability found in the conversational mode of speaking.

Eventually some large auditoriums were equipped with overhead metal deflectors that helped carry the voice. The huge Billy Sunday Tabernacle at Winona Lake, Indiana, used such a device for many years to bring the evangelist's colorful and energetic sermons to eager listeners in the rear and in the doorways of that auditorium.

The development of electronic aids brought the answer to earlier wishes, and the effectiveness of various forms of persuasive speech was extended almost unbelievably. Now the political campaigner can address with ease a capacity audience in Madison Square Garden, and a nation's president can be heard by virtually the entire citizenry. It is of interest to review briefly the chief electronic aids, their values and limitations as media of persuasion.

THE PUBLIC ADDRESS SYSTEM.   Public address systems are used to (a) make a speech easily audible to all in a large auditorium, (b) to reach those extended audiences that gather outside the speaker's view, and (c) to arrest the attention of that unpolarized or pedestrian audience found on the streets of a city, the midway of a fairground, or on a campus.

In the first case, the job of the persuader is essentially the same as for any direct public address situation, but this job becomes more complex in the latter two cases. The extended audience usually cannot see the speaker. The visual aspects of the speaker's persuasion are lacking, so his voice and composition must gain the desired response from the audience. The greatest test for the persuader comes in attempting to influence the "pedestrian audience." Whereas the first two cases involve situations where the audience has a definite location and some singularity of purpose, the pedestrian or scattered audience has practically no homogeneity. In the former two situations the persuasion can be sustained; in the latter the persuasion is momentary and must compete with many distracting stimuli. To meet such situations, the persuader must rely on the loud stimulus of a powerful amplifier, the arresting value of startling statements, introductory music of a stirring variety, and short, succinct appeals.

The enterprising persuader hangs loudspeakers along busy streets and in large stores to direct the shopper; at county fairs he blasts at us from every booth; and he cruises about town with a loudspeaker on top of his car telling us to vote for Nicodemus Noodledumps, to attend the Military Ball next Saturday evening, or to support a student rally at the fieldhouse.

During World War II we saw the P.A. system used in still another manner: to persuade the enemy to surrender immediately rather than risk certain death later, and to discourage the pressed Japanese from leaping over Suicide Cliff on Saipan.

RADIO.   Although it has been overshadowed by public interest in television, radio remains a very active carrier of persuasive messages and is by no means a dying medium. In 1972 there were 4,381 AM radio stations and 2,401 commercial FM stations having an estimated total time sales of $1,258,000,000. There were 64,100,000 radio homes in 1972.[15] Virtually every home in the United States has one or more radio receivers. In addition there are uncounted thousands of car, truck, and in-hand portable models.

In general, radio is thought to function primarily as a diverting companion, helping "to fill the voids created by (1) routine and boring tasks and (2) feelings of social isolation and loneliness."[16] As such it occupies many hours of listening time per day, even though it often is the most casually attended of the mass media. It can be concluded that domestic radio remains a significant carrier of persuasive messages because of its coverage, its commercial support, and its ability to reach many differing groups and moods of people as a result of the many and varying types of stations available.

In addition to its domestic role, radio has been, and continues to be, a significant vehicle of national governments in peace and war. Virtually every nation has its national and international radio propaganda broadcasts, and some privately sponsored stations also exist on the international scene. Some of the more familiar examples are the Voice of America, Radio Free Europe, Radio Moscow, Radio Cairo, and the foreign broadcasts of the British Broadcasting Corporation.

Radio persists as a significant channel for the promotion of a large variety of products, services, and ideas locally and nationally. Because of the local nature of many stations, a greater number of persuaders, such as small merchants and local promotion organizations, can purchase broadcast time; these small groups are not interested in covering a large geographic area nor could they afford to buy large network time.

TELEVISION.   The growth of television broadcasting in the United States in the last twenty years has been phenomenal. In 1972 there were 701 commercial TV stations on the air, and the total time sales of stations and networks was $2,750,300,000. With 64,800,000 TV homes in the United States and an average of six hours, twenty minutes total view-

---

[15] *1973 Broadcasting Yearbook.*

[16] H. Mendelsohn, "The Roles of Radio" in A. Casty, *Mass Media and Mass Man* (New York: Holt, Rinehart and Winston, 1968), p. 87.

ing time per home per day, we must conclude that television is indeed an important means of promotion.[17]

By combining auditory and visual stimulation, television is capable of creating a greater sense of viewer participation and of commanding more complete attention than other electronic communication aids. Marshall McLuhan has sensitized modern America to the possible effects of the mass media on the total culture. His thesis is that the information a message conveys is not as significant as the medium or vehicle carrying that information, that the electronic and technical forms are more informative than the verbal messages themselves.[18] Much of his discussion has focused on television.

In addition to the usual product commercials, television is now used as the chief vehicle in political campaigns, in campaigns sponsored by such service organizations as the National Safety Council, the American Cancer Society, and the Heart Association. Churches are frequently employing television, as well as radio, in preaching their messages. And, of course, government is using television to legitimate its policies at home and abroad. With satellite telecasting now possible, the potential of international broadcasting is certain to expand greatly in the future.

The academic study of television is in its infancy. Scholars in the field are attempting to establish a sufficient body of research to support basic theory regarding the nature and effects of this medium. Television promises to become an even more significant means of engineering consent and of influencing our total way of life. Those who wish to influence mass audiences and who have the financial ability to do so should study this vehicle carefully.

THE FILM.   There is much written on the film as an art form and as a source of information and entertainment. Our concern here, however, is with film as an attitude-change agent, and much less theory and research are available on this topic.

Through its ability to combine art and the latest technology, the film can be an arresting and probing adventure. But can it persuade? In the hope that it can and does, many groups have prepared films to persuade directly or to present information selectively so that it persuades indirectly. Thus, we have the films of large corporations that are shown to school classes in their study of some manufacturing process, the films used by churches to form religious attitudes on a variety of topics, the travelogues of famous resort areas, and the films shown to servicemen in orientation courses.

[17] *1973 Broadcasting Yearbook.*

[18] M. McLuhan, *Understanding Media* (New York: McGraw-Hill, 1964).

But research on the film as a communications medium awards it a much higher mark as a conveyer of information than as an agent of attitude change. In 1951 Cooper and Dinerman reported an elaborate study designed to test the film as a means of influencing attitudes on discrimination. The results of the study showed that prejudice remained as much within the experimental groups as among the control groups.[19]

Probably the most detailed study of the film was the study of the *Why We Fight* series of films shown to American soldiers entering World War II.[20] These films were to provide background facts about the war, to create favorable attitudes toward America's participation in the war, and to arouse the soldier's motivation as well as willingness to serve in the armed forces at that time. The films were found to be quite effective in teaching information but were ineffective in changing attitudes. The men's motivation to serve as soldiers—which was the chief objective of the films—was not changed.

These studies suggest that in the area of basic attitudes the film cannot be relied upon to produce change. In the areas of product and service sales, the evidence is insufficient to conclude whether the film is an effective vehicle of persuasive messages. The reader would do well to keep in mind that the varied conditions in which the promotional film is used will doubtless produce varied results.

Printed media

In addition to the speech vehicles, the persuader may use media made possible by the modern printing press, including books, newspapers, magazines, pamphlets, leaflets, photographs, cartoons, comic strips, banners, mottos, and billboards. Of all the vehicles that can carry persuasive messages, print alone permits the reader to determine the occasion, duration, and direction of his exposure to the message. Through print, the subject matter can be developed briefly or extensively, simply or complexly. It can reach small and specialized receivers at little cost, and it permits the reader to supply his own interpretations because a speaker is not structuring the message through his interpretations. The printed media have an enduring quality, can be sampled repeatedly and at one's

---

[19] E. Cooper and H. Dinerman, "Analysis of the Film 'Don't be a Sucker': A Study in Communication," *Public Opinion Quarterly* 15 (1951): 243–64.

[20] C. I. Hovland, A. A. Lumsdaine, and F. D. Sheffield, *Experiments on Mass Communication: Studies in Social Psychology in World War II*, Vol. 3, (Princeton, N.J.: Princeton University Press, 1949).

own pace, and can be shared with others; in addition, the printed word is associated with learning in our intellectual tradition.

On the debit side, however, we are inundated with the printed matter of a thousand missionaries to our minds. The printed word must compete not only with this flood of printed messages but also with radio, television, and film messages that many people find more appealing than the printed word. In addition, research indicates that face-to-face persuasion is generally more effective than the printed word.

For the reader interested specifically in the nature and effectiveness of the printed word—and in comparison to the other mass media—there is an extensive body of literature available. Here, however, we will consider only briefly some of the chief points of the printed media as carriers of persuasive messages.

Books

Traditionally books have held a place of respect in the average home. They are the records of the intellectual progress of man; they represent his artistic and literary attempts; they inform him; they suggest solutions to his problems. The prestige books have attained gives them a psychological advantage in the process of persuasion. "If it's published in a book, it must be true" is all too often thought.

Many writers find they can speak from the library shelf to those who do not attend public speeches. If the book is well written, the author can take much more time than the public speaker to develop his persuasion carefully and at length. In addition, books have the ability to reach a wide variety of people over a period of many years.

A list of the persuasive books would be almost endless. Children's books often are designed to teach lessons of moral and social behavior. Religious, political, economic, and social leaders use the bound volume to modify the conduct of their readers. A moment's reflection brings to the reader's mind the effectiveness such early books as Harriet Beecher Stowe's *Uncle Tom's Cabin* which was influential in the antislavery movement, the indictment Hawthorne's *Scarlet Letter* brought against vicious gossip and bigoted mores of a community, the political persuasiveness of books by such revolutionaries as Karl Marx and Adolf Hitler, the internationalism urged by Wendell Wilkie's *One World* and Clarence Streit's *Union Now,* and arousal of public concern for the plight of the sharecropper by Steinbeck's *Grapes of Wrath.* More recently Harold Taylor's *Students Without Teachers* urged campus reform and Eldridge Cleaver's *Soul on Ice* espoused the case for the black militant.

The persuader who wishes to use the book to carry his message to people must make certain he can write well and must be concerned with adequate marketing of the book. He must realize, too, that books are still an expensive, therefore infrequent, purchase for many people. Bookshops are not distributed evenly. There are numerous circulating libraries in the United States, but only a small proportion of the population uses them. Through mass buying, book clubs have been able to bring books to more readers for less cost, and the recent increase in cheaply bound reprint editions has brought more books to more people. Nonetheless, the book market does not approach the number of readers reached by newspapers and magazines.

Newspapers

Modern newspapers are ranked among the most important means of opinion formation. In ancient civilizations news was transmitted crudely by placards placed in public places. The kings of ancient Assyria and Babylonia were the only ones to receive the news tablets. In 60 B.C. Julius Caesar, as consul, began his *Acta Diurna* ("Daily Events") which gave notice of games, fires, religious rites, and news of the armies and Senate. During the Middle Ages the Roman Catholic Church employed messengers to gather and distribute news to the higher clergy. Roving troubadours brought news of remote regions to the townspeople. Gradually newsmongers arose and began selling news to clients, such as those engaged in commerce and politics.

In the latest survey of newspapers (1972) there were 1,761 dailies in the United States, with a total circulation of 62,510,242 and advertising sales of $6,960,000,000.[21] The use of the modern newspaper can be attributed essentially to the Industrial Revolution and the rise of democratic nationalism. Today, with widespread literacy, the voice of the common man is becoming more effective in our political and economic life, and the newspaper has become one of the chief vehicles in the marketplace of public opinion.

The public has the right to expect a newspaper to report news in an impartial manner, and many papers make an honest effort to satisfy this expectation. Nonetheless, news is often presented in a manner designed to influence belief and conduct. Historically, this "personal journalism" has linked with it such names as Horace Greeley, Charles A. Dana, Joseph

[21] *Facts about Newspapers—1973* (Newspaper Information Service, American Newspaper Publishers Association, Dulles International Airport, Washington, D.C. 20000).

Pulitzer, and William Randolph Hearst. Newspapers become known for their political leanings—Republican, Democratic, liberal, conservative, radical. The headlines they formulate as well as the space and priority given to news items are excellent indices of their policies. Thus, the news on the front page may be used to persuade in a relatively concealed manner while the editorial page persuades openly.

The editorial page, of course, allows the editor to interpret the news for his readers in a manner suited to his purposes. And when the editorial staff is pressed for time or ideas, agencies in the hire of vested interests are only too anxious to supply free editorials designed to disseminate propaganda favorable to their clients.

Although the exact extent to which the newspaper influences conduct is in much dispute, there is general agreement that it does exert an over-all social influence, which, over a period of time, is very strong. Political tyrants have realized this and have consistently attempted to control the press. It has been reported that within one year after Hitler came to power, about 600 German dailies disappeared.[22] Russia did not have a free press under the czars, nor does she have a free press now under the Communist party. The elimination of a representative democracy usually brings with it the death of a free press.

Nevertheless, the persuasive influence of the newspaper should not be overestimated. In recent years we have seen indications that the average reader may be using the newspaper largely for its news value and may remain skeptical of the arrangement or development of the news and the editorial policies of the paper. We must not forget that in recent presidential elections voters have often acted counter to the avowed editorial policies of many newspapers. Nor must we forget that the revolutionary movements of Lenin, Mussolini, and Hitler grew and finally achieved complete power in the face of strong opposition from leading newspapers in each country.

The national and international news channels have been reduced to specialized agencies—the Associated Press, United Press International, the International News Service, Reuters, and Tass. Because newspapers usually gather only local news themselves, these national news sources have considerable opportunity to control thought.

Like the radio and motion picture, the newspaper is an expensive vehicle of persuasion, available only to those of considerable financial backing. Financial, political, religious, and other interests thus own and control many of our newspapers.

[22] F. M. Marx, "Propaganda and Dictatorships," *Annals of American Academy of Political and Social Science* 179 (1935): 211–18.

Magazines

The approximately 700–800 magazines published in the United States seek readers interested in romance, fashions, fishing, photography, tennis, literary criticism, movies, science, fiction, politics, health, real estate, banking, antiques, music, mechanics, sex, history, and on through an amazing variety of interest areas. Publishers and editors have learned to adapt to the public opinion of almost every social group, whether the adaptation is made merely to increase circulation of the magazine or intentionally to propagandize the readers. Since magazines are adapted to special groups, the editor or publisher intent on persuading his readers can tailor his persuasive appeals more directly to the motivational structure of his readers than can the persuader who employs vehicles that reach a larger, heterogeneous, unspecialized group.

The magazines of political, economic, religious, and other areas of controversy usually publish articles that support the policy of the publication. Magazine stories can often be powerful, subtle propaganda by catching the reader's interest in the web of a well-woven plot and simultaneously building attitudes useful to the purposes of the writer and publisher. Nor must we forget that those magazines carrying book reviews and criticisms of various plays and motion pictures dispose the readers for or against certain other vehicles, thus serving as directors of human thought. This type of influence is either unintentional or intentional, depending on the integrity and policy of the reviewer or critic.

The neat, dignified, colorful format of most modern magazines and their price tend to win them a greater prestige value than that extended to the newspaper.

Pamphlets, leaflets, and handbills

Small printed handouts have been employed by the persuader ever since the invention of the printing press. Classic examples of their use usually include Voltaire's anonymously written pamphlets designed to arouse the French people against Louis XV and Thomas Paine's pamphleteering for the federal Constitution. In more recent times the development of numerous print shops and the consequent decrease in printing costs have made the pamphlet, leaflet, and handbill available to persuaders of all types. The morning mail brings a small pamphlet from a book club, a political party, or a retailers' association. Along the busy downtown streets, leaflets are distributed by religious sects, health societies, or theater groups; handbills are thrust upon passersby urging them to take advantage of a certain sale, to patronize a certain restaurant, or to attend a political rally. By the close of any day in the city, no observing person can be oblivious to the role played by these media of manipulation.

Like the radio, these vehicles have gone to war. The "leaflet bomb" has become an effective weapon in modern warfare. A leaflet in the hands of an enemy, if persuasively written, may be more effective than many machine guns. Leaflets were prepared during World War II to arouse the French people against their German conquerors; this propaganda included President Roosevelt's D-Day radio message to the French people, statements by General Eisenhower, and the joint messages of the British and American governments. Another leaflet containing pictures of General Pershing arriving in France, American troops moving up to the front in 1917 and 1918, and the final rejoicing in victory was distributed, carrying with it the promise that those days of victory would soon come again. A total of 24 million leaflets was dropped in metropolitan France.[23] The "safe conduct" leaflet (the handbill floated over enemy lines, which guarantees an enemy soldier safe conduct to surrender if he waves the leaflet) has been known to have important results.[24]

Pamphlets, leaflets, and handbills are considered by most people as intentional influence. Such vehicles do not have the prestige accorded books and magazines. Generally they are used to reach people of a given area as inexpensively as possible. These printed materials may be the only vehicle available to the persuader of limited means, or they may be the supplementary carriers of a large, expensive plan of promotion.

The pamphlet can develop its persuasion at some length; the leaflet of several unbound pages can present only a few appeals; and the handbill can at best make a few terse statements in bold type. The leaflet and handbill can be prepared quickly and thus adapted to the changing conditions within a continuing persuasive situation. Often, however, the source of the handout is not revealed, and the credibility quotient is quite low.

Photographs, drawings, cartoons, and comic strips

Pictorial vehicles, such as photographs, drawings, cartoons, and comic strips, present stories, events, or ideas readily perceived by those of

---

[23] W. Carroll, *Persuade or Perish* (Boston: Houghton-Mifflin Co., 1948), pp. 29–30.

[24] M. F. Herz, "Some Psychological Lessons from Leaflet Propaganda in World War II," *Public Opinion Quarterly* 13: 3 (1949).

all educational levels, an advantage over those media which require a greater reading ability. These means of persuasion are sometimes called secondary or dependent types because they must rely on other vehicles—such as newspapers, books, magazines, pamphlets, leaflets, billboards, or posters—to bring their messages to the persuadees.

The actual photograph of a car accident with its scattered human flesh and blood may be more persuasive in a safety campaign than 10,000 words. A drawing of a kindly, simple, motherly, honest-looking, elderly woman may lend great credibility to an advertisement of "home-cooked" foods. A newspaper or magazine publisher may print only those pictures that put his candidate in the most favorable light; the unfavorable or convict-type picture of the political opponent is frequently printed. In order to assure the desired responses, only authorized photographs of some families, such as a royal family, are distributed to the press.

In general, photographs are accorded a degree of prestige, for they are considered true reflections of reality. It should not be forgotten, however, that pictures can be retouched to better serve the purposes of the publisher. Certain atrocity pictures used in wartime to convince a people of the barbarism of the enemy are examples of this practice.

The artist creating a drawing or cartoon can formulate his own reality; he can distort actuality to fit his own ends. Most people realize this fact and therefore do not give the drawing and the cartoon the same prestige value as the photograph. Political figures are most subject to the propagandistic distortions of the cartoon and the caricature. Few men of controversy escape them. Those newspapers and news magazines unable to hire their own artists usually have available the free drawings and cartoons provided by agencies in the hire of special interests.

Comic strips are a disarming means of propaganda; they depict almost every phase of contemporary life, subtly championing, satirizing, or obviously pooh-poohing certain aspects of it. In recent years many of the comic strips have taken up the to-be-continued story with emphasis on the love, hate, intrigue, and conflict of life rather than on the humor of human conduct. Many have left the "Mutt and Jeff" and "Blondie" approach and have become the thriller-type, such as "Dick Tracy," "Superman," and "Smiling Jack." During World War II some villains in these comics were dressed as Nazis and Japanese. The author can indoctrinate his readers according to his purposes; he can try to change readers' attitudes toward enemies outside the country or toward social, political, and economic types within the country. When used on a large scale in a concerted plan of promotion, the *simulated reality* of the photograph, drawing, cartoon, and comic strip can become actuality in the minds of many readers.

Billboards, posters, banners, and mottos

No matter where we turn, we are confronted with the persuasion of a billboard along the street or highway, a poster stuck on a post, fence, city bus, subway, or store window, an array of banners flying from a gasoline station, a circus, or a store where a special sale is in progress, a motto hanging in your hotel room, stuck on your windshield, or placed in the window of your bank.

These vehicles play an important part in the promotion of many ends. The large billboard meets you head-on at an abrupt turn in the road to ask "Have you tried the Uncola?"—and the local church demands to know "Where will you spend eternity?" The poster may ask you to buy war bonds or attend the senior prom. The banner may herald a slash in a store's sirloin steak prices or a future homecoming celebration. The motto in the Boy Scouts' den may advocate preparedness and a good deed a day; in the parlor it may praise the pleasures of home. The uses of posters, banners, and mottos are almost endless.

Such vehicles are not prohibitively expensive and, if placed properly and prepared with artistry, can be quite effective. They have a definite space limitation, and therefore the appeals must be brief and succinct. They must be content to identify a product or to state a brief slogan. In general, advertisers and other persuaders use such vehicles to supplement the more completely developed persuasion they use in newspapers, magazines, on the radio, television, from the public platform, and by still other means.

Mass nonverbal vehicles

Mass demonstrations are the vehicles of persuaders who wish to appropriate the dynamic nature of crowds to exert pressure toward desired ends. Throughout history the use of such methods has appeared periodically. The march on Washington in 1890 by Coxey's "army of the unemployed" and the "bonus march" on Washington by veterans of World War I were cases of national concern. There have been hunger marches, political marches, religious marches, marches by the American Legion and by teachers seeking increased salaries. Abroad, Mussolini and Hitler staged frequent mass demonstrations to form and then to solidify their power. In a 1930–34 study of Communist activities in Chicago, it was found that "during the first five years of the depression the Communist Party led, organized, or participated in 2,088 mass demonstrations in the city of Chicago."[25] This number did not include the regular public meetings held by the party and its affiliated units.

In recent years mass demonstrations have increased in the cities, on campuses, and outside churches, legislative halls, and factories. The exposure by television and press has made every citizen very aware of how "body rhetoric" can promote ideas. It is important, therefore, that the student of persuasion give careful study to this method of carrying persuasive messages.

Although mass demonstrations frequently have an oral dimension, we are concerned here primarily with the use of physical bodies in communicating a point of view. This is not to suggest that we consider the verbal component insignificant. Frequently, the oral language prior to or accompanying a mass demonstration is a type of coercive rhetoric, one that involves ultimatums or non-negotiable demands. Too, the demonstrations are sometimes merely preludes to violence. We simply consider such coercive rhetoric and violence as outside the spirit and method of persuasion and therefore outside the domain of our present study. We are quite aware, however, that these methods can be strong modes of influence and deserve the careful study and concern of every citizen who is pledged to the more thoughtful considerations of, and solutions to, social problems.

Mass demonstrations frequently result from a feeling that the channels of normal protest procedures are either inaccessible or ineffectual. Their values, though not established by as much careful research as might be desired, are thought to be as follows: (1) to bring attention to grievances by disrupting normal modes of living and providing a dynamic and dramatic stimulus, (2) to coalesce a broad spectrum of dissent and thus provide the movement with an identity, (3) to utilize a boldness of protest not usually found in individual behavior, (4) to suggest at least the illusion of universality, and (5) to pose the threat of power and potential violence. In sum, the overall purpose is to provide a channel of communication in a situation where conventional channels are thought to provide little or no opportunity for a fair hearing.

Let us look briefly at the chief types of mass demonstrations.

Parades and marches

The parade is the type of march that usually has a very general overall purpose, such as the purpose of commemorating Veterans'

---

25 H. D. Lasswell and D. Blumenstock, *World Revolutionary Propaganda* (New York: Alfred A. Knopf, 1939), p. 44.

Day, Independence Day, May Day, or Homecoming; it may be used to promote the strength of a political movement, as used by Hitler. Banners, music, floats, and marchers are frequently included. The parade can be an irresistible spectacle and tends to command attention quite readily. It serves to reenforce attitudes and customs relative to a cultural value, and frequently it provides members of special-interest groups in the parade the opportunity to carry persuasive messages on the banners or floats. Thus not only a general purpose, but many separate and individual purposes may be served. Parades are a worldwide source of interest and diversion, they help create group identity, and they provide a dramatic method of promoting a cause.

A march, in contrast to a parade, is more specific, is singular in purpose, and is usually linked with an immediate and urgent problem. It may be accompanied by banners, placards, or singing, but normally its purpose does not permit the gaiety and the disarming mood of the parade. A Milwaukee priest has recently completed a march of welfare recipients from Milwaukee to the state capitol in Madison, Wisconsin, in an attempt to influence welfare legislation. In this case the march ended in physical violence by temporarily taking over the Assembly Hall. Many student marches have been held recently on campuses throughout the country and abroad. Labor groups continue to use picketing marches, housewives have used marches against food prices, and the unemployed have marched in efforts to secure jobs. Abroad the most widespread and violent marches were used by the youth in the Red Guard movement in efforts to spread the cultural revolution promulgated by Communist China's leader, Mao Tse-tung.

The march thus persists as a form of promotion in today's societies and should be given careful study by every scholar in the field of persuasion.

Sit-ins and kneel-ins

Other less active mass demonstrations include the sit-in and the kneel-in. The sit-in was popularized in the Civil Rights movement when blacks sat down at lunch counters, in the front seats of buses or trains, and in other places where their presence was not traditionally accepted. More recently some student groups have staged sit-ins in university buildings to protest some existing policy.

The kneel-in has also been used in attempts to desegregate churches and other places. This "religious sit-in" has sought to employ the respect for religious worship as an attitude-change agent.

In the study assessing the values of the sit-in and kneel-in, Carolyn Calloway summarizes:

> . . . various psychological devices such as the together device, common ground, and prestige were instruments in persuading the masses (Negro) to action.
> The demonstrations were characterized by those factors of attention such as novelty, movement and change, and repetition which sustained the attention of the receivers. By gaining attention the demonstrators were able to present their grievances to the American people. They appealed to courage and self-discipline, morality and sympathy. The demonstrators hoped that these appeals would influence white Americans to reassess their value systems and commit themselves to alleviating the problem of the Negro.
> . . . The mass media contributed significantly to the Negro struggle. Newspapers and magazines carried the messages of the demonstrators to the local, national, and international community. Television, being a visual medium, dramatically portrayed the injustices imposed on Negroes throughout the South.[26]

Conclusion

Our purpose in this chapter has been to alert the reader to the vital roles played by the chief carriers of persuasive messages and to suggest that the message must be suited to the medium, and that both must be adapted to the audience if possible. We have not attempted to provide detailed analyses of the nature, values, and limitations of these media as carriers of persuasive messages. There is a sizable body of literature on most of these vehicles, and students of persuasion should consider this literature as necessary supplementary reading. Our point here has been that careful study should be made in the selection and use of the vehicles in terms of their ability to reach the desired audience, their credibility as assigned by the audience, and their capacity to help move that audience toward some attitudinal or behavioral change.

Research measurements of the media as agents in the process of persuasion are lacking in some cases, sketchy in others, and are becoming quite fruitful in still others. The reader will understand that those vehicles operating in mass situations are difficult to assess; they do not lend them-

[26] C. R. Calloway, "An Analysis of the Non-Verbal Means of Persuasion in the Civil Rights Movement—1960–1963: Sit-ins, Marches, and Kneel-ins," (Master's thesis, University of Wisconsin, 1968), pp. 101–2.

selves to the controls of the laboratory. Nonetheless, the student would be well advised to become familiar with the research literature on those media of interest to him.

In closing this discussion let us review briefly what the research indicates in general about the media.

Apparently the introduction of new media does not reduce the use of the old. This may be surprising to those who would reason that with new media would come a corresponding reduction in the use of the old media. The studies by Wilbur Schramm and others indicate that people who use one vehicle or medium tend also to use the other, older media to a greater extent. This may explain in part why there are more newspapers and books than there were prior to radio and television and more radio stations since the coming of television.

Audiences tend to regard the mass media with a certain degree of prestige. Lazarsfeld and Merton hold that:

> The mass media bestow prestige and enhance the authority of individuals and groups by *legitimizing their status.* Recognition by the press or radio or magazines or newsreels testifies that one has arrived, that one is important enough to have been singled out from the large anonymous masses, that one's behavior and opinions are significant enough to require public notice. The operation of this status conferral may be witnessed most vividly in the advertising pattern of testimonials to a product by "prominent people." Within wide circles of the population (though not within certain selected social strata), such testimonials not only enhance the prestige of the product but also reflect prestige on the persons who provide the testimonials.[27]

Another point of interest is that persons having some definite interest in a subject tend to follow this interest in the media that assure the most complete treatment, and usually this means the printed media. It is of interest, too, to note that the responses to the media tend to vary with level of education; those of a higher level of education rely more on print than on the other media, and those with a lower level of education rely more on radio and television.

Finally, when the composition of the audience is held constant, the media tend to differ in effectiveness as carriers of persuasive messages. Klapper provides, in part, this summary of studies.

[27] P. F. Lazarsfeld and R. K. Merton, "Mass Communication, Popular Taste, and Organized Social Actions" in L. Bryson, ed., *The Communication of Ideas* (New York: Harper and Row, 1948), p. 95.

In laboratory experiments, wherein all conditions other than the media are kept constant, formal personal appeal is typically found more effective than radio, which is in turn found more effective than print. Television and films may be hypothesized to fall between personal appeal and radio.

In real life situations, informal personal appeal has been consistently found to be more effective than any mass medium, but it is nevertheless not essential to successful persuasion. The relative efficacy of the mass media varies so widely from one topical area to another as to defy generalization. Multimedia usage supplemented by face-to-face contact is believed to be peculiarly effective and has characterized various highly successful propaganda campaigns.[28]

[28] J. T. Klapper, *The Effects of Mass Communication* (New York: The Free Press, 1960), pp. 129–30.

II

Exploring
the bases of persuasion

Theory and practice of effective persuasion must rest securely on knowledge of the bases of human motivation and the rhetorical means of using this knowledge in persuasive messages. The chapters in part 2 attempt to provide these bases.

Chapter 3 traces the chief steps that have been made in the search for the sources of motivation and persuasion. Chapters 4, 5, and 6 consider the natures and roles of drives, motives, emotions, and attitudes in persuasion. Chapter 7 assesses the influences of man's social behavior on motivation and persuasion. Chapter 8 provides a new approach regarding the role of critical thinking in persuasion. Chapter 9 treats the frequently neglected part culture plays in human persuasion. Finally, chapter 10 closes part 2 by pointing the reader toward the ethical dimensions of persuasion.

3

The search for a theory of persuasion

Introduction

We are all "people watchers." From time immemorial no subject has been more fascinating, occupied more discussion and debate than the study of man himself. Through the centuries the great philosophers, theologians, rhetoricians, and poets, as well as the unskilled and untutored, have made their pronouncements regarding the behavior of that puzzling creature called man. In recent history the vast field of the behavioral sciences has brought the methods of science to bear upon this complex and intriguing subject.

Inability to provide an adequate explanation of man's behavior did not deter early man from developing—largely through trial, error, and astute observations—some theories about, and practical skills in, dealing with others. Over 3,000 years ago, Egyptian wise men suggested principles for influencing people. The courtesans, politicians, and traders of every age developed some skills in recognizing the sources of human response and in manipulating these to their own ends. The advertisers were among the early persuaders, and the earliest known advertisement (3,000 B.C.) was written on a sheet of papyrus in Thebes and urged the return of a runaway slave. Advertisements of gladiatorial contests and of baths have been found on the walls of old Pompeii.

From the earliest attempts to use the available modest knowledge of persuasion to our present abundance of research and data regarding human motivation and highly intricate systems of influence, many notable theories concerning the nature of persuasion have evolved. The sincere student of persuasive discourse can best understand the subject if he attempts first to understand the foundations on which contemporary theory and practice are based. This knowledge of the heritage of persuasion theory will provide a framework for one's future study. Although countless people use persuasive techniques, few are skilled in the analysis of human behavior.

This chapter, therefore, presents a brief survey of some of the chief attempts to answer the great human riddle. Our purpose here is not to present a comprehensive treatment of the various approaches to the understanding of human behavior, but to highlight briefly some of the chief guideposts that have pointed us toward the present paths of inquiry into the subject. From this survey the reader should glean some insight into those theories that help form the bases upon which our present approach to the study of persuasion rests and to appreciate the problem of formulating a modern theory.

Early theories of human nature

Platonic and Aristotelian views[1]

Although Plato and his famous pupil, Aristotle, are best known to students of rhetoric and public address for their views on rhetoric, let us first sketch briefly their differing philosophical views regarding the nature of man; then we will follow with a summary of their contributions to rhetorical theory. Some claim that Plato might be considered one of the founders of social psychology. An idealist who was interested in reforming what he thought was decadence in Greek society, he developed a concept of human behavior that claims people behave as they do because society teaches them to so behave. The total education of the individual, from shortly after birth until death, determines his behavior. Thus, seeing behavior that was distasteful to him, Plato believed that the training of the individual should be so adjusted as to produce the desirable type. To Plato the ideal person was the philosopher-king, the only one who could know truth and establish civilization as it ought to be.

Aristotle, on the other hand, claimed that the cause of society was to be found in the "nature" of the individual. He thought that the individual behaves instinctively and has a rather unchangeable character because he found the people of Greece tended to behave in a relatively uniform manner. Critics have observed that had Aristotle looked further, he would have found that other people lived social patterns that were quite different from the Athenians. These two great philosophers espoused differing theories of human behavior that still persist.

Fifth century B.C. Greek society gave a prominent place to oral persuasion. The political system operated to a great extent through speech. It is quite understandable, therefore, that these two men should concern

[1] R. T. LaPiere and P. R. Farnsworth, *Social Psychology* (New York: McGraw-Hill, 1936), pp. 6–7.

themselves with rhetoric. Out of the need for effective oral discourse it was to be expected that there should arise those who sought to teach others how to speak effectively. These *sophists*, as they came to be called, accepted fees and professed to teach knowledge and skills adequate to the practical needs of their pupils. Plato, in his distrust of the masses, severely criticized the sophists as providers of false knowledge, fallacious arguments, and downright demagoguery. They were corrupting the youth. Plato seemingly heaped on the sophists all the disdain he felt for the ills of Greek society and its training system. His indictment of the rhetoric of the courts and political assemblies as being concerned merely with probabilities—not with truth—has persevered until today when some consider the rhetoric used in these places as suspect, artificial, or "sophistic." Thus he argued the need for the philosopher-king whose knowledge of truth could make of society (and the individual) what it ought to be.

Although Plato's lofty ideals are probably not to be realized in society, although his criticism of the sophists may not have been entirely justified, his insistence upon the search for truth, his analyses of individual sophists in his *Dialogues*, his suggestions that a persuader should become an astute student of human nature and society, and his pointing ever to a nobler rhetoric are enduring contributions to our study.

With his theory of the nature of man, Aristotle seemed less interested than his teacher in reforming Greek life and more interested in observing relatively fixed behavior and reorganizing theory regarding life (and rhetoric) in terms of principles and classifications. In siding more with the rhetoricians of the day, his *Rhetoric* claimed that rhetoric is an art (not a pseudoart, as Plato claimed), that it has a subject matter of its own, that it is not a vulgar technique used only by demagogues, and that it is an essential part of education and government. Defining rhetoric as "the faculty of observing in any given case the available means of persuasion," Aristotle claimed that rhetoric properly dealt with probabilities and contingencies, that no one deliberates about certainties. We shall later refer to the more specific modes of persuasion used by Aristotle and other classical writers.

Hedonism

Another classic behavioral theory is the view that man by nature seeks pleasure and avoids pain. Started among the Greeks and prominent during the eighteenth and nineteenth centuries, this philosophy was later criticized and for the most part rejected by psychologists because of its dependence on knowledge of an individual's private experiences. To assume knowledge of a person's pleasure sensations seemed precarious indeed. What to one is pleasure may not be so to another, even though the stimulus situations may be identical. To argue that it is "natural" for man to do some things and equally "natural" for him to avoid doing other things ignores the fact that behavior to a great extent is socially determined. Another criticism has been that hedonism tends to become circular. Murray points this out:

> A man is said to seek pleasure; if he seeks something, then, it must be pleasurable. But what about a man who seems to seek failure? Or what about suicide? There are those people who appear to reject pleasure-seeking as a way of life. The Puritans, for example, avoided pleasure as a sinful thing. Of course, you could say that the Puritans obtained pleasure from abstention, but with this sort of argument one can explain behavior only after the fact, and hedonism loses all predictive power.[2]

It should be pointed out, however, that there has been some revival of hedonistic theory in more recent years by such psychologists as Paul T. Young[3] and David C. McClelland[4] who have brought more sophistication to the field by using objective means of measurement—an experimental hedonism, if you will. The student of persuasion will need to study this approach for potential answers to the question of motivation.

Early religious theories

Medieval theologians postulated that man's behavior was not due to nature, but to God. Behavior that was not acceptable to the church, it was reasoned, was motivated by an opposing force—Satan. Man, it was contended, had the right to choose whom he would serve. This was sometimes called the "free-will" theory.

Another early religious answer to behavior was the "doctrine of original sin," a doctrine still accepted by some today. This theory holds that from birth man is possessed of degrading influences and that his personal behavior and his society are direct evidences of this fact.

Critics of these theories point out that these attempts at single postulates designed to explain man's behavior tend to neglect the important

[2] E. J. Murray, *Motivation and Emotion* (Englewood Cliffs, N.J.: Prentice-Hall, 1964), p. 4.

[3] P. T. Young, "The Role of 'Hedonic Processes' in Motivation" in M. R. Jones, ed., *Nebraska Symposium on Motivation* (Lincoln, Neb.: University of Nebraska Press, 1955), pp. 193–238.

[4] D. C. McClelland, *Studies in Motivation* (New York: Appleton-Century-Crofts, 1955).

influences of training and socialization. Persuaders who have based their persuasion on these theories have been successful chiefly among those who are willing to grant the doctrinal assumptions involved.

Machiavellianism

Niccolo Machiavelli (1467–1527), Italian statesman and advisor to Italian princes, was known for his philosophy of expediency and, according to some writers, was the father of chauvinistic political theory. In defiance of the free will doctrine of the theologians, he contended that man by nature is a bad creature, that he has no choice in the matter. Therefore, Machiavelli advised princes that if man is not to do evil he must be persuaded to do good by wily political leadership and thus tricked into thinking he is gaining his evil ends. In *The Prince* (1513) Machiavelli outlines various stratagems a politician may use to gain his goals. This book was one of the earliest manuals of political craftsmanship.

If we were to adopt Machiavelli's theory of the debased nature of man, then our persuasion to get men to do good necessarily would employ deceptive methods.

Rationalism

The view that man is essentially a rational creature was held in varying degrees by some ancient philosophers (Plato, Aristotle), by certain medieval philosophers (St. Thomas Aquinas), by more recent thinkers (Descartes, Hobbes, Spinoza), and by many average citizens today.[5] In our tendency to make wish the father of thought we may see ourselves as highly rational, reflective, fact-finding creatures. If this were so, a persuader need only present the facts, reason cogently from them, and the persuadee will respond as expected.

Critics of this point of view are quick to suggest that frequently our alleged *reasons* for our behavior are not necessarily the real determinants, that man much of the time acts upon the promptings of desire, and that what is considered rational conduct in one society may not be so regarded in another.

It is probably true that modern man in some settings is demanding more rational appeals in attempts to persuade him, but the claim that man is *innately* rational has not been adequately supported. Rather than saying man is a rational creature, it is more accurate to say he is a *rationalizing* one.

[5] For a discussion of rationalism, see W. E. H. Lecky, *History of the Rise and Influence of the Spirit of Rationalism in Europe* (New York: Appleton, 1914).

Racial determinism

Closely linked to the theory of rationalism is that which claims that by the slow process of biological selection more rational races have tended to emerge.[6] Some protagonists have concluded that certain races are therefore inferior and incapable of as much rationality as others. This belief has led dictators to proclaim that certain people are destined to rule over others and, as Adolf Hitler demonstrated, this persuasion can achieve certain temporary successes. Modern science, however, has repudiated the theory of racial determinism as a valid or sufficient explanation of human conduct.

Personality type and trait theories

Each individual manifests a certain unique style or configuration of personal characteristics and adjustment patterns in dealing with his environment; this configuration is termed *personality*, and this important concept has opened an area of research into man's behavior. To classify phenomena has always been the beginning of science, and so it has been with the ordering of personality characteristics into types and traits. From the ancient to the present day this approach has sought to provide clues to the prediction of behavior. What reader has not "typed" the personalities of others in attempts to explain or predict behavior? This is a great pastime for many of us. Let us look at a few representative examples.

Type theories

BODY TYPES. Kretschmer (1925) projected one of the early theories of body types and their relation to personality characteristics.[7] He concluded that there are three rather distinct physical types: (1) the *asthenic* type, characterized by a lean, narrowly built frame, poor blood, inadequate skin secretion, narrow shoulders, long, thin arms with delicately shaped hands, a long narrow chest, thick stomach, and angular face; (2) the *athletic* type, characterized by strong development of the skeleton and the muscles, firm and healthy skin, broad shoulders, thick chest, muscled abdomen, trunk tapering toward mid-section, narrow

---

[6] See J. A. deGobineau, *The Inequality of Human Races,* trans. by A. Collins, (New York: Putnam, 1915). See also Paul Radin, *The Racial Myth* (New York: McGraw-Hill, 1934).

[7] E. Kretschmer, *Physique and Character* (New York: Harcourt, Brace, 1925).

pelvis, tapering and shapely legs, muscular arms, firm face and jaw, and short, snubby nose; and (3) the *pyknic* type, which does not reach its highest development until middle age and is characterized by a rounded figure, fatness about the trunk, a deep, vaulted chest which tends to broaden out toward the lower part of the body, soft and rounded shoulders pushed slightly forward.

After classifying people morphologically, Kretschmer then related physical attributes to particular psychological traits. Undoubtedly one's physical construction and one's health provided a basis for some personality manifestations. However, studies have found little significant relationship between body type and personality.

PHYSIOLOGICAL TYPES.   The ancient Greeks classified people's temperaments according to body chemistry and the prominence of one fluid in the body.[8] Four types were indicated—(1) the *sanguine,* characterized by being cheerful, pleasant, warmhearted; (2) the *phlegmatic,* characterized as having a sluggish, apathetic disposition; (3) the *melancholic,* marked by a sad and depressed nature; and (4) the *choleric,* characterized by a rather irascible, easily angered nature.

In recent times personality characteristics have been linked with hormones and to other endocrinal explanations. However, even though more accurate measurements have been devised, it seems clear that the differences in individual physiology do not demonstrate distinct "types," but rather continuities.

SOCIOLOGICAL TYPES.   While some were seeking the answer to personality and behavior in terms of body and physiological types, others were exploring the possibility of classifying people in terms of their social roles or *social types.* Thomas and Znaniecki were among the pioneer theorists and researchers in this area in their study of the Polish peasant in Europe and in America.[9] Three types were said to exist: (1) the *Philistine,* or practical man, who has a strong wish for security and safety; (2) the *Bohemian,* who tends toward new experiences, flightiness, and pleasurable activities; and (3) the *Creative* man, who is relatively stable, yet possesses the capacity for changing his attitudes and desires in terms of some goal of a creative nature as found in art, religion, mechanical invention, politics, or economics.

Though this line of research has not produced many subsequent investigations, it should be said that this approach has tended to focus

---

[8] Kimball Young, *Personality and Problems of Adjustment* (New York: Appleton-Century-Crofts, 1940), pp. 302–3.

[9] W. I. Thomas and F. Znaniecki, *Polish Peasant in Europe and America* (Boston: Badger, 1918, 1920).

The search for a theory of persuasion

upon the relationship between the social order and the individual's behavior patterns.

PSYCHOLOGICAL TYPES. Perhaps the best known theory of psychological types is the *introvert-extrovert* classifications advanced by Jung (1922). [10] The *introvert* is said to focus his attention on himself and to create an inner, subjective world, while the *extrovert* is primarily interested in the world outside himself and how to relate to it. Jung did not claim that all people should be so classified, but he did contend that everyone has tendencies toward both introversion and extroversion, and that one generally predominates. The two major classifications were divided into the subclasses of thinking, feeling, sensation, and intuition. Thus we have the extroverted thinking type, the extroverted feeling type, and so on.

As critics have pointed out, certain social conditions surrounding a person can produce one or the other of these manifestations, but to say that these traits lie inevitably within the *natural* makeup of a person seems to go beyond known facts.

Trait theories

Trait theory may be said to be the opposite of type theory in that persons are not grouped according to a few types but are classified according to a large number of traits. As the reader knows, it is an everyday game for people to label others according to their own unscientific scales as energetic, lazy, shy, or aggressive. Some social scientists have attempted to bring scientific methods into observations of those rather consistent patterns people demonstrate in various situations. Scales are developed—each representing a trait—on which persons may be located. Thus a *psychogram* may be made showing in a schematic way how an individual's traits may vary when compared with others as a norm. This response-oriented approach looks for characteristics that are not governed by the context of the stimulus, that tend to recur under varied conditions. Stimuli, therefore, are cancelled out so that the *traits* can be said to be truly those of the individual and not resident in a given situation.

ALLPORT'S THEORY OF DISPOSITIONS.[11] Gordon W. Allport (1937, 1961), in what may be called a trait theory, distinguishes between two broad trait classifications: (1) *common traits,* those that are comparable among persons, and (2) *personal traits,* those that are unique to a person. In their *Scale of Values* (1960), Allport, Vernon, and Lindzey

[10] C. G. Jung, *Psychological Types* (New York: Harcourt, Brace, 1922).

[11] G. W. Allport, *Personality* (New York: Henry Holt, 1937).

indicate how people may be measured in terms of *common traits*.[12] One person may be compared to another according to preferred values, such as theoretical, esthetic, social, economic, political, and religious. *Personal traits,* however, cannot be used in comparing one person with another because they are unique to a given person. Even though two people might demonstrate what appears to be a common trait—say, submissiveness—each will be submissive in his own unique way because of his personal capacities and experiences. It seems accurate to say that Allport would contend that common traits exist only in a rather crude or broadly comparable way.

Allport views personal traits (dispositions) as organized in a hierarchal manner. In this connection he identifies personal traits as *cardinal, central,* and *secondary* dispositions. The *cardinal disposition* is one which is so predominant that it influences virtually all the behavioral patterns of an individual. When a person stands out because he is so dominated or possessed by a single cardinal disposition, he may well become a reference point, a prototype, by which we tend to describe others. Thus we may say a person is a *Tarzan* or a *Beatle,* comparing him with a known reference disposition. It should be clear that there are few who demonstrate a *cardinal disposition.* Many, however, have at least a few *central dispositions,* that small number of dispositions that can characterize a person. The *secondary dispositions* are those many characteristics that demonstrate a person's more isolated interests or response tendencies.

CATTELL'S THEORY OF SURFACE AND SOURCE TRAITS.[13]   In attempting to reduce the great number of trait names used to distinguish individual personalities, the researcher may find traits that seem to cluster together; he may then use one name for the cluster and thus reduce the total number of traits to a manageable size which would permit the creation of a *trait profile* for an individual. Cattell used this approach in a very comprehensive study that arrived at 171 personality variable names which were said to cover the entire "personality sphere." Most of these traits were expressed as polar opposites—such as loyal vs. fickle, wise vs. foolish. The interrelationships that were found to exist among traits led Cattell to distinguish between two types of traits: *surface* traits and *source* traits. All traits that showed an intercorrelation of .60 or higher were assumed to indicate one cluster or *surface* trait. *Source* traits were

[12] G. W. Allport, P. E. Vernon, and G. Lindzey, *A Study of Values: A Scale for Measuring the Dominant Interests in Personality,* 3rd ed., (Boston: Houghton-Mifflin, 1960).

[13] R. B. Cattell, *Description and Measurement of Personality* (New York: World Book Co., 1946). See also R. B. Cattell, *The Scientific Analysis of Personality* (Baltimore, Md.: Penguin Books, 1965).

found through *factor analysis,* a more refined method than *cluster analysis.* In addition to showing what traits cluster together, this method is capable also of explaining clusters of surface traits and of identifying the "purer" examples of a basic trait. Thus Cattell was able to arrive at lists of both surface and source traits which could be used in measuring personalities.

This approach lends itself conveniently to experimentation, but trait theory does not account for traits that express themselves differently as the result of varying environmental conditions. Nonetheless, the student of persuasion must keep in mind that research in this area may reveal information useful to his study.

Early general theories of motivation

Instinct theory

"Just appeal to their basic instincts" has been the offhand advice given to many budding persuaders. And man has been thought to have many instincts—pugalistic, maternal, self-preservative, and on through an almost endless list of names assigned as instincts to behavior that could not be explained otherwise. Charles Darwin probably provided the start of a scientific approach to motivation. He held that certain complex actions of birds and animals were inherited, instinctive, and that these arise out of natural selection. Soon the explanation was related to human beings, and a great debate started. About 1900 certain psychologists theorized that man, too, behaves according to a set of instincts. Among these were William James, Sigmund Freud, and William McDougall who argued that the instinct doctrine provides a useful concept in psychology. To McDougall certain conducts in man—such as flight, pugnacity, curiosity, mating, food-getting, acquisitiveness, self-assertion, gregariousness, and constructiveness are instincts.[14] By 1924 the list of so-called instincts had grown so large that Bernard found in a survey of approximately 400 authors that the term instinct had been applied to almost 6,000 different urges and activities of man.[15]

Some of the difficulty in the controversy over instinct theory was caused by a lack of clear definition. More recently instinctive behavior has been redefined as behavior in which the underlying biological pat-

[14] W. McDougall, *An Introduction to Social Psychology* (London: Methuen, 1908).

[15] L. L. Bernard, *Instinct: A Study in Social Psychology* (New York: Henry Holt, 1924).

terns have been produced by maturation rather than through learning. Even with this definition, studies have shown that it is doubtful, and indeed rare, that the human adult demonstrates any purely instinctive behavior patterns. Thus we may say that for our purposes, instinct theory is probably only of historic value.

Drive theory

In 1918 Robert S. Woodworth introduced the concept of drive to describe that body of energy that actuates the organism into behavior patterns not produced by habit.[16] This general concept was soon enlarged to signify different drives such as hunger, thirst, sex, and freedom from fatigue. Significant, careful subsequent research studies have tended to support drive theory and have given it more scientific respectability.

In 1932 physiologist Walter B. Cannon offered the concept of *homeostasis*, which suggested that deviations from the normal, steady organic state caused the individual to do those things that would return the body to a state of equilibrium and thus increase the chances for biological survival.[17] Soon it was thought that homeostasis may well be the basis for all motivation, that drives give rise to psychological motives.

It would appear, however, that there is a very complex relationship between psychological motivation and physiological needs and that homeostasis does not provide a complete explanation of physical drives or social motives. Regardless of the criticism leveled at drive theory in terms of how much behavior can be explained by the theory, it is rather generally agreed that our physiological imperatives do play a significant role in our motivation. Surely no one will doubt that a person is basically an organism with its own function and perpetuation at stake, that organic deficits can and do arouse activities fundamental to the study of motivation. Attempts, however, to explain all human behavior in these terms are destined to err, for they neglect the fact that man is also a social creature and that he may delay or redirect his physical drives so that his social desires may be gratified.

Psychoanalytic theory

A Viennese neurologist, Sigmund Freud, originated psychoanalysis as a method for treating the emotionally disturbed.[18] His experi-

---

[16] R. S. Woodworth, *Dynamic Psychology* (New York: Columbia University Press, 1918).

[17] W. B. Cannon, *The Wisdom of the Body* (New York: Norton, 1932).

[18] S. Freud, *The Interpretation of Dreams*, Vols. 4 and 5 (London: Hogarth Press, 1900).

ence with his patients led him to conclude that sexual problems seemed to be at the root of many disturbances. In a theory akin to the instinct school of thought and to drive theory, Freud held that the fundamental source of human energy comes from a drive—sexual in nature—which he called the *libido*. To Freud the term *sexual* was used quite broadly and includes all types of activities that are physically pleasurable. The complete self is divided into three parts: (1) the *id*, characterized by man's more primitive, unrestrained impulses; (2) the *ego*, which is the "rational self" and which strives to control the basic urges of the *id;* and (3) the *super-ego*, which is that part of a person in charge of moral ideas and ideals. The *super-ego* and the *id* are thus in constant conflict, a conflict resolved successfully in the normal person but quite unsuccessfully in the abnormal personality.

Modern scholars have criticized Freud's theory, chiefly as being too biological and as not taking into sufficient account the significance of man's social experiences and development. Certain neo-Freudians have emerged who emphasize not only the social development but also the "growth force" of man. These neo-Freudians say that man's desirable potentialities are too often thwarted by his poorly designed social environment.

Nonetheless, Freud's formulations have had a considerable impact on man's search for himself. Even today our speech reflects the influence of compartmentalizing personality by references to "appeals to our better selves," to "our rational selves," or to our "animal nature." And who can deny that psychoanalysis has sensitized us all to the psychic states that can beset us and awakened us to the problems that can arise in that complex labyrinth which is the mind of man.

Contemporary approaches to the study of motivation

In the contemporary study of motivation the concept of *attitude*—referring to a state of preparedness or a set to initiate a particular response—has become a central, complex concept in socio-psychological theory and research. Gordon Allport has stated that "the concept of attitude is probably the most distinctive and indispensable concept in contemporary American social psychology. No other term appears more frequently in experimental and theoretical literature."[19] With this great interest in such a broad, multidimensional concept, it is not surprising that varied theorists and researchers have developed varied approaches and theories regarding

[19] G. W. Allport, "Attitudes in the History of Social Psychology" in G. Lindzey, ed., *Handbook of Social Psychology*, Vol. 1 (Reading, Mass.: Addison-Wesley, 1954), p. 43.

it. Our purpose here is merely to sketch a few of the best known theories in general; in chapter 6 we explore in detail the matter of attitudes in relation to persuasion.

Consistency theory

In recent years there has been considerable concern with the theory that man desires to have logically consistent attitudes in reference to various life situations. An approach that has commanded the efforts of a number of social psychologists for over a decade is known as *consistency theory*, a theory that a person strives to have consistent beliefs and behavior, and that when he is aware of some discrepancy he strives to rectify the inconsistency by making some change in his beliefs, his behavior, of perhaps both. The approaches surveyed below can be said to represent three variants of consistency theory: (1) balance; (2) congruity; and (3) cognitive dissonance.

BALANCE THEORY.   Heider (1946, 1958) may be credited with pioneering in the area of consistency theory with his *balance theory* and model.[20] He contended that people strive for balance, for harmonious relations between their attitudes and their behavior, and that they sense frustration or psychological upset when such a balance is not present. He theorized using essentially two types of relationships between people and between people and events: (1) *sentiment relations* such as admiration, approbation, or love and (2) *unit relations* which result in a unity of persons or persons and related events, such as proximity, similarity, causality, or ownership. Thus when a person likes two other people, he tends to expect that the other two like each other. In a model using a number of interrelationships among people, Heider attempted to demonstrate how attitudes cognitively are adjusted to create a balance between attitudes and behavior.

Though this approach seems to provide no answer regarding which of the numerous possible avenues may be taken to reduce the imbalance in any given situation, it should be said that Heider's theory opened up a great variety of applications that could be pursued in other research.

CONGRUITY THEORY.   The congruity theory of attitude change developed by Osgood and Tannenbaum (1955) grew out of their work on the measurement of meaning using their semantic differential scales.[21]

[20] F. Heider, "Attitudes and Cognitive Organization," *Journal of Psychology* 21 (1946): 107–12.

[21] C. Osgood and P. Tannenbaum, "The Principle of Congruity in the Prediction of Attitude Change," *Psychological Review* 62 (1955): 42–55.

The principle of congruity asserts that when two attitude objects with different evaluations are linked by an assertion, there will result a tendency for the evaluations of each of the objects to shift toward a position of balance or congruity. If, for instance, President Ford were to praise Cuba's Castro, the tendency would be to evaluate the president less highly and Castro more highly. For Ford to praise the United States and Castro to praise Cuba, no shift toward congruity is indicated because the attitude objects would suggest no incongruity.

A complete study of this theory reveals a very notable attempt to demonstrate with mathematical precision what some might still prefer to have presented verbally. The mathematical statement of the theory allows for an exact testing of the theory. We shall explore this theory in greater detail in chapter 6.

COGNITIVE DISSONANCE THEORY.   The theory of cognitive dissonance was advanced by Festinger (1957) and has generated no small amount of experimentation and criticism.[22] This theory, though closely related to other consistency theories, stresses the after effects that may follow a decision a person has made that produced a discrepancy or inconsistency between a belief and an action; to put it differently, this theory stresses what happens to individuals when their experiences do not coincide with what they had previously believed. Cognition or awareness of such a state of affairs, it is presumed, will cause the person to make any one of various responses—such as refusing to believe that the discrepancy exists, belittling its significance, adjusting his life to the fact, or seeking out justifications for the decision. A person may seek reassurance from others that his decision was correct, read only those advertisements or articles that further justify his position, become highly partisan for the product he bought or for the position he took, and so on. All salesmen know that they must continue to reenforce the decision a buyer has made lest the buyer's fear of making a mistake keep him from consummating the transaction. The cigarette advertisement that assures the smoker he "is no longer alone" surely seeks to keep the person who has decided to smoke the cigarette from experiencing the dissonance that may come from making the decision in full knowledge of lung cancer research.

In terms of the large body of literature related to dissonance theory we may conclude that this theory is possibly the most popular. It has many supporters and active researchers, but it also has many critics. The advanced student of persuasion should become familiar with the sizable

[22] L. Festinger, *A Theory of Cognitive Dissonance* (Evanston, Ill.: Row, Peterson, 1957).

body of literature related to the theory and should keep in mind its potential worth to a theory of persuasion.

Self-actualization theory

Consistency theories of attitude change considered briefly above tend to emphasize that motivation results from a need to be consistent, that attitude changes result from deficit tensions, and that behavior therefore departs from a state of equilibrium and then returns to it. In contrast with this approach is the theory that an individual has a fundamental need to develop himself to his greatest potential, that there are *positive* aspects of human motivation. The term that is used to designate this pervasive type of motivation is *self-actualization*, a seeking for complete self-fulfillment. A brief look at the views of two notable theorists in this area should suggest still another approach in seeking the sources of persuasion.

MASLOW.   Working on the premise that individuals are constantly striving to realize their potentialities, Maslow states that he was looking for a "humanly usable theory of motivation," and agreed that deficit theory is not the whole picture. He wrote "if the motivational life consists essentially of a defensive removal of irritating tensions, and if the only end product of tension reduction is a state of passive waiting for more unwelcome irritations to arise and in their turn to be dispelled, then how does change or development or movement or direction come about? Why do people improve? Get wiser? What does zest in living mean?"[23] Thus, to Maslow, creativity becomes something more than the removal of some deficiency or inconsistency.

To show man's progression toward self-actualization, Maslow contends that there exists a hierarchy of human needs which may be depicted in the form of a pyramid to indicate that certain needs take priority over others. At the base of the pyramid are our physiological needs, then progressing upward we have in turn security needs, social needs, esteem needs, and, at the apex, the need for self-actualization as may be expressed in the search for knowledge, desire for beauty, and creativity. In short, man's hierarchy of needs and values range from the basic or primitive organic needs to those values that are the most advanced forms of being and achieving. This approach argues that the higher needs will not be met until those lower in the hierarchy are satisfied.

[23] A. H. Maslow, *Motivation and Personality*, 2nd ed. (New York: Harper and Row, 1970). See also A. H. Maslow, "A Theory of Motivation," *Psychological Review* 50 (1943): 370–96.

ROGERS.   Like Maslow, Carl Rogers regards the need for self-actualization as inherent in the nature of man. As a therapist, Rogers has inquired into the private world of the individual, the world of experiences he calls the *phenomenal* field. This approach involves analyzing one's perceptions and interpretations because they determine the individual's behavior and form his attitudes. A self-concept tends to emerge from these perceptions and interpretations, and it is in terms of this concept that a person will accept or reject information, ideas, and propositions. To Rogers the most basic drive of the organism is toward this self-actualization. "The organism," he contends, "has one basic tendency and striving —to actualize, maintain, and enhance the experiencing organism."[24] According to this theory, in problems of human adjustment it is this growth for wholeness that makes recovery possible.

The social judgment–involvement approach[25]

For many years Muzafer Sherif has contributed notably to our knowledge of attitudes and the problems involved in changing them. His investigation of the processes of social judgments have added significantly to our understanding of the variations that can occur among individuals in accepting or rejecting propositions. Sherif's emphasis on the role of ego-involvement in attitude change has introduced a highly important dimension into our study. It suggests that attitudes based on social norms cannot be depicted as a given point on a continuum or attitude scale but are more accurately represented in terms of having a *latitude of acceptance, rejection,* or *noncommitment.* The range or size of the latitude will depend on the amount of ego-involvement connected with the attitude in question. Attitudes related to the basic values (family, religion) will have considerable ego-involvement. When propositions to change such attitudes are advanced, a judgmental process discriminates between alternatives. Hence we have the *social judgment–ego-involvement* approach to the study of attitudes as most recently advanced by Sherif, Sherif, and Nebergall.

Since the authors of the present book discuss the uses of this approach in chapter 6, we shall be content here merely to suggest the basic approach. Later we shall elaborate on the significance of the approach to students of persuasion.

---

[24] C. R. Rogers, *Client-Centered Therapy: Its Current Practice, Implications, and Theory* (Boston: Houghton-Mifflin, 1951).

[25] C. W. Sherif, M. Sherif, and R. Nebergall, *Attitude and Attitude Change: The Social Judgment-Involvement Approach* (Philadelphia: W. B. Saunders, 1965).

Attitude type and function theories

A smaller group of theorists contends that to change attitudes one must first know the *type* and/or *functions* of the attitude one is attempting to change and that this knowledge is necessary to the persuader. Such an approach assumes the burden of providing bases upon which attitudes may be justifiably classified. Let us review briefly several of these theories.

SMITH, BRUNER, AND WHITE.[26]   In a theory that is not based on experimental research but on a series of comprehensive case studies of subjects' attitudes toward Russia, the authors attempt to determine the roles played by opinions and attitudes in personality. Using a broad definition of attitude that includes opinion, they contend that an opinion or attitude may serve three types of functions: *object appraisal, social adjustment,* and *externalization. Object appraisal* provides the individual with an orientation toward objects in his environment; in classifying objects the individual is in a better position to determine what response is appropriate for him. The *social adjustment* function of attitudes permits the person to adjust appropriately to various social relationships; a person may voice only favorable opinions in situations where he wishes to be accepted and may express unacceptable opinions in situations where he wishes to remain independent or to remain outside the acceptance circle. Social adjustment attitudes can thus serve a very useful role in social relationships. The *externalization* function of opinions is served when they protect one's ego from the frustrations and anxieties resulting from inner problems. Thus a person may project onto some external group his own objectionable characteristics or desires. Some contend that racial prejudice may arise in this manner.

According to this approach attitudes or opinions may change because of a shift in one or all of the three functional purposes of attitudes or opinions. New information or argument may cause a change relative to an appraisal of an object or person, group pressures may produce a change in the social adjustment function, and an attitude based on the externalization function may be changed by the psychotherapist who provides "reassurance and permissiveness."

This theory contends that to change attitudes one must know their functional bases and what support such bases give to people's opinions on the issues in question.

[26] M. Smith, J. Bruner, and R. White, *Opinions and Personality* (New York: Wiley, 1956).

KATZ. In his functional approach to the study of attitudes, Katz states:

> ... the functional approach is the attempt to understand the reasons people hold the attitudes they do. The reasons, however, are at the level of psychological motivations and not of the accidents of external events and circumstances. Unless we know the psychological need which is met by the holding of an attitude we are in a poor position to predict when and how it will change.[27]

Katz lists four functions that attitudes may serve for the personality: (1) the *instrumental, adjustive,* or *utilitarian* function; (2) the *ego-defensive* function; (3) the *value-expressive* function; and (4) the *knowledge* function. These are described by Katz as follows:

> 1. The *instrumental, adjustive,* or *utilitarian function* upon which Jeremy Bentham and the utilitarians constructed their model of man. A modern expression of the approach can be found in behavioristic learning theory.
> 2. The *ego-defensive function* in which the person protects himself from acknowledging the basic truths about himself or the harsh realities in his external world. Freudian psychology and neo-Freudian thinking have been preoccupied with this type of motivation and its outcome.
> 3. The *value-expressive function* in which the individual derives satisfactions from expressing attitudes appropriate to his personal values and to his concept of himself. This function is central to doctrines of ego psychology which stress the importance of self-expression, self-importance, self-development, and self-realization.
> 4. The *knowledge function* based upon the individual's need to give adequate structure to his universe. The search for meaning, the need to understand, the trend toward better organization of perceptions and beliefs to provide clarity and consistency for the individual, are other descriptions of this function. The development of principles about perceptual and cognitive structure have been the contribution of Gestalt psychology.[28]

KELMAN. Kelman's functional approach to the study of attitudes is based on "the assumption that opinions adopted under different conditions of social influence, and based on different motivations, will

[27] D. Katz, "The Functional Approach to the Study of Attitudes," *Public Opinion Quarterly* 24 (1960): 163–204.

[28] D. Katz, "The Functional Approach to the Study of Attitudes" in T. D. Beisecker and D. W. Parson, eds., *The Process of Social Influence* (Englewood Cliffs, N.J.: Prentice-Hall, 1972), p. 21.

differ in terms of their qualitative characteristics and their subsequent histories."[29] Thus Kelman discusses the functional basis not only in terms of motives but also in terms of antecedent social influences, and his approach is unique in this regard. He identifies three processes of social influence: *compliance, identification,* and *internalization. Compliance* is said to occur when a person accepts influence from another person or group not because he accepts the content of a message but because he anticipates some approval or reward which is a social effect. *Identification* occurs when one accepts influence because he wishes to establish or maintain a "satisfying self-definition" relationship with another person or group. Here the act of conforming to another's influence is the satisfying part, even though he may also agree with the message content of the other person. *Internalization,* as you might expect, comes when a person accepts influence because the content (ideas and prescribed actions) of the induced behavior is the reward factor. Adoption is based on congruity of the influence idea with the individual's own set of values.

For each of the three processes mentioned, Kelman provides a set of antecedents and consequents. The determinants (antecedents) of compliance, identification, and internalization are: (1) the motivational basis for the influence or the nature of the anticipated effects; (2) the source of power of the influencing agent; and (3) the manner in which the prepotency takes place. The consequents distinguished by Kelman are: (1) the conditions in which the attitude will be manifest; (2) the conditions in which it can be changed; and (3) the type of behavior system in which it exists. Thus each of the three processes (compliance, identification, and internalization) operates between a set of antecedents and consequents and can be treated by relating the postulated antecedents in a given case to the postulated consequents. If a given attitude has certain antecedents it will necessarily have certain consequents.

From our brief survey of the three attitude type and function theories it should be clear that he who would change the attitudes or opinions of others must know something of the type or function of attitudes he wishes to change. These theories should provide a basis for learning more about the nature of attitudes and opinions.

Modern rhetorical approaches to persuasion

For many years students of rhetoric and public address depended on the classical, medieval, and Renaissance philosophers and theologians for the bases of their approaches to persuasive discourse. These approaches

---

[29] H. C. Kelman, "Processes of Opinion Change," *Public Opinion Quarterly* 25 (1961): 58–78.

tended to be essentially message-centered with some concern from philosophic and intuitive insights for the roles played by the speaker and the audience in the communication process. Though the contributions of the early writers on rhetoric have provided highly significant concepts, certain modern scholars in the field have sought to incorporate into the study the knowledge that has come from the more recently developed and scientifically oriented fields of psychology, social psychology, sociology, and communication theory. These scholars have attempted to use the insights of behavioral theory and research in the hope of developing a more complete and soundly based theory of suasive rhetoric.

Below we survey briefly the contributions of some writers who have helped in pointing the way toward using such new knowledge in the study of persuasive discourse.

James A. Winans

James A. Winans (1917), long an esteemed professor of public speaking at Cornell University, pioneered in attempts to identify the technique of persuasion and to place the processes of persuasion upon a clearly defined psychological foundation. Reflecting the influence of early psychologists E. B. Tichener and William James, Winans claimed that "what holds attention determines action." He therefore defined persuasion as the "process of inducing others to give fair, favorable, or undivided attention to propositions."[30] He pointed out that ideas which "arouse emotions" hold attention, and that the most evident way to fix attention is by awakening desire for the end sought. Motives and knowledge were related to attention. Apparently considering an analysis of motives to be unnecessary for students of public speaking, Winans adopted the list of *motive appeals* given earlier by Phillips[31] which include appeals to man's spiritual, intellectual, moral, and material wants. Wants were classified as self-preservation, property, power, reputation, affections, sentiments, and tastes.

Winans' attempt to add to the standard rhetorical tradition those insights of emerging behavioral science, plus his comprehensive treatment of the techniques of persuasion, make his contribution to our historical survey a notable one.

William Norwood Brigance

Acknowledging respect for the pioneering work of Winans, William Norwood Brigance suggested that more recent psychological re-

---

[30] J. A. Winans, *Public Speaking* (New York: The Century Co., 1917), p. 194.

[31] A. E. Phillips, *Effective Speaking* (Chicago: The Newton Co., 1908), chapter 5.

search provided a better insight into the nature of persuasion. As a background for his subsequent writing, Brigance in 1931 posited his *genetic* approach to persuasion in which he argues that "the tools of persuasion are best understood and most effectively used if we view them in the order of their origin and development in the race."[32] He points out that *authority* was the oldest mode of persuasion and therefore was the strongest with primitive man. *Experience* became the second mode of persuasion acquired by the race; as man's scope of experience increased, so did the body of accumulated knowledge man could use. The third development is *reason* which, because it is the most recent, is the weakest mode of persuasion.

In 1935 Brigance suggested that whereas James and Winans viewed persuasion as a *mental process*, "the generally accepted view today, however, is that persuasion takes place, not on an intellectual, but rather on a motor level." He claimed that even though the psychologists were often divided on technical points they agreed that the dominant basis for human belief is *desire*. This compelled Brigance to redefine the James-Winans theory of persuasion and to state his own definitions of persuasion as follows:

> 1.   When the aim is to arouse from indifference, to inspire, or to stimulate lagging enthusiasm and faiths, *persuasion is a process of vitalizing old desires, purposes, or ideals.*
> 2.   When the aim is to secure the acceptance of new beliefs *or courses of action, persuasion is a process of substituting new desires, purposes, or ideals for old ones.*[33]

In pointing the student of persuasion in the direction of a primary concern for the desire systems of the audience, Brigance was presaging the receiver-centered, behaviorally oriented emphasis of today's scholars in persuasion.

Robert T. Oliver

Robert T. Oliver was among the first scholars in the field of public address to attempt to blend the knowledge of rhetoric and public address with the insights of the contemporary behavioral sciences in such a way as to produce a body of theory and practice that could result

[32] W. N. Brigance, "A Genetic Approach to Persuasion," *Quarterly Journal of Speech* 17 (1931): 329–39.

[33] W. N. Brigance, "Can We Re-Define the James-Winans Theory of Persuasion?" *Quarterly Journal of Speech* 21 (1935): 19–26.

in the teaching of a formal course in persuasive speech. Contending that persuasion is not just a set of techniques, Oliver holds that the foundations of persuasion lie in the careful study of motivation.

In defining persuasion, Oliver states that "in a broad sense, persuasion is any form of discourse that influences thought, feelings, or conduct." In noting that such a definition might seem to suggest that "all speech is persuasive—for all speech is influential," he hastens to add that the fundamental basis for distinguishing persuasion from other forms of discourse is the conscious *purpose of the speaker*.[34] Thus only by determining the purpose of the speaker can one distinguish persuasion as a special mode of discourse.

The chief principles of persuasion, according to Oliver, are *attention, suggestion,* and *identification*; the modes of appeal are *evidence and authority, dynamic logic, emotion,* and *rationalization.*

In his two editions of *The Psychology of Persuasive Speech,* Professor Oliver has contributed commendably to our knowledge of that form of discourse called persuasion.

Wayne C. Minnick

In two editions of *The Art of Persuasion,* Wayne C. Minnick has sought to bring still more of the insights of contemporary behavioral science into a rhetoric of persuasion. His second edition has set forth a non-Aristotelian approach, one with greater emphasis on behavioral studies and theoretic constructs in the fields of communication and psychology. He emphasizes the interaction of man's perceptual-cognitive processes and his motivational system. Rather than viewing proofs in the traditional manner—logical, emotional, and ethical—Minnick views message support materials in persuasive discourse as cognitive, consensual, and motivational. This position shifts the emphasis from a message-centered to a response-centered orientation in which the total psychological equipment of the listener is brought to bear on the message received. Minnick defines persuasion as "discourse, written or oral, in which the author controls all appropriate communication variables in an attempt to determine the response of the receiver toward a particular choice of belief or conduct."[35]

The student of persuasion will be sensitized to the modern emphasis

[34] R. T. Oliver, *The Psychology of Persuasive Speech,* 2nd ed. (New York: Longmans, Green and Co., 1957), p. 8.

[35] W. C. Minnick, *The Art of Persuasion,* 2nd ed. (Boston: Houghton-Mifflin, 1968), p. 19.

in persuasion and will become acquainted with some of its significant research by studying the work of Professor Minnick.

Chaim Perelman

In 1958 *La Nouvelle Rhétorique Traité de L'Argumentation* by Chaim Perelman and L. Olbrechts-Tyteca was published in France, but not until its publication in English in the United States in 1969 as *The New Rhetoric: A Treatise on Argumentation*,[36] was its impact felt in America. The book presented argument as an everyday working form of communication rather than as an academic exercise. Argument as treated by Perelman and Olbrechts-Tyteca resembles audience-centered persuasion, with a new flexible rationality determined in part by participants and occasion.

Perelman extended and enlarged the concept of reason in argument. He rejected limiting "reason" to formal logic, and called attention to the fact that different men in different cultures have their own ways of being reasonable. Arguing reasonably according to Perelman consisted of using the system of critical deliberation characteristic of the individual auditor and satisfying its demands. He approached but did not cross the threshold of asserting that what is believed to be supported logically *is* supported logically, the perceptual criterion of critical thought. Certainly this modern interpretation was implied by his situational and individualistic approach to the reasoning processes in discourse.

Another contribution of Perelman was the distinction between the particular and the universal audience, and their reciprocal interaction.[37] Similar to his expansion of the concept "reason," the development of the notion of universal audience was taken from the real, work-a-day world, a formulation of immediate usefulness to practicing persuaders and active receivers of persuasion. Identifying universal and particular audiences to a certain message, analyzing their relationship in a persuasive interaction, and designing elements of the message and context with both in mind became productive procedures.

Truly the influence of Chaim Perelman and his coauthor, Mme. Olbrechts-Tyteca has changed our thinking about thoughtful persuasion. As a result, we deal with individual and cultural differences more realistically and competently.

[36] C. Perelman and L. Olbrechts-Tyteca, *The New Rhetoric: A Treatise on Argumentation* (South Bend, Ind.: University of Notre Dame Press, 1969).

[37] The concepts of universal and particular audiences are developed in some detail in chapter 8.

Conclusion

In this chapter we have attempted to provide the student of persuasion with a sufficient survey of the various attempts to explain the nature of human motivation to enable him to see his study in a more meaningful framework, to know something of its legacy. One basic conclusion should be immediately clear: the study of human motivation has been a major concern throughout the recorded history of man and, in recent years, even though the field may be said to be in a state of some disorder, there is burgeoning creativity in both theory and research that will increase our understanding of man and thus lead us to new and more astute theory and practice of persuasive rhetoric.

From this survey of the search for the sources of persuasion it should also be clear why we argued in chapter 1 that a modern approach to persuasion must be eclectic, pluralistic, and integrative in nature. In the succeeding chapters the reader will note that the present approach seeks to draw upon a number of the varied materials—only sketched in this chapter—that seem most relevant to the theory and practice suggested by your authors. Additional significant contributions not included in this chapter's survey will also be used.

4

The drives and motives in motivation

Introduction

Motivation: a basic consideration in the study of persuasion

If from some high vantage point in outer space a researcher from another planet could view the human species as we know it, he would see that this form of life lives in little boxes of various sizes, shapes, and materials. He would note that shortly after light comes to their portion of the planet many of these creatures leave their little boxes, rush in a little mobile mechanism to other boxes where they may manipulate some other mechanisms, lean over an elevated wooden plane and shuffle papers about, meet with other members of the species where they may make funny loud sounds and wave parts of their bodies at others. Our researcher may note that still others are building these boxes, still others are scraping the surface of the planet with belching machines, some females of the species collect in other little boxes where they sit with their heads under hot hoods and make sounds and signs to others doing the same thing, the smaller members of the species are running around chasing each other or batting little spheres, and many others are doing all sorts of queer things. And then as the daylight is fading, these odd creatures engage in a frenzied rush to return to the little boxes they had left earlier. Here, after watching a moving bright light in a little box for a while, they lie down inertly on a raised platform until the morning light reappears, whereupon these odd creatures repeat the the whole process again.

As our objective researcher views all this activity he would begin to suspect that there must be some type of energy that propels this little creature day after day, year after year. And, indeed, our hypothetical researcher would be right, for he has been observing a *motivated* creature, one who engages in a great variety of forms of behavior as he strives toward an equally great variety of goals. What can we learn about this complex subject of motivation that will be of help to the persuader? Certainly in a receiver-centered approach to persuasion the persuader must know as much as possible about human motivation if he is to develop messages designed to utilize the motivational processes of the persuadee. For him to study language, speech style, organization, and the modes of presentation without concern for their relation to motivation is to reduce rhetoric to simply a demonstrative art rather than a mode of persuasion. Since the study of motivation is, in sum, a study of determinants of behavior, such a study is of continuing concern for the persuader whose goals usually are centered upon modifying human behavior in some way.

Behavioral scientists hold differing views regarding the nature of human motivation. Man's capacity for learning is so great and his behavioral patterns are so varied and complex that it is to be expected that different approaches (biological, psychological, social) will lead to differing emphases and yield varied results. It is our belief that the biologically orientated and the socially orientated approaches will eventually begin to merge, and a more complete psychology of motivation will result. In the meantime, we are not disposed to attempt to demonstrate that one approach or field of behavioral study has all or even most of the answers regarding human motivation. Our primary allegiance is to those who seek to understand and practice persuasive discourse. Our purposes, therefore, will be served best by borrowing those insights from all approaches that seem to provide information useful as a foundation on which a theory of persuasion may be constructed. This means we will be less interested in the motivational processes themselves than in the ways these processes shed insights into the means of rhetorically finding and utilizing the available means of persuasion. It is hoped, however, that the limited treatment of motivation within this volume will be sufficient to provide a fundamental grasp of its nature and its role in persuasion.

We cannot refrain from adding the hope that the following discussion of human motivation will forever lay to rest the notion that people can *motivate* other people. This is a misuse of the term. Attempts to influence through language the behavior of another should be referred to as *persuasion*. The motivational process lies *within* the receiver of the message. Through persuasion the attempt is made to influence this process.

In our discussion that follows, we have attempted, as in the other parts of this book, to rest our conclusions on those theories and researches that have had considerable acceptance and in which we, too, have confidence. In this chapter we shall explore two of the basic factors in the nature of motivation, discuss the concepts related to their study, and suggest some implications for the study and practice of persuasion. In chapter 5 we discuss the nature and role of emotion in persuasion. In chapter 6 the nature of attitudes, the chief theories of attitude change and the ways people attempt to resist attitude change are discussed. In chapter 7 the influences of social behavior on motivation and their implications for persuasion are treated. Together these chapters should provide a foundation of a receiver-centered approach to persuasion.

The general nature of human motivation

The human being is characterized by *activating* or *energizing* *forces*, and these activations have *directions* or *goals*. Here we have the two basic aspects of motivated behavior: *activation* and *direction*. Ancient theorists noted these two aspects of behavior and attempted to explain them by a variety of explanations. Some ascribed the basic energizing forces to some supernatural external power, others to some inherent *life force* within all organisms. Today students of behavior have discarded early speculations in favor of more scientific approaches. The study of motivation now involves researches that examine the conditions that *arouse, sustain,* and give *direction* to behavior. When the reward or goal of the motivated behavior is attained, we may say that the given motivated act has been completed. In saying this, however, one must not conclude that behavior then becomes quiescent, for many types of motivated behavior can be operative simultaneously or sequentially.

Motivated behavior, then, may be considered as all the various forms of behavior in which people engage in seeking goals, whether these goals are to be found in winning satisfying rewards or in avoiding unpleasant experiences. Its origins may be either in the biological or physiological needs of the organism, the socio-psychological desires of the individual, or both.

The concepts of drive, motive, emotion, attitude, and value

In order to gain insights into motivated behavior, it is necessary first to become familiar with the chief terms used in describing the various dimensions or components of such behavior. We refer to *drives, motives, emotions, attitudes, and values.* Here we provide brief initial explanations of these terms as we shall use them, so that the reader can conceptualize their relationships and therefore be better prepared to understand more readily the more detailed discussion of these concepts which follows.

DRIVES. Drives have their origin in the biological requirements or basic needs of the organism. They are those bodily conditions (such as hunger and thirst) that are characterized by unlearned tensions, restlessness, and general activity. Drives are those aroused states of the organism resulting from an imbalance or deprivation of needs.

MOTIVES. Whereas a drive goads the organism into general activity, a motive is that psychological, learned state that directs the individual toward the means of satisfying not only his physiological or drive needs, but his socio-psychological goals as well. Thus, we may speak of physiological motives and social motives.

EMOTIONS.   Emotions are those conscious forms of affective or aroused behavior that range from mild to very intense physiological and psychological responses to stimuli, usually of external origin; they are motivational in nature insofar as they help in directing behavior toward some goal.

ATTITUDES.   An attitude is a predisposition, a polarized re-action tendency, created through learning or experience, to respond in a certain manner to some person, object, place, or situation. Attitudes dispose the individual to *become motivated toward a given goal.*

VALUES.   In time attitudes tend to cluster around a few rather broad attitudinal patterns relative to very inclusive goals. When this occurs we have what frequently are called *values.* A series of such clusters are spoken of as *value systems.* Values may be centered around one's religious faith, his views of the democratic way of life, or of the nature of success.

The relationship of these basic concepts of motivation may be understood more readily by placing them in the schematization shown in figure 4–1, which shows the organization of the factors playing significant roles in motivating behavior. They constitute the foundation materials upon which an approach to the study of persuasion must be based. In a receiver-centered approach the study of the organization of motivated behavior is, of course, basic to, and must precede, the study of the symbols and methods that can direct it rhetorically.

The bodily bases of motivation

In our search for the springs of human response it seems wise to start with the lowest common denominator of all human beings, indeed of all primates—the basic physical needs of the organism. If the organism is to survive, certain conditions must be met. It is here, then, that our discussion must start.

Drives

All of us have heard it said that "physical survival is the first law of life" and—though your authors shy away from absolutes—this statement may come close to being one. *Undeniably, man's behavior*

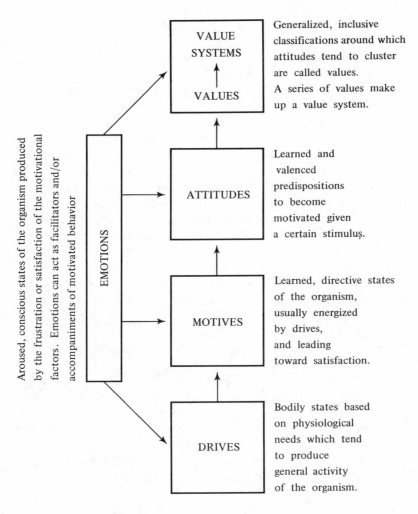

Figure 4–1. Organization of factors in motivation

is modified to a great extent by his biological requirements. These include food, water, oxygen, rest, proper temperature, avoidance of tissue injury, and elimination of body wastes. When one or more of the basic needs are experienced they become high priority items in our motivation. Mohandas Gandhi was reported once to have observed, "God Himself dare not appear to a starving man except in the form of bread."

Drives, then, are based on physical needs. They are energy states characterized by tensions, restlessness, or general bodily activity. As such they indicate behavior that, when linked with the directionality of motives, leads toward satisfactions of basic needs.

To understand more fully drive theory, one needs to be aware of the *theory of homeostasis*, a concept introduced in 1932 by W. B. Cannon.[1] This theory posits that physical drives are regulatory mechanisms that attempt to maintain a certain physiological balance or equilibrium within the organism. These mechanisms are said to seek to establish a consistency in the normal functions of the body in order to permit the individual to achieve goals not directly related to bodily functions. Some homeostatic processes are quite automatic, such as body temperature and a balance between the amount of oxygen and carbon dioxide in the blood. Others require the production of tensions and other activities that lead to behavior necessary to tension reduction, such as rest from fatigue, food-getting, and the like.

Drive theory and the doctrine of homeostasis for many years have had a significant place in discussions of motivation. Regardless of this fact, we must caution against the notion held by some that all behavior can be explained ultimately in these terms, that drives will assure survival needs. It seems to us that it would be inaccurate always to equate physiological needs with drives. For instance, we are unaware normally of vitamin or oxygen deficiencies; chemical imbalance in the body may not produce a drive. It has been demonstrated, too, that in cases of extreme deficiencies of food and temperature the drive initially created may cease to exist. Thus after a given point a person may not be aware that he is starving or that he is freezing to death. We must remember also that man can and does on occasion delay satisfaction of his physical needs, and he sometimes redirects these drive energies into learned patterns of social behavior.

Regardless of the reservations we have relative to the *need-drive* formulation and the doctrine of homeostasis, we believe that the physiological demands of the organism and its modes of expressing them remain a fundamental consideration in the study of persuasion. We would add, however, that in the contemporary treatments of motivation emphasis has shifted to increased considerations of the socio-psychological and environmental conditions that play roles in our motivated behavior. This increased concern for incentives external to the organism receives considerable attention in the discussion that follows.

---

[1] W. B. Cannon, *The Wisdom of the Body* (New York: Norton, 1932).

The implications of drive theory for persuasion

Fundamentally man is a biological organism, despite his other capacities and attributes that distinguish him greatly from the lower animals. This organism is not a self-perpetuating instrument. Rather, it is dependent on learning and on its physical and social environment for its well-being. A persuader can thus be assured that, in general, the satisfactions of drives based on basic physiological needs will be of continuing concern to the persuadee. Man's vast systems of food and water production, preservation, and distribution, his concern for medical care whatever the cost, his insistence on clean air, his laws demanding safety devices in factory, car, and home, his demands for adequate fuel to heat his home, and a host of other examples the reader could name, all attest to a basic concern for the preservation of the organism. Indeed, the broadly defined and often used phrase "social security" means basically "organism security." These basic drives are so great that even in affluent societies, where a person is not apt to experience real deprivation, there is, nevertheless, the vague fear or anxiety that deprivations might occur, and activities are ordered in ways intended to avoid such an eventuality. It is reasonable to conclude, therefore, that persuasive appeals designed to assure the satisfactions of basic needs will, in general, be given a favorable hearing.

Granting the general effectiveness of such appeals, we must not conclude that when basic needs (food, water) exist they will always constitute a strong drive or that they demand top priority on our satisfaction list. There is a certain interdependence among drive states and between physical needs and social desires. Deprivation of water has been shown to reduce a hunger drive. Prolonged hunger tends to result in a weakened sex drive. Emotional situations can cause a person to "forget" that he is hungry or thirsty. People may endure great physical hardships, or risk survival itself to help a loved one. They may pierce their ears or noses, wear painful shoes, diet to the point of physical harm, and ignore bodily needs and drives in many other ways to reap psychological and social rewards. Hence a persuader must not assume that active drives, as basic as they are, will always be the most urgent motivational factor to appeal to at a given time. The relative dominance or strength of our drives is largely dependent on specific circumstances operative at a specific time.

But regardless of the social motives that may cause an individual to depreciate or ignore temporarily the thrust of a drive, it must be understood that the motivational power of needs and drives should always be considered as potentially strong. A hungry or thirsty persuadee, an audience in a room that is too hot or too cold, or a receiver who is ill presents a very real problem to a speaker trying to persuade such individuals to study the *Dialogues* of Plato. To preach the values of democracy to an underfed and disease-ridden tribe is certainly an exercise in futility, if not stupidity. One cannot extend people's motivational reaches to the heights when their feet are in the mire of poverty and physical deprivation.

Motives—the learned directive energies of motivation

The general nature of motives

We know that at birth, an infant has a set of physical needs and drives, that it develops a set of primary emotions (love, rage, fear) as it attempts to adjust to its environment. We know, too, that the infant is not a miniature man or woman with an adult's motivations. Rather, the infant at birth is an unsocialized organism; it must develop *motives* that direct its behavior toward satisfying goals. As the child matures, learns, and experiences, we soon see indications of the development of many new behavioral patterns that tend to satisfy not only his physical needs (as discussed above), but also his psychological ones. The parents try to understand desires and behaviors of their child; soon the child becomes an adult with a still more complex system of motivation.

What is the nature, then, of the motives that become the mainsprings of our responses? Ask a man why he goes to work each morning and he will probably reply simply that he must live. When pressed further, he may recite that all men go to work, or that he has a duty to his family, company, and so on. However, these may not be the real or sole reasons. What we enjoy today, we may reject tomorrow. An attractive co-ed may be too busy with her school work to go out with a common sophomore, but she will easily find time to sneak away for two precious hours with the senior class president. Mrs. Hopeful's splitting headache may keep her from accepting an invitation to tea with Mrs. Nobody, but her headache is mild enough for her to go for a ride with Mrs. Plushpurse in a new Continental convertible. The salesman's prospect may see no need for additional life insurance until he learns his social rival has such a policy. And why is it that a fellow will postpone a dental appointment but risk his life racing a locomotive to the crossing? Why is it that we display contradictory behaviors within ourselves? How can a person be philanthropic at one time and greedy at another? As one writer put it, "Each day becomes either a theatre in which many motives work together in playing their roles in the drama of our lives or is a prize ring where motives compete, singly or in teams, for supremacy in our life patterns."[2]

The answers to these questions are found somewhere in the complex constellations of human motives. We turn now to a discussion of the general nature of motives in the hope of answering at least some of the questions of the human riddle. In order to prepare rhetorical appeals, the persuader must understand the receiver's motives.

GENERAL DEFINITIONS OF MOTIVES. To understand the nature of motives it is first essential to define the term *motive* in relation to its function in the motivational process and to distinguish it from the term *drive*. Frequently these terms are used interchangeably. Some speak of a person's *drive* for social prestige, while others may speak of his *motive* to gain such recognition. Some scholars define the term motive to include what we earlier have called drive. In order to achieve some understanding of the term's general usage, it will be helpful to draw upon several generally accepted definitions.

Murray states, "It is clear that different theorists have different conceptions about motivation. Nevertheless, there is general agreement that motivation arouses, directs, and integrates a person's behavior. It is not observed directly but inferred from his behavior or simply assumed to exist in order to explain behavior."[3] From this statement it would appear that Murray views a motive as including the aroused behavior of drives, the direction of this energy, and the reduction or satisfaction of the individual's needs. Psychologists Hilgard, Atkinson, and Atkinson provide the following general definition which stresses the directive qualities of a motive. "By a *motive* we mean something that incites the organism to action or that sustains and gives direction to action once the organism has been aroused."[4] Social psychologists Newcomb, Turner, and Converse state, "More specifically, we shall use the term 'motive' to refer to a state of the organism in which bodily energy is mobilized and directed in a selective fashion toward states of affairs, often though not necessarily in the external environment, called goals. Motive, then, is a concept that joins together a state of energy mobilization and a goal."[5] This definition,

[2] F. C. Dockeray, *Psychology* (Englewood Cliffs, N.J.: Prentice-Hall, 1945), p. 143.

[3] Edward J. Murray, *Motivation and Emotion* (Englewood Cliffs, N.J.: Prentice-Hall, 1964), p. 7.

[4] E. R. Hilgard, R. C. Atkinson, and R. L. Atkinson, *Introduction to Psychology* (New York: Harcourt Brace Jovanovich, 1971), p. 294.

[5] T. M. Newcomb, R. H. Turner, and P. E. Converse, *Social Psychology* (New York: Holt, Rinehart and Winston, 1956), p. 22.

too, includes the mobilization and direction of energy states plus the matter of selectivity relative to the goal being sought.

Although they differ slightly in scope and emphasis, these well-regarded definitions have some useful ideas in common. To these definitions we would add more specifically that a motive involves learning. Therefore, we shall here conceive of a motive as based on a drive and as giving direction toward a goal or satisfactory tension reduction through learning. The learning process tells us what directions leading to what goals have provided past satisfactions of our physiological or social needs. Because motives tend to be named in terms of the goals being sought, we would speak of a *hunger drive* and a *food motive*, as Newcomb, Turner, and Converse point out.

Now that a general framework for conceptualizing the term motive has been given, we would be less than honest if we were to lead the reader to believe that this rather traditional approach can explain all motivated behavior. We must remind ourselves that the study of motivation still has some disarray and that no one approach, no single definition can answer all questions. Granting this, let us look at a few limitations. Harlow's studies of man and monkeys have shown that monkeys do solve problems without any reward that conceivably could reduce an organic drive state, and that in children whose hunger drive has been reduced by food, curiosity often prompts the child to learn without the reward of tension reduction. The motive involved in the absence of a drive state was termed *curiosity-manipulation.*[6]

Then, too, we know that man does not always try to satisfy his physiological needs in whatever direct manner is most convenient. As chapter 7 discusses at length, man is a social creature who develops motives that lead to numerous sociogenic satisfactions. We suspect that man's great capacity for learning obscures the connection between his basic drives and his social motives. It is easy to see the connection between a food motive and a hunger drive, but it becomes more difficult to accept that physical needs may be satisfied directly by the motive that leads us toward some patriotic gesture or prompts us to engage in a charitable act toward someone else in need.

The answer may well lie in viewing some motives as *physiological motives* (those leading to the reduction of a drive based on a physiological need) and others as *social motives* which lead toward the satisfactions of our socio-psychological needs. If social motives play such significant roles in motivation, and we believe they do, what has been theorized as to their derivation? Below we shall consider this question briefly.

[6] H. F. Harlow, "Mice, Monkeys, Men and Motives," *Psychological Review* 60 (1953): 23–32.

THE GREAT DEBATE: THE DERIVATION OF SOCIAL MOTIVES. The question of the derivation of social motives has caused considerable debate among theorists. It is not within our purposes or competence to attempt to resolve the controversy. From the point of view of persuasion, our chief concerns are the knowledge of the presence and functions of social motives and skills in using them to communicate. Their precise derivations are of secondary interest. Nevertheless, the serious student of persuasion will want to know something of the rival schools of thought on the matter. The theorists most prominent in the debate have been Sigmund Freud, Gordon W. Allport, and Neal E. Miller.

As most readers know, Freud contended that social motives are derived from man's basic biological needs.[7] To him man is an organism energized by primitive instincts that tend to be inhibited by the restrictions of society. Through sublimation, man directs these basic impulses (essentially, sexual and aggressive) into socially acceptable channels. Thus the child's love motive for the mother is basically of sexual origin. The male sexual impulse is what may lead him into becoming a dress designer. The aggressive impulse becomes the reason for the young man's interest in becoming a star athlete. The friendly ties which bind a group together are derived from the sexual impulses in a family situation, and so on. Critics of this view have tended to doubt that such feelings as love, tenderness, and social dependence are actually sublimations of basic sexual motivation. This remains the most serious question of Freud's theory.

Allport's theory of the *functional autonomy* of social motives for years has been applauded and criticized.[8] He disagreed with the notion that adult behavior is motivated entirely by innate needs and that adult social motives are simply sublimations of infantile impulses of sex and aggression. Agreeing that an infant is motivated by some primitive drives, he believes that in the human adult many motives become disassociated from any infantile or primitive origins and tend to become functionally autonomous. To Allport, therefore, such traits as gregariousness are acquired. To him the many social motivations are transformations of basic needs. Thus it is argued that after repeated performances an activity tends to become independent of any relationship with the conditions instrumental in the development of that activity or behavior, and such activity tends to become self-perpetuating. Critics of the theory have contended that the examples of social motivation given by Allport as autonomous are actually cases where *secondary drives* are

[7] Sigmund Freud, *The Interpretation of Dreams*, Vols. 4 and 5 (London: Hogarth Press, 1900).

[8] Gordon W. Allport, *Personality, A Psychological Interpretation* (New York: Henry Holt, 1937).

operating to produce the behavior. Some of these critics do grant, however, that some motivated activities of man may be partially autonomous under certain conditions.

Neal E. Miller (in collaboration with John Dollard) postulates that social motives are learned as a result of acquired drives and rewards.[9] Thus affection attachments to a mother are not sexually based as Freud would have it but are the result of the mother's care for the child's basic needs over a period of time. The motives seeking social approval, conformity, honesty, and pride have been learned because they are rewarded in a given social or cultural setting. In one culture the motive to compete may be strong, while in another cooperation has strong motive value. This approach is based on careful research, and it seems to provide a reasonable explanation of the many and varied social motives of which man is capable.

DIFFICULTIES IN INFERRING THE FUNCTIONS OF MOTIVES IN SPECIFIC BEHAVIORAL ACTS. We said earlier that motives are generally labeled according to their goals; a *food motive* directs us toward *food*. This practice, however, carries with it certain hazards. For instance, one goal may be served by different behaviors. Satisfaction of the motive of personal achievement may be sought by one person by amassing great wealth, but by another by enduring poverty in order to administer to the underprivileged in a remote country. Then, too, we may have the reverse situation, where different motives may be fulfilled by the same behavior. To the writer, going fishing may please his wife who wants him to find time for relaxation by engaging in his favorite sport. The same act of fishing, however, may be used to annoy the writer's coauthor who wants him to get on with writing this book. Then, again, we must remember that a given behavior can be used to satisfy a series of motives. To climb Mount Everest may be motivated by the need for adventure, personal achievement, a craving for social recognition, and for the money to be made from the television coverage, public lectures, and published articles on the climb. And, finally, it must be remembered that human motives are expressed differently among cultures.

The implications of these difficulties in inferring the functions of motives should be clear. If the salesman's message assumes that the customer wants a new car as a status symbol when, in fact, he wants it as a potential long-term economy measure, the salesman has reduced his chances of a sale by a considerable margin.

---

[9]Neal E. Miller, "Studies of Fear as an Acquired Drive: I. Fear as Motivation and Fear-Reduction as Reinforcement in the Learning of New Responses," *Journal of Experimental Psychology* 38 (1948): 89–101.

Identifying and classifying human motives

Regardless of the debate as to their derivation, numerous motives have been identified. As stated before, man's unusual capacity for learning has resulted in the development of many motivational factors that have been studied experimentally. It is to be expected, therefore, that attempts would be made to catalog these many motives. A complete and satisfactory inventory is virtually impossible because of man's motivational complexity and because of the disagreements among scholars regarding what energy states can properly be called motives. Nevertheless, several attempts have produced useful inventories. These not only provide a checklist for the student of persuasion, but also serve to emphasize the complexity and extensiveness of motivational factors as available means of persuasion. In this section we wish to present several well known composite lists and then single out for more discussion a few motives that are quite commonly used as appeals in suasive discourse.

MURRAY'S INVENTORY OF PSYCHOGENIC NEEDS. A list of motives that has had considerable influence was prepared by Murray who identified twelve "viscerogenic needs" (physiological needs) and twenty-eight "psychogenic needs," which may be said to be our socio-psychological needs or motives. Below we reproduce Murray's list of the psychogenic motives as adapted by Hilgard, Atkinson, and Atkinson.[10]

A. Needs associated chiefly with inanimate objects
   1. Acquisition: the need to gain possessions and property.
   2. Conservation: the need to collect, repair, clean, and preserve things.
   3. Orderliness: the need to arrange, organize, put away objects; to be tidy and clean; to be precise.
   4. Retention: the need to retain possession of things; to hoard; to be frugal, economical, and miserly.
   5. Construction: the need to organize and build.
B. Needs expressing ambition, will power, desire for accomplishment, and prestige
   6. Superiority: the need to excel, a composite of achievement and recognition.
   7. Achievement: the need to overcome obstacles, to exercise power,

[10] E. R. Hilgard, R. C. Atkinson, and R. L. Atkinson, *Introduction to Psychology*, 5th ed. (New York: Harcourt Brace Jovanovich, 1971), p. 316.

to strive to do something difficult as well and as quickly as possible.

8. Recognition: the need to excite praise and commendation; to command respect.

9. Exhibition: the need for self-dramatization; to excite, amuse, stir, shock, thrill others.

10. Inviolacy: the need to remain inviolate, to prevent a depreciation of self-respect, to preserve one's "good name."

11. Avoidance of inferiority: the need to avoid failure, shame, humiliation, ridicule.

12. Defensiveness: the need to defend oneself against blame or belittlement; to justify one's actions.

13. Counteraction: the need to overcome defeat by striving again and retaliating.

C. Needs having to do with human power exerted, resisted, or yielded to

14. Dominance: the need to influence or control others.

15. Deference: the need to admire and willingly follow a superior; to serve gladly.

16. Similance: the need to imitate or emulate others; to agree and believe.

17. Autonomy: the need to resist influence, to strive for independence.

18. Contrariness: the need to act differently from others, to be unique, to take the opposite side.

D. Needs having to do with injuring others or oneself

19. Aggression: the need to assault or injure another; to belittle, harm, or maliciously ridicule a person.

20. Abasement: the need to comply and accept punishment; self-depreciation.

21. Avoidance of blame: the need to avoid blame, ostracism, or punishment by inhibiting unconventional impulses; to be well behaved and obey the law.

E. Needs having to do with affection between people

22. Affiliation: the need to form friendships and associations.

23. Rejection: the need to be discriminating; to snub, ignore, or exclude another.

24. Nurturance: the need to nourish, aid, or protect another.

25. Succorance: the need to seek aid, protection, or sympathy; to be dependent.

F. Additional socially relevant needs

26. Play: the need to relax, amuse oneself, seek diversion and entertainment.

27. Cognizance: the need to explore, ask questions, satisfy curiosity.

28. Exposition: the need to point and demonstrate; to give information, explain, interpret, lecture.[11]

THE KRECH AND CRUTCHFIELD INVENTORY OF MOTIVES.   Another inventory was made by Krech and Crutchfield. They make a relatively brief but excellent summary of those motives based upon man's physiological *and* his social needs.(See table 4–1.)

MASLOW'S HIERARCHAL INVENTORY OF MOTIVES.[12]   Believing that too frequently psychology has emphasized man's abnormalities and neglected his strengths, Maslow focuses on the well-adjusted, emotionally healthy individual. Not denying the importance of man's innate needs, he stresses the urge toward self-actualization (peak experiences of happiness and fulfillment) as found in his study of both historical and contemporary persons. He has contended that a general motivational hierarchy exists where the needs of certain lower or *deficiency motives* must be satisfied before the needs of the higher or *being motives* can be met. First one's *physiological* requirements must be satisfied, then one's *safety needs,* followed by, in turn, *belongingness and love needs, esteem needs,* and, finally, assuming the motives lower on the scale have been satisfied, the need for *self-actualization*—the development of full individuality or the experience of being—must be fulfilled.

Maslow's discussion of the basic physiological needs parallels the treatment given them earlier in the chapter. The safety needs, which must be satisfied next, refer to our need for security, for freedom from harm, anxiety, fear, and the like. The satisfaction of this deficiency motive provides us with stability in living and with a predictable world. The belonging and love needs refer to our need for affiliation with others, affection, and social cohesion. When these prior needs have been met, one strives for esteem, which may be characterized by achievement, adequacy, mastery, competence, independence, and freedom, as well as the desires for social recognition, prestige, and status. This broad class of esteem needs is of great significance in social persuasion. Finally, according to Maslow, when all the prior needs are met, the motivational channels are cleared for the seeking of true fulfillment of the individual. As Maslow puts it, "What a man *can* be, he *must* be."

This inventory by Maslow attempts to reduce the size of a list of motives to those considered basic and to place them in an hierarchal order in man's ascent toward the highest motivation—self-actualization.

---

[11] From *Explorations in Personality* edited by Henry A. Murray. Copyright 1938 by Oxford University Press, Inc. Renewed 1966 by Henry A. Murray. Reprinted by permission of the publisher.

[12] A. H. Maslow, "A Theory of Motivation," *Psychological Review* 50 (1943): 370–96. See also A. H. Maslow, *Motivation and Personality,* 2nd ed. (New York: Harper and Row, 1970).

Table 4–1

The Krech and Crutchfield Inventory of Motives

	SURVIVAL AND SECURITY (DEFICIENCY MOTIVES)	SATISFACTION AND STIMULATION (ABUNDANCY MOTIVES)
Pertaining to the body	Avoiding of hunger, thirst, oxygen lack, excess heat and cold, pain, overfull bladder and colon, fatigue, over-tense muscles, illness and other disagreeable bodily states, etc.	Attaining pleasurable sensory experiences of tastes, smells, sounds, etc.; sexual pleasure; bodily comfort; exercise of muscles, rhythmical body movements, etc.
Pertaining to relations with environment	Avoiding of dangerous objects and horrible, ugly and disgusting objects; seeking objects necessary to future survival and security; maintaining a stable, clear, certain environment, etc.	Attaining enjoyable possessions; constructing and inventing objects; understanding the environment; solving problems; playing games; seeking environmental novelty and change, etc.
Pertaining to relations with other people	Avoiding interpersonal conflict and hostility; maintaining group membership, prestige, and status; being taken care of by others; conforming to group standards and value; gaining power and dominance over others, etc.	Attaining love and positive identifications with people and groups, enjoying other people's company; helping and understanding other people; being independent, etc.
Pertaining to self	Avoiding feelings of inferiority and failure in comparing the self with others or with the ideal self; avoiding loss of identity; avoiding feelings of shame, guilt, fear, anxiety, sadness, etc.	Attaining feelings of self-respect and self-confidence; expressing oneself; feeling sense of achievement; feeling challenged; establishing moral and other values; discovering meaningful place of self in the universe.

SOCIAL MOTIVES OF SPECIAL CONCERN TO THE PERSUADER. In addition to the inventories given above, we wish to single out several motives for special consideration because of their frequency of use in persuasion.

ACHIEVEMENT MOTIVE. "Achievers" and "doers" hold a revered place in our value system. Most of us would like to be thought of as accomplished, successful people. This achievement motive, referred to in the inventories above, is characterized by a disposition to set and reach goals and to meet certain standards of excellence. This motive is considered first here because it has been studied more extensively than others.

McClelland and his associates have conducted the most notable researches on achievement.[13] They used the Thematic Apperception Test (TAT) which asked subjects to write fantasy stories about scenes they saw flashed on a screen. These pictures suggested life situations, such as two men working at a machine, a boy seated at a desk with a book, and a father-son situation. The subject's stories were to suggest what was happening in the scene, what led up to the situation, what was being thought, and what will happen. It was assumed the stories would reveal the motivations of the writer. These stories were analyzed for indications of the importance of achievement or success. This method was used to separate the subjects in terms of high and low achievement scores. Other studies followed that used the two groups in task-oriented situations in order to learn more about the functions of achievement motivation.

These excellent studies, as well as others, support quite convincingly that in general those with high achievement motivation learn and perform tasks faster and better than those of low achievement. It should be noted, however, that this is not true when the task is a rather routine, boring one. Apparently such a task does not present the challenge needed by the subjects motivated by high achievement. As French discovered in a study involving Air Force cadets, when the high- and low-achievement men were involved in a routine, relaxed, informal experiment the two groups demonstrated no real difference in the tasks performed.[14] However, in the experiment linked with matters of intelligence and career success where the high achievement subjects were

---

[13] D. C. McClelland, J. W. Atkinson, R. A. Clark, and E. L. Lowell, *The Achievement Motive* (New York: Appleton-Century-Crofts, 1953). See also J. W. Atkinson, ed., *Motives in Fantasy, Action, and Society* (New York: Van Nostrand, 1958).

[14] E. G. French, "Effects of the Interaction of Motivation and Feedback on Performance" in J. W. Atkinson, ed. *Motives in Fantasy, Action, and Society* (New York: Van Nostrand, 1958), pp. 400–408.

challenged, the high achievers did perform better than those with low achievement scores. A related part of the experiment showed that the high achievers were not readily moved by offers of rewards for those best scores who completed the testing an hour early. The satisfaction of achievement apparently was related more to the value of achieving and doing it in terms of certain standards of excellence than to other rewards. High achievers also prefer any feedback to be in reference to the task being performed and not simply a "feeling feedback" where someone praises the subject but provides no specific comments on the quality of the work being done. Also, the high achievers tend to prefer experts rather than nonexperts or friends as partners in performing a task.

The development of the achievement motive is thought to have its origins in the home where parents determine the amount of emphasis that is placed on achievement in rearing the child. Parents of high achievement subjects were found to have encouraged excellence and the values of achievement. Low achievers were not so encouraged, as the study by Winterbottom has shown.[15]

It is thus quite well established that the achievement motive has been clearly identified and shown to be a very important motivational factor in many individuals, in our whole culture, and, indeed, in achieving nations. The persuader must keep in mind that the strength of this motive varies among people, that the individual with high motivation tends to be more independent, and that the low achiever usually prefers affiliation with others to independence and a task orientation.

AFFILIATION MOTIVE.   The affiliation motive, like achievement, is defined in Murray's inventory of motives given above. We believe the importance of this social motive also deserves further comment here, although chapter 7 presents more material related to this motive.

Undoubtedly the dependence of the infant on the mother and then on others in the family provides the origins of the affiliative motive. Affections, companionships, and close group relations result in satisfying rewards and tend to be perpetuated. During the nurturing process the parents who place more emphasis on the dependencies and loyalties of group living are establishing the foundations of a potentially strong affiliation motive. Research by Sears and his associates confirms this point.[16] They found that preschool children tend to develop a normal amount of dependency, but if the mother, in the feeding and weaning

[15] M. R. Winterbottom, "The Relation of Need for Achievement to Learning Experiences in Independence and Mastery" in J. W. Atkinson, ed., Motives in Fantasy, Action, and Society (New York: Van Nostrand, 1958), pp. 453–78.

[16] R. R. Sears, J. W. M. Whiting, V. Nowlis, and P. S. Sears, "Some Child Rearing Antecedents of Aggression and Dependency in Young Children," Genetic Psychology Monographs 47 (1953): 135–234.

process that produces frustration in the child, proceeds to use caresses and otherwise comforts the child, the youngster may be shifted to considerable dependence on and affiliation with others. Schacter's study found that apparently the affiliation motive in adults is related to such childhood experiences that encourage dependence.[17] The studies referred to in our discussion of achievement also indicate that the affiliation motivated person is more concerned with companionship than in excellence of performance in a task situation.

It appears well established, then, that all people have some degree of affiliation motivation, but that some have very high affiliation motivation which becomes a dominant factor in their behavior, while others have a weak affiliation need. Nonetheless, as has been said many times, we are social creatures and we learn, in no small measure, who we are through our relationships with others. The persuader must gain insights into the persuadee's greater or lesser reliance on affiliation motivation in the conduct of his affairs.

SOCIAL APPROVAL MOTIVE. *Social approval* and *conformity* motives are related to the achievement and affiliation motives and to each other. These broad areas of motivation may involve a number of other more specific motives. Social approval is necessary to increase our chances of gaining those conditions necessary for physical survival, for gaining leadership, recognition for skills and masteries, for satisfying affiliations, and for the establishment and protection of a self-hood. So it is that of all the objects that acquire power to act as motivational sources, the approving individual is among the most important. As the great psychologist William James once said:

> No more fiendish punishment could be devised, were such a thing physically possible, than that one should be turned loose in society and remain unnoticed by all the members thereof. If no one turned around when we entered, answered when we spoke, or minded what we did, but if every person we met "cut us dead," and acted as if we were non-existent things, a kind of rage and impotent despair would ere long well up in us, from which the cruelest bodily tortures would be a relief; for these would make us feel that, however bad might our plight be, we had not sunk to such a depth as to be unworthy of attention at all.[18]

Persuaders throughout history have urged courses of action by suggesting the social approvals that will be the receiver's reward.

---

[17] S. Schacter, *Psychology of Affiliation* (Stanford, Calif.: Stanford University Press, 1959).

[18] William James, *Principles of Psychology* (New York: Henry Holt and Company, 1890, I.), pp. 293–94.

SOCIAL CONFORMITY MOTIVES. *Conformity motives* operate within every individual and society. Whereas personal independence has a useful role in a creative, achieving society, a certain degree of conformity must exist if that society is to function smoothly and with a certain stability. The achiever, as discussed above, will conform less and the affiliator more, but both will conform under certain conditions. The individual who needs much social approval for psychological adequacy will more actively seek this approval through various types of social behavior than will the more independent "loner" who gets his satisfactions through more personal achievements. Nevertheless, if a person is not disposed actively to seek social approval, he will usually conform to the extent that he does not reap discomforts because of his deviations from some social norm.

An extended treatment of conformity and supporting research is given in chapter 7. All types of political, religious, economic, labor, and educational persuaders have made us aware of the effectiveness of appeals to conformity. "This is what *they* are wearing this fall," says the clerk; "All good Americans fly the flag," says the mayor to his con-stituents; "What will your fellow Democrats say if you support that Republican?" asks the partisan. Conform and you win; deviate and you lose.

Habits as motives

In any discussion of motivation we dare not forget the role of *habit.* This is not a motive in a strict sense, but it seems to us to act *as* a motive in fostering continued behavioral patterns within which motives often are satisfied. Psychological literature has reported many researches that establish the existence of habit and how it functions in general. Habits, mechanisms of ordering and reenforcing our satis-factions, seem to play an important role in motivating behavior. The mechanism tends to furnish its own motivation. In a sense we may call this the "functional autonomy of habit."

The role of habit has considerable significance to the persuader. When asked why he bought another Ford, an acquaintance of the writer replied, "Oh, I've just always bought Fords." That seemed to sum up the matter for him. Car dealers know that between 60–70 percent of their customers will continue to buy the same make of car. Pollution experts know the force of habit when they attempt to persuade a farmer to change his procedures of fertilizing the land so that runoff is not so harmful to our lakes and streams. In a fuel shortage it takes first-rate persuasion to get drivers to change a driving habit of 70 mph to a 55 mph lope. "I've always done it this way" summarizes for most of us the role of habit in meeting many of our daily satisfactions. The persuader who can demonstrate that his proposal can fit neatly and readily into our tried and comfortable ways has won an important point. Appeals to the new, the innovative, the highly irregular can be effective to those less routinized and more individualized lives, but not to the highly habituated. In this matter, too, whole communities and cultures vary. Some pride themselves in their traditional habits; others are more quick to innovate, to experiment, and to be *progressive*.

A summary of the chief implications for persuasion of the nature and role of motives in human motivation

After the persuadee's motives have been carefully identified, the useful ones selected, and their strengths determined, the persuader must prepare and present his message in such a way that these motives are fully engaged and used in the message delivered. The link between the selected motives and the message purpose must be forged unmistakably. To help assure this procedure, it should be helpful to list some of the chief implications for persuasion of the materials discussed above. The important role of attitudes and their relationships to motives are discussed in the following chapter.

1. Man is a complex motivational creature who, through his innate and great learning capacities, develops a multimotivated system. This system can become so complex as to baffle the most skilled clinical psychologist, yet its essential nature contains those raw materials out of which effective persuasion is made.

2. Man develops motives that lead to the satisfaction of his physiological and his socio-psychological needs. The physiological needs frequently, though not necessarily, make prior demands on our behavior.

3. The strength or intensity of an individual motive tends to vary in relation to other motives and will itself vary in different situations. Likewise motives differ among age, vocational, and cultural groups.

4. Even though a given person is unique in many ways in his motivational makeup and in his responses to situations, he nonetheless has much in common motivationally with others of his community and culture. Man is quite predictable in his general motivational behaviors.

5. A persuader must remember that motives within an individual frequently come into conflict. A customer may want the comfort and safety of a large, heavy car, yet finds it difficult to ignore the motivation to be that good citizen who buys a small compact which helps conserve gas during a national fuel emergency.

6.   Many of the things we seek are learned desires. Through the sales-man's message a formerly neutral object may become a reward object. The uses of language can greatly increase the number of responses that become associated with different types of rewards or goals.

7.   We must look to early training for the origins of such social mo-tives as achievement and affiliation.

8.   The need to achieve seems to be in all people to some degree. In some the need is great and expresses itself in more independence, more striving for excellence, more tenacity in overcoming obstacles. In others the need may be low and the concern greater for affiliation with others than with tasks and standards of excellence.

9.   Affiliation-oriented persons tend to respond more favorably to offerings of more and more satisfying friendships. They tend to be more dependent on others.

10.   Normally our general need for social approval is strong, except perhaps for those who are very independent and high achievers. Even here we wonder if an unexpressed desire for such approval does not exist. Social living makes appeals to social approval rather common in modern life.

11.   The persuader must be very cautious in imputing a given motive to a given behavior. A motive may find satisfaction in more than one behavioral act. Then, too, a given behavioral act may satisfy more than one motive.

12.   Habits can be reenforcers of our motives. For a persuader to recommend a course of action that interrupts a persuadee's comfortable ways of satisfying one or a number of motives is to meet with great resistance. However, there are many times a persuader will need to try to establish a new habit pattern by stressing other strong motives that can be satisfied.

13.   In the selection of motives to appeal to in a given message, it is usually wise to consider first the potential use of one or more of the basic needs of all people as suggested by Maslow in his hierarchal system. Then one might proceed to less basic motive appeals that are still ap-propriate to the receiver and the goal of the message.

14.   Before the receiver's motives can be engaged, his attention must be gained, and the link between the satisfaction of his aroused motives and the speaker's recommendation must be accurately perceived.

15.   Throughout the process of rhetorically arousing and employing a receiver's motives in ways useful to the persuader, it must be remem-bered that the credibility of the persuader is at work, either helping or hindering this process.

16. Finally, it should be eminently clear that audience or persuadee analysis cannot rely upon guesswork. If the persuasive effort is to succeed, a thorough analysis must be made.

Conclusion

An extended set of conclusions is unnecessary here because a summary of the implications of the material has been made at the end of each major part of the chapter. One overall conclusion from the content of the chapter is inescapable: he who would persuade must be a careful student of human motivation in general and of the intended receiver's motivations in particular.

The present chapter has discussed only two of those factors that play roles in motivation and that were defined and schematized earlier in the chapter. Succeeding chapters consider the other motivational factors.

5

Emotions—
the affective dimensions of motivation

Introduction

Woodrow Wilson once said, "We speak of this as an age in which the mind is monarch, but I take it for granted that, if this is true, mind is one of those modern monarchs who reign but do not govern. As a matter of fact, the world is governed in every generation by a great House of Commons made up of the passions; and we can only be careful to see to it that the handsome passions are in the majority." This statement speaks a fundamental truth about the role of our emotions and adds a wise admonition. Had Wilson, once a university president, been on some college and university campuses in the late 1960s he would have seen more evidence of the truth of his statement, even though students in these centers of higher learning are presumed to be trained in the more rational proc-

104

esses of reflective thought. Intense expressions of emotion have not been confined to our campuses, however, but have been found throughout history in many aspects of human enterprise. Feelings and emotions in varying degrees are a part of every human situation. Any discussion of persuasion, therefore, must necessarily explore the nature of the emotions and attempt to discover the role they play in motivation and thus in persuasion. Aristotle, Cicero, and other ancient and medieval writers, as well as many contemporary scholars interested in suasive rhetoric have shown concern for human emotions.

During our discussion of drives and motives in the preceding chapter it must have occurred to the reader as a result of his own experiences that when the physical needs of the organism are thwarted or safety jeopardized, when motives are kept from fulfillment (be it avoidance of the unpleasant or achievement of the pleasant) *emotions* are experienced. All of us have experienced, too, the emotions that can be aroused not only by the direct experiencing of some event but by the words and actions of an actor, political orator, or evangelist, by the words of a novelist, or by the pictures and words of an advertiser. Indeed, from infancy until death we see about us and experience within us innumerable emotion-arousing events.

Our concern here, of course, is to look at emotional behavior from the point of view of the student of persuasion. We will therefore be less concerned with the bodily bases and theories of the nature of emotion and more concerned with social motives, the relationship between emotion and motivation, and what this relationship can mean to the study and practice of persuasive discourse.

A final introductory word is in order. For many years the fields of rhetoric and speech communication considered the nature of man as split into two distinct parts. We refer to the frequent references to the "logical" and the "emotional" dimensions of man, and to the "appeals to reason" and "appeals to emotion" categories of some students of rhetoric. Our study of the human motivational process does not warrant any such simple, clear-cut dichotomy. Emotion and reason are not distinctly different and separable, not distinct entities that produce a particular type of behavior. Instances of motivation and behavior are more accurately the products of both emotion and reason, used in varying proportions and suited to situational needs. Misunderstanding of the nature of motivation has permitted some to suggest that "appeals to emotion" are suspect— if not downright unethical—and "appeals to reason" are of the highest order. It may well be that some persuaders overemphasize the *affective* dimension of a situation, or, on occasion, a persuader may insist unwisely on behavior based on a highly rational process, but we would contend that to label one dimension as necessarily good and the other bad, or to separate the two, is to distort the essential unity of the motivational and resultant behavioral processes.

The reader will understand that when we use the terms *emotion* and *reason* we are using the available terminology and not suggesting that their referents are separate entities. For pedagogical reasons we have separated the various elements to help demonstrate the organization of human motivation. Our discussion of reason or critical thought will be found in chapter 8.

We now turn to a brief look at the nature of emotion, followed by a more detailed account of the relationship of emotions and motivation, and conclude with some suggestions for applying knowledge of emotions to persuasion.

The nature of emotions

Traditionally many scholars of human motivation have discussed man's experiences of pleasantness and unpleasantness as *affective* states, labelling the relatively mild affective states *feelings* and the more intense affective states *emotions*. In a sense these affective conditions can be arranged on a continuum ranging from the very mild affects to the most aroused and intensive states such as rage or terror. In our discussion we shall consider emotion as being *that type of affective state characterized by considerable intensity and where the organism is experiencing more widespread visceral and somatic changes than is true of the more mild feelings we may have over some person, object, or event; it is both a physiological and a psychological response to a stimulus.*

The physiological basis of emotion

In considering emotions as intense affective behavior, or the more stirred-up condition of the organism, certain symptoms reflect this physiological condition. The rather profound changes that normally take place in the body include increased heartbeat and breathing rate, a tensing of the muscles, increased perspiration, a flushed face, a blanched face, tears, laughter, and excited, even incoherent speech. The relationship of emotion and physiology is supported by modern research and apparently has long been recognized, as suggested by such words and phrases as "sweetheart," "cold-hearted," and "breathless with surprise."

Research tends to indicate, however, that the physiological bases of emotion seem to be common to a number of emotions (particularly the more intense ones), and thus differentiation at times can be difficult, if not impossible.

In considering the physiological bases of emotion, one should not think that all emotions are innate. Although infants usually cry when pained or experience fear when confronted with some sudden lack of physical support or other unusual stimulus, emotional expressions in general tend to develop through learning and maturation. Since our concern is essentially with adults, let us look briefly at the role of learning in emotions.

Learning and emotional expression

As the child matures he learns through experience to fear more events and objects, and he learns about the situations, objects, and people that make him happy, loving, frustrated, or angry. Through simple conditioning, emotions often become associated with other and new objects or events. The young lover may come to associate a certain popular song with a young lady because the love emotion was expressed most while dancing to this song. Thereafter, hearing the song alone can arouse the emotion. Undoubtedly many of our irrational fears also come about through conditioning.

Also, through social learning we learn *how* to express emotions; a culture dictates the acceptable and unacceptable ways of expressing them. A child may be permitted to throw a temper tantrum, but an adult is expected to display his anger more by the language he uses, by avoiding or leaving the inflammatory situation, or perhaps by visual gestures which demonstrate his displeasure. The college student learns to become more blasé, more sophisticated in his emotional responses; the intelligent person does not lose his head. In many cultivated social circles, in the more formal churches, in many conventionalized secular gatherings, the "mature" individual is supposed to mask his feelings. On certain occasions, however, an overt display of emotions is considered appropriate, as in meetings of very young people, at sporting events, political rallies, evangelistic meetings, and informal social parties.

Some cultures consider the more free expression of emotion normal. Italian and Spanish people, for example, are often described as more interesting and having greater color and vivacity than nationalities who mask their emotions. On the other hand, the American Indian and the Eskimo are thought to be less emotionally expressive; they seem imperturbable, or even inscrutable. The role of cultural learning in emotional expression was demonstrated well by Klineberg who studied Chinese novels to find how a Chinese writer would portray various human emotions.[1] Although many of the bodily changes in emotion (flushing, paling, trembling) were used as symptoms of emotion in Chinese fiction in much the same way as in Western fiction, the study indicated the Chinese had very different ways of expressing the emotions. For instance a Chinese novelist wrote, "Her eyes grew round and opened wide" (meaning she became angry); another wrote, "They stretched out their tongues" (meaning they showed signs of surprise); and still another wrote, "He scratched his ears and cheeks" (meaning he was happy). Would you have interpreted the emotions accurately had you read the novels?

Finally, through learning we are able, regardless of the culture in which we live, to place ourselves in situations that lead to pleasurable emotional responses or that avoid the unpleasurable ones. This capacity makes life more satisfying.

The way in which the learning process affects the expression of emotions is of enormous importance in the study of persuasion. The persuader must be able (1) to demonstrate orally and visually that he is participating —in type and intensity—in the emotion he wishes his audience to experience, (2) to use descriptive language so skillfully as to create a situation or event with such reality as to arouse the desired emotional response, and (3) to identify with some accuracy the emotions of the receivers prior to and during the message.

The reader will note that these skills rely on the accurate identification of emotional responses. Within a given culture, it is generally assumed that people can make such judgments with considerable accuracy, particularly in instances of intensive emotion. Unfortunately much of the research testing this assumption has involved only appraisals of photographs and drawings of facial expressions. The total physical being and the total social context of the emotional subject were overlooked. Early research in such perceptions was conducted by Woodworth who found that the judges seldom made a mistake in placing a picture of an emotionalized subject in one of the following six broad categories: (1) love, happiness, mirth, (2) surprise, (3) fear and suffering, (4) anger and determination, (5) disgust, and (6) contempt.[2] It would appear that in posed pictures considerable accuracy in perception is possible when categories are broad and group together emotions that are sometimes confused with

[1] Otto Klineberg, "Emotional Expression in Chinese Literature," *Journal of Abnormal and Social Psychology* 33 (1938): 517–20.

[2] R. S. Woodworth, *Experimental Psychology* (New York: Holt, Rinehart and Winston, 1938).

each other. Judgmental accuracy might also be helped by the fact that stereotyped expressions of emotions are used.

Our judgment of such researches is that they are of limited value because in everyday situations there are many more variables at work. Landis found that in using photographs depicting people being subjected to actual emotion-arousing situations, judgments of the emotions were not consistent.[3] Research evidence is still needed concerning the perception of emotions expressed in their total situational contexts. In view of the difficulty in perceiving emotional behavior with confident accuracy, the persuader is well advised to make his judgments with considerable care. For additional information on perception, see chapter 12.

Classifying the emotions

It is rather common practice among psychologists first to classify emotions into two broad categories—the pleasurable and the unpleasurable. Such a classification rests on the premise that the individual's physical and psychological welfare is sought through the processes of acceptance and rejection, of approach and avoidance. Within these broad classes, more specific emotional behaviors can be identified. Although our purpose here is simply to prepare a list of the chief emotions that have been studied most and that are frequently aroused or utilized in suasive rhetoric, our reader should first be made aware that to arrive at such a list is not easy and in the last analysis must necessarily be somewhat arbitrary.

The behaviorist John Watson held that children experience three basic emotions—fear, rage, and love.[4] Some of his critics suggested that at birth the infant shows only two states—excitation and quiescence, but that the generalized excitement or emotion becomes differentiated as the infant matures. Through differentiation and subdivisions of broad emotional patterns, innumerable adult emotions to be identified and classified could result.

Plutchik proposed an "emotional mixture" theory that postulated eight basic emotional expressions—anticipation, anger, joy, acceptance, surprise, fear, sorrow, and disgust.[5] These basic reactions are said to have shown

[3] C. Landis, "Studies of Emotional Reactions. II. General Behavior and Facial Expression," *Journal of Comparative Psychology* 4 (1924): 447–509.

[4] J. B. Watson, *Psychology from the Standpoint of a Behaviorist* (Philadelphia: Lippincott, 1919).

[5] R. Plutchik, *The Emotions: Facts, Theories, and a New Model* (New York: Random House, 1962).

evolutionary changes and may depend on maturation of the individual. The many complex emotional experiences of an adult are supposed to result from various mixtures of the eight basic emotional responses. Plutchik assumed, too, that each of these eight reactions can vary in intensity; thus fear may range from a mild timidity, into apprehension, fear, panic, and finally terror. He experimented to determine how language usage reflects differences in identifiable emotional intensity and asked his subjects to rank six groups of emotional synonyms in ascending intensity order. The responses were: (1) annoyance, anger, rage; (2) pleasure, happiness, joy, ecstasy; (3) surprise, amazement, astonishment; (4) apprehension, fear, panic, terror; (5) gloominess, dejection, sorrow, grief; and (6) dislike, disgust, loathing.

That emotions have varying intensities and levels of arousal is generally agreed; this identification of emotions as variations in intensity of a basic emotion is a useful approach. It may indicate, too, how a mixture of emotions may produce a third. A college student's Saturday night escapade may involve a mixture of joy and mild fear, resulting in a feeling of guilt.

Some contend, however, that the *only* significant difference between emotions is to be found in intensity. To classify emotions solely in this manner would assume that if happiness and sorrow had the same intensity, one could not distinguish between them, a claim we cannot accept. Level of intensity is only one of many criteria for describing and classifying emotion. Pleasantness or unpleasantness is not necessarily dependent on intensity or level of arousal, yet these two terms do help differentiate emotions. Likewise, the approach-avoidance dimension of an emotion is useful, because emotions can be characterized in terms of their tendency to urge us either toward some source of stimulation or away from it. Fear leads to avoidance, anger frequently leads to aggressive behavior.

In his excellent book on motivation and emotion, Murray summarizes well the difficulties in identifying and classifying emotions. "In general, the bewildering variety of emotions can be classified according to several principles. The generalized emotional reaction at birth is *differentiated* during development. On the adult level, we can distinguish a few basic emotions which *combine* in various ways to produce subtle emotions. Finally, emotional experience can be described in terms of several *dimensions*, such as level of intensity, pleasantness-unpleasantness, and approach-avoidance."[6]

---

[6] E. J. Murray, *Motivation and Emotion* (Englewood Cliffs, N.J.: Prentice-Hall 1964), p. 58.

In light of what has been said above, it should be clear that a sizeable list of emotions could be compiled, depending on one's skills at fine differentiations and one's vocabulary. It seems wise, therefore, to urge the student of persuasion to become an astute observer of the fewer and basic human emotional responses, to become more accurate in perceiving them and more skillful in arousing them rhetorically when it seems necessary and justified. In the pleasant classification we would put the basic emotions of *joy* and *love*; in the negative or unpleasant classification we would put *anger, fear, sorrow,* and *disgust*. To attempt to make many sharp distinctions among the complex and highly differentiated emotions of adult life seems unproductive for our purposes.

In our discussion given below of the relationship of emotion and motivation we explore more fully several of the basic emotions as they contribute to the process of motivation. Ethical problems resulting from use of the emotional condition for purposes of persuasion are treated in chapter 10.

Emotion and motivation

If there is no connection between emotions and motivation, there is little, if any, reason to encourage the student of persuasion to become acquainted with the nature of emotions. Do emotions play a role in the motivational process, or are they merely behavioral side effects with no real motivational power? How can we confirm our intuitive answers to this question?

As we have seen earlier, emotions have both a physiological and a psychological dimension. They influence our perceptions, are influenced by learning, and affect behavior. But do they direct behavior toward goals? Because the study of emotions is a very complex one, it is to be expected that scholars with differing interests and approaches in the matter will also differ on the relation, if any, between emotion and motivation. Some contend that emotion is a process different from that of motivation. Others hold that emotions are highly related to motivation, that they actually are one class of motives. Still others view emotional behavior as a dimension of various aspects of the motivational process.

It is our judgment that even though *very extreme* emotions can be disruptive and unorganized, less extreme emotions play significant motivational, directive roles in our behavior and, as such, must be considered relevant to our subject. The theory that captures best the perceptual-motivational nature of the emotions has been advanced by Magda

Arnold.[7] She suggests the following sequence (paraphrased by your authors): (1) First, there is a neutral perception of some event, object, or person; (2) then follows an appraisal or judgment of the stimulus as being good or bad, pleasurable or harmful; (3) the second step leads to a felt (emotional) tendency in regard to such a good or bad stimulus; (4) then follow those physiological changes organized toward approach or avoidance; and (5) finally the action (approach or avoidance) takes place. This theory recognizes that emotion is linked to motivation; it postulates that the tendency toward an approach to or avoidance of the stimulus has not only activation qualities, but also the capacity to direct behavior. Leeper also confirms this view in a similar perceptual-motivational theory.[8] He holds that the emotional and motivational significance of the generally widespread bodily changes that characterize emotions come about because these bodily changes affect the organization of the cortical processes which, by virtue of their perceptual functions, are indeed motivational processes. He contends, therefore, that emotions *are* motives.

The view held generally among scholars is that emotion is a dimension of the motivational process. Hilgard, Atkinson, and Atkinson conclude that, "Emotional states are aroused states. An unpleasant emotional state corresponds to the tension state in aroused drive, and the organism seeks to terminate it. . . . Reduction of the tension aroused in unpleasant emotion is equivalent to the reduction of drive tension. Actually in this situation emotion *is* drive."[9] Long a student of motivation, Bindra states that, "The term *emotional behavior* is used as a collective name for the behavior of anger, fear, joy, and the like, and *motivated behavior* as a general label for the phenomena such as hunger behavior (food seeking and eating), sex behavior, and drug addiction behavior. Now, although emotional behavior and motivated behavior are often treated as if they were distinct classes of behavior, they are not so in fact."[10] In a more qualified statement that reminds us of both the disruptive as well as the organized capacities of the emotions, Murray concludes of emotion, "It can disrupt ongoing behavior but it can also produce new, goal-directed forms of behavior. Moderate levels of emotion are generally

[7] M. Arnold, *Emotion and Personality, vol. 1. Psychological Aspects, vol 2. Neurological and Psychological Aspects.* (New York: Columbia University Press, 1960).

[8] R. W. Leeper, "Some Needed Development in the Motivational Theory of Emotion" in *Nebraska Symposium on Motivation* 13 (Lincoln, Neb.: University of Nebraska Press, 1965): 25–122.

[9] E. R. Hilgard, R. C. Atkinson, and R. L. Atkinson, *Introduction to Psychology,* 5th ed. (New York: Harcourt Brace Jovanovich, 1971), pp. 345–46.

[10] D. Bindra, *Motivation—A Systematic Reinterpretation* (New York: The Ronald Press, 1959), p. 26.

facilitating but extreme emotion is more disruptive. . . . In all these effects, emotion is very much like motivation, which can also organize or disorganize behavior."[11]

We trust the above discussion is sufficient to establish a general and theoretical case for considering the emotions as important motivational factors in the direction of behavior; when aroused and directed through rhetorical means, emotions thus become elements of persuasion. Granting, then, these justifications, let us now explore the researches that evaluate more specifically the effectiveness of motion arousal in changing attitudes and behavior.

Evaluating the effectiveness of emotional arousal in modifying attitudes and behavior

The persuader wishing to increase his skills in arousing and using the receiver's emotional responses must know the conditions for their effective use. Human emotions are complex, highly sensitive psychological expressions. They are not to be toyed with recklessly if they are to be employed in purposeful manners. Because of the complexities of emotional behavior and the many unanswered questions concerning it, we hope every student of persuasion will make the topic a continuing study. We survey below a number of important research studies that have helped bring our knowledge of the role of emotion in motivation to its present status. We have confined this survey to a discussion of the three most common emotions: fear, anger, and love.

The effectiveness of fear appeals

Since much of the research on emotion relates to the study of fear, we will begin with this emotion. In one of the earliest studies, Janis and Feshbach tested the effects on audiences of fear-arousing messages. Using equivalent size groups of high-school students as subjects, they presented three fifteen-minute, illustrated speeches on the topic of tooth decay and oral hygiene. One group heard a speech using very strong fear appeals, the second group heard the speech using moderate fear appeals, and the third group heard the speech using minimum or mild fear appeals. The greatest conformity to the speaker's recommendation was produced by the speech using the minimum fear appeals. There was, however, no statistically reliable difference between the

---

[11] E. J. Murray, *Motivation and Emotion* (Englewood Cliffs, N.J.: Prentice-Hall, 1964), p. 64.

effectiveness of the speech using the minimum fear appeals and that using moderate appeals. The researchers explained the results in part by suggesting that "the overall effectiveness of a persuasive communication will tend to be reduced by a strong fear appeal if it evokes high emotional tension without adequately satisfying the need for reassurance."[12] This explanation suggests that there may be a number of variables (such as in the nature of the message) that may relate to the effectiveness of the degrees of emotional intensity used; this may help explain the studies that follow which contradict the results of the Janis and Feshbach research.

Kraus, El-Assal, and DeFleur conducted a field study to judge the threat appeals carried by the mass media regarding potential eye injury from observing an eclipse of the sun in an improper manner.[13] They concluded that at least in some cases strong fear appeals may be used successfully. Likewise, strong threat or fear appeals were found by Berkowitz and Cottingham to be more effective than mild fear appeals in persuading inexperienced drivers to wear seat belts.[14] Leventhal, Singer, and Jones[15] conducted a study that provides an "escape route" from fear. The subjects (Yale seniors) read a health bulletin on tetanus inoculation and then completed a questionnaire that included items on various other types of inoculation as well plus items on the emotions experienced while reading the prepared bulletin. Some read a bulletin that included high fear appeals, and another group read a bulletin that included similar information, but which used low-fear appeals. Both types of bulletins included an identical paragraph on the control of tetanus and informed the subjects that the university health service was making shots available to all students interested in being inoculated. Half of the bulletins (high-availability messages) provided specific directions regarding the location of the health service and the daily hours of the service. It was found that the high-fear message bulletins caused the subjects to feel the tetanus shots were more important than did the low-fear message bulletins, although the low-fear message readers had originally expressed

[12] I. Janis and S. Feshbach, "Effects of Fear-Arousing Communications," *Journal of Abnormal and Social Psychology* 48 (1953): 88.

[13] S. Kraus, E. El-Assal, and M. DeFleur, "Fear-Threat Appeals in Mass Communication," *Speech Monographs* 33 (1966): 23–29.

[14] L. Berkowitz and D. Cottingham, "The Interest Value and Relevance of Fear-Arousing Communications," *Journal of Abnormal and Social Psychology* 60 (1960): 37–43.

[15] H. Leventhal, R. Singer, and S. Jones, "Effects of Fear and Specificity of Recommendation upon Attitudes and Behavior," *Journal of Personality and Social Psychology* 2 (1965): 20–29.

stronger intentions of getting the shots. It is interesting to note that of the nine subjects who actually got the shots all but one had read the high-availability message. Four of these eight had read the high-fear bulletin and four the low-fear bulletin. This evidence suggests that both low- and high-fear appeals can produce attitude change, but that *both fear arousal and specific recommendations for its reduction are needed to result in action.*

Another study that also suggests the effectiveness of fear appeals when combined with readily available means of escape was conducted by Leventhal and Niles at the New York City Health Exposition in 1964.[16] In this study, movies were prepared to arouse three levels of fear relative to lung cancer. The movies were shown to eighteen groups ranging in size from fifteen to forty subjects attending the exposition. No film was shown to a control group. After showing the films (and after showing no film to the control group), chest X-rays were encouraged. It was stated that the X-ray unit, which was seen by the subjects as they entered the room, was down the hall and ready to serve. The subjects were also given a booklet ("To Smoke or Not To Smoke") and asked to read it. After reading the booklet, the subjects were asked to fill out a questionnaire covering such items as degree of fear aroused, relation of smoking to lung cancer, the desire to have a chest X-ray, intention to stop smoking, number of cigarettes smoked per day, and the length of time since the last X-ray. The results showed that fear does facilitate persuasion. Those subjects who took the X-rays were those who had reported greater fear aroused, and they included a higher proportion of those who saw the film (regardless of the level of fear used) than of subjects in the control group. On the whole, the smokers reported a *greater intention* to have the X-rays than did the nonsmokers. However, the smokers who saw the films reported less desire to stop the habit than those in the control group. Interestingly, those who witnessed the high-fear film reported greater fear and a stronger belief that smoking does cause cancer, but those people expressed *less intention* to stop smoking than was reported by those who saw the low-fear movie. The researchers suggested that the readily available X-ray unit provided a "quick and easy escape" from fear, but that the more difficult and perhaps longer-term task of stopping smoking was not adopted in many cases.

Additional studies tend to support the notion that the persuasive value of varying intensities of emotional arousal is dependent upon other vari-

[16] H. Leventhal and P. Niles, "A Field Experiment on Fear Arousal with Data on the Validity of Questionnaire Measures," *Journal of Personality* 32 (1964): 459–79.

ables. For instance, fear-arousing appeals can be significant when extended over a long period of time. DeWolfe and Governale, inducing a high degree of fear in student nurses during a six-week study of tuberculosis, produced greater attitudinal change toward the disease and the methods to fight it than they did in those who were subjected to a lesser degree of fear.[17] Also, in a varied-time study, Leventhal and Niles studied the duration of exposure to fear appeals in relation to the amount of effectiveness.[18] They administered technicolor sound films of durations of eight, sixteen, twenty-four, and thirty-two minutes, each to a different group. The films showed the plights of the victims of serious car accidents. It was found that the longer duration of exposure produced greater concern about driving and greater desire to take some preventive action. Powell tested hypotheses which assumed a significant interaction between the persuasiveness of fear appeals and the object of the threat.[19] He found that a strong fear appeal that posed a real threat to the family of the listener produced greater attitude change than a mild appeal. However, it was not confirmed that such appeals directed at the receiver's family would produce a greater attitude change than when directed at the receiver himself.

The study of fear appeals may be approached from still another point of view. Goldstein studied fear appeals in relation to receiver personality types and found that those who were able to cope well with their own needs and emotions were able to handle greater fear appeals than the avoiders who did not recognize the personal implications of the aggressive and sexual items used in the study.[20] The minimum fear appeals were given greater acceptance by the avoider personality who usually avoids unpleasantness as much as possible. In a study also concerned with personality differences in relation to fear appeals, Janis and Feshbach used an Anxiety Symptoms Inventory to divide audiences into high- and low-anxiety groups.[21] It was found that high-anxiety audience members were influenced less by the strong fear messages than were the members of the low-anxiety audience. It was concluded that mild fear or threat

[17] A. S. DeWolfe and C. N. Governale, "Fear and Attitude Change," *Journal of Abnormal and Social Psychology* 69 (1964): 119–23.

[18] H. Leventhal and P. Niles, "Persistence of Influence for Varying Durations of Exposure to Threat Stimuli," *Psychological Reports* 16 (1965): 223–33.

[19] F. Powell, "The Effect of Anxiety-Arousing Messages When Related to Personal, Familial, and Impersonal Referents," *Speech Monographs* 32 (1965): 102–6.

[20] M. J. Goldstein, "The Relationship Between Coping and Avoiding Behavior and Response to Fear-Arousing Propaganda," *Journal of Abnormal and Social Psychology* 59 (1959): 252.

[21] I. Janis and S. Feshbach, "Personality Differences Associated with Responsiveness to Fear-Arousing Communications," *Journal of Personality* 23 (1954): 154–69.

appeals may be especially effective when high-anxiety (vague fear) people are the receivers. In a related study that used the Q-methodology, Miller and Hewgill were able to fit subjects into two categories of fear types: (1) those students primarily fearful of career failure, and (2) those students fearful of separation from valued others. This study simply confirms, as the authors pointed out, "the notion that there are numerous individual differences which influence fear arousal."[22]

Finally, we would point out that the word *anxiety* frequently appears in treatments of the fear emotion, but it is not always used in a consistent manner. Most commonly it is considered a *vague fear* that, unlike general fear, is not related to a specific object. It may result from a series of mild fears, and it may have only a vague object as its stimulus. A series of social rebuffs, the noting of the punishments others receive for behavior like one's own, or a series of job or financial failures may well result in arousing anxiety which, in turn, can produce motivational behavior designed to alleviate the tension of the anxiety.

Jealousy may be considered a form of anxiety based on fear of losing the affections of a loved one. This special case of anxiety, however, is related to a specific object, and it is often expressed as aggression toward the rival of the object's attentions rather than as withdrawal or avoidance behavior that generally accompanies fear-arousing situations.

The effectiveness of arousal of anger

As mentioned earlier, whenever some motivated behavioral sequence leading toward some desired goal is thwarted, frustration results; it is frequently expressed in the emotion of anger and leads toward aggression. Insults to your self-esteem or to a loved one, the failing grade that keeps you from getting into law school, or the denial of a promotion or salary increase toward which you have worked diligently frequently produces considerable frustration and anger as its expression. Independent truckers in the United States, feeling that their economic survival was threatened by a shortage of diesel oil and by higher fuel prices expressed their frustration in no small amount of anger and with some violence. The experiment conducted by Amsel supports the point that angry, aggressive action tends to result from interferences with the seeking of goals, even when the interferences are only mild.[23] Research

---

[22] G. Miller and M. Hewgill, "Some Recent Research on Fear-Arousing Message Appeals," *Speech Monographs* 33 (1965): 390.

[23] A. Amsel, "Partial Reinforcement Effects on Vigor and Persistence" in K. W. Spence and J. T. Spence, eds., *The Psychology of Learning and Motivation*, Vol. 1 (New York: Academic Press, 1967), pp. 1–65.

also shows that frustration, like fear, can be conditioned, as demonstrated by Wagner.[24]

Of course, the expression of anger is subject to social and cultural expectations. Aggression born of anger is taboo in many situations, even penalized by law. So it is that anger at times will not be expressed in readily observable manners. In an early study by Gates, college women were asked to keep records of those occasions where they experienced anger or great irritation.[25] They also were to record the impulses they had to express their anger. The 51 subjects made a total of 135 reports on anger situations. The following impulses were reported: to make a verbal retort—530; to do physical injury to the offender—40; to injure inanimate objects—20; to run away, leave the room—12; and to cry, scream, or swear—10.

Although the research is not as extensive as that dealing with fear, the available data and common experience demonstrate quite convincingly the role that frustration and its frequent emotional expression—anger— can play in motivation. It has been the practice of many persuaders throughout history to use the existing frustration of a receiver or audience, perhaps magnify it, and then direct the aggressive behavior toward some target person or group, or to rhetorically create frustration based on some situation that has not been perceived by the receiver and then to show how the tension created can be reduced or eliminated by accepting the persuader's recommendation.

The effectiveness of appeals to love, joy, and delight

In view of the lack of specific research in this area, one might conclude that there is more concern among researchers for our unpleasant emotional experiences than for our pleasant ones. The pleasant feelings of joy and delight are frequently accompaniments of the successful satisfactions of such goal-directed motives and emotions as achievement, social approval, and love. Research thus focuses on the goal itself. But regardless of the lack of rigorous evidence on the motivational values of these pleasurable sensations, we know from experience and related motive studies that they do affect behavior purposefully. Let us look at some of the ways this is done.

Pleasurable feelings are the result of both real and anticipated satis-

[24] A. R. Wagner, "Conditioned Frustration as a Learned Drive," *Journal of Experimental Psychology* 66 (1963): 142–48.

[25] G. S. Gates, "An Observational Study of Anger," *Journal of Experimental Psychology* 9 (1926): 325–36.

factions of one's drives and motives. The release from tensions (such as fear) can produce joy and, as such, has motivating power. Humor—and its frequent accompaniment laughter—are common expressions of joy and delight and are used as releases from fears, anxieties, and tensions. President Lincoln often used jokes to reduce tensions in his cabinet meetings. The famous Will Rogers used humor to reduce tensions and to disarm potential antagonists as he made his more critical points. Ethnic humorists have used the arousal of mirth and laughter through humor for many years in attempts to plead for tolerance and to reduce tendencies toward aggression or potential violence. A very popular contemporary television show, *All in the Family*, uses this method in exposing bigotry and prejudice. Humor is often used to redirect personal tensions and frustrations toward some outside target or scapegoat, a tactic that provides the release. It also may be used as an aid to personal security or even superiority. The British philosopher, Thomas Hobbes, said, "Laughter is caused either by some sudden act of their own that pleaseth them; or by the apprehension of some deformed thing in another, by comparison whereof they suddenly applaud themselves."[26] Thus we may experience a happy feeling when a dignified, egotistical person slips on the ice. If a persuader thinks his receivers regard him or her as too formal, cold, or distant, he can make fun of himself to disarm them and enhance his credibility.

Appeals to joy and delight are most generally useful, however, in persuading people to accept recommended social and personal goals. The joy generated in anticipation of becoming great, of overcoming a present obstacle, and of gaining social approval can be very motivating. The preacher's assurance that God loves everyone can be a joyful experience to one who feels despised, rejected, and a personal failure. And when joy is experienced on actual achievement of goals, we may continue to do those things that perpetuate the conditions of joy or great pleasure. The emotion aroused during a successful political rally not only helps unify those present but also spurs the party workers to new dedication in their future efforts to get the ticket elected.

Although we cannot investigate here all emotions from a persuasive point of view, we must not forget that feelings such as sympathy, sorrow, and surprise or astonishment can play important roles in human motivation. However, we trust our survey of some of the evidence in support of the effectiveness of the emotional states of fear, anger, and love has been sufficient to establish feelings and emotions as important factors in persuasion.

[26] T. Hobbes, *Leviathan*, Everyman's Library edition, 1914, p. 27.

A summary of the practical implications for persuasion
of theory and research in emotional behavior

Thus far we have been concerned primarily with acquainting the reader
with the basic nature of the emotions, their roles in the motivational
process, and the effectiveness of appeals designed to arouse emotion. The
occasional references to the implications of this knowledge for persuasion
have been made only to help clarify the points under discussion. In this
final section we summarize the chief points made regarding the emotions
as aspects of motivation and discuss briefly their more specific and practical implications for persuasion.

1.   Emotions are aroused states of man that can range from mild to
extreme intensities. The stimulation of emotions can be of internal or
external origin. In persuasive messages, we are primarily interested, of
course, in the external, rhetorical stimulation of the emotions.

2.   It is quite well established that emotions are related to motivation in that they can function not only as accompaniments but as facilitators or directors of behavior.

3.   In persuasion one deals with the motivational values of drives,
motives, attitudes, *and the emotions*. Emotions are the *affective* components of the other motivational factors. Even though an emotion can act *as*
a motive, the emotion itself is aroused initially by one or more basic
needs or motives that direct the individual toward some desired goal.
For example, the stimulus that triggered the emotion of anger in a person
may have been caused by some business competitor whose unfair practices kept the angry individual from receiving the coveted Outstanding
Young Businessman's Award given by the Junior Chamber of Commerce.
In this hypothetical case, the social approval, achievement, or other
motive was frustrated and anger developed. This could lead to aggression.
In rhetorically creating or using any such situation, the persuader must
decide what emotion he wishes to arouse and to what extent it should
be aroused for maximum effectiveness. An attempt to arouse great emotion in conjunction with an appeal to a motive of average salience to the
receiver will probably be received coolly if not rejected. Mild frustration
of a motive based on some relatively weak human need will normally
result in only a weak emotion. In preparing his message, the persuader
should keep in mind that he must maintain a certain balance between
the need strength of the motive on which his appeal is based and the
intensity of the emotional dimension he wishes to add to the appeal.

4. If the persuader's goal calls for a relatively well organized task to be performed, the arousal of emotion must not exceed the amount of intensity that permits organized, adaptive behavior on the part of the persuadee. Extreme emotional intensity leads to disruptive, disorganized behavior.

5. If the persuader desires an intellectual commitment to a proposition, he must remember that reflective thought generally thrives best in a calm, dispassionate condition. It should be pointed out, however, that if there are any completely emotionless acts, they are those acts so highly habituated as to be virtually automatic.

6. In terms of responsible rhetoric, undue or irrelevant emotional arousal is a poor substitute for facts. Reverend Lyman Beecher is supposed to have said, "The less I have to say, the louder I yell." Similarly, in the margin of an orator's manuscript was found, "Argument weak here, yell like hell!" To increase emotional arousal when the real substance of the message is decreasing is a sign of a crippled rhetorician. Extreme emotional arousal is frequently the technique of the demagogue.

7. The persuader who uses intensity of some very unpleasant emotion to the extent that it causes the receiver to experience great psychological pain is engaging in a hazardous discourse, indeed, for the frustration the receiver feels may well be blamed on the communicator. Your authors have seen this occur in their classes in persuasion.

8. The persuadee by no means always follows behavioral patterns that have become habituated responses to motivational stimuli. Frequently he is prompted to approach problems in a very thoughtful, rational manner in order to discover new and better modes of satisfying his needs. Reasoned discourse with a minimum of emotional appeal is suggested to help him do this.

9. On occasion the receiver of a message will act very impulsively, prompted in large measure by the emotional stimulation of the situation. The impulse buyer allows the dominant motive and its emotional components to trigger his behavior.

10. Our emotions affect our perceptions. By his message a persuader can minimize or maximize our emotional responses to threatening situations.

11. Some receivers are personally prone to exhibit and act on emotion; others are distrustful of emotional behavior and tend to inhibit its expression and depreciate its value.

12. Social customs and expectations influence the ways in which and the degrees to which emotions are expressed. To know these customs is

essential for the persuader who tries to interpret the feedback of emotional responses in his audience.

13. Heightened emotion can reduce the amount of attention to the overall message content but can increase attention to the more personal implications of the message.

14. Through learning we attach certain emotional responses to certain objects, places, ideas, and people. The persuader should attempt to learn the attachments of his receiver so that he can use these favorably.

15. The feelings of joy and delight can be aroused and used motivationally by demonstrating that the persuader's recommendation will satisfy some strong desire or avoid that which is unpleasant.

16. It is difficult to make generalizations regarding the effectiveness of fear appeals in persuasion, but one certainty seems warranted: fear appeals in general have persuasive value in changing attitudes and behavior. In some cases and under some conditions strong fear appeals are effective. This is especially true in dealing with the "copers" rather than with the "avoiders" of the difficulties of life. It has been shown that high-anxiety subjects conformed less to the persuader's goal when strong fear appeals were used than did the low-anxiety subjects.

17. When the message provides a ready and not too difficult means of escape from a fear stimulus, change is likely to be produced.

18. The credibility of the persuader has been shown to be related to the use of fear appeals. The high-credibility source can be more effective in using strong fear appeals than can the low-credibility source.

19. Humor and laughter can be used to reduce frustrating, tense situations and can disarm the antagonistic receiver.

20. Fear can be aroused in many ways. To show that some courses of action opposed by the speaker would deprive us of our basic necessities (food, water, safety), bring harm to a loved one, a revered object, or keep us from attaining other necessary goals can produce the fear emotion.

21. Fear appeals seem to retain their effectiveness when extended over a period of time.

22. The persuader should be aware of emotional dispositions other than those we have discussed thus far. The person who has a *phobia* exhibits extreme or pathological fear of some stimulus. The word *temperament* is usually used to describe the general differences among people in their emotionality. We say some are even-tempered and others are hot-tempered. Finally, a *mood* is a state of emotion that tends to persist through a limited period of time. It is akin to a temperament but does not persist as long.

23. Emotional appeals in suasive discourse must be used ethically. On occasion a speaker arouses emotions completely irrelevant to the point under consideration in order to cloud the point and shift the issues. A classic case was the "eulogy of a dog" by Senator George C. Vest of Missouri. While awaiting the trial of his own client, the senator was asked to help the prosecution attorneys win in a dog case. A dog had been killed, the presumed killer was on trial, and damages were being asked. The senator consented to help and spoke as follows:

> Gentlemen of the Jury—The best friend a man has in the world may turn against him and become his enemy. The son or daughter that he has reared with loving care may prove ungrateful. Those who are nearest and dearest to us, those whom we trust with our happiness and our good name may become traitors to their faith. The money that a man has he may lose. It flies away from him, perhaps, when he needs it most. A man's reputation may be sacrificed in a moment of ill-considered action. The people who are prone to fall on their knees to do us honor when success is with us may be the first to throw the stone of malice when failure settles its cloud on our heads. The one absolutely unselfish friend that man can have in this selfish world, the one that never proves ungrateful or treacherous, is his dog. A man's dog stands by him in prosperity and poverty, in health and sickness. He will sleep on the cold ground, where the wintry winds blow, and the snow drives fiercely, if only he may be near his master's side. He will kiss the hand that has no food to offer; he will lick the wounds and sores that come in encounter with the roughness of the world. He guards the sleep of his pauper master as if he were a prince. When all other friends desert, he remains. When riches take wings and reputation falls to pieces, he is as constant in his love as the sun in its journeys through the heavens. If fortune drives the master forth an outcast in the world, friendless and homeless, the faithful dog asks no higher privilege than that of accompanying him, to guard against danger, to fight against his enemies. And when the last scene of all comes, and death takes the master in his embrace, and his body is laid away in the cold ground, no matter if all other friends pursue their way, there, by the graveside, will the noble dog be found, his head between his paws, his eyes sad, but open to alert watchfulness, faithful and true, even to death.[27]

You will note that no argument was made regarding whether the defendant killed the dog or the financial worth of the animal. Nonetheless, at the close of the speech the judge and the jury were wiping tears away.

---

[27] Quoted in the Indianapolis *News*, 12 September 1924.

The jury filed out and returned soon with a verdict favoring the plaintiff. They awarded him $500; he had sued for $200.

How should emotional arousal be used in persuasive discourse? This is a question the reader must answer.

Conclusion

From the discussion of the nature, types, and the motivational values of emotion and their implications for persuasion, the reader has surely concluded that the role of emotion in persuasion can be highly significant and that the arousal and uses of emotional responses present complex rhetorical and ethical problems. It should not be concluded, however, that persuasion as a mode of discourse operates to the neglect of critical thought. Chapter 8 considers this matter in detail.

6

Attitudes and attitude change: theory and practice

Introduction

A reminder of our present purposes

Throughout this book we have attempted to keep in mind our chief purposes of equipping the reader with basic knowledge about the field of persuasion as an academic study, providing him with those theories, principles, and methods requisite to the effective practice of persuasion, and to assist him as a consumer of persuasive messages in evaluating them intelligently. We remind ourselves and the reader to keep these goals in mind because many researchers in attitude and behavioral change are not interested primarily in actually producing change —as is the persuader—but in using the researches to gain further knowledge of basic psychological and social psychological processes and to refine their methodologies. This text is not simply a compendium of the most relevant studies in attitude and attitude modification; such reviews are reported quite carefully and more completely elsewhere.[1] For our present purposes we will use relevant researches to clarify and to support points useful to the student of persuasive communication. It is hoped, of course, that within the limits of a single chapter the reader will achieve some insights into the methods of investigation used and the larger implications of theory. The main purpose, however, is to help the reader combine the knowledge of the behavioral sciences and of suasive discourse into a more complete, receiver-centerd approach to rhetoric.

As we begin this chapter the reader is encouraged to review those materials on attitude theory briefly sketched in chapter 3.

The study of attitudes

Nothing is more interesting than other people. We all enjoy that great human game of imputing motives and attitudes to others and drawing our own satisfying conclusions about them, however unscientific and unskilled we may be. We glibly label a person a Red, Radical, Liberal, Conservative, Hippie, or ill-bred Yokel. The persuader, however, must seek to base his understanding of the persuadee on the most tenable knowledge from research in human behavior and suasive rhetoric.

---

[1] See M. Fishbein, *Readings in Attitude Theory and Measurement* (New York: John Wiley and Sons, 1967). See also C. A. Insko, *Theories of Attitude Change* (New York: Appleton-Century-Crofts, 1967).

Since persuaders are primarily interested in modifying existing attitudes, creating new ones, or influencing behavior linked with attitudes, we must first consider the nature of attitudes and then look at the theories and modes of attitude change, the basic conditions of attitude change, the relation of attitude change to behavioral change, the resistances to attitude change, and, finally, some practical suggestions for the persuader in making such changes.

The concept of attitude is only one factor—though a central one—of many that play a role in human behavior. Many people work in fields related to persuasion, and they hold many different opinions, and use varying terminology. We have sought to rest our views on these points of considerable agreement among varying fields and on those theories and researches in which we have some confidence.

The nature of attitudes

Definition of the concept of attitude

An attitude is an abstract concept, a construct, and a complex psychological phenomenon of great social significance. Because an attitude cannot be measured directly, it is inferred and studied in indirect ways. Allport's definition of attitude is accepted widely: "*a mental and neural state of readiness, organized through experience, exerting a directive or dynamic influence upon an individual's response to all objects and situations with which it is related.*"[2]

Attitudes, motives, and values

Although motives and attitudes are alike in some respects, it is important to understand that they possess significant differences. We have seen that motives depend on some drive state of the organism, that they are learned ways to achieve certain rather specific goals, and that they only persist until the goal is achieved. Attitudes, on the other hand, though also learned, do not depend on a given drive state nor are they characteristically of temporal duration. Rather, they are persistent predispositions or reaction tendencies of a more generalized sort, and they are likely to arouse certain motives. Attitudes generally provide a more stable, continuing organization of one's behavior and are not normally related to specific goals.

[2] G. W. Allport, "Attitudes" in C. Murchison, ed., *Handbook of Social Psychology* (Worcester, Mass.: Clark University Press, 1935), p. 810.

When attitudes become organized into larger, more general classes of things and when these vital attitudinal patterns come to play enduring roles among individuals and in society, *values,* or *value systems* emerge. As Newcomb, Turner, and Converse point out,

> Attitudes toward certain things appear to become dominant over attitudes toward an increasing variety of things. Thus a person may come to orient a very large part of his waking behavior around a core of religious convictions, or around the pursuit of occupational success. The term *value* is used by some social psychologists to refer to the common objects of such inclusive attitudes. For many people, entire systems of thought and "philosophies of life" are organized around values that become, for them, more and more inclusive.[3]

In chapter 4 we indicated the relationship between drives, motives, emotions, attitudes, and values.

Attitudes and opinions

Although there is no great difference between attitudes and opinions, they are not precisely the same. As we point out in the succeeding section, attitudes constitute a certain predisposition, preference, or general orientation toward a given person or object; attitudes may not be entirely conscious. We tend to agree with Hovland, Janis, and Kelley that an *opinion* involves some type of *expectation* or *prediction*—not merely a preference—and that it can be verbalized.[4] A person may not choose to voice his opinions or he may express them in a distorted or inaccurate fashion, but, nonetheless, we see opinions as verbalizable modifications of an attitude.

Opinions expressed in public do not necessarily correspond precisely with one's real attitude. Gorden has demonstrated that the public expression of opinion is likely to represent a compromise between the person's true attitude and what he believes to be the prevailing attitude(s) of the group in which he finds himself.[5]

It should be clear that measurements seeking opinion responses do not necessarily yield accurate information regarding attitudes. Many current investigations are not interested in private attitudes but in public opinion.

[3] T. M. Newcomb, R. H. Turner, and P. E. Converse, *Social Psychology* (New York: Holt, Rinehart and Winston, 1965), pp. 44–45.

[4] C. I. Hovland, I. L. Janis, and H. H. Kelley, *Communication and Persuasion* (New Haven, Conn.: Yale University Press, 1953), pp. 6–10.

[5] R. L. Gorden, "Interaction between Attitudes and the Definition of the Situation in the Expression of Opinion," *American Sociological Review* 17 (1952): 50–58.

The formation and general characteristics of attitudes

Before discussing specific attitudes, it should be helpful to discuss first the general characteristics of attitudes.

1. First, an attitude might be considered a storehouse of our past experiences and their meanings to us. As we attempt to adjust to our social environments, we develop rather consistent manners of thinking and feeling about the people, objects, and issues within this environment. Attitudes are thus formed as a result of learning. This learning usually takes place through association and through the satisfactions of our needs.

2. As a result of this conditioning or learning process, attitudes become organized, relatively stable, and consistent or generalized ways of assessing the people and objects in our environment. They can become dominating forces in our lives; they provide us with a certain regularity in our reactions and adjustments to the world about us. In their early stages of formation they may be flexible, but in later life we may become prisoners of the restraints they impose on us. Those who have attempted "brainwashing" prisoners of war by persuasion, coercion, and violence have found how difficult it is to change basic attitudes.

3. Attitudes have valence. Early in infancy we come to associate certain people or objects with pleasantness or unpleasantness. Attitudes vary in the degree to which they are attracted to a given object or person.

4. Attitudes are predispositions or reaction tendencies; they constitute a readiness to become motivated in relation to a certain attitude object. They thus differ from motives because they are not dependent on any drive state. You may have a positive attitude toward a loved one as you sit reading this book, but you will not be motivated to protect this person until you receive a report that his or her life is in jeopardy because of a fire in another building. In short, an attitude normally persists, but a motive does not.

5. Attitudes may be *dominant* at a given time; that is, at one moment certain attitudes may be active and ready to urge a person to react to some stimulus. Or attitudes may be *latent*, not ready to provide an immediate impetus to some type of reactive behavior. The persuader must learn the specific nature of the attitude(s) with which he is dealing before he can determine the nature of the rhetoric he must use to accomplish his goal.

6. Attitudes also vary in intensity; they may assign to people or objects *degrees* of favorableness or unfavorableness, positiveness or nega-

tiveness, goodness or badness. Take an audit of your attitudes toward your fraternity or sorority, your dorm president, a Japanese, a Chinese, a black, the tennis team, and your local car dealer, and we think you will detect differing intensities of attitudes at work. Thus we can see that attitudes may lie along a scale from very positive to very negative values even though, as we shall see later, these attitudes should not be thought of as a fixed point on the scale but as having ranges or latitudes.

7.   Research indicates that frequently we are not completely aware of the presence or operation of attitudes. By careful self-examination, however, one can become conscious of at least some hidden attitudes. You may note the presence of a negative attitude toward people of other races, for instance, as you attempt to explain to yourself why you feel a certain way about a person of another race despite experiences with him that indicate he is a first-rate human being. In a sense, an attitude is like an iceberg; only a small part of it may be detected while the major portion lies hidden beneath the surface of complex experiences and associations.

Even when we are aware of our attitudes we may be quite reluctant to reveal them. Experience has taught us that there are certain rewards in keeping our true attitudes hidden from other people in general and—on occasion—even from our close friends. The researcher must often devise very subtle methods to test what he hopes are real attitudes.

8.   Finally, it is generally agreed that attitudes have two components: (a) a *cognitive* and (b) an *affective* dimension. The cognitive aspect refers to a set of beliefs or more rational appraisal of the attitude object, while the affective component refers to an emotional or feeling response toward the person or object. For instance, you might attempt to justify in a cognitive manner your negative response toward a prospective fraternity brother; your emotional or affective response might be real anger or hatred for the person. When the affective and cognitive components of an attitude are consistent with each other, the attitude may be said to be in a stable state.

In summary, we have said that attitudes are to a great extent the products of learning; they reflect the beliefs and feelings we have as individuals, the values of our culture, and our experiences in family, religious, educational, and general social life. As such, attitudes become those predispositions, those reaction tendencies we have either for or against people and objects in our environment. Attitudes, therefore, affect our perceptions, our judgments, our learning efficiency, indeed our whole philosophy of life. They provide us with a relatively stable or fixed self-image.

In chapter 7 we discuss how attitudes are influenced by social behavior.

Theories of attitude change

As mentioned earlier, the concept of attitude has become a pervasive and indispensable concept in contemporary social psychology. Various theorists and researchers have approached the study of attitudes in many different ways, and they have posited many different theories. In chapter 4 we sketched the views of a few approaches and theories in order to suggest some contemporary trends in the search for the sources of persuasion. Our purpose here is (a) to consider these theories in more detail, (b) to add additional approaches that are of significance, and (c) to provide more practical aid in using these theories in persuasive communication.

Two additional introductory notes are in order. First, the persuader primarily interested in practical techniques of influencing others is apt to be distressed by the seemingly inconsistent conceptual definitions of attitude and the differing methods for using the concept of attitude in research studies. Until more standardization is achieved in controlling the experimental bias and conceptual definitions, we must understand and appreciate these variations as the inevitable products of a growing complex area of investigation rather than as reflections on the validity of the research.

Second, the reader should keep in mind that a theory is a representation, a model, or a set of rules conceived to show how events operate in the real world. A theory lends itself to verification and to prediction of variables within the scope studied. Thus Einstein's theory of relativity provided an explanation of the relation and movement of celestial bodies. To a person prone to dismiss such a construct by saying: "it's only a theory," we would rejoin, "there's nothing more practical than a sound theory." We encourage the serious student of persuasion to study carefully the theories we discuss below and to be alert to the ever-enlarging body of literature in attitude and behavioral change.

Learning theory

In our discussion of motives and emotions in the preceding chapter, as well as in our discussion of the development and change of attitudes in the present chapter, the reader will have noted references to the role of learning. Those psychologists who emphasize the stimulus-response relationships are committed to what is frequently called *behavior theory*, in which learning of the S-R sort formerly was of central concern. We shall use the term *learning theory* (also used by many) in referring to essentially the same approach. However, we agree with Clark Hull and others who contend that the state of the organism also plays a significant role in the conditioning process, and thus we prefer the S-O-R (stimulus-organism-response) learning theories.[6]

The literature on learning is extensive and, in some cases, complex. Our purpose here is not to review this material but simply to point out that learning processes pervade much of the theory regarding attitudes and attitude change. We have, for example, said that the components of an attitude may be learned by the principles of transfer, association, and need satisfaction. Thus attitude change may be brought about through *transfer* when the source of influence (family, church, speaker) demonstrates attitudes the receiver desires to imitate. If certain conditions cause the individual to learn new ways of feeling or reacting to others by *associations* with them, attitude change can take place. Research has shown that prejudiced attitudes can be changed by integrating varied types of people in housing projects and in military camps.[7] Also, when it can be demonstrated that an individual will gain some advantage or reward by changing his attitudes, his attitude change is related to his *need satisfaction*.

Learning theory can thus be a useful approach to the study of motivation. One must keep in mind, of course, that people differ in their ability and readiness to respond to stimuli, that their motivations to respond vary, and that a repetition of responses tends to increase the chances of predicting future responses, as in habit formation. *The persuader will often need to provide learning situations to help produce the desired attitude or behavior change.* His results will be no better than his ability to make this learning clear and motivating. The final part of this chapter gives practical suggestions to help the persuader in this regard.

Consistency theories

Since the early 1950s there have been a number of independent theories advanced with the same general premise that people tend to do

---

[6] C. L. Hull, *A Behavior System: An Introduction to Behavior Theory Concerning the Individual Organism* (New Haven, Conn.: Yale University Press, 1952).

[7] For a review of some of these studies see D. Krech, R. S. Crutchfield, and E. L. Ballachey, *Individual in Society* (New York: McGraw-Hill, 1962), chapter 7.

those things that reduce (if not eliminate) any internal inconsistencies among attitudes, feelings, and overt behavior. These theories may be broadly labeled "consistency theories." They assume that a consistent or balanced cognitive, psychological state is constantly sought and that inconsistencies or imbalance lead to attitude or behavioral changes tending to reduce the inconsistencies. In recent years, therefore, scholars have expressed considerable interest in consistency research. It is our guess that this emphasis is dwindling. Nonetheless, the influence of this approach has been so great and the subsequent researches generated by it so numerous that the student of persuasion should be familiar with at least the chief examples of consistency theory. As mentioned in chapter 4, consistency theory may be divided into three variants: balance theory, theory of cognitive dissonance, and congruity theory. Let us look at these theories in more detail and suggest their useful points to the student of persuasive discourse.

BALANCE THEORY. We have pointed out that attitudes tend to become more fixed or stabilized in time because they become organized into systems. A number of attitudes may thus become related to one another because of interdependence or sharing of attitude objects. As a simple example, a student may have a favorable attitude toward his fraternity, his school, the school's football team, and the student newspaper. To him these attitude objects may be linked together effectively in a system of attitudes. As long as these attitudes are not endangered by new, contrary information, they are *balanced*; harmony reigns. If, however, the football team lets him down, or a speaker provides persuasive materials regarding the subversive activities of the school paper, an imbalance occurs causing him to rearrange his attitudinal structure in order to restore psychological harmony. So persuaders do not actually deal in single attitudes but in systems of attitudes where a change in one attitude is reflected in adjustments of the other attitudes in the system. The systems are held together by this *balance principle*, thus guaranteeing attitude organization and stability within the individual.

This general idea is the basis of *balance theory*: the need for harmonious relationships among attitudes within a system of interdependent ones. Heider (1946, 1958) may be considered the modern pioneer in this area, and his work has stimulated much thought and research.[8] He was primarily interested in the relationships between people and between people and events. These relationships were of two types: sentiment relations and unit relations. The sentiment relationship has to do with liking, loving,

---

[8] F. Heider, "Attitudes and Cognitive Organization," *Journal of Psychology* 21 (1946): 107–12. See also F. Heider, *The Psychology of Interpersonal Relations* (New York: Wiley, 1958).

approving, admiring. The unit relationship is a perceived unity between people or between people and events. Such unit relationships are characterized by their similarity, proximity, causability, and memberships. In short, Heider is primarily interested in interpersonal perceptions. Thus, a *sentiment relationship* is one person liking or approving of another person or an event. The *unit relation* is the perception of one person as similar to another individual or a given object. To Heider, in a "balanced" state all these relationships fit together in a harmonious manner. For example, if one person likes two other persons, the first person tends to expect that the other two like each other. If such is the case, balance exists. In more complex fashion Heider discusses the various possible relationships among two people and an object or event and the relationships among triads, both positive and negative. In these situations the person perceiving the relationships tends to attribute psychological states to the other person that are like his own.

In explanation of his theory, Heider assumes that the first person (P) has attitudes toward a second person (O) and toward the object (X) that are either favorable or unfavorable. Secondly, Heider assumes that P actually knows or thinks he knows that the attitude of O toward the object is either favorable or unfavorable. Thus, if all of these three attitudes are favorable, or if two are unfavorable and the other is favorable, a condition of balance exists. In such a situation where the two persons have favorable attitudes toward each other and toward the object in question, no attitude change is necessary. On the other hand, if any two of the attitudes are favorable and the other unfavorable, a condition of imbalance is said to exist. In such a situation, balance can be gained by a change of attitude on the part of the first person, (P) by the first person (P) changing the attitude of the second person (O) toward the object, or by changing his perception of the second person's (O's) attitude toward the object in question. Figure 6–1 shows balanced and unbalanced situations graphically.

The basic assumption, it must be remembered, is that an unbalanced situation produces psychological tension that strives to restore balance. In small interpersonal relationships this cognitive balance theory has some useful implications for the persuader. When two youngsters are irritated by a state of imbalance, one may roll the other in the dirt until he changes his attitude toward the bully or toward the toy, the object in question. In the adult world, however, persuasion is the more acceptable way of restoring balance.

This theory can be criticized for its limited situations; many real life situations include a much more comprehensive social setting. Then, too, this theory does not predict which means will be used to restore balance.

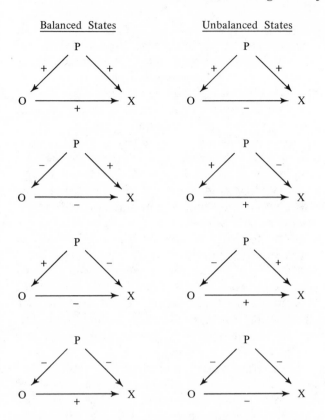

Figure 6–1. Balanced and unbalanced states.

Finally, the first person's attitude may remain unchanged despite likes or dislikes of the second person for the object.

Another approach similar to that of Heider was advanced by Newcomb.[9] He postulated that in Heider's "unbalanced situations" there is a "strain toward symmetry" that influences the two people related to some object. A *system of orientation* involves the first person (P), his orientation toward the other person (O), and the object (X). In the unbalanced state the strain is toward communality through communication; thus communication becomes an important means of reducing the strain. The degree of strain is determined by the degree of orientation discrepancy,

[9] T. M. Newcomb, "An Approach to the Study of Communicative Acts," *Psychological Review* 60 (1953): 393–404; see also T. M. Newcomb, "Individual Systems of Orientation," in *Psychology: A Study of a Science*, Vol. 3, S. Koch, ed. (New York: McGraw-Hill, 1959), 384–422.

the sign (for or against) and degree of attraction, the importance of the object, the degree of commitment or importance of the orientation, and the relevance of the object. Strain can be reduced by communication or other means that change the variables producing the strain.

Newcomb's approach is of particular interest to students of persuasive communication because it emphasizes the many variables involved in the orientational nature of what some might think a simple situation.

COGNITIVE DISSONANCE THEORY.   The theory of cognitive dissonance, formulated by Leon Festinger, probably has encouraged the most discussion (favorable and unfavorable) and research (over 300 studies) in the area of attitude change.[10] He suggests that cognitive elements are "knowledges" about facts, objects, behaviors, circumstances, etc. It would appear that Festinger includes beliefs, opinions, and attitudes in a general category. He holds that people tend to resolve or reduce any inconsistencies between their attitudes and their behaviors. Thus any two cognitions may be either relevant or irrelevant to each other. Any relevant relationships may be of two types: consonant or dissonant. For example, to the nonsmoker, the reports by the American Cancer Society create no dissonance, for his behavior and the cancer information are in consonance. To the smoker, however, the cancer reports and his decision to continue smoking can produce considerable dissonance because consistency is absent. The dissonance will be great when the relevant elements involved are of great significance to the individual, such as one's health, a grade on a final examination, or behavior related to a loved one. The dissonance will increase with the number of cognitive elements that are in dissonance, such as more reasons why you should not have bought the particular car.

You will note that cognitive dissonance is assumed to occur *after* some decision or choice. In clarifying the difference between dissonance and the conflict felt prior to making a decision, Festinger makes the following distinction:

> The person is in a conflict situation before making the decision. After having made the decision he is no longer in conflict; he has made his choice; he has, so to speak, resolved the conflict; he is no longer being pushed in two or more directions simultaneously. He is now committed to the chosen course of action. It is only here that dissonance exists, and the pressure to reduce this dissonance is *not* pushing the person in two directions simultaneously.[11]

[10] L. Festinger, *A Theory of Cognitive Dissonance* (Stanford, Calif.: Stanford University Press, 1957).

[11] L. Festinger, *A Theory of Cognitive Dissonance*, p. 39.

This theory holds that cognitive dissonance is a tension state varying in accordance with the significance or centrality of the elements involved and the degree of conflict present. The state of tension resulting from the dissonance provides the motivational power to seek the elimination or reduction of the dissonance.

Let us look at some of the implications of this theory for the student of persuasion.

When a persuader seeks to change an attitude, create a new one, or change overt behavior in any way, he could demonstrate to his receiver that the suggested attitude or behavioral change (decision) will not result in some dissonance or inconsistency between the receiver's cognitive elements.

The speaker may seek out and emphasize existing inconsistencies between, let us say, a professed attitude and a given behavior. He, then, can indicate how the dissonance can be reduced or resolved by the adoption of his proposal. The clergyman, for example, may show how the Christian's religious attitudes and his decision not to give to the church's missionary budget result in great dissonance; the person must change his mind and donate money to the church if he is to eliminate the dissonance.

The persuader must consider what is called "cognitive overlap." For instance, using the above example, the parishioner might reply that he "had given generously to the local welfare budget, and welfare is *akin to the missionary enterprise.*" Thus, he may not sense any dissonance because missionaries and welfare have much in common (cognitive overlap). One may experience less dissonance when a choice is made between a beagle and a basset hound than making a choice between a beagle and a parakeet as a pet.

The speaker should remember that dissonance can be reduced by showing the listener the advantages of his chosen alternative or the disadvantages of the unchosen alternative. Car salesmen for years have sent follow-up letters to the buyer congratulating him on his good judgment in buying the car and furnishing other reinforcements of the original decision. Even mothers-in-law keep telling the new son-in-law what a great girl he married.

Festinger points out that "forced compliance"(public pressure without or before a change in private opinion) may result from a threat concerning noncompliance or from a reward for compliance. If such forced compliance does take place, dissonance results between the private opinion (still held) and the behavior granted. The amount of the dissonance will again depend on the significance of the reward or punishment used to gain the desired behavior and on the significance of the opinion or behavior involved. As in other cases of dissonance, the individual in a forced compliance situation may attempt to reduce the dissonance tension by downgrading the significance of the decision he has made or the behavior he has taken on, by changing his private attitude or opinion to make it consistent with his behavior, or by magnifying the particular rewards or punishments that produced the behavior.

The persuader should consider the rhetorical problems and opportunities in using cognitive dissonance as a motivating principle. Several valid criticisms may be made of Festinger's work. Most important is that the term dissonance is very vague. Then, too, more precision in the conceptualization of cognitive elements is needed. More evidence is required to make confident dissonance predictions in specific situations, particularly in regard to forced compliance situations. The student of persuasion should thus regard this theory as fruitful but not final.

CONGRUITY THEORY.   The congruity theory of attitude change was developed by Osgood and Tannenbaum in an attempt to bring greater mathematical precision into the nature and prediction of attitude change.[12] This theory holds that when two attitude objects with different evaluations are linked by an assertion, the person's evaluations of each of the attitude objects will tend to shift toward a position of congruity. The assumption, therefore, is that any changes in evaluation "are always in the direction of increased congruity." For example, if the astronaut Neil Armstrong is evaluated favorably and the necessity for further space tests is also evaluated positively, then a speech by Armstrong favoring further space tests would indicate that a state of congruity exists. But if Armstrong were evaluated negatively and he were to speak for space travel, a state of incongruity would exist. A series of congruous and incongruous situations could be diagramed similarly to the balanced and unbalanced states of the Heider theory shown in figure 6–1.

Tannenbaum secured evaluative scores from 405 college students regarding their attitudes toward the *Chicago Tribune*, labor leaders, and Senator Robert Taft as sources, and on legalized gambling, abstract art, and accelerated college programs as objects. Later the students were given "highly realistic" newspaper clippings that included assertions made by the several sources on the concepts or objects. It was found that in general there were no significant attitude changes when the original attitudes toward the source and the object were favorable or positive and when the assertion made was also positive. However, when a positive source was linked with a positive assertion about a negatively evaluated object, the attitude toward the source of the message became less favor-

12 C. Osgood and P. Tannenbaum, "The Principle of Congruity in the Prediction of Attitude Change," *Psychological Review* 62 (1955): 42–55.

able, and the attitude toward the negative object became more favorable. The converse was also true.

The researchers recognized that incredulity could enter into the subjects' evaluations. A subject highly favorable to a political candidate could tell himself, "My candidate would never make a speech or statement of that sort." Osgood and Tannenbaum included a "correction for incredulity" in their formulae to account for this possibility.

The congruity principle represents a significant step in attitude research. It brings considerable mathematical precision in dealing with the problem of the *direction* of attitude change and the *extent* of the change. These useful predictive qualities are not present in Heider's theory.

The social judgment–involvement approach

Another approach to the study of attitudes and attitude change referred to only briefly in chapter 4 is the *social judgment–involvement theory* as proposed by Sherif, Sherif, and Nebergall.[13] This well-conceived and well-executed study challenged a long-standing view that a person could compare two statements on a given issue and judge which of the two statements was more favorable (or unfavorable) to that issue. Does the individual's view on an issue exert influence on his ability to discriminate among positions taken in regard to that issue? Does an individual's attitude toward an issue act as an "anchor" point from which he evaluates other views toward the issue? These types of questions gave rise to earlier researches involving Muzafer Sherif and others, and to the research on which the present approach is based.

The extensive research study by Sherif, Sherif, and Nebergall found that an attitude cannot be viewed simply as a single fixed point on a scale; any adequate theory, the researchers contend, must provide conceptual tools to evaluate the discrepancy between the attitude and the communication, in terms of the position of the individual, the position of the communication, and the individual's assessment of the communication (placement), specifying the stimulus conditions under which the discrepancy was experienced. Any discrepancy that a receiver may experience results from the individual's own position on the issue in question and the position the message presented to him takes. This discrepancy produces an appraisal of the message position in terms of the receiver's own position and results in a judgment that places an evaluation of this situation "as close to or distant from his own position in some degree." The attitude of an individual actually represents a *range* of things he will

[13] C. W. Sherif, M. Sherif, and R. Nebergall, *Attitude and Attitude Change: The Social Judgment-Involvement Approach* (Philadelphia: W. B. Saunders Co., 1965).

accept, a *range* of things he will *reject,* and possibly some positions to which he is *noncommittal.* This approach postulates that attitudes have latitudes—a *latitude of acceptance,* a *latitude of rejection,* and a *latitude of noncommitment.*

Granting the latitude concept, it follows that if the position advocated by a persuasive message does not fall much beyond the latitude of those positions that are acceptable, the advocated position likely will be *assimilated* into the acceptance range. If the advocated position lies quite beyond the acceptable range, however, the receiver will tend to evaluate the discrepancy greater than it actually is—the *contrast effect*—and place the advocated position well into the latitude of rejection. The degree of a person's ego-involvement in his position is of great importance in this whole process of attitude change. An anchor position involving considerable ego-involvement will reduce the size of the latitude of acceptance (fewer other positions will be acceptable), and thus the latitude of the rejected positions will be increased. The latitude of acceptance of theological positions, for instance, may be very narrow for the fundamentalist but much broader for the theologically liberal individual. This approach to attitude change certainly suggests that a person's persuasibility decreases in proportion to the increase in ego-involvement of his own position.

In situations involving matters of less ego-involvement on the part of the receiver of a message, the authors wisely point out that other *situational* considerations become of more concern—such as the prestige of the speaker, delivery elements, and so forth.

An excellent conclusion of this theory is provided by Sherif, Sherif, and Nebergall:

> A change in attitude, therefore, implies a change in his categories
> for evaluation, which amounts to changing a part of himself; and it
> implies manifest change in the patterned behaviors from which
> they are inferred. The frame of reference for studying attitude change,
> therefore, includes the individual's stand and his degree of involvement
> in it, which affects the extent to which it is the major anchor in a
> communication situation. It includes the communication itself, its form,
> and the order of arguments. It includes the communicator and the
> source, both of which affect the extent to which the position presented
> in communication anchors the individual's subsequent appraisals of
> the issue. Thus, a source and speaker with high standing or prestige
> in the person's eyes, in effect, enhances the anchoring function of the
> advocated position. Similarly, any event or procedure that successfully
> involves the individual in a position presented to him, such as the
> necessity of doing a good job of presenting it or defending it himself,

increases the salience of that position as an anchor when he subsequently evaluates the issue.[14]

Functional theories

Functional theories concerning attitudes and attitude change tend to focus on the functions attitudes serve in helping individuals reach satisfying goals. Assuming that human behavior can be classified and that attitudes can be related to such classifications, functional theorists dwell on the identification and function of those attitudes that affect a person's basic motivational needs and seem less concerned with the person's information level and perceptions of the attitude object.

KATZ'S FUNCTIONAL APPROACH. Katz's theory may be said to fit best into a functional classification.[15] He introduces his approach by reminding the reader of the dimensions of attitudes and the distinction he makes between beliefs, feelings, attitudes, and value systems. Attitude is a predisposition of the person to evaluate objects, a view rather generally held. Opinion, to Katz, is the verbal expression of an attitude that may also be expressed nonverbally. Attitudes have an affective dimension as well as a cognitive or belief component. All attitudes include beliefs, but all beliefs are not necessarily attitudes. Value systems arise when specific attitudes become organized into a *hierarchal* structure.

Katz then proceeds to identify the major functions attitudes serve, and he groups them according to their motivational basis. These functions are (1) the instrumental, adjustive, or utilitarian function, (2) the ego-defensive function, (3) the value-expressive function, and (4) the knowledge function. The definitions of these functions were given in chapter 4 and therefore will not be repeated here. In order to see more clearly the origin and dynamics, the arousal conditions, and change conditions in relation to each of the four functions, we have given Katz's summary in table 6-1.

Katz's functional theory represents still another approach to the role of attitudes in human motivation. The validity of this approach rests, of course, on the accuracy of the classifications used.

KELMAN'S PROCESSES OF OPINION CHANGE.[16] Katz determined

---

[14] C. W. Sherif, M. Sherif, and R. Nebergall, *Attitude and Attitude Change: The Social Judgment-Involvement Approach*, pp. 242–43.

[15] D. Katz, "The Functional Approach to the Study of Attitudes," *Public Opinion Quarterly* 24 (1960): 163–204.

[16] H. C. Kelman, "Processes of Opinion Change," *Public Opinion Quarterly* 25 (1961): 58–78.

Table 6-1 Determinants of Attitude Formation, Arousal, and Change in Relation to Type of Function

FUNCTION	ORIGIN AND DYNAMICS	AROUSAL CONDITIONS	CHANGE CONDITIONS
Adjustment	Utility of attitudinal object in need satisfaction. Maximizing external rewards and minimizing punishments.	1. Activation of needs 2. Salience of cues associated with need satisfaction	1. Need deprivation 2. Creation of new needs and new levels of aspiration 3. Shifting rewards and punishments 4. Emphasis on new and better paths for need satisfaction
Ego defense	Protecting against internal conflicts and external dangers	1. Posing of threats 2. Appeals to hatred and repressed impulses 3. Rise in frustrations 4. Use of authoritarian suggestion	1. Removal of threats 2. Catharsis 3. Development of self-insight
Value expression	Maintaining self-identity; enhancing favorable self-image; self-expression and self-determination	1. Salience of cues associated with values 2. Appeals to individual to reassert self image 3. Ambiguities which threaten self-concept	1. Some degree of dissatisfaction with self 2. Greater appropriateness of new attitude for the self 3. Control of all environmental supports to undermine old values
Knowledge	Need for understanding, for meaningful cognitive organization, for consistency and clarity	1. Reinstatement of cues associated with old problem or old problem itself	1. Ambiguity created by new information or change in environment 2. More meaningful information about problems

From *Public Opinion Quarterly* 24(1960): 163–204.

his classifications of functions according to their aid in meeting a person's individual needs; Kelman's classifications, on the other hand, are chosen on the basis of their relationships to the sources of influence external to the individual. These processes of *social* influences are *compliance, identification,* and *internalization.* As mentioned earlier (chapter 4), *compliance* occurs when a person accepts attitudinal influence from another person or group because he anticipates some social reward, not because he accepts the content of the message. *Identification* occurs when one accepts influence because he wishes to establish or maintain a "satisfying self-definition" relationship with another person or a group. Here satisfaction is found in conforming to another's influence, even though the individual also may agree with the message. *Internalization* occurs when a person accepts influence because the ideas or prescribed actions of the message are based on congruity with the person's own set of values. For each of these three processes Kelman stipulates a set of *antecedents* (determinants) and a set of *consequents.* In table 6–2 Kelman summarizes how these three processes work in terms of their antecedents and consequents.

Table 6–2 shows that if a given attitude has certain antecedents it will necessarily have certain consequents. The reader should keep in mind that the processes of compliance, identification, and internalization are not mutually exclusive. In everyday life they seldom occur as pure cases.

In Kelman's aproach we see again the functions attitudes may serve and under what conditions. Anyone intent on changing attitudes would do well to determine first what functions the attitudes of his receiver are serving, what new behaviors can serve these functions better, and what antecedent and consequent conditions can be controlled.

Brown's principle of differentiation[17]

After grappling with the theories involving imbalance, incongruity, and dissonance, with their relatively difficult prescriptions for analyzing attitude differences and their associated human problems, the reader should find comfort in the psychological technique advanced by Roger Brown called *differentiation.* This theory suggests that a specific case or segment of larger attitude objects may be differentiated out of the larger framework; this allows the general attitude toward the larger object or group to be maintained while an attitude toward the specific case can change to prevent or reduce tension. For example, if a young man who has a very negative attitude toward the Women's Liberation

[17] R. Brown, *Social Psychology* (New York: Free Press, 1962), chapter 11.

Table 6–2

Kelman's Summary of the Distinctions Among the Three Social Influence Processes

	COMPLIANCE	IDENTIFICATION	INTERNALIZATION
Antecedents:			
1. Basis for the importance of the induction	Concern with social effect of behavior	Concern with social anchorage of behavior	Concern with value congruence of behavior
2. Source of power of the influencing agent	Means control	Attractiveness	Credibility
3. Manner of achieving prepotency of the induced response	Limitation of choice behavior	Delineation of role requirements	Reorganization of means-ends framework
Consequents:			
1. Conditions of performance of induced response	Surveillance by influencing agent	Salience of relationship to agent	Relevance of values to issue
2. Conditions of change and extinction of induced response	Changed perception of conditions for social rewards	Changed perception of conditions for satisfying self-defining relationships	Changed perception of conditions for value maximization.
3. Type of behavior system in which induced response is embedded	External demands of a specific setting	Expectations defining a specific role	Person's value system

From *Public Opinion Quarterly* 25(1961): 58–78.

movement finds himself attracted to a young lady who, he finds out, is a Women's Libber, he will experience a certain psychological tension or discomfort. But by telling himself that this woman is different—more intelligent, more rational than other "libbers"—he can maintain his negative attitude toward the movement in general and at the same time reduce his discomfort by differentiating the one woman from the larger group.

Political persuaders have used this principle of differentiation many times in attempts to influence, for example, a Democrat to vote for the Republican candidate and still preserve the voter's party loyalty. Individuals rationalize many personal problems in this manner.

Conditions facilitating attitude change

Now that we have looked at the basic nature of attitudes and reviewed some of the chief theories of attitude change, we are ready to discuss the more practical points a persuader may consider as he attempts to change these rather persistent, complexly organized reaction tendencies that exert such dynamic and directive influences on our responses to other people, ideas, and objects. We now consider suggestions the creator of persuasive discourse should ponder carefully if he wishes to prepare messages that have a predictable chance of changing attitudes and behavior in some manner.

Focusing discourse on the attitude object

As we continue our receiver-centered approach to the study of persuasion, we must keep in mind that the receiver's existing attitudes are related—favorably or unfavorably—to some person, idea, or other object of appraisal and that his attitudes are essentially the result of past learning experiences. The speaker must first demonstrate rhetorically that the receiver's attitude toward the attitude object is incorrect or inadequate. As Solomon Asch wisely observed, we should distinguish change in the "object of judgment" from change in the "judgment of the object."[18] Here we are concerned with treating the object of judgment or the *attitude object*, as we shall call it.

If the receiver analysis indicates no knowledge that the attitude object has changed and is thus quite different than the receiver believes, the

[18] S. Asch, "Studies in the Principles of Judgments and Attitudes: II. Determination of Judgments by Group and Ego Standards," *Journal of Social Psychology* 12 (1940): 432–65.

persuader may demonstrate there has been *actual change in the object itself*. For instance, if I know you have a negative or unfavorable attitude toward a political leader for whom I am campaigning because you knew him in his younger, irresponsible years, I may try to change your attitude by providing information that the candidate (attitude object) is quite a different man now. I would present proofs that he is a serious, purposeful, highly trained, and thoroughly reliable fellow. For you, the receiver, to change to a favorable attitude toward the man would be to bring this attitude into consistency with the favorable attitudes you hold toward such virtues; to put it differently, your attitude would be assimilated into your latitude of acceptance.

Now let us assume that there has been no actual change in the attitude object—and this is often the case—but that the receiver's attitude toward the object is known to be incomplete or inaccurate. Then the attempt at attitude change becomes one of *providing new and more accurate information regarding the unchanged cognized object*. For example, you might hold a very negative or unfavorable attitude toward a person with long, shaggy hair, shabby dress, and rather sour features until I inform you that the person is the noted author whose works you admire. This attitude change does not necessarily mean that you have changed your general attitude toward such personal appearance. Rather, I have inserted new information of greater positive valence in reference to this particular individual, the attitude object. A major premise underlying the proposals for integration of the races in housing and in various organizations is that the mutual learning of new information about people of other races will lead to attitude change.[19] One should keep in mind, however, that simply to provide what is considered by the speaker as germane new information about the attitude object does not automatically produce attitude change. The new information, however well supported and presented, can meet with many resistances or distortions as indicated later in this chapter.

Focusing discourse on the attitude itself

We have discussed ways in which attitudes might be changed by centering persuasive discourse on the attitude object. Now let us see how one may seek change by centering his discourse on the attitude or feelings the receiver has toward the attitude object. In short, we now

---

[19] M. Deutsch and M. E. Collins, *Interracial Housing and a Psychological Evaluation of a Social Experiment* (Minneapolis: University of Minnesota Press, 1951).

turn from "object of judgment" to "judgment of the object." Here the task becomes more difficult because the persuader seeks to revise the affective (feeling) relationship between the receiver or audience member and the object of his attitude. Discourse will need to be adjusted even more carefully and specifically to the motivational systems of the receivers. If the attitude object itself has not changed, and the persuadee understands the object accurately and fully, the persuader must find the available means of persuasion within the motives and functions of the attitude toward the given person, idea, or object.

We turn now to answer some questions concerning this approach to attitude change.

First, try to discover the conditions under which the attitude to be changed was formed. Can it be shown that these conditions provided unfair or distorted learning experiences in relation to the attitude object? Or, if the attitude was acquired essentially by transfer from other people, can it be argued that these sources were biased or otherwise incapable of formulating an acceptable attitude?

Secondly, will an investigation of the functions of the attitude(s) held by the receiver serve as useful means of persuasion by indicating that these functions are not in the best interests of the receiver? Can it be shown that the attitude change proposed will better serve his interests or motivations, that it is actually more consistent with the attitudes now held, or that it fits harmoniously within the receiver's value system? This area of investigation should prompt discovery of a number of profitable lines of persuasion.

Thirdly, what is the intensity of the attitude(s) you wish to modify? If the attitude is of central concern to the persuadee, the intensity with which it is held will be quite great and tenaciously defended. In this event, the discourse must include the most persuasive case possible.

Fourthly, can the use of group influence facilitate attitude or behavioral change? This point is discussed in detail in chapter 7. Here we simply want to remind the reader that evidence indicates that individuals within group situations are often influenced by the observed reactions of others in the group.

A fifth consideration is of utmost importance to the speaker: what have you done to assure that the message itself has qualities that will make the lines of persuasion effective? The nature of the message, as well as the vehicle used to carry the message and the credibility of the source of the message, can exert great influence toward attitude change. The *nature* of the message includes the word choice, style, organization, and the manner in which arguments are developed or appeals made in the attitude change attempt. This point is of considerable importance because often the public speech is the only (or at least the chief) means of influence that can be controlled or manipulated in reference to the persons you wish to influence.

Finally, try to create a participating situation to strengthen a weak commitment. It has been found that participation following a weak or even a negative commitment to a belief or behavioral change can result in a more certain or fixed attitude and/or behavioral change.

Attitude change and overt behavioral change

In our discussion of attitudes thus far, the reader might be tempted to think that a direct relationship always exists between one's attitudes and his overt behavior. In fact, some writers on the subject have contended that attitudes have not only affective and cognitive components but related behavioral components as well. Because persuaders frequently seek an overt behavioral change (buying a Chevrolet, working for the campus blood drive, or giving money to the Community Chest), it is vital that we ask whether a changed attitude necessarily leads to a corresponding overt behavioral change. Unfortunately, this predictable correlation does not exist. All of us have observed (in others, of course) discrepancies between a professed attitude and overt behavior. Let us see if there may be some explanation for these seemingly contradictory stances.

We should remember that most studies of attitudes (formal and informal) ask the subject to indicate his attitude either orally or in writing. Since we cannot test attitudes directly, we must try to learn about them through some such overt *behavioral* act (written or oral). Thus, the researcher cannot be absolutely sure that he has determined the *true* attitudes of his subjects, even though refinements in these methods do increase their reliability. We would suggest that attitude research try new methods involving a focus on the subjects' willingness to engage in real-life behavioral acts (giving money, joining a campaign, voting for a certain candidate). Some initial steps have been made in this direction.[20] Your authors presently are working on this problem.

Regardless of this limitation, other explanations obtain irrespective of the methodology used in determining attitudes. One such explanation is that *overt behavior is not only the result of the attitudes held toward some object but also the product of the current situation in which the individual finds himself.* The perceived situation, which will differ among

[20] G. R. Miller, "A Crucial Problem in Attitude Research," *Quarterly Journal of Speech* 53 (1967): 235–40.

individuals' perceptions, involves other realities, other attitudinal linkages as the person judges his overt behavior; these judgments are not called into play when he is simply asked to register his attitudes by some oral or written method. For instance, when asked in a group of students to join a demonstration against some campus practice, you may agree to join not because you really have a negative attitude toward the practice but because you are in a situation where to do otherwise you feel you may lose the respect of a fraternity brother, a girl friend, or that you might lose the group's votes in the forthcoming election in which you are a candidate. The unprejudiced businessman may discourage certain races from doing business with him because he fears losing other customers. You will note, however, that we have given only one way the situation might be perceived. Another person might perceive that he would be regarded favorably by others if he did *not* join the demonstration.

Overt behavior thus results both from attitudes and from the perception of a particular situation. A persuader should consider carefully whether his call for some behavior change takes both these points into account.

He may choose to explain differently the discrepancy existing between one's professed attitudes and his overt behavior. We have focused on the *current situation* in which the behavior occurs, and we have seen how this focus introduced additional variables to which the person had to accommodate his motivational system. Here, let us look at the attitude with which the overt behavior in a given situation may be expected to correspond. Because it is complex, *the situation will normally arouse a series of attitudes at the same time.* Behavior is frequently the result of many attitudes. Thus, the persuader's attempt to change the receiver's behavior may fail if the persuader's message attempted to change only one of the receiver's attitudes. As Newcomb, Turner, and Converse point out, "It is particularly useful to know the total system of attitudes, even though some are 'overruled' in a given situation, for situations are constantly changing, and we are interested in long-range trends in behavior."[21]

This point was supported well in a study of the 1952 and 1956 presidential elections by Campbell and his associates.[22] It was found that Dwight D. Eisenhower had a very great personal popularity; only a very small segment of the population indicated a negative attitude. Had the

[21] T. M. Newcomb, R. H. Turner, and P. E. Converse, *Social Psychology* (New York: Holt, Rinehart and Winston, 1965), p. 71.

[22] A. Campbell, P. Converse, W. E. Miller, and D. Stokes, *The American Voter* (New York: Wiley, 1960).

overt behavior (voting) in those elections corresponded to the favorable attitude, Eisenhower would have been elected both times in landslide fashion with from two-thirds to three-fourths of the vote. Although he was elected by a comfortable margin, the landslide did not occur. Why? The answer is that voting behavior is the result of a number of attitudes, not simply of the attitude toward one man. Other attitudes regarding the Democratic Party, party loyalty, and so on, play a vital role in the ultimate vote cast.

Festinger suggests that the discrepancy between attitude and behavior could be due to the brevity of a single exposure to some persuasive speech.[23] It is reasoned that since a person's attitude at a given moment toward a person, object, or issue is a complex orientation serving a number of functions, a persuasive message may produce only a momentary shift in attitude. If no additional reinforcement to this isolated message is provided, the shift can readily regress toward the original attitude. So it is that the sinner may be converted upon hearing a single, rousing evangelistic sermon, but he will backslide readily if no reinforcing influences are met.

This review of some of the possible explanations for inconsistencies between indicated attitudes and overt behavior should be sufficient not only to highlight a major problem in attitude research but also to emphasize additional points with which the persuader must be concerned as he prepares his messages.

Resistance to attitude change

Keeping in mind the nature of attitudes and the theories and conditions of attitude and behavioral change we have just discussed, it should be helpful to list quite specifically some of the chief *sources* and *means* of resistance to attitude change. Keep in mind, too, that these sources and means of resistance to change may present themselves singly or in any combination; in general, however, receivers tend to select one mode of resistance from the options available.

The following list tends to capsulate in a practical way much of the substantive materials on attitudes given earlier. It is our hope that this procedure will forewarn the persuader and help him formulate a message that uses the available means of persuasion effectively.

[23] L. Festinger, "Behavioral Support for Opinion Change," *Public Opinion Quarterly* 28 (Fall, 1964): 404–18.

Sources of resistance to attitude change

1. People with extreme attitudes on matters of central concern—that is, where there is likely to be considerable ego-involvement—are quite resistant to change. In fact, a speech threatening this extreme position may cause the attitude to become even more firmly fixed as the receiver seeks to defend it. A persuader may be well advised not to ask for too great an attitude change at a given time. Such extreme attitudes usually can be changed only in time and by repeated exposures to change attempts.

2. Receivers of persuasive messages generally are more resistant to change when the source of the message is held in low esteem. The matter of the persuader's credibility is discussed at length in chapter 11.

3. People are quite resistant to change when the persuader asks for a change in attitudes that is contrary to the receiver's experiences. If a person "knows a thing to be true," he would have to deny the trustworthiness of his own senses in order to change his attitude, and will be very reluctant to do so.

4. Attitudes developed early in life—as in the home or other primary groups—usually become quite fixed and are therefore very resistant to change.

5. Attitudes that in later social life have become anchored in membership and/or reference groups can be quite difficult to change. To permit change would be to give up many socio-psychological rewards provided by such groups.

6. A person who has publicly "gone on record" as holding a given attitude on a given topic is likely to be quite resistant to change, for the public commitment usually provides certain social rewards and is bound up with self-identity as well. An old legislative maxim says: "get to the senator before he has committed himself publicly; don't ask him to jeopardize his public reputation."

7. An attitude based on opinion sources held in higher regard than those supporting an argument for a change will be resistant to change, as any debater knows.

8. Attitudes may provide a useful target for one's aggressions or a respectable front for things one is ashamed of or has repressed. Such attitudes serving an intra-psychic function can be quite resistant to change.

9.   On occasion an attitude may be used to avoid psychological pain and is therefore resistant to change. Evidence that a friend has been false to you may be discredited in order to avoid the psychological pain of changing your attitude toward the person.

10.   Suggestions for attitude change that are contrary to our logical reasons for holding them will be resisted.

11.   Requests for change of an attitude that is of central value in a whole constellation of interdependent attitudes will meet with great resistance because attitudes do not exist in a vacuum. Thus, a changed attitude may well require a number of compensatory changes in other attitudes to regain the original psychological balance.

12.   The self is also an attitude object, and the self-image tends to become extremely strong. As you well know, one's attitude toward himself as an individual is usually quite favorable. Attitudes linked vitally with this self image—or to put it differently, attitudes with considerable ego-involvement—are very resistant to change.

13.   Messages seeking attitude changes that are carried via some channel or vehicle of low credibility will meet with great resistance. The receiver will be more reluctant to accept change if the message is carried by an untrusted newspaper, magazine, radio or television station, or other vehicle which to him is of dubious merit.

14.   Although the research is not absolutely conclusive, it seems to be generally true that attitudes are more resistant to change by persuasive appeals that create very strong anxieties or fears than those that create moderate fear appeals. The very high anxiety appeal is more apt to be perceived as a thing "that couldn't ever happen to me," or as an excess of horror having no basis in reality. Some of the sermons of early evangelists who damned sinners to a hell worse than Dante's *Inferno* probably were dismissed by many hearers for this reason.

15.   Attitudes that are near a neutral or a moderately favorable or unfavorable position toward a proposition can still be resistant to change but are generally less resistant than stronger attitudes.

The means people use to resist attitude change

We have looked at some of the chief *sources* of resistance to attitude change. Now let us examine briefly some of the *means* people use to resist such change. In chapter 1 we discussed how a receiver of a persuasive message perceives and interprets the message in ways that "make sense" to him in terms of his attitudes, motives, feelings, and beliefs, and how he may perceive the original message in manners that make it suitable to his own experiences and needs. Keep this in mind as we list a few of the means a receiver or audience may use to resist attitude and possibly behavioral change.

1. Studies generally support the premise that individuals tend to avoid information contrary to their attitudes and opinions, although the research does not consistently support it. Apparently people will listen more readily to arguments in favor of their position, read articles in support of it, and attempt to avoid information dissonant or inconsistent with their opinions. Thus simply to obtain a hearing for contrary information can be a major job for the persuader.

2. Another means of resistance to attitude change is to listen to opposing arguments but depreciate them by dwelling on their poor logic or other weaknesses. This keeps opposing views from threatening our own. We are sure our reader has witnessed such attempts to resist attitude change.

3. When a message seeks an attitude change that does not agree with our experiences and needs, we may misperceive the information and thus distort it to our own advantage. At best the new information may be considered a minimal contradiction of our attitude or behavior. Research agrees that we tend to misperceive and forget those bits of information inconsistent or dissonant with our own attitudes or behaviors.

4. A person may add elements to a perceived message that can make the whole point objectionable. He may say the speaker has not given the whole picture and that when additional information is supplied the position of the speaker becomes untenable. To help achieve this end, the receiver or listener may seek out the additional information that tends to weaken the speaker's position and strengthen the original position of the receiver. The well-prepared speaker can forfend against such barriers by anticipating them and incorporating refutative materials in his message, leaving no place to hide for the person who is disposed to seek such shelter.

5. Finally, as discussed in detail in chapter 11, the audience or receiver may seek to make the attitude change attempt suspect by focusing on the dubious character of the speaker or his background. This means of resistance to attitude change has been used ever since the opponents of Christ asked: "What good can come out of Nazareth?"

Attitude change and the persuader's specific audience and purpose

In concluding our discussion of attitudes and attitude change it should be useful to relate this material to the persuader's specific purpose and the demands of his audience. Throughout this book, the authors have stated directly and implied that a specific and clearly formulated purpose in the mind of the persuader or speaker is an essential prerequisite to the preparation and presentation of persuasive discourse. In chapter 1 the general types of persuasive purposes were discussed. Because most persuasive messages seek some form of attitude modification, let us (1) look briefly at some of the ways our knowledge of attitudes and attitude change can help sharpen the speaker's goal and (2) help him discover the rhetorical means of achieving it. We will consider some of the basic questions a persuader should ask himself in preparing his message. This list of questions should provide a practical summary of many of the foregoing materials.

1. First, of course, one must ask: What have I done to assure that the people whose attitudes or behavior I wish to influence are present? People tend to avoid exposure to messages that are likely to try to change their existing attitudes. Thus the clergyman frequently finds himself addressing those already committed, the political candidate finds only the partisans have come to hear him, and the editorial is read essentially by those who have frequently agreed with its position. To reach those most needed can be a big task indeed. The persuader must always consider carefully how he will reach his desired receiver, as discussed in chapter 2.

2. What specific attitude(s) do I wish to change? Is it an attitude that relates to some specific instance (one's attitude toward your campus chapter of Sigma Chi) or is it an attitude toward a general class or group of objects or people (one's attitude toward all Greek societies)? The answers to such questions can present quite different sets of problems. For instance, the functions and intensities of the attitude held by a member of a local fraternity can be different from those the member holds of the national organization, and more different still from the independent, non-affiliated student.

3. Is the attitude I wish to change a strong, central one, or is it a weak and more remote one? The strong attitude and its constellation of related attitudes offers a big job indeed for the persuader. He must present his most effective case.

4. How was the attitude learned? Was it essentially a product of experiences in the home, school, church, a gang? Was the learning adequate, accurate, sketchy, inaccurate?

5. What functions are being served by the existing attitude(s) held by your audience? Keeping in mind the functional approach to the study of attitudes by Katz, given earlier, one can ask: is the attitude to be

changed now serving an instrumental or adjustive function, an ego-defensive function, a value-expressive function, or a knowledge function, or any combination of these? Or, according to Kelman, is the listener using his present attitude in a compliance manner to gain some social approval, as an identification to establish a satisfying self-definition relationship with others, or as an internalization function wherein the attitude is held because the ideas involved are the reward?

6. What specific component of the attitude do I wish to change? It is important to know whether or not a change is sought in how the receiver thinks (his cognitions) or feels (affective behavior) about the attitude objects, or how he behaves either verbally or nonverbally. To seek cognitive change you will need to present sufficient evidence and cogent reasoning to establish belief; to seek affective change will require more nonlogical motivational appeals, as discussed in the preceding chapter.

7. Do I seek a short- or long-term attitude or overt behavioral change? For a short-term change, controlling the current variables may be sufficient. For a long-term change, adequate means of reinforcement are needed.

8. What have I done to forfend against the receiver's use of one or more of the sources and means of resistance to attitude change? The reader is encouraged to review carefully the list of the resistance sources and means as given earlier.

9. Have I related wisely the new information on the topic with the information already known by the receiver? Because attitude change depends on the introduction of new information, such information must be presented so that it makes the prior information inadequate.

10. If I am speaking to a group or audience, do the people present share rather common attitudes (a partisan or hostile group), or is the group a very heterogeneous one where I will need to contend with a variety of differing attitudes toward the goal I seek?

11. Because attitude change is dependent not only on the nature and functions of the attitude(s) relative to the subject or object under consideration but also on the perceived credibility of the source of the message and the message itself, the persuader must ask himself: what attitude does the receiver have of me as a person, as a speaker on the given subject, or as a representative of a given organization? And what can I do in preparing the message that will relate clearly and effectively the content materials to the receiver? Other parts of this book offer help in answering these questions.

12. Finally, if the attitude change I produced during the message was not great or the behavior I asked for was rather distasteful, what can I do to create some post-message participation by my receivers that conceivably could strengthen the attitude change and legitimate the behavioral change? Such acts of participation have been found capable of creating greater attitude change at a later date.

Conclusion

Within the confines of a single chapter we have attempted to select and discuss some of the chief points regarding the nature of attitudes, the theories of attitude change, and some practical suggestions for using this information. We have assumed throughout this chapter that the reader will link this information with the materials given in the two preceding chapters as he continues to develop a more complete grasp of those factors involved in human motivation that are basic to finding the available means of persuasion.

In this chapter we have attempted to demonstrate that attitudes and persuasion are related and that, since persuasion is primarily concerned with producing attitude change and frequently behavioral change, the study of attitudes becomes essential knowledge to theorist and practitioner alike.

In the following chapter, we discuss the influences of social behavior on persuasion.

7

The influences of social behavior

on persuasion

Introduction

No one is an island separated from the mainland of humanity. Man is inescapably a social creature. From infancy until death he depends on others, and it is largely in relation to others that he knows who he is. He influences others and is influenced by them; his motives, attitudes, values, and behavior reflect this influence system. Thus it is hardly accurate for anyone to say he has a strictly *personal* opinion on something or that he has a truly *individual* style of life. This social interaction is carried on by a complex system of communication, which is studied by those in the field of *speech-communication*. Since much human interaction is designed to influence others, the study of groups and collective behavior and their modification of the individual's motivational system becomes essential information for the student of persuasion.

In previous chapters we have considered the matters of drives, motives, attitudes, values, and behavior largely from the point of view of the individual. Although we have suggested on occasion the individual's social context, we have not dealt specifically with the role others play in modifying the individual's motivation. In this chapter we explore (1) how modern society is built on social relationships, (2) the persuader's approach to the study of social behavior, and (3) the purposes and general characteristics of conventional interaction groups.

The reader will note that the information to follow links with, and should provide additional understanding of, the materials treated in the preceding two chapters.

Modern society—a structure built on interrelationships

In every culture, man creates a whole constellation of affiliations in which he participates in varying degrees, depending on his needs and desires. In our modern mass society, characterized by considerable specialization of skills, division of labor, and impersonal and transitory relationships among people, we tend to feel a loss of personal intimacy and solidarity. In our quest for personal reenforcements, for economic, political, and social gains, and for still other reasons, we have become dependent on group memberships. By the time we are in elementary school we are members of the Cub Scouts, 4-H Club, Little League ball team, a Sunday School class, a neighborhood gang, and a glee club.

By the time we are adults, the number of group memberships is greatly increased. We may be a member of the Presbyterian church, the Veterans of Foreign Wars, the Rotarians, the local Taxpayer's League, the National Education Association, the Speech Communication Association, the Republican Party, the Teamsters Union, Sigma Chi fraternity, the League of Women Voters, the State Assembly, the National Association for the Advancement of Colored People, the Student Co-op, and a host of other groups. Most of our society's social, political, economic, religious, educational, and governmental business is carried on by the use of groups. Persuasive messages emanate from numerous collections of people who have found that their desires can be served best through associational rather than individual efforts.

It should be clear that the persuader must understand how groups affect human motivation and the manner in which groups themselves are used as attitudinal and behavioral change agents. The greatest persuaders of people are the motives, attitudes, opinions, and behaviors of other people.

The persuader's approach to the study of social behavior

If a persuader is to find the available means of persuasion he must know the social allegiances of the individual he wants to influence, and he must learn how to use groups to move other individuals and other groups. What are the motivational factors within groups and in individuals involved in the groups? is the basic question to which he seeks answers. This knowledge becomes an important part of the persuader's audience or receiver analysis, his market research. His interests, therefore, do not lie primarily with the mechanics of the flow of communicative interactions among members of a group nor with the many other descriptive approaches to interpersonal and group behavior being conducted today. He sees knowledge of social behavior as instrumental information, not consummatory knowledge, as he seeks to develop a theory of persuasion and modes of applying this theory to practical problems in persuasion.

The subject of social behavior is a large discipline and involves many subareas of study. There are those interested in small groups, large groups, crowd behavior, group leadership, educational groups, and therapy groups. We will try to distill from this large field those concepts and research data of chief concern to the persuader. Nonetheless, we suggest that the serious student engage in a continuing study of the many facets of social behavior and their implications for the understanding and development of suasive discourse.

Social behavior in conventional groups

The purposes of conventional groups

We are concerned here with the purposes of those groups that exist primarily to serve persuasive goals. Let us list and discuss briefly the general purposes of such groups.

1. Some groups are created and joined to provide a sense of kinship, a means of personal and social reenforcement. Bridge groups, knife and fork clubs, neighborhood groups, and other social organizations serve a personal-social function; they strive to modify attitudes and behavior in ways that lead to self-fulfillment and social adjustment.

2. Groups may be created to serve as perpetuators of existing standards and values. These groups seek the stability of an existing order or the continuity of values jeopardized by an ever-changing, dynamic society. The Young Americans for Freedom was created to combat the militant, revolutionary groups on college campuses. Groups like the American Legion, the Daughters of the American Revolution, the National Rifle Association, and the Society for the Preservation of our National Environment are examples of groups seeking stability of an existing order.

3. Groups can act as change agents upon individuals who are wooed into membership and influenced by the group. Many groups or organizations (religious, political, economic, educational, and social) engage in persuasion in this manner. Many individuals are persuaded through group influences who would not have been influenced through other means.

4. Groups frequently are formed to affect change in, or actual overthrow of an existing order. Such groups have operated throughout history in evolutionary or revolutionary manners.

The general characteristics of conventional interaction groups

It is common knowledge that individuals affect each other psychologically as they interact; this has been known in a general, intuitive way ever since man's tribal beginnings. It must be said, however, that our century deserves the credit for pursuing in scholarly investigations the ways in which people interact and influence each other, how groups are created and structured, and how they behave.

Undoubtedly, much of the impetus for beginning study of group phenomena came from French sociologist Gustav LeBon's classic book, *The Crowd* (1895), an astute though unscientific treatment of the behavior of people in crowds and mobs.[1] Early concern for this area of study also was generated by Triplett, an American psychologist, who reported in an 1897 study of children that the subjects tended to work faster in groups than when alone.[2] But to F. H. Allport must go much of the credit for opening many experimental doors as the result of his research on the effects of others on individual tasks.[3] The tasks were performed under three situations: completely alone, alone but in awareness of others working on the tasks elsewhere, and together. The subjects demonstrated greater speed in tasks performed when together but with less accuracy, and a different orientation when together. The general value of this pioneer study is that the presence of others makes a definite psychological difference that is experimentally demonstrable.

We turn now to the general characteristics of groups.

GROUP NORMS. A group-level concept that has been given considerable study in social psychology is that of *norm*. A social norm exists when a given type of social behavior attains a certain regularity that can be understood only in reference to the group to which it belongs. "In its most general sense," says Davis, "a norm is a standard against which the appropriateness of behavior is to be judged. Some norms are pervasive, in that they are widely shared by the bulk of the members of a culture; others are local, in the sense that they apply specifically to the members of a particular group."[4] A norm exists when group members agree (and are aware that they agree) that the given regularity is regarded as a virtual rule. To rest when fatigued is not a norm, but for the British to have tea each day at four o'clock or for the brothers of a campus fraternity to meet daily for a short beer at 4:30 is a norm.

Norms, therefore, can keep life from being chaotic. They provide it with predictive qualities which lend stability and a certain regularity. Indeed, successful communication presupposes the participants share norms of symbols (visual and oral) and their referents. Thus group norms involving our motives, attitudes, values, and behavioral patterns constitute important information to a person striving to influence one or more

1 Gustav LeBon, *The Crowd* (London: T. Fisher Unwin, 1895).

2 Norman Triplett, "The Dynamogenic Factors in Pacemaking and Competition," *American Journal of Psychology* 9 (1897): 507–33.

3 Floyd H. Allport, "The Influence of the Group upon Association and Thought," *Journal of Experimental Psychology* 3 (1920): 159–82.

4 James H. Davis, *Group Performance* (Reading, Mass.: Addison-Wesley Publishing Company, 1969), p. 82.

members of a group. Such a group has a well-established set of norms, even though it is not yet definitely established how rapidly or under what conditions norms are formed. Understand and respect these norms and you gain valuable insights into the means of persuasion; disregard them and you neglect a frequently significant aspect of the persuadee's social motivation.

GROUP COHESIVENESS. Our readers will have noticed that some groups seem to have a quality of closeness, a vital commonality of purpose not found in other groups. This group spirit, as it is often called by laymen, is labeled *group cohesiveness* by social scientists. Literally, cohesiveness is a sticking together, a unifying property of the group membership. Thus, in high cohesive groups the unifying properties or cementing elements far outweigh those divisive factors that press toward disaffiliation with the group. Back's experiment with low and high cohesive groups demonstrated that the following factors are related to cohesiveness:

1. Interpersonal attraction of the members.
2. Individual motivation to succeed in group tasks.
3. Pride of membership.
4. Group size—smaller groups tend to be more cohesive than large groups.
5. Structural integration—facilitates smooth, coordinated activities among members.
6. Group sharing.[5]

The persuader who wishes to influence some or all members of a group or to use groups as a vehicle for promotion must assess not only the group's norms but also the degree of cohesiveness present. Then he can proceed to use those factors that support cohesiveness, keeping in mind that cohesiveness is a *class* of phenomena and that behavior leading to cohesiveness in a group may not be meaningful in another setting. A high cohesive group can influence its members more effectively than a low cohesive group. Because its members are highly motivated, a high cohesive group usually performs tasks with greater chance of success and is more likely to agree on common goals than a low cohesive group. Finally, as we shall see later, increased cohesiveness normally results in greater pressures on the members to conform.

The cohesiveness of a group contains many sources of and resistances to persuasion because the factors leading to cohesiveness also contribute

[5] K. Back, "Influence Through Social Communication," *Journal of Abnormal and Social Psychology* 46 (1951): 9–23.

to the satisfactions of the individual member through his interaction with the group. If a member of a labor union local attempts to persuade his fellow members to go on strike by showing how the action would enhance the pride the members feel for their union as well as further their economic goals, he will probably meet with much favorable response. But if an owner of the plant attempts to persuade the union members by ignoring or jeopardizing the cohesiveness of the group, he will probably encounter considerable resistance, if not certain failure.

INTERGROUP RIVALRY. Another concept, similar to group cohesiveness, is intergroup rivalry. A person may belong to a number of compatible groups or to groups whose interest areas are so different that they do not compete with each other. Groups may conflict, however, either inadvertently or by design. Many groups in the areas of religion, social life, politics, business and finance, industry, labor, and education are in constant competition. Rival groups establish the "ins" and the "outs," much as youngsters in their neighborhood gangs. This emergence of group rivalries is the understandable result of group cohesiveness and strongly revered norms in areas of central concern.

Two specific (though questionable) practices in human thinking and persuasion have risen from group rivalry: stereotyping and scapegoating.

Members of one group tend to hold rather arbitrary, and often oversimplified and inaccurate, mental pictures of other groups. Superficial and uncritical evaluation of other people often identifies them with the incorrect group, or wrongly attributes certain characteristics to them. This *stereotyping* often leads to narrow, faulty images of people and ideas that do not conform closely with one's own experience.

The Old Testament history provides an early record of the *scapegoat*. According to tribal custom, a goat was periodically assigned the accumulated sins of the tribe who then proceeded to destroy or drive the unhappy creature into the wilderness. This action cleansed the tribe. Persuaders throughout history have used the scapegoat technique to court an audience's or group's good will by providing them with useful scapegoats. Hitler found the Jews useful scapegoats, many youths today find the Establishment or their upbringing similarly useful, and political parties and orators usually find scapegoats in the opposition party and its leaders.

How do persuaders interested in leadership select scapegoats? Allport points out some characteristics that make people and groups easy targets:

1. The target must be easily identifiable. White, black, red, or brown skins are readily identifiable, as is long and short hair, or different forms of religious worship. On occasion a desired scapegoat not readily iden-

tifiable is made so, as in the case of Hitler compelling the Jews to wear a special insignia.

2. Out-groups (scapegoats) must be accessible. Police, for instance, are much more accessible for the frustrated, the disenchanted, or the revolutionary than are those who make the laws the police are required to enforce.

3. Scapegoats must not be able to retaliate in any effective way. For Nero, the Christians served as perfect scapegoats.

4. Scapegoats have usually been so before because antagonisms tend to persist.[6]

Group rivalry (and its attendant stereotyping and scapegoating) has been a source of much suasive rhetoric. Such rivalry has been used throughout history from the first tribal conflicts, the religious and feudal wars, the legendary Martins and the Coys, to the most recent conflicts on your campus between political conservatives and revolutionaries.

The influence of the group on the individual

Above we have discussed conventional interactive groups as groups, units, or entities. We now focus on the individual within such groups and how group life influences her or him.

Social conformity

"When in Rome do as the Romans do" is a familiar admonition, and persons in groups do indeed tend to conform to the actions of the group. Prevailing group norms, the elements of group cohesion, influence the individual greatly because the pressure to conform is often very strong. In a classic study, Asch found that individuals will go against the dictates of their own senses in judging the length of straight lines in order to conform to a group judgment.[7] Bovard found that the opinion of a leader frequently is less influential than the group's opinions in changing the opinions of group members.[8] Festinger, Schacter, and Back studied the less formal communication networks of people in a housing development and found that those who lived physically closest to one another tended to share the group's opinions, while those living on the

---

[6] Gordon W. Allport, *ABC's of Scapegoating* (Chicago: Central Y.M.C.A. College, 1944).

[7] S. E. Asch, *Social Psychology* (Englewood Cliffs, N.J.: Prentice-Hall, 1952).

[8] Everett W. Bovard, Jr., "Group Structure and Perception," *Journal of Abnormal and Social Psychology* 46 (1951): 398–405.

periphery of the group were more likely to deviate from the dominant group opinion.[9]

The tug to fit a norm is great and, in general, we can conclude that persons succumb to this social influence. But what is the nature of the conformity? Does conformity represent actual attitudinal change, or is it simply a convenience posture taken to achieve certain desired goals? The answer is that conformity often involves *compliance* attitudes and behavior. Kelman suggests that when an attitude change is made for conformity and when it does not occur in private, it is a *compliance change*.[10] Of course, in many instances conformity is not simply the result of compliance; the individual member may have *internalized* the attitudes and values espoused by the group, or he may have held these positions before he joined the group. This matter of *public compliance* and *private acceptance* is of considerable concern to the persuader. Often the persuader does not care whether the change is based on public compliance or private acceptance as long as his goal is achieved. The proponents of the mandatory use of car seat belts do not care whether a driver believes such a law is correct or not, as long as he uses the belts. Surely the American Cancer Society's primary concern is that the smoker quit the habit and is much less concerned with whether the decision to quit was based on public compliance or private acceptance of the harmful claims made.

On the other hand, the persuader is often concerned with producing basic belief or private acceptance. The preacher wants his parishioner to maintain the same religious attitudinal and behavioral stances when he is away from the group pressures of his local church. The parent wants the son or daughter to maintain a given moral code after the youngster is free of the home influence. The politician wants the voter to keep voting the party ticket after he has moved away from the predominantly Democratic neighborhood and its political pressures.

Clearly the *type* of commitment the persuader desires must be formulated as he considers his persuasive purpose or goal, and his message must be prepared to produce the type of attitude change desired. Regardless of the type of acceptance sought, persuasion frequently involves appeals to social conformity, and it should therefore, be useful to examine more fully the reasons why members of a group tend to conform.

THE REWARDS OF CONFORMITY. To say that an individual conforms to the group because of a general motive to do so could lead readily to circular reasoning; people don't conform to every group nor

[9] Leon Festinger, S. Schacter, and K. Back, *Social Pressures in Informal Groups* (New York: Harper, 1950).

[10] H. Kelman, "Compliance, Identification and Internalization," *Journal of Conflict Resolution* 2 (1958): 57–60.

to all the goals or practices within a given group. A more reasonable explanation is that conformity results from a satisfying accommodation between the group's expectations (group pressures) of the individual and the individual's expectations of rewards from the group. The person who has accepted the goals and standards of the group to which he belongs will strive to help the group gain and maintain them. In turn, the individual member can receive from the group a satisfying level of prestige or status, of interpersonal affections, of shared goals, and still other rewards he desires. This reciprocal accommodation strengthens the group norms and cohesiveness, which in turn lead to ever greater conformity.

If the persuader demonstrates that his demands will result in greater conformity rewards for the persuadee, he may have positive results. But if the persuader supports a goal that has the potential of denying such rewards, he risks failure. To ask a person to betray his group as well as what it stands for is a formidable rhetorical task for even the most persuasive speaker.

THE PENALTIES OF DEVIATION.   The group dispenses rewards for conformity, and it can also exact penalties for deviations from its norms. These penalties range from the "cold shoulder" treatment to outright expulsion. The fraternity brother whose grades have fallen below a standard established in pride by the brothers can receive social sanctions until his grades are brought up. The street gang may withhold full status from a member until he has successfully pulled off "a big job." The union bricklayer who is laying too many bricks per hour may receive a poor rating by his steward. The reader undoubtedly has noticed many ways in which a group may apply sanctions (penalties) to a deviant.

Because groups usually have penalties for deviation, the persuader has two general means of persuasion: (1) he may attempt to show that what he is asking will assure freedom from such penalties, or (2) he may try to demonstrate that the penalties—particularly the severe ones—suggest that the norms and values of the group are suspect, knowing that behavior performed merely to avoid social punishment is not internalized (privately accepted) and that often sanctions cause the individual to reconsider his attitudes, behavior, and specific reasons for being affiliated with the group.

Nonconformity as a means of persuasion

Although individuals generally conform to the group, certain individuals, under certain circumstances, do not conform to group standards, norms, and goals. Some of these nonconformists see social groups as opportunities for gaining leadership roles or as instrumental means in seeking other ultimate goals. They wish to set standards; sometimes they seek to enlist the group's aid in the promotion of some personal or social cause. In an interesting study Hollander suggests that a nonconformist must earn the right to behave as a nonconformist.[11] If the nonconformist's ideas and suggestions have been shown to be valuable in the past, the group tends to give this individual "idiosyncracy points or credits." If, on the other hand, the nonconformist's ideas or behavior require too much adjustment on the part of the group members, or if the ideas prove to be ill-advised or unusable, he loses his credits and his ability to lead and may receive severe sanctions.

In his work in interaction process analysis, Robert F. Bales found that those who attempt to gain leadership are motivated by a strong desire to influence others and at the same time to keep themselves relatively free from external control.[12] Those who assume the role of leader can gain a certain level of respect but are not likely to gain genuine affection. It is difficult for a leader to play the role of "best-idea" member and the "best-liked" member at the same time. Nonetheless, the person who is able to enlist the group's influence capacities to serve some predetermined goal has a greater chance of success than if he attempts to persuade each individual without the aid of group pressures or sanctions, or both.

We turn now to examine additional motivating roles groups can play for the individual.

The role of reference groups in persuasion

THE NATURE OF MEMBERSHIP AND REFERENCE GROUPS.   In our discussion of attitudes and attitude change (chapter 6) we said a persuader may attempt attitude change by focusing on the attitude object and providing additional useful information about the attitude object, by focusing primarily on the receiver's attitude or judgment of the attitude object, or by doing both. Here we wish to point out that the receiver's attitude toward the object of judgment is frequently conditioned by the attitudes *others* have of that object. For instance, if a political campaigner points out to the voter that the candidate for whom he speaks has been endorsed by the other brothers in the voter's cherished

---

11 E. P. Hollander, "Conformity, Status, and Idiosyncrasy Credit," *Psychological Review* 65 (March, 1958): 117–27.

12 Robert F. Bales, "Interaction Process Analysis" in D. L. Sills, ed., *International Encyclopedia of the Social Sciences* (New York: Macmillan, 1968), vol. 7, pp. 465–71.

fraternity, the campaigner has increased his chances of getting one more vote for his candidate. The *reference group* appealed to in this case is also a *membership group* of the voter. When a membership or a non-membership group's standards, goals, or norms act as *referent points* in the functions of an attitude of a person, we call that group a *reference group*. If an individual holds membership in a group in which he finds considerable motive satisfaction, if the goals of the group are quite compatible with his own attitudes and values, and if he therefore desires to remain a group member, this membership group is also a reference group. If, on the other hand, a membership group does not supply these satisfactions and he is a member in name only, then this membership group is not a reference group.

THE MOTIVATIONAL POWERS OF REFERENCE GROUPS. When a group's standards and goals act as true referent points for an individual, that reference group can exert great influence on this person's motivational system. A person may desire membership in a certain reference group but may never achieve it. This does not keep the reference group from having a significant influence on the attitudes and behavioral patterns of the individual using the group as a referent. The stage-struck drama student may have the Broadway Set as a reference group and may assume the attitudes and dress of his or her favorite stage personalities, even though the hopeful's chances of joining the group are slim. To the sand-lot football player, the Green Bay Packers or the Minnesota Vikings may be a reference group par excellence. Upon a moment's reflection, the reader can list several groups which are reference groups—perhaps in business and finance, in social life, or in educational circles—that account for at least some of his or her attitudes and behaviors. Perhaps you are studying persuasion in order to eventually become a member of a positive reference group.

While we are thinking about the power of reference groups, we must keep in mind that these referent points can act both positively and negatively. A person who holds the National Association of Manufacturers as a positive reference group may regard the AFL-CIO negatively. You may favor pending legislation if your favorable reference group favors that position, but you may reject the legislation if it is supported by a negative reference group.

For centuries, persuaders of all sorts have used appeals to reference groups. The social worker points out that "no good Lion's Club member would desert a needy boy." The truant officer asks Johnny, "What will your father and mother say if you flunk out?" In an attempt to get the labor vote back in the Democratic column, the 1972 campaigners repeatedly exhorted that "Labor always votes Democratic." "You'll never own a home on Nob Hill or Canterbury Drive if you don't study hard," says the professor to a lazy freshman. Or, if some positive reference group is not readily available to the political orator, he sometimes generates the hope of history by saying, "If you support me in this bold venture the generations yet unborn will one day rise up and call you blessed!"

REFERENCE GROUPS IN CONFLICT. In our complex society and with our multiple allegiances reference groups create very real conflict situations. This fact is frequently learned early in life when the youngster's gang (a positive reference and a membership group) engages in activities that contradict the values held by another of his reference groups—his family. In the 1960 presidential campaign, which pitted a Democratic, Catholic candidate against a Republican, Protestant candidate, the pollsters found it very difficult to predict how two types of voters would vote: (1) the fundamentalist Protestant who was also a Democrat, and (2) the Catholic who was also a Republican. Here, indeed, positive reference groups were in conflict, and some shift in attitudes was necessary to resolve the dissonance experienced by such voters.

Many college students experience conflict between the standards of the family and those of the newer reference group, the campus peer group. This can be an agonizing experience, indeed, until attitudes and behaviors are adjusted to avoid or at least reduce the dissonance.

In a classic study of college students, Newcomb studied the female students at Bennington College from 1935–1939.[13] The women had come from well-to-do families with quite conservative political and social values. The young faculty members, however, were quite liberal, although the school at that time was not known as a liberal school. The student body was small (250 female students) and the faculty was also small (50). The campus, therefore, was a small, highly cohesive community.

In the 1930s there was considerable political tension between the "haves" and the "have-nots." Leaving their conservative homes, the students discovered that this college community had a liberal faculty, and they found the older students, particularly those with high prestige, subscribed to liberal ideas. The incoming freshmen experienced this conflict immediately. Through tests, Newcomb studied the students during the four-year period. In the election of 1936, 66 percent of the parents of the coeds favored the conservative candidate, Republican Alfred Landon, over the liberal Democratic candidate, Franklin D. Roosevelt. The freshmen favored the conservative candidate by 62 percent, 47 percent of the sophomores, and only 15 percent of the juniors and seniors favored the conservative candidate. Newcomb studied

---

[13] Theodore M. Newcomb, *Personality and Social Change* (New York: Dryden Press, 1943).

intensively the most and least conservative sixths of the three consecutive graduating classes and found that the most liberal coeds were very popular, had been elected to leadership roles, and played a central role in this community. In contrast, those women who maintained a conservative stance were described by other students as "indifferent to the activities of student committees," they resisted the expectations of the college community, tended to be the least popular, and socialized mostly with other conservative students. The faculty members tended to perceive these students as overly dependent on parents and other home ties.

In such a correlational study it is difficult to distinguish cause from effect with certainty. Did students adopt more liberal attitudes in order to gain recognition on campus? Were the attitude changes *compliance* attitudes or were the new positions internalized? To help answer this question, Newcomb interviewed a large number of the students years later and found that they were much less conservative in 1960 than one could reasonably expect from their age and economic status. Their husbands, too, were more liberal than one would expect considering their standard of living.[14] It would appear, therefore, that the liberal point of view nurtured during the college years became an enduring value system. What started as a conflict in reference groups had now taken on at least partial, if not complete, resolution. Here, too, is evidence of the motivational power of group life.

In our open, pluralistic society people increasingly accept multiple loyalties that inevitably conflict. Our schools cultivate in children the capacity for such multiple loyalties and a certain tolerance for the differing loyalties (reference groups) among students. This, of course, introduces the youngsters to an important norm of a truly free society.

When the majority of our membership and reference groups agree on certain general values and standards of behavior, there is little or no conflict. It is in this manner that a *culture*, with its generally shared patterns of thought and conduct, acts as persuasion in a virtually out-of-awareness manner.

Implications of group behavior for the persuader

In analyzing the potential receiver of a persuasive message, the persuader must be as thorough as possible. In this chapter we have added still another area to be analyzed—the influence of social behavior, particularly that found in the conventional, interactive groups and in reference

[14] Theodore M. Newcomb, "Persistence and Regression of Changed Attitudes: Long Range Studies," *Journal of Social Issues* 19 (1963): 3–14.

groups. These areas of study suggest many lines of rhetorical appeal that can be designed to change social attitudes, values, and behavior. To help synthesize the materials presented in this chapter, and to add a few points, it should be useful to survey briefly the chief points to be remembered by a persuader and to indicate their implications for persuasion.

1. Groups exist to serve purposes or goals. Some groups fulfill social and personal adjustment needs, some help perpetuate existing standards, values, and customs, some act as change agents of individuals, while still others are formed to change or overthrow an existing order. The persuader must know the purpose of the group when attempting to persuade the group or an individual affiliated with the group. To know the group's purpose is to know much about the attitudes and values of the group members.

2. The influence of the group on the attitudes and behavior of its members is clearly established; individuals are affected psychologically as they interact. The persuader who thinks his persuadee is simply an isolated individual with no social attachments is making a colossal mistake.

3. Groups give rise to norms or standards which dictate the appropriate attitudes and behaviors of their members. To know these norms is to gain insights into the available means of persuasion.

4. Groups have cohesiveness in varying degree. High cohesive groups have members highly motivated in performing tasks and pursuing goals. The persuader must first know the degree of cohesiveness within the group and then formulate his message in a way that can use this knowledge.

5. Groups frequently compete with each other. This tends to increase cohesiveness and the pressures of conformity within the group. To know and use these rivalries for persuasive ends has been a common tool of the persuader.

6. Although individuals tend to conform to the group, it should be remembered that the smaller the group, the greater is the pressure to conform. To contradict the values of a small, cohesive group (such as the family) presents a formidable task for any persuader. Attempting to have your proposal assimilated into the small group's latitude of acceptance is a much wiser approach.

7. In groups where there is considerable frequency of contact and interaction among members, one may expect a stronger pressure to conform. The persuader can determine the frequency of contact of the group members he wishes to influence, and he should be aware of the constraint this pressure places on his message preparation.

8. The longer the members of a group have been interacting with each other, the greater is the pressure to conform.

9. If a group is group-centered or democratic, rather than leader-centered, there tends to be greater pressures toward conformity. When group members are able to participate in the decision-making process, they are most likely to accept the group's decision.

10. In general the closer the group's goals are to those of the individual, the greater is the pressure to conform. Persuadee analysis must attempt to determine whether the group's goals are very close to or the same as those of the individual to be persuaded.

11. Groups with clearly defined norms normally exert greater pressure to conform. When norms are free from ambiguity, the conforming process is easy. The persuader must know the pressures that urge the individual toward conformity as well as the degree to which the group norms are defined for its members.

12. In situations where the opinion of the membership on some issue is a prevailing or homogeneous one, there is more pressure to conform on that individual whose opinion might be outside this norm. Usually appeals concerning the good of the group or suggestions of isolation are sufficient to persuade the individual to conform on the issue. For an outsider trying to break up the group, this nonconforming individual is, of course, the place to start.

13. When a particular issue can be demonstrated to be very close to the goals of the group, there is considerable pressure to accept the point.

14. A persuader should know the social status of the group he wishes to influence. Normally the higher the group status, the greater is the pressure to conform.

15. Nonconformity can be used to gain leadership or persuasive positions within a group. It must be remembered, however, that a certain level of respect must be achieved by advancing useful ideas and that to be the best-idea person and the best-liked person at the same time is difficult, indeed.

16. The persuader must remember that reference groups also play a major role in our motivational systems. Therefore, he must learn the existence of such groups and their influence on the persuadee.

Conclusion

Throughout this chapter we have stressed that the persuader is never dealing with a completely isolated individual free from social influence, because every human being has a number of affiliations with different groups, each with its own set of expectations, purposes, sanctions, and rewards. It has been our purpose to alert the student of persuasion to the nature of such social behavior in the hope of broadening his theoretical knowledge of the bases of human persuasion and his skills in the practice of persuasion.

8

Critical thinking in persuasion

Introduction

A persuader can adapt to the motives, attitudes and emotional needs of his audience, but if his message does not meet their standards of reasonableness he will fail. "I wanted to believe him, but he didn't give me any good reasons." "That salesman didn't have the facts to justify buying his brand of television, so I went elsewhere." "My husband said his back hurt too much to mow the lawn, but he went to play golf." "His proposition looked pretty good until I figured where we would be five years from now." "That speaker had me completely won over until I asked myself, *what* did he say?" "He failed to mention just one disadvantage of his proposal, but man, that was a big one!" These reactions are typical of thoughtful responses that sound the death knell for many persuasive purposes.

Receivers test persuasive messages to be sure they "make sense," and the message that falls short of being sensible is unlikely to win acceptance. Thus, we can conclude that a prerequisite to success in persuasion is to satisfy the critical thinking requirements imposed by the persuadee.

The present chapter examines the role of critical thought in the process of persuasion. Before we proceed to a discussion of the elements that lend reasonableness to persuasion, however, we should review some important and recent changes in the concept of reasoned argument.

In the twentieth century, critical thinking in persuasion has evolved through three distinct phases. First "textbook in logic" standards were accepted, and it was assumed that if a message met the academic criteria of soundness it would be effective with any audience. This approach was totally message-centered.

The second phase emphasized adapting a message to an intended audience. The popular model was that of sender and receiver. The sender accepted a responsibility to so design his message that particular receivers would *probably* be able to decode it. Adaptation consisted of choosing certain verifiable facts and methods of reasoning that *in the persuader's judgment* would be persuasive to his listeners.

With the recognition that persuasion is an interaction and the discovery of astounding variability in human perceptions, reasoned discourse came to include the many contributions of persuadees to the act of influence. In this third stage persuasion was conceptualized as a joint venture between speaker and receiver. This present phase says that people think about all percepts that can influence outcomes, including fantasy, rhetorical vision, and varied information and misinformation which they supply. Replacing textbook standards, the dominant criterion of effective reasoned discourse then becomes the extent to which a persuader succeeds in being perceived as reasonable by particular participants. Facts and traditional logic are still useful, but in most instances they are subordinate to using reasoned procedures of decision making of the individual persuadee.

Replacing "objective reality" with "perception is meaning" has restructured applications of critical thinking in persuasion. The word and the fantasy become the relevant reality. Ways of being reasonable about the new reality are indeed relative. The ideal reasoned discourse is attainable only when a persuader and persuadee reason together within the boundaries of their resources.

The above sweeping changes in the conceptualization of reasoned persuasion resulted in large part from the study of perception. Perceivers of a message were found to be adding not only interpretation but also an abundance of associations. The wealth of materials contributed by receivers was found to be integrated with the content of the message, and the combination was processed to produce response. Knowledge of the elements of human perception proved the insufficiency of a message-centered approach to thoughtful communication. Because an understanding of perception is essential to the student of persuasion, chapter 12 treats this topic in some detail.

When we agree that the receiver attaches his own meanings to the words he hears and enriches a message with his own additives, it seems sensible to interpret his response in terms of the composite perceptions that produce it. Certainly such a perceptual orientation is preferable to an analysis based on what a bystander thinks is in the *message*. Concentrating on perception in an interaction contributes to increased understanding of elements important to that event.

To summarize, our treatment of critical thinking in persuasion assumes that response of a receiver results from what he *believes to be* true more than from what *is* true. For him, perception is meaning. Necessarily, then, the criteria we use to examine and evaluate reasoned discourse are perceptual and process-oriented.

Using process-oriented criteria to classify persuasive interactions

We have discussed how the responses of an audience are shaped by their perceptions. To predict the responses of persuadees, then, a persuader should know their perceptual potential, that is, the meanings they are able to read into his message. To help with this difficult task we now recommend a system of classifying persuasive interactions that is based on different kinds of perceptions.

Three modes of response are possible in communication: deliberative, automated, and emotional. Often all three operate concurrently, and each contributes to the overall response of a receiver in varying amounts. To classify the predominant perceptions of an individual or of a group of receivers involved in the process of persuasion we need the following four categories: reasoned, reasoned-emotional, unemotional-suggestive, and suggestive-emotional.

Reasoned

When the interaction in persuasion causes participants to be thoughtful with little automatic reaction or emotion entering into ongoing responses, we can label the act "reasoned persuasion."

Reasoned-emotional

If significant emotion is produced as a result of critical deliberation, and indeed, would not have occurred if a receiver had not subjected a message to thoughtful examination, we can label the communication "reasoned-emotional." For example, citing facts of social injustice and asking an audience to ponder them may be a highly effective way to arouse their anger against irresponsible, corrupt officials. Critical thinking and emotional arousal may be equally important to this outcome.

Unemotional-suggestive

When a predominantly automated interaction occurs in the process of persuasion the receiver uses habit responses to incoming stimuli. The process of suggestion substitutes for deliberation. The interaction has much in common with that of a hypnotist and his willing subject. What is said by the persuader is accepted by the persuadee, and requested responses are given immediately and uncritically, in push-button fashion.

As in hypnosis, the use of suggestion need not arouse emotion in eliciting responses. A regular churchgoer can listen to oft-repeated suggestions of ways to improve the quality of his life and accept them as desirable goals without the slightest twinge of emotion or more than a trace of deliberation. The interaction between the minister and such a member of his congregation is properly labeled "unemotional-suggestive."

Suggestive-emotional

Rabble-rousing is a typical example of an attempt to produce suggestive-emotional response. A persuader bypasses the critical faculties of his audience and achieves his intended response by touching on topics that are known to be laden with emotion. A quick burst of anger or fear makes it unlikely that thoughtful examination of the message can take place. When the anti-abortion speaker begins his speech to the Anti-Abortion League by saying that the bill pending in the legislature is designed to "encourage the wanton murder of helpless children," the interaction that results will probably be one that could be accurately labeled "suggestive-emotional."

Persons who plan persuasion and those who study it in action will find the above process-oriented categories helpful. People in persuasive interactions are deliberative, automated, or emotional, each to some degree. A persuader attempts to achieve one of the four resulting categories as his predominant audience response. Elements in the interaction can be analyzed to find how they contribute to or detract from that calculated objective.

The nature of proof in persuasion

We now turn our attention to the elements contributing rationality to those persuasive interactions we can classify as "reasoned," and "reasoned-emotional." The ingredient necessary to produce thoughtful consideration of a proposal has long been designated "proof." Our emphasis on individual perceptions and a process orientation can be seen in the following definition: *Proof is any element in communication perceived by an individual receiver as reasoned support for a proposition.* The model of the process of persuasive communication in chapter 1 (figure 1–1) can be used to clarify the development and implementation of proof in persuasion.

As an example, let us use a two person relationship. The source, after deciding to rely on reasoned discourse as a major method in his persuasion, formulates his persuasive proposition in unemotional language, using words that are familiar to his receiver. Before preparing his message he asks himself, how does my particular receiver set about being reasonable? His analysis of the receiver (box B in the model) begins with an inventory of the critical thinking habits characteristic of the persuadee. While he can presume that his listener's techniques of deliberation *probably* resemble accepted methods of inductive and deductive logic, he is careful not to so conclude without evidence that such is the case.

Let us illustrate this analytical procedure concretely by examining a specific persuadee. In analyzing this individual receiver's reasoning potential, our source discovers these useful bits of information:

1. The receiver is a "delayed decision maker." No matter how conclusive an argument may be, a substantial time interval must elapse before this person is ready to express preference for an option.

2. Statistical information is given great weight by this receiver. If evidence can be expressed in numbers, including tables and formulas, he is impressed favorably.

3. The receiver is predictably skeptical about opinion evidence. One authority to him is as good as another, since he has long ago concluded, "Opinions are a dime a dozen."

4. The receiver reveres structure (main heads, subheads, and documentation) in argument. The familiar and orderly arrangement of the elements that makes up a unit of evidence and reasoning may outweigh its substance in his assessment.

5. For him, language reinforces a reasoned appeal powerfully. When a persuader confidently and appropriately inserts many "therefores" and "whereases" and speaks knowingly of premises, dilemmas, conditional relationships and syllogisms, this receiver finds it difficult to challenge the soundness of the accompanying argument.

The above information completes the analysis of our hypothetical persuadee's program for processing data "logically." While certain processes of interpretation and assessment therein fail to meet conventional standards, and other important criteria of rational argument are not recognized, his is *the only system that is available to him* to fashion judgments on the quality of the argument he perceives. Consequently, to the extent the source succeeds in adapting his message to the criteria used by this receiver in separating the meritorious from the spurious, the resulting reasoned discourse is of high quality.

We should note that analysis of critical thinking is but a part of the collection of needed information about the receiver. Information concerning the ways the receiver attempts to be reasonable is useful only if the source knows also the habits, interests, needs, desires, and goals of the receiver that relate to the persuasive purpose. With this further information the source can proceed to box C of the model, message preparation. He can now develop message units that show the receiver how the recommendation will satisfy needs with reasons and evidence that make sense to the individual receiver.

We will deal only briefly with the remainder of the model, since source preparation for the interaction, steps A, B, and C, demonstrated how proof is planned and developed. Carrying out the plan involves steps D through G, accompanied by continuous feedback. The receiver's responses will be viewed primarily as indicators of critical acceptance. Where necessary, message units will be revised to increase their reasonableness to this receiver. It may be necessary to change the source's analysis of the data processing procedures of the receiver and possibly to ask for a lesser attitude change than was originally planned in the interest of promoting reasoned acceptance. Emphasizing the thoughtful, deliberative dimension of the interaction implements the persuader's intention to rely on reasoned discourse in this instance rather than on the psychology of suggestion or emotional appeals.

Treating proof as a contingent and relative concept with characteristics dependent on context may seem strange to some of our readers. We submit that acceptance of a perceptual criterion for reasoned discourse leads logically to this interpretation. The case for reducing reliance on absolute standards and moving to the position we have delineated is ably described by Delia:

> Whereas *logos* has traditionally been viewed as following the laws
> of logical form, this framework suggests that it should be understood as
> based on the natural adaptive tendency of the psychological field
> to maintain a coherent and harmonious relationship among its affective,
> cognitive and behavioral elements. Reasoned discourse thus becomes
> discourse that makes application of inductive and deductive reasoning
> and evidence within the context of the listener's field of predispositions.
> The criterion for selection of premises, examples, analogies, authorities
> and statistics is ultimately, "Will the listener accept it?" The persuader's
> only real guide in evaluating the reasonableness of his arguments is
> the degree to which the components of proof are congruent with the
> listener's total predispositional field. Logical proof is thus proof adapted
> to man's natural rational process.[1]

Support contributed by the receiver of persuasion

Our concept of *proof* implies that an argument which to one receiver is perceived to be without support to another may be adequately supported. Incoming messages are processed so differently by different people that

[1] Jesse G. Delia, "The Logic Fallacy, Cognitive Theory, and the Enthymeme: A Search for the Foundations of Reasoned Discourse," *Quarterly Journal of Speech* 56 (April, 1970): 144.

one person's suggestion can be another person's reasoned discourse. Thus, to speak of an argument as "supported" or "unsupported" is to renounce the perceptual criterion and revert to a message-content orientation. Since proof is conceptualized by the receiver, we can never be certain that a human being at a particular moment will perceive or fail to perceive support in any given message. A message may be loaded with statements of fact and statistics, but we have no assurance that proof will or will not result. Consequently, the notion that an argument in isolation can be categorized as "supported" or "unsupported" is untenable.

Every receiver is his own data bank. A genuinely active interchange stimulates participants to "plug in" their own facts, examples, and analogies and facilitates their filling logical gaps with reasons. Because the game of interpretation is played partly with supplied data and partly with home-based resources, an amount of support in a given instance can be estimated only by assessing what is supplied by whom, when, and how it is perceived.

A further item of receiver-centered support in the delivery of a message is the thoughtful processing of elements of ethos or credibility. Not all the impact of a speaker's reputation is accomplished through automated, uncritical response. The receiver is at liberty to *consciously* review the expertise of a persuader and use it as a corrective factor in assigning weight to his argument. Similarly, circumstances such as effects of physical surroundings or preceding events can be evaluated critically and become part of the ongoing reasoned interaction. In short, we should add to our list of items incorporated in proof two important variables, credibility and circumstantiality.

Thoughtful reactions to a message by groups and individuals are influenced by prevailing interpretations of events of general interest. Only recently have rhetorical critics recognized the power of what they term "fantasy themes" and "rhetorical visions" to affect persuasive interactions. Since these constructs are significant elements in everyone's reasoning about society's problems, we must consider their role in reasoned discourse.

Information supplied by persuadees

The information used in thinking about a message comes from internal (stored) and external inputs. That from the outside reaches everyone and contributes uniformity to audience responses. Information from the data banks of receivers is almost infinitely varied and contributes to differing interpretations of the message.

It should be noted that "stored information" is not limited to so-called

factual knowledge. Techniques of testing reliability and validity of arguments, logical forms or patterns into which an incoming unit can be
fitted, premises from past arguments, related, previously tested generalizations, and familiar words to be substituted for strange, imprecise or
loaded words are examples of kinds of stored materials that can be
retrieved and fed into the building of percepts.

Systems of reasonableness imposed upon received messages vary from
person to person, from situation to situation, and from textbook standards. Cronen and Mihevc report a study in evaluation of deductive argument which concludes ". . . the selection of evaluative strategies is, in
part, a situation bound behavior."[2] In reviewing previous research as well
as their own they state the following implications:

> 1.   There is no real contradiction between the existence of general
> validity patterns in the population and the frequent acceptance of
> fallaciously derived conclusions. From the fact that both communicator
> and listener accept the same conclusion we cannot assume that both
> employed the same data or the same evaluative strategies. Argument,
> including the logical *form* of argument, exists in the mind of the listener.
>
> 2.   It is useful to conceive of the listener as possessing hierarchies
> of perceptual rules and evaluative strategies. Both are functional in the
> evaluation of messages.[3]

A circumstance that "primes the pump" for a receiver is the reception
of information without explanation or interpretation. What is enigmatic
is challenging. When an active mind receives an ambiguous or vague
message an attempt is made to fit it into a meaningful pattern. Probably
the presumption is that the content would not have been transmitted
without a worthy purpose. Exposure to information is a powerful stimulus
to retrieval of stored materials from internal resources in the receiver.

Very similar to "mere exposure" is Perelman's concept of "presence":

> By the very fact of selecting certain elements and presenting them
> to the audience, their importance and pertinency to the discussion
> are implied. Indeed, such a choice endows these elements with a
> *presence*, which is an essential factor in argumentation and one that is
> far too much neglected in rationalistic conceptions of reasoning.[4]

[2] Vernon E. Cronen and Nancy Mihevc, "The Evaluation of Deductive Argument:
A Process Analysis," *Speech Monographs* 39 (June, 1972): 131.

[3] Ibid.

[4] Chaim Perelman and L. Olbrechts-Tyteca, *The New Rhetoric: A Treatise on
Argumentation* (University of Notre Dame Press, 1969), p. 116.

Perelman elaborates on the uses of "presence," noting the ability of a speaker to make what is actually absent seem to be present through what Perelman terms "verbal magic." Certainly this act draws heavily upon an audience's resources of experience and imagination. He mentions the use of concrete objects, noting their power to command attention and stimulate interpretation. He discusses the influence of time, place, and circumstances on the receiver's ability to respond to a particular presence. And, finally, he suggests that suppressing presence has argumentative utility:

> The importance of presence in argumentation has a negative as well as a positive aspect: deliberate suppression of presence is an equally noteworthy phenomenon, deserving of detailed study.[5]

Perhaps an example will clarify "suppression of presence." In December 1972 when Paris peace negotiations to settle the Vietnam War had broken down, President Richard M. Nixon of the United States ordered a "carpet bombing" of Hanoi. Many Americans felt the "presence" of North Vietnamese civilians who were killed and injured in the bombing, and because they could see no consequences that would justify the wholesale killing of nonparticipants, Americans tended to oppose the assault. President Nixon's spokesmen countered the sympathetic reaction by designating all those bombed as the "Communist enemy." For many in the United States this suppressed the presence of suffering human beings, and the spectre of napalmed children and maimed elderly citizens of Hanoi ceased to exist. A more literal suppression occurred after the Bach Mai Hospital in Hanoi was destroyed by American bombs. When asked about this, Jerry Friedheim, a Pentagon spokesman, answered: "I don't know what the other side may refer to as the Bach Mai Hospital, if indeed there is one."[6] For persons in the United States who were disturbed by the "presence" of sick and wounded people in a hospital being blown to bits, the denial of the existence of the hospital may well have "suppressed the presence."

Very briefly, we have touched upon a variety of ways in which information is supplied by receivers in the process of persuasion. It would be quite unrealistic to think that information important to a persuasive interaction is limited to the content of the message. As yet we have few techniques for finding out what particular audiences can be relied on to contribute or what the persuader can do to control this dimension of

---

[5] Ibid., p. 118.

[6] "The Talk of the Town," *The New Yorker*, 13 January 1973, p. 22.

communication. Now that we recognize the role of information furnished by the receiver, research to add to our understanding of this phenomenon is urgently needed.

Proof derived from credibility

Different from the concept of presence, but related to it is the classical concept of "ethos," or "credibility."[7] While universally recognized as important to persuasion, its effect is usually assumed to result from suggestive communication. Here we concentrate on those effects of ethos that are consequences of thoughtful deliberation. Basic to critical thinking about ethos is making distinctions between a person and his acts.

If we assume that a persuasive interchange begins with a definite ethos of the persuader in the mind of the persuadee, then the utterances and actions of the persuader will be measured against this initial ethos. Actions and utterances will be consciously judged as consistent or inconsistent with expectations, and the credibility at the beginning of the interaction will be reinforced or changed as the message continues.

It is difficult to fix boundaries of credibility. If the percept of a source's ethos is shaped by all that has been and is known of that person, and if everything he does and says in a communication may be used to revise the receiver's estimates of his credibility, then all variables in a persuasive interaction have an "ethos dimension."

As currently used, "ethos" and "credibility" are source-oriented terms. We treat them as characteristics that are thought by the receiver to reside in the communicator and which limit or enhance his effectiveness. An interaction-based concept, one that specifies a process-influenced variable, would be more useful to the study of persuasion. Such a construct emerges from a pioneering study of interaction in selling, done by Evans at the University of Chicago.[8]

In an unusually comprehensive collection of information about interviews in the selling of life insurance, Evans found that the familiar variables of the salesman's product knowledge, personality, and speaking ability, or the prospect's need for insurance and ability to pay for it singly or in combination were not predictive of the outcome of the selling effort. Significantly, the *quality* of the personal interaction between salesman and prospect related positively to the outcome. Evans stated this finding succinctly: "The most important data are how the prospect

---

[7] The concept of credibility is treated in some detail in chapter 11.

[8] Franklyn B. Evans, "Dyadic Interaction in Selling—A New Approach," an unpublished study, University of Chicago, 1964.

perceives the particular agent and the similarities between agent and prospect that help the situation to be free and pleasant."[9]

Relationship in interpersonal communication may be evaluated in terms of the *quality* of an interaction. The Evans study demonstrated that high quality interaction was associated with more favorable assessment of the persuader's arguments. How people feel about each other in casual contacts, such as sales interviews, is apparently an important factor in determining the estimate of source credibility, which in turn affects the interpretation of a message.

Sources and receivers will benefit from thoughtful assessment of elements of interaction that have qualitative consequences. For example, the Evans study found that the more similar two people were, the greater was the probability that they would develop a high quality dyadic interaction. As other hypotheses are tested and knowledge accumulates, it will be increasingly possible for us to reason about the means of obtaining the quality of interaction we want, or to identify the causes of low quality relationships. The consciously competent communicator of the future will be as reasonable about planning the quality of interpersonal interaction as his predecessor was in making sure that his conclusion followed logically from his premises.

As we review the role of credibility in proof we can conclude (1) that trust and credibility in persuasive interaction are similar if not synonymous, (2) that while thoughtful assessment of credibility undoubtedly affects the weight assigned to a unit of persuasion, much of the impact of source credibility is through other-than-rational processes, (3) that the quality of interaction is a major factor in enhancing or reducing credibility, and (4) that elements affecting the quality of interaction can be understood, analyzed and to some extent, controlled. Hence, the receiver can reason about credibility and use it deliberately. The persuader can design and implement his persuasion to encourage his audience to make thoughtful use of his assessed credibility.

Proof developed from circumstantiality

The speaker as a person interacts with his audience to generate credibility, while the effects of the context on the audience create circumstantiality. Some of these nonpersonal circumstances are in the message, and others are in the setting. All may precipitate deliberative, automated, or emotional response. Usually circumstantial factors are assumed to operate without awareness and to produce only automated or emotional

[9] Ibid., p. 215.

reactions. But any element of circumstance can be called into conscious-ness for deliberation and be subjected to thoughtful examination. The often accepted assumption that the context affects persuasion *only* through subconscious processes seems to us unwarranted.

Circumstances other than those in the context of the message include immediate situation, prior and subsequent events, and persons present. In the immediate situation a few influential factors are physical condi-tions that determine comfort, audibility, seeing, temperature, ventilation, showmanship, adherence to time schedule, difficulties in producing the program, use of films and other aids, coverage by radio, TV, or printed media, appropriateness of physical setting, and sponsorship of the oc-casion.

Prior and subsequent events help the audience interpret their experi-ences in any act of persuasion. If this event is one of a series, then it is affected by those earlier in the series and by those still to come. Members of an audience check related incidents to make judgments of consistency. Perhaps unrelated events coincidentally changed the context and caused facilitation or obstruction of persuasion. Perception of a speaker's argu-ment for no-fault divorce could be changed by his wife's filing for divorce and charging adultery. Any persuasive attempt can be made easier or more difficult by the uncontrollable march of related and un-related events.

Persons present affect perception of the message. In a dyad or a small group the presence of an observer will change not only reactions but also content of messages. In a large group, the realization that one is a mem-ber of a minority or is an isolate causes one to be very hesitant to accept arguments contrary to majority opinion. Conversely, the discovery that one is in agreement with the majority of an audience causes relaxation of critical standards as far as pro-majority contentions are concerned. When two hostile factions make up an audience, each faction will apply more exacting tests to arguments opposing its position than they will to those favoring it. Truly, every audience, because of its composition, presents a different perceptual problem to the persuader.

Factors of circumstantiality in the message per se are those mechanics of arrangement and selection that contribute to or detract from the believability of its content. Associated with increased believability are such items as abundant detail, use of revealing pictures, concrete and specific language, precision in exposition, and the appearance of impartial objectivity. The opposites of these characteristics lower the believability of a message. The effects of these and other circumstantial details of a message are summarized by Rosenthal. He notes "apparent verifiability" as contributing to the quality of reasoned discourse and mentions that empirical statements, " . . . assertions about persons, events or conditions in the real world," carry with them the presumption that verification is possible.[10] Whether verification actually takes place or not is unimportant. When a receiver decides that a statement *could* be "checked on" he finds it more believable than another statement lacking the potential of being verified. The *difficulty* of putting a statement to the test seems not to affect its apparent verifiability.

An item of circumstance becomes proof when the receiver of a message is conscious of its impact and decides that the item helps to support a proposition. If circumstances enhance a persuasive message through automated or emotive processes without conscious deliberation by a receiver, then their effect, although it may be substantial, is other than proof.

Fantasy themes and rhetorical visions as components of proof

In a rhetorical interaction it becomes possible to identify "fantasy themes." Individuals supply elements of clarification and interpretation from their rich store of rumors, wishful thinking, and stereotypes. In a continuing interaction, such as in a political campaign, related fantasy themes interweave and form a fabric of fact and fiction in which the participant is unable to tell where reality ends and fantasy begins. The resulting shared visualization of a complex situation may lead to Bormann's "rhetorical vision."

> A rhetorical vision is constructed from fantasy themes that chain
> out in face-to-face interacting groups, in speaker-audience transactions,
> in viewers of television broadcasts, in listeners to radio programs,
> and in all the diverse settings for public and intimate communication in
> a given society. Once a rhetorical vision emerges it contains dramatic
> personae and typical plot lines that can be alluded to in all
> communication contexts and spark a response reminiscent of the
> original emotional chain. (In the small group context the "inside joke"
> is an instance of an allusion to a previous chaining fantasy theme.)
> The same dramas can be developed in detail when the occasion
> demands to generate emotional response.
>
> The relationship between a rhetorical vision and a specific fantasy
> theme within a message explains why so much "persuasive"
> communication simply repeats what the audience already knows.[11]

When the cease fire agreement to conclude the Vietnam War was signed in Paris on January 27, 1973, it served as a key element that

---

[10] Paul I. Rosenthal, "Specificity, Verifiability, and Message Credibility," *Quarterly Journal of Speech* 57 (December, 1971): 393–401.

[11] Ernest G. Bormann, "Fantasy and Rhetorical Vision: The Rhetorical Criticism of Social Reality," *Quarterly Journal of Speech* 58 (December, 1972): 398–99.

completed two contrasting rhetorical visions. Those who believed that United States participation in the conflict was necessary to save the world from Communism interpreted the provisions of the agreement as a victory for South Vietnam and agreed with President Nixon that it represented "peace with honor." Those whose rhetorical vision had pictured the United States military efforts as gratuitous interference in the internal affairs of another sovereign state saw no gains in the specifics of the agreement over the previous provisions the United States had rejected. They perceived the settlement as a victory for the Viet Cong and North Vietnam. The "chaining out" of related fantasies in the two rhetorical visions made the opposite interpretations of the Paris pact easily predictable.

The processes by which fantasies chain out and rhetorical visions are built are deserving of further study. Quite helpful to an understanding of these phenomena at an intuitive level is the analysis of what happens as a rumor spreads. It seems clear to the present authors that a rumor is a fantasy theme and that the development of a rumor over time might well represent the typical growth of a fantasy theme.

In 1947 Allport and Postman[12] presented an analysis of the normal "processes" of rumor spreading. These are patterns of distortion, principally, leveling, sharpening, and assimilation, and secondarily, exaggeration, condensation, and conventionalization.

Leveling is a process of omitting systematically details of the rumor that do not conform to the stereotypes of the person transmitting the rumor. *Sharpening* stresses the details that remain in the familiar pattern and is partly a result of the leveling operation; since fewer details remain, those left are more prominent. *Assimilation* adapts the rumor to the most available frames of reference. It is given local and timely significance.

Exaggeration is evident in the imputation of motives, the tendency to increase numbers, and the emphasis on an incidental item. *Condensation* reduces the rumor to a few easily remembered details. If the original rumor is complex, a synopsis soon evolves. *Conventionalization* removes unfamiliar elements from the rumor, such as strange words, subtle shadings of meaning, and so on. "The story sinks in verbal simplicity to the level of the least educated, and verbally least gifted member in the chain of transmission."[13] Allport and Postman conclude that hearsay is an important social influence. Deliberate use of rumor spreading for social control is cited, and tribute is paid to its effectiveness.

Clearly, rumor, rhetorical vision, and fantasy themes exert much

[12] Gordon W. Allport and Leo Postman, *The Psychology of Rumor* (New York: Henry Holt & Co., 1947).

[13] Ibid., p. 156.

influence through unemotional-suggestive and suggestive-emotional receiver responses; and a rational analysis of these elements of persuasion is necessary, since they are critical variables in the act of influence. A "facts of the case" analysis, however, would omit them entirely. Bormann argues that undue attention to "life facts" may cause the critic to overlook other kinds of social reality that may be of equal or greater importance:

> When a critic makes a rhetorical analysis he or she should start from the assumption that when there is a discrepancy between the word and the thing the most important cultural artifact for understanding the events may not be the things or "reality" but the words or the symbols.
> Indeed, in many vital instances the words, that is the rhetoric, are the social reality and to try to distinguish one symbolic reality from another is a fallacy widespread in historical and sociological scholarship which the rhetorical critic can do much to analyze and dispel.[14]

Quite clearly, any system of critical thinking useful in the planning, implementation, and analysis of modern persuasion must encompass elements of fantasy. Perceptions are structured and decisions are shaped by nonfactual evidence in processes similar to those described above. The principal product of the "other-than-reality" content of persuasion appears to be the formulation of basic premises, to be reasoned with in conventional patterns. The student of persuasion, then, cannot disregard apparently unsubstantiated assumptions which are relevant to an issue and are generally believed.

Fantasy as a force in human affairs has been directly and indirectly recognized for many years. Eric Hoffer in 1951 wrote eloquently on make-believe as necessary to the waging of war:

> The indispensability of play-acting in the grim business of dying and killing is particularly evident in the case of armies. Their uniforms, flags, emblems, parades, music and elaborate etiquette and ritual are designed to separate the soldier from his flesh-and-blood self and mask the overwhelming reality of life and death. We speak of the theatre of war and of battle scenes. In their battle orders army leaders invariably remind their soldiers that the eyes of the world are on them, that their ancestors are watching them and posterity shall hear of them. The great general knows how to conjure an audience out of the sands of the desert and the waves of the ocean.
> Glory is largely a theatrical concept. There is no striving for glory

---

[14] Bormann, "Fantasy and Rhetorical Vision," pp. 400–401.

without a vivid awareness of an audience—the knowledge that our
mighty deeds will come to the ears of our contemporaries or "those who
are to be." We are ready to sacrifice our true, transitory self for the
imaginary eternal self we are building up, by our heroic deeds in
the opinion and imagination of others.[15]

We conclude our discussion of the role of fantasy in critical thinking
by relating an actual experience. A dean of a college of education grap-
pled with the problem of distinguishing reality from fantasy at a human
relations conference for a period of two weeks and continued his thinking
and reading for the month that followed the conference. At the end of
this prolonged study period he had resolved his difficulty. "My fantasy,"
he said, "is reality." He had decided that, in an immediate and action-
related sense, what one perceives to be, is.

In summary, a significant proportion of argument lies outside the
boundaries of the tangible. Our incomplete list of these nonmaterialistic
sources of support for reasoned persuasion includes information supplied
by receivers, the thoughtful use of elements of credibility and circumstantiality, and the fantasy themes and rhetorical visions of individuals
and groups.[16]

A role for absolute standards of critical thinking in persuasion

To this point our frame of reference for the consideration of critical
thinking in persuasion has been the almost infinite variability of human
reasonableness. Consequently, adapting to the thinking of a particular
audience or receiver has been our chief concern. Now we turn to cultural
norms that influence particular audiences. Cultural norms of critical
thinking are established by the common practices of the majority of the
educated members of a community. Here we ask the reader to join us in
recognizing that relative and absolute standards can coexist and that
both can be useful.

Reasoned discourse, like most of the tools of communication, benefits
from the flexibility to adjust to certain people and circumstances. However, it is equally beneficial to persuader and persuadee to know the
patterns of thinking shared by members of diverse groups. To reach a
large group we often talk to a hypothetical person we have constructed

[15] Eric Hoffer, *The True Believer* (New York: Harper and Row, 1951; Perennial
Library Edition, 1966), p. 65, Perennial Library Edition.

[16] For further material on the reasoning process in groups, see chapter 7.

out of interests, motives, and knowledge we assume to be common to most of the collective. Certain reasoning patterns and criteria of interpreting information we assume to be generally understood and followed. And, finally, we can postulate that particular ideals and goals are held throughout a society, and we can use them in our appeals to its members. In effect, we are treating some generalizations about the reasoning process as absolutes, expecting people to conform to them. If our selection of apparent universals is wise, then conformity will indeed occur often enough to reward us for treating groups of people as though they resembled each other, which, of course, they do.

The universal audience

What happens when an argument tailored to one audience is overheard by another? Often unanticipated and sometimes disastrous consequences, as many a speaker who failed to remember that his talk was to be covered by radio or television can testify. Often it is rewarding to prepare for a universal audience.

> Argumentation aimed exclusively at a particular audience has the drawback that the speaker, by the very fact of adapting to the views of his listeners, might rely on arguments that are foreign or even directly opposed to what is acceptable to persons other than those he is presently addressing.[17]

Without challenging the desirability of maintaining the perceptual criterion of good argument, namely, that the highest quality of reasoned discourse for a particular receiver is that adapted to his unique system of reflective thinking, we must recognize that it is often impractical to give other audiences receiving the same message similar individual treatment. When this situation is recognized, the persuader supplements adaptation to a particular audience with adjustment to more fixed norms, the commonalities of a culture that a variety of audiences may agree upon. Perelman postulates the concept of "universal audience" as a companion to the "particular audience." The interaction of these two somewhat dissimilar audiences must be understood for optimum use of thoughtful persuasion in a given instance.

Perhaps an example will clarify the somewhat complicated functions of particular and universal audiences. Let us suppose that the U. S. Supreme Court and the Supreme Court of the State of Minnesota have declared the anti-abortion laws of Minnesota to be unconstitutional,

17 Perelman and Olbrechts-Tyteca, *The New Rhetoric*, p. 31.

hence null and void. In our hypothetical situation, Dr. Jane Hodgson, whose test case precipitated the court decisions, is addressing Minneapolis gynecologists urging the establishment of abortion clinics in the Twin Cities.

Dr. Hodgson's particular audience of physicians must be reasoned with by using their existing stereotypes and perceptions of gynecological care, both what it is and what it ought to be. Further, she must select lines of argument acceptable to the broader community of newspaper readers, radio listeners, and TV viewers. The primary medical audience will be very thoughtful about the arguments designed for the remote, more universal audience, and this outside audience will inspect critically, and be influenced by, the in-house arguments aimed at the gynecologists. Truly, universal and particular audiences interact, and in the words of Perelman "pass judgment on one another."

How universal does a universal audience need to be? In the above hypothetical case, perhaps large numbers of outsiders would have received Dr. Hodgson's message or reports of the interaction she had with the gynecologists, but not *everybody*, not even everybody in the immediate geographical area. What entitles us to call the outside audience *universal* is the universality of the opportunity for everyone in a specified large community to receive it. From the point of view of Dr. Hodgson, *everybody* in the Twin City area might as well have been reading, listening, and viewing.

Distinguishing between universal and particular audiences is an extraordinarily useful device in planning, conducting, and analyzing persuasion. Not only can relative standards be applied to accomplish a particular purpose, but normative standards in a culture or subculture become equally important. Appeals directed to unique and to generalized audiences are interwoven in proportions dictated by topics, situations, and people affected. Any unit of persuasion that is not completely private will fall somewhere on the continuum shown in table 8–1.

Finally, the specific purpose of the persuader enters into his treatment of universal and particular audiences. If his purpose is immediate, then

Table 8–1

**Percentage of Reliance upon Criteria
of Particular and Universal Audiences**

Particular	0	25	50	75	100
Universal	100	75	50	25	0

his concern usually lies predominantly with his particular audience. With his desired short-term consequence achieved it is unlikely that a later response of the universal audience could make much difference. Long-range purposes, however, usually necessitate much greater reliance on responses of the universal audience. Interaction of particular and universal audiences over time affects the reactions of both, and this complicates the planning and implementation of persuasion.

Universals of thoughtful deliberation in America

Methods of critical thinking are culture bound. Within a culture, approved norms exist that function as universals. In modern America, a universal in this category is *orderliness*. A perceived systematic arrangement of parts of an argument has a value greater than that of an arrangement of the same ingredients that appears to be random. We do not need to know the historical derivation of this preference. It is sufficient to understand that our living together for a few hundred years has led us to a general agreement that, other things being equal, it is better to have things in order.

Clarity and *directness* are plus-rated universals in American culture. Unclear and obscure arguments are usually given little weight. Lest we forget the cultural limits of universals, perhaps we should mention that in most of the Far East, clarity and directness are negative, inhibiting factors in reasoned discourse.

Concreteness and *specificity* are highly regarded by most Americans in preference to abstract and imprecise citations. Though there is reason to doubt that *all* of the universal audience can tell an abstraction from a specific instance, there is the general desire to think with definite concepts rather than with vague generalities.

Finally, a universal of thoughtful deliberation in American culture is *accuracy*, freedom from distortion. When we reason about a problem, we would prefer not to ignore important aspects, or work with concepts that are untrue. All of us would like to deal with the relevant variables in our varied ways of thinking critically. The following tests of validity represent dimensions of accuracy generally endorsed in America:

1. Is all wording simple and clear?
2. Are opposing points of view recognized?
3. Are units compared really comparable?
4. Are statistics representative?
5. Are bases of all percentages supplied?
6. Do examples and illustrations represent the situation fairly?

7. Are generalizations adequately supported?
8. Are quoted authorities reliable and qualified?
9. Is concealment and other deception avoided?
10. Are all relevant facts of the case acknowledged?
11. Is appropriate documentation supplied?[18]

And, of course, Western rhetoricians have long agreed that the principles of *unity, emphasis,* and *coherence* should be observed in arguments that purport to be reasonable.

The above brief listing of certain universals of thoughtful deliberation that are generally characteristic of modern America is, of course, incomplete. Our reader can supply other items in greater detail.

The function of the unattainable ideal

A prime mover in shaping critical evaluation of argument is the influence of the ultimate objective or "ideal." The testing of intermediate objectives and methods against long-range outcomes is a true universal, for it is characteristic of all human societies. The particular ideals toward which people strive vary from culture to culture, but individual and social utopian goals are "built into" human affairs everywhere.

During the second half of the twentieth century some American ideals in programs of social action are: the end of racial and religious discrimination, universal education, the Great Society, rehabilitation of criminals, equality for women, a balanced diet for everyone, control of pollution, safe automobiles, a balanced national budget, peace.

If you reflect a moment about what the mentioned long-range goals have in common, you will conclude that in the foreseeable future each is unattainable. The critically thoughtful reader will find it interesting that attainability is unrelated to the power of a goal to modify behavior. Common sense might suggest that it is fruitless to work toward something that cannot be had, but such is obviously not the case.

Some insight into the dynamic of the unattainable ideal comes from the American belief that "success" is continued movement toward a selected objective. *Progress* is the essential element, and a goal provides direction. As long as an individual or group continues to pass checkpoints on the way, he or it is successful. When a person or group stops moving ahead, failure begins.

---

[18] William Howell and Ernest Bormann, *Presentational Speaking for Business and the Professions* (New York: Harper and Row, 1971), p. 210.

The positive influence of unattainable ideals has been neglected in the study of persuasion. Just as the Ten Commandments have made a rational contribution to the lives of millions of people, so have a host of other desirable, remote eventualities structured our institutions and our life styles. We urge that our reader incorporate these distant but powerful influences in his analyses of ongoing persuasion. In other words, he should calculate the usefulness of the unattainable ideal. He becomes a critical thinker when he uses his goals to test appropriateness and productivity of particular activities.

The importance of reasoned discourse in persuasion

Many people believe that thoughtful, methodical processing of information in the process of social control has been tried and found wanting. For them, the pendulum has swung from a blanket faith in reasoning to an equally total trust in feelings and emotions. Because of this apparent de-emphasis of rationality in interpersonal communication, we must confront the question of whether critical thinking is important to persuasion, and hence, worthy of our time and effort in its study.

We believe that much of the disillusionment with efforts to persuade through reasoned discourse comes from a message or content orientation. If perceptual differences of receivers are ignored and *only* absolutes of logical correctness are relied upon, then it is not surprising that attempts to use reason to persuade have often failed. When we appeal to the particular system of reasonableness we find in our audience, we can expect response patterns to change drastically. This approach can show us how to "be believable."

Probably the distinctive advantage of settling a social problem via reasoning rather than through feelings and emotions is the quality of the resulting decision. On the average, thoughtful reflection ensures more accurate assessment of variables and a more thorough analysis of relationships than occurs with an emotional solution. But this is substantive rather than a persuasive advantage, a valuable by-product of reasoned persuasion. We now proceed to those advantages that accrue to the deliberate use of reasoned discourse to secure desired responses from individuals and groups.

Reasoned persuasion has prestige values

Apparently reasoned discourse has unique prestige values. People have high regard for "horse sense," brains, problem-solving ability, ability to suspend judgment, and insistence on sound evidence as a prerequisite to decision. Our democratic form of government and Anglo-American jurisprudence have encouraged widespread respect for evidence and its systematic interpretation. Scientific advance and wide acceptance of scientific method in modern industry, plus the transfer of laboratory principles to education, have helped create the stereotype of "the educated man" as a thorough, methodical problem-solver. This inclusion of reasoning power at the heart of our "educated man" concept is termed by some authors the "idealization of the rational."

Reasoned discourse can be an antidote to emotion

Perhaps you have heard a speaker who relied on reasoning follow a speaker who relied on emotionalized appeals. Actually or by implication he said to his audience, "Let's sit back and look over the facts of the situation. Let's consider them objectively and see exactly what their significance may be." If done simply and sincerely, this technique can be effective because of its striking contrast. Our consciences bother us a bit when we indulge in flights of fancy. Similarly when we "go along for the ride" with a highly emotionalized speech, we do not feel quite right about it. Somewhere inside of us a censor continually reminds us that there are items of evidence and reasoning to be considered that we may be overlooking. The highly emotionalized speaker may be so effective that he causes us to forget the censor; the reasonable speaker helps the censor by reminding us of the values of sound evidence and valid reasoning.

Reasoned discourse has lasting effects

A student of persuasion provided an interesting testimonial concerning this attribute of reasoned discourse. He explained that when he began his study of persuasion he had little faith in the powers of reasoned discourse to persuade. He preferred to place his faith in visual imagery, human interest, and dramatic devices. At the conclusion of a case study of reasoned persuasion he made approximately this statement: "I am amazed to find that when you advance primarily emotional appeal you have to keep 'pushing' it all the time, but if you do a good job of building a logical argument you can sit back and relax; it will stand by itself."

This student's observation would seem to be verified by the experience of others. Persuaders of the past have found that a good reason tends to be remembered long after impulses based on emotion have been forgotten.

Reasoned persuasion is difficult to refute

A unit of reasoned discourse makes severe demands of anyone who would disagree because it cannot be adequately answered by assertion or innuendo. Because this argument accepts rigorous standards of evidence and reasoning, these standards are inferentially applied to any opponent. He is challenged to demonstrate equal or superior evidence and reasoning. In this sense the proper use of reasoned discourse throws a burden of proof on the opposition.

Reasoning is an effective way to resolve conflict

We all feel "high pressure" competing persuasions impinging upon us from all directions. We are urged in the language of dynamic action to act immediately without taking time for deliberation.

The categorical nature of advertising and political appeals makes compromise within them impossible. For example, when the Democrats agree that "the Democratic administration has great integrity" and the Republicans assert that "the Democratic administration is the most corrupt in our history," the citizen being indoctrinated with these conclusions is understandably confused. Apparently this circumstance comes about because politicians and advertisers want their statements as strong as possible and thus make them unconditional. But because Mr. Citizen is incapable of believing that an issue is both black and white at the same time, he is resentful. Both advertising and politics present such strong demands in opposite directions.

As the media of mass communication intensify the campaigns of advertising and other propaganda, the need for a means of resolving contradictions increases. We have at present some agencies that sell the services of resolving conflicts produced by conflicting claims. These agencies attempt to discover and propagate reliable information about nationally advertised products. This is reasoned discourse in action, not for purposes of persuasion, but to help the receiver of the information to make a better decision.

In persuasion the psychological consequence of being reasoned with in a situation of conflict has a similar advantage. When the persuadee is satisfied that a recommended course of action has logical superiority, his distress over conflict subsides and his choice becomes clear and easy.

These five advantages of using reasoned discourse in persuasion seem to be both obvious and important. Bypassing these critical tendencies in an audience might indeed be a severe handicap to a persuader.

Further, the persuader has the power to encourage his audience to be critical. By calling attention to possible weaknesses in his argument, by requesting his audience to defer judgment, by directly asking his listeners to be hard-nosed and demanding, he can improve the quality of reasoned discourse. In chapter 1 we voiced our concern over the many problems and limitations of persuasion. Certainly a persuader can avoid many of these pitfalls by putting his audience on guard and helping them to resist his persuasion in every reasonable way possible. The greatest and most famous persuaders dedicated themselves to the production of critical, deliberate responses, with consequent benefits to mankind.

Conclusion

Reexaminations of the role of reasoning in communication are few. A leader in exploring the revision of reasoned discourse assumptions to make them compatible with an interactive process of persuasion has been Carroll Arnold of Pennsylvania State University. We are indebted to him for a modern rationale of thoughtful communication that incorporates a perceptual criterion and the concept of universal standards; its substance argues eloquently for the importance of reasoning in persuasion.

> I first want to define the terms carefully. In general communication, "reasonable" and "logical" occur as terms people use when they want to report that something "hangs together" for them, seems adequately developed for their purposes, seems free of inconsistencies insofar as they noticed. It seems to me we must admit that in rhetoric and drama at least, "reasonable" is in the final analysis what the consumer is willing to call "reasonable."
>
> But I would hasten on to make a second point: that it is a general characteristic of men and women that they hunt for inter-connections among things and ideas, especially when they are uncertain or begin to doubt. That is part of their nature—a fact well documented. It isn't all of their nature, of course. We must admit that, too. Maybe we need not be uniformly regretful. I, for one, think it is rather nice to illogically allow people to fall in love instead of logically mating them by bloodlines as we do with apparently more important creatures like dogs and horses! I do not really see that admitting that people do not always hunt for reasons denies that relation-hunting is there in people; and communicators must be ready to deal with these "rational" demands or they will almost surely fail whenever they encounter the indifferent or the doubters. Accept that much, and now, there is reason to reason!
>
> Thirdly, I would want to drive home the most practical point I believe I know about making communications reasonable, as I have defined the term That point is that when listeners want reasons spelled

out, they mercilessly put down as stupid or too sloppy to be trusted communicators who do not reason or who do it badly. It is easy to show that general absence of clarity, consistency, completeness, and consecutiveness in discourse is, in the world's eye, the mark of the fool.[19]

[19] Carroll Arnold, "What's Reasonable," *Today's Speech* 19:3 (Summer, 1971): 22.

9

The cultural bases of persuasion

I. Introduction

II. Culture and the process of persuasive communication
  A. The linguistic approach to the study of transcultural persuasion
  B. Identifying characteristic nonverbal patterns in intercultural communication
  C. Categories of nonverbal communication important to persuasion within and across cultures
    1. Kinesics
    2. Proxemics
    3. Haptics
    4. Paralanguage
    5. Nervantics

III. Intercultural research and the study of persuasion
  A. The study of values and perceptions as a basis for intercultural persuasion
    1. A duocultural approach
    2. The study of self and contrasting group stereotypes
    3. Descriptions of patterns of thinking and modes of social discourse
  B. Applying results of research to intercultural persuasion

IV. Conclusion

Introduction

As noted in previous chapters, all constituents of the process of persuasion are influenced, subtly or obviously, by their cultural environment. Thus the roles played by persuasion vary markedly from place to place. These variations involve vehicles, values, attitudes, and motives; a relative reliance on reason or feeling in persuasive appeals, and even standards of ethics. Hence, a theory of persuasion is incomplete without a cultural dimension. This chapter endeavors to supply basic theory and the results of research necessary to an elementary understanding of cultural forces that shape varied acts of persuasion.

The cultural differences that concern us can be placed on a continuum from "minor and local" to "distant and exotic." Blue collar and white collar workers live in contrasting cultures, as do artists and engineers. Perhaps our reader on first thinking about intercultural persuasion pictures himself overseas among people of other races, customs, and religions. Here the cultural contrast is striking because of strangeness. Sights, sounds, and smells are new to us, so we expect behavioral patterns to be different from ours. But the more or less familiar cultures at home present problems to the persuader that are as perplexing as the more dramatic far-away situations. Consequently, a cultural approach to persuasion is necessary and helpful to persuader and persuadee within community, state, and nation as well as abroad.

A concept basic to consideration of culture in persuasive communication is that of sets of expectations. We will explain and exemplify that concept, encouraging the reader to recall from his experience further examples and analogs of our examples. He will find that behaviors which seem strange in other cultures can often be found in his own, the difference being of degree rather than of kind.

"Sets of expectations" specify appropriate behavior and define the norms of human interaction in a homogeneous group, in particular situations. For people from contrasting groups (cultures) to communicate effectively, each needs insight into his own culturally patterned behavior as well as knowledge of the relevant behavioral constructs in the culture represented by the other person. The differing expectations in a given interaction can then be better understood, and misinterpretations can be reduced.

Several examples will make these statements more meaningful. A North American manager in a factory in Bombay, India, found himself developing a dangerously high level of frustration over his failure to persuade the men working under his supervision to follow simple instructions. He knew that the men who received the message were sufficiently competent in spoken English to perceive his intended meaning. He rationalized his lack of success by saying that his men were "unreasonable," but the *reason* for their unreasonableness eluded him.

What the manager needed to know was that in India in the supervisor-employee relationship direct suggestion is inappropriate. Meanings are routinely implied and inferred. The men receiving his direct instruction either ignored it because it was explicit, or tried to read into the simple instruction a more complicated indirect message. The manager increased his efforts to be more direct and more specific and hence behaved even more inappropriately than before. Finally he decided to preface an instruction by saying, "Now, I mean exactly what I'm going to say, and nothing else," whereupon his Indian receiver retired to a quiet place and asked himself, "I wonder what the boss really meant when he said that he was going to say *exactly* what he meant?"

One of the authors, while investigating task-oriented communication between North Americans and host nationals in Japan, encountered a constellation of related behaviors that caused difficulties for the Americans. A Japanese resists saying "No" to an American; he will say he understands when he does not, and he will seldom ask for more information when he needs it. These tendencies have deep roots in the Japanese concept of politeness. Culturally, these behavioral patterns make sense, but in an American frame of reference, they are absurd. An American's ability to adjust his communication to these probable responses will be increased by superficial knowledge that they are to be expected. But some understanding of their origin in Japanese assumptions and values will help the American visitor to a less mechanical, more sensitive procedure of adapting to them in face-to-face communication.

The examples from India and Japan might be categorized respectively under "directness" and "politeness." Another set of expectations with profound consequences for interpersonal communication is "personal trust." Gardner supplies a relevant illustration from still another culture:

> One facet can be made clear if we suppose, for example, that an American expert has been basically socialized to trust people (openness, frankness, honesty, etc.) and not to inquire into, or not to be interested in, or even to denigrate such interest in, the motives of others. Put in a negative statement, he has been taught not to be always suspiciously on guard. A man is to be tested by the results of his work. On the other hand, a Middle Easterner has been basically socialized to be always suspiciously on guard in his dealings with his fellow men. Survival, for him, depends upon the sensitive probing and accurate evaluation of the hidden motives behind every action. How can two such people interact and communicate successfully in such a common social situation? The American has neither taste nor skill for operating with covert motives, and the Middle Easterner cannot be convinced about the overtness of the American.[1]

Our three diverse instances suggest how sets of expectations differ and why this difference often influences communication. Now we will

[1] G. H. Gardner, "Cross-Cultural Communication," *The Journal of Social Psychology* 58 (1962): 247.

examine in some detail the overall concept of culture and the way it dictates the conduct of persuasion.

Culture and the process of persuasive communication

As was the case with the term *persuasion,* the term *culture* is defined in many ways by varied authorities. A definition suited to our requirements and one which represents a central tendency in usage is provided by John and Ruth Useem and John Donoghue: "Culture has been defined in a number of ways, but most simply, as *the learned and shared behavior of a community of interacting human beings.*"[2]

Since culture encompasses all learned and shared behavior, it includes formal language as well as other forms of communication. The definition is purposely vague about minimum numbers of people to constitute a culture. The important requirement for referring to a grouping of persons as "a culture" is the uniformity of their behavioral pattern in specified human interactions, the boundary of that uniformity becoming the boundary of the culture.

The belief that cultural and national boundaries coincide is widely held, but in light of our definition of culture, it is obviously false. The Soviet Union is composed of widely dissimilar cultures, Czechoslovakia is both Czech and Slovak, India's mosaic of religious faiths incorporates so many differences in shared behaviors that we could refer to each of them as "cultures," and Canada has French communities where the way of life resembles that of France more than that of North America. In the United States, various ethnic groups attempt to preserve their "cultural identity." Among these are American Indians of several diverse origins, urban clusters composed, for example, of blacks, Chicanos, Jews, or Italians, and communities settled by homogeneous groups of immigrants, as the Finns on Minnesota's Iron Range. Perhaps one should consider certain regions of the United States as cultures because of their distinctive behavior patterns. Regional cultures would be the Eastern Seaboard, the Upper Midwest, the Deep South, the Far West, and the Pacific Northwest. Regional United States cultures have resulted from a blending of differing value systems into distinctive patterns.

We stress that a single culture accommodates many degrees of difference. Whenever one encounters a distinctive set of shared behavior patterns that characterize a group of people, it can be viewed as another

[2] J. Useem, R. Useem, and J. Donoghue, "Men in the Middle of the Third Culture: The Roles of American and Non-Western People in Cross-Cultural Administration," *Human Organization* (Fall 1963): 169.

culture, whether it is halfway around the globe or only a block away. There is value in adding the cultural dimension to the process of communication. Because of the "out-of-awareness" nature of cultural influences, we tend to project upon other people our own approved patterns without thinking that theirs may be different. Assuming (unconsciously) that others are like ourselves has caused many a well-intentioned tourist to be labeled an "ugly American" and many a police officer to get into trouble in a black community of his city.

A modern theory of persuasion must incorporate elements of comparison of domestic and remote cultures that affect communication among peoples of those cultures. An extensive area involving several disciplines is immediately opened for study. We will mention briefly several approaches to a comparative examination of cultural influences that can help to establish a multi-cultural basis for persuasion.

The linguistic approach
to the study of transcultural persuasion

The oldest technique of intercultural interaction is the learning of the other fellow's language; little significant intercultural communication can be accomplished otherwise. Either sender or receiver must translate one set of symbols into a common system of symbols. At least one bilingual participant is essential, and he has both a difficult task and a heavy responsibility in creating a representation of the message in the second language that will be perceived by the receiver with minimum distortion.

In the process of translation, whether it is done by sender or receiver, culture cannot be separated from language. Words and phrases are perceived in context, and context is supplied by culture. Colloquial expressions and figurative language are particularly hazardous to intercultural communication.

Sen Nishiyama, a skilled interpreter who was employed by the United States Information Agency in Tokyo in the spring of 1966, related an incident of translation that shows the involvement of culture and language. Mr. Nishiyama was interpreting for two American astronauts, Frank Bormann and Walter Shirra, and on this occasion they were in a television studio, as guests on a children's program. Japanese children in the studio were asking questions. One asked, "Will you get to the moon?" Bormann answered, " We hope to, in 1970. I hope to be on the first trip, and when I return, I will tell you that the moon isn't made of green cheese." Mr. Nishiyama said that his translation told the children, "Mr. Bormann hopes to reach the moon in 1970, and then will return and tell you that there are no rabbits on the moon." The green cheese myth is unknown in Japan, but the belief that rabbits inhabit the moon is an established legend.

But Mr. Nishiyama later concluded that he had made a bad translation! Bormann's remark had been a happy one, and since Japanese children enjoy thinking about rabbits on the moon, the translation had been sad. "What I should have said," Nishiyama concluded, "was, Mr. Bormann will tell you that he talked with the rabbits on the moon!" A delightful part of Japanese folklore is the belief that the rabbits on the moon can talk.

Scholars are systematizing the study of other languages and securing more efficient learning and deeper understanding through methodologies of structural linguistics. Programmed instruction, use of native speakers of the language as instructors, intensive learning procedures, much stress on spoken usage, and use of voice-recorded and videotaped interactions are a few of the innovations that help one acquire some facility in a "foreign" language. But language alone is not enough to ensure effective communication in a strange community. In the words of Ray Gorden, an expert in Latin America and a sociologist at Antioch College, "If you know the language but not the culture in a country you visit, you will be able to make a fluent fool of yourself."[3]

Most of us are sensitive to problems in communication caused by dissimilar languages. When the languages look and sound alike, but usages and meanings differ, pitfalls in the road to understanding are treacherous because they are so inconspicuous. A wise observation points out that "the Americans and the English are divided by a common language." Communicating with minority groups is, at least to some extent, a problem of learning the particular meanings they have assigned to familiar words. Vocations and professions similarly stipulate meanings for their own vocabulary. When a banker communicates with a physician, substantial problems in finding common elements in language must be solved, even though both speak English.

It is a safe assumption that whenever two individuals from different cultures interact there will be misunderstandings, whether the two people speak the "same language" or not. A message written or spoken by one will need some *translation* if it is to be perceived accurately by the other. All of us should become more sensitive to variations in usage among others who speak our language and try to adapt our messages and perceptions to their frames of reference. A substantial amount of

[3] From an interview in the spring of 1966, with Professor Gorden of CEUCA, a bi-national university, sponsored by the Great Lakes College Association in Bogota, Colombia.

the "generation gap" can be attributed to such semantic elements that are not common to oldsters and youngsters. Perhaps it would be stretching our elastic definition of culture too far to refer to those under twenty-five and those over forty as belonging to different cultures, but shared behavior patterns and linguistic habits may be sufficiently different to justify that usage.

Identifying characteristic nonverbal patterns in intercultural communication

Another approach to better communication among cultures is the location of specific behaviors with different meanings important to communication. Lists of these have been accumulated over many years, principally by field anthropologists. Because these symbolic acts caught the attention of the visitor they tend to be fragmentary and are often dramatic contrasts to comparable behaviors in the visitor's culture. Hence they impress us as "bizarre bits" of behavior. We should understand that the described behavior is "bizarre" only when compared to the visitor's culture and is entirely appropriate and usual in the setting where it is found.[4]

Many "bizarre bits" brought home from far places by sociologists, anthropologists, and other behavioral scientists are nonverbal. Gestures indicating "yes" and "no" differ widely around the world. Europeans and North Americans generally nod the head for "yes" and shake it from side to side for "no." Eskimos flick the eyebrows for "yes" and wrinkle the nose for "no," Indians near Hyderabab have a complex head movement with a slight distinction between affirmation and negotiation, while the Lebanese toss the head up and to the side and click the tongue for "no."

Other gestures are no more uniform. Pointing is done with the finger in one culture, with the lips in another, and any pointing gesture whatsoever is extremely rude in a third. The American "A-OK" gesture which makes a circle of thumb and a finger is pornographic in the Middle East *if* it happens to use the middle finger. Made with the thumb and index finger, it is "A-OK." Japanese show sensitive facial responses to conversation in private, informal settings, while in public and on formal occasions they are careful to inhibit any facial gesture. Americans and most cultures make no similar distinction.

Nonverbal behaviors have claimed the attention of scholars in intercultural speech-communication in recent years because they are highly

---

[4] See Edward T. Hall, *The Silent Language* (New York: Fawcett World Library, 1966), chapter 8.

significant in determining outcomes of communication, they vary so widely from culture to culture, and until the past decade or two they were largely ignored. Now they are being described and classified, culture by culture, but much remains to be done. In spoken persuasion, for example, we need "micro" studies, to quantify nonverbal elements of intercultural interaction associated with success and with lack of success of the persuader.

Categories of nonverbal communication important to persuasion within and across cultures

Five identifiable and distinct kinds or categories of nonverbal communication have been described and used to increase our understanding of nonlinguistic interactions. These are dependent or independent variables for study. By "breaking down" nonverbal communication into its parts we can separate critical from less essential elements. Quantitative comparative studies are possible, and the reader can subjectively assess the roles of each of the five types of "silent language" in his own or observed interpersonal interactions.

Kinesics includes all purposeful body movement to add meaning to spoken language. A skilled speaker's use of facial expression, gesture, and movement would be predominantly kinesic activity. Any unintended physical actions such as nervous mannerisms are *not* kinesics. The "bizarre bits" of behavior mentioned above are examples of kinesics.

Proxemics is the use of space and the physical relationships of people to implement interpersonal communication. Proxemic elements in a conversation include the distance that separates the conversationalists, their directness of eye contact, bodily attitudes such as leaning towards or away from each other, use of sitting or standing posture, or turning away or toward each other. Cultural differences in proxemics are striking. Middle Easterners prefer a close conversational distance that makes North Americans uncomfortable. Taking a position which turns the sole of your shoe toward a citizen of the Arab world with whom you are conversing is, to him, an insult. Americans tend to slouch and assume relaxed, informal postures at even formal functions. In most cultures such behavior is undignified and inappropriate. Often this informality is interpreted as an intended put-down to the members of another culture. As we study physical relationships of people talking with each other we are discovering that their cultures structure proxemic elements to a surprising degree. Appropriate positions, distances, and bodily attitudes are uniformly practiced. Yet, few people recognize that any standardization exists. Truly, the important codes of proxemics exert rigid control over communicators, even though they are "out of awareness."

Haptics is that part of interpersonal communication which is accomplished through the sense of touch. Sometimes totally nonverbal, more often incidental to words and/or music, touch is an eloquent and indispensable means of communicative interaction. Conventions on appropriate uses of tactile stimulation to convey meaning differ widely from culture to culture.

In Thailand, physical contact between adults in public is strongly disapproved. Violating this convention has severe consequences; typically the person touched considers himself to have been slighted. The head of a person is almost completely off-limits. Touching a Thai male on the head may be interpreted as a mortal insult. During American participation in the war in Vietnam hostility was generated among the Thai when American soldiers held hands with or caressed Thai girls in the streets. Apparently the American command failed to understand the seriousness of this offense. Had it been able to measure the ill will resulting from public physical contact between Thai girls and members of the occupation forces, a regulation forbidding this practice could have been enacted and enforced.

Physical contact supplementing speech communication is used freely in India. Men hold hands and embrace and, to the amazement of Americans, kiss each other, as they do also in the Middle East. Where abundant physical contact between members of the same sex is the norm, touch is used extensively to supplement language in even formal instances of speech communication. Typically, North Americans in Latin America are somewhat perturbed the first time they are grasped, rubbed, and patted in the course of a business interview. Americans reject interpersonal touching except between members of opposite sexes, with a slight relaxation that permits ladies, especially young girls, to hold hands and hug one another. While the United States is not as strict about public body contact as Thailand, it is still far less permissive in this regard than is most of the rest of the world.

Where bodily contact is part of an accepted pattern of interaction, the manner in which the touching takes place is often meticulously specified by the culture. Social dancing in Western cultures routinely permits partners to assume a posture of embrace to some degree, at least occasionally. In North America a girl dancing with a boy can place her right arm lightly over her partner's shoulder and around his neck, which current etiquette endorses as a proper position. In Latin America, in particular in Colombia, a girl placing her arm in this identical position is signaling her partner that she has decided to sleep with him. Many United States girls of college age, spending a semester or a year in South America, have been amazed at the change in behavior of a local boyfriend, after they danced together. In Colombia the correct (and safe) place for a girl's hand while she dances is flat against the boy's lapel.

Then she can control the distance between them by pushing, and at the same time supply mute but convincing testimony of her virtue.

Communication through physical contact, haptics, like proxemics, is assuming a position of importance in the study of interpersonal interaction. It is essential to analysis of intercultural persuasion, for the touching relationship is a culturally determined variable that encompasses a vast range, and is usually a critical factor in influencing responses to messages.

Paralanguage, the fourth category of nonverbal communication, is the use of voice in ways that affect the receiver's responses to words in the message, yet which are not linked to discrete meanings of words, phrases, and sentences. Hence, a rising inflection to ask a question or a falling inflection to indicate the end of a thought are *not* paralanguage. These and similar vocalizations become a part of the particular symbolized thought, hence are treated as "verbal" by the linguist.

The essence of the concept "paralanguage" is summarized by Trager: "Paralanguage is divided into voice set as background for, and voice qualities and vocalizations as accompaniments of, language proper."[5]

The loudness or softness of voice is a phenomenon of paralanguage, as are gutteral, nasal, breathy, or harsh voice qualities. Affective states (emotional conditions) are often revealed to the perceptive listener by changes in vocalization independent of linguistic structure. In North America, an unusual level of volume, evidenced by shouting or almost whispered speech, often indicates a significant psychological disturbance. "Normal" vocal intensities vary from culture to culture. A person coming from a soft-spoken society (e.g., Japan) and visiting a culture where voices are normally loud and strident (e.g., Lebanon) may find himself concluding that all the people around him are perpetually excited, perhaps hysterical. A good interpreter acting as intermediary between a Japanese and a citizen of the Arab world will talk loudly while converting Japanese to Arabic and softly while speaking in Japanese.

When a person says he is interested in hearing about your trip to the Taj Mahal and asks the proper questions, and yet you know he is not interested, the information probably comes to you via paralanguage. Similarly, your friend may say, "What, me upset? I couldn't care less," and tell you that he cares very much indeed, through paralanguage. When the husband returns home at 5:45 in the afternoon, only to learn that he must be ready at 6:00 to go out for cocktails and dinner, paralanguage enables him to articulate "I'm glad we can go" and be understood by his wife as having said, "I hate the whole bloody business."

Most paralanguage phenomena are out-of-awareness. Nevertheless,

[5] G. L. Trager, "Paralanguage: A First Appreciation" in Dell Hymes, ed., *Language in Culture and Society* (New York: Harper and Row, 1964), p. 276.

they are learned behavior patterns, and in a homogeneous group, one person's paralanguage vocalizations resemble those of another. Every culture has very complicated expectations for paralanguage appropriate to many different situations. Anthropological linguists seem to agree that paralanguage patterns are sufficiently intricate that it is unlikely that any person will master the paralanguage in a culture other than his own.

As yet, little has been done to specify and quantify cultural norms in paralanguage. This will be done by scholars of intercultural communication in the coming decades. But until more information is available, the individual taking residence in an unfamiliar culture will be wise to observe paralanguage manifestations and discuss these with natives. Paralanguage cues associated with sincerity and insincerity, with direct and indirect suggestion differ interculturally, and these distinctions are frequently critically important to the interpretation of a message. The visitor needs to know the tone of voice appropriate to the leader and the tone used by the follower. These and many other facts about vocalization in different situations can be learned superficially, and, once acquired, can be used readily.

Nervantics is the most recent addition to the forms of nonverbal communication. Nervantics is fidget behavior, not purposeful but often prominent. It becomes important because, like the other kinds of nonverbal communication, it is both culturally determined and an important influence in causing the consequences of communication.

An American businessman in Japan picks up nonverbal feedback cues *not* from watching the face of his host, as he would at home, but by watching the Japanese associate's hands because the only way a Japanese person in a formal situation is permitted to fidget is with his hands. All other parts of the body, including the face, are so carefully controlled that no expression escapes. If the hands are in normal position, side by side in the lap, all is well. When they clasp, tension is developing, and if the hands grip together so tightly they shake, their owner is profoundly disturbed. At this point the wise American finds an excuse to adjourn the meeting, to give him some time to discover what has gone wrong!

Learning to fidget with cultural appropriateness has obvious utility in interpersonal communication. If an American in Japan uses the nervous mannerisms acceptable in the United States, such as slouching, scratching his head, and pulling his ear, the Japanese observing him are likely to dismiss him as an awkward and unmannered person. Because the judgment of "jitters" is largely out-of-awareness, they will not analyze their reasons for not respecting him, but will feel certain that he is not deserving of respect.

Since conforming to expectations of fidget behavior facilitates cross-cultural interpersonal communication, the individual entering another culture should investigate the nervantics of that society and take steps to control his habitual nervous mannerisms if they would be perceived as inappropriate.

Intercultural research and the study of persuasion

When one contemplates the research in intercultural and international relations that has implications for the process of communication, one is tempted to concur with the anthropologists' observation that culture is essentially communication. Certainly all interactions involve communications, hence the study of intercultural relations is, to a significant degree, the study of intercultural communication. In most research into international procedures and problems, the communication analysis is incidental rather than central, however. The authors of this book firmly believe that the time has come to move in the direction of establishing a system of research efforts oriented to the analysis of intercultural communication as a central objective. Ultimately, we may be able to build a science or at least a discipline, devoted to the problems of communication across cultural, ethnic, and national boundaries.

Significant beginnings of a discipline have been made. Rather than attempting to be comprehensive in cataloging helpful researches into intercultural communication, we will mention three kinds of study that show great promise and supply examples of each. These are (1) the study of values and perceptions, (2) the study of self and contrasting group stereotypes, and (3) description of patterns of thinking and social discourse.

The study of values and perceptions as a basis for intercultural persuasion

The nature of problems encountered while communicating with members of another society can be better understood if the outsider has insight into its values and resulting perceptions. A knowledge of specific values and perceptions in context, characteristic of a homogeneous group of people in particular circumstances, can be an empirical asset to the communicator. Only recently have studies with this narrow, particularized approach been undertaken. Because it is the first of its kind, and because it illustrates the measurement of specific values and perceptions with obvious implications to persuasive and nonpersuasive communication, we will discuss at some length a study by Whitehill and Takezawa, *The Other Worker*.[6] To us it seems a prototype, the kind

[6] A. M. Whitehill, Jr., and S. Takezawa, *The Other Worker* (Honolulu, Hawaii: East-West Center Press, 1968).

of study that might profitably be replicated in other contexts, with different pairs of cultures.

A DUOCULTURAL APPROACH. *The Other Worker* is a study of the values and perceptions of Japanese and United States factory employees. It implements what the study terms "the duocultural approach." Only two cultures are involved, and these are compared in context; the specified circumstances are the role of a worker in a large successful manufacturing industry. Data for the comparison are "worker perceptions," collected from 2,000 rank and file production workers (958 Japanese and 1,042 United States) by questionnaire. Each of the thirty questions in the questionnaire provides four concrete behavioral responses of which the worker chooses one. The "situational-choice" format avoids semantic ambiguities in using abstract value words like "commitment," "loyalty," "obligation," or "fairness." All responses were familiar and acceptable in both cultures.

In *The Other Worker* results of each of the thirty items in the questionnaire are consolidated in a single table. We will cite findings from eight tables, to suggest the nature of the findings and the possibility of using this sort of information in communicating with members of the two populations.

Much more than their United States counterparts, the Japanese workers are motivated to work by a desire "to live up to the expectations of their family, friends and society." United States workers are predominantly motivated by "their responsibility to the company and to co-workers to do whatever is assigned to them."[7]

Sixty-six percent of the Japanese thought of their company as "equal in importance to my personal life," or "of greater importance" as compared with 23 percent of United States workers.[8]

Japanese workers were more willing to accept "rules and disciplinary penalties established by management" (60 percent to 38 percent).[9]

Twenty-three percent of United States workers felt that an unqualified but willing worker should be continued in his position "until he retires or dies" as compared to 55 percent of Japanese workers.[10]

When a worker wishes to marry, 70 percent of Japanese workers believed that his or her superior should "offer personal advice to the worker if requested," while 60 percent of United States workers thought the superior should "not be involved in such a personal matter."[11]

Thirty-two percent of Japanese respondents said that the best manage-

[7] Ibid., p. 106.
[8] Ibid., p. 111.
[9] Ibid., p. 115.
[10] Ibid., p. 139.
[11] Ibid., p. 171.

ment policy is to "avoid, whenever possible, evaluation and comparison of individual performance," compared to 11 percent of United States workers. Seventy-eight percent of United States workers thought management should "make evaluations and comparisons, and inform each worker of both his strengths and weaknesses so he will know where he stands." Thirty-nine percent of Japanese workers shared this belief.[12]

Wages should include extra compensation for either a limited number, or for all members of the family, believed 14 percent of the United States workers and 61 percent of the Japanese.[13]

Forty-nine percent of the Japanese and 21 percent of the United States respondents believed that decisions on problems of promotions, transfer, hours of work, etc., should be by "discussions among supervisors and managers concerning each such problem at the time it arises," while 60 percent of the United States workers and 35 percent of the Japanese wanted "a clearly stated written policy."[14]

When we put together even the few selected fragments of *The Other Worker* study it begins to become apparent that Japanese and American factory workers attach different importance to the same belief, circumstances, or procedure, and that a positive value for one group may be negative for the other. Answers to the questions in the two thousand questionnaires enable us to construct a "value and perception profile" for each group. Studying the profiles makes possible predictions about successful and unsuccessful means of communicating with members of either group, as well as about probable difficulties that will occur when the groups communicate with each other. For the persuader, the profiles supply essential information concerning what is important to the members of the two populations in the context of their work situations. He can treat the heirarchy of values in each profile as a rank order listing of motives to which his messages can appeal.

As we accumulate information concerning the perceptions and values people in varied cultures have about the social, vocational, and professional institutions and organizations in which they play their roles, their messages will take on added meaning for us and our messages to them can be tailored to trigger more predictable responses.

THE STUDY OF SELF AND CONTRASTING GROUP STEREOTYPES. A research project is now underway to ascertain the influence of membership in culture clusters upon intra- and cross-cultural interaction.[15] The

12 Ibid., p. 207.

13 Ibid., p. 249.

14 Ibid., p. 297.

15 F. B. Evans and W. S. Howell, "Exploratory Study of Intercultural Communication in Hawaii" (Project HOE), supported by University of Hawaii, University of Minnesota, and the Ford Foundation.

objective of the study is "to identify and describe barriers to and facilitators of face-to-face communication in the Hawaiian Islands that are caused by the existence of ethnic and religious groups." Professional interviewers collected personal information about each member of a panel representing several ethnic groups. Subjects were male undergraduate students at the University of Hawaii.

The Hawaiian Islands are an excellent place to study intercultural communication because many distinct ethnic groupings are present and each preserves its identity, its customs, and its costumes. In addition, members of all groups speak English, making it possible to study communication within and between cultures without the troublesome language barrier. As an example of the separateness of the ethnic groups, the annual spring beauty contest at the University of Hawaii (Kapalapala) has seven divisions: Chinese, Japanese, Hawaiian, Filipino, Korean, Caucasian, and for those whose ancestry is thoroughly mixed, Cosmopolitan. Each division is a separate contest, and winners do not compete against each other.

An important category of data is the self-perception (self-image) of the "in-group" and the image its members have of contrasting ethnic groups. The investigator can tabulate the discrepancies between the way a group perceives itself and the manner in which a contrasting cultural group perceives it. Since to some extent we see and hear what we expect, communication is distorted by discrepancies between self-image and the perceptions of a different ethnic group. Members of the "in-group," without thinking about it, assume that the outsider perceives them as they see themselves.

To assess self and contrasting ethnic group images the semantic differential was used. A subject rated himself, his best friend, and a typical member of a contrasting ethnic group on the scale. The twenty semantic differential items were adjusted to the population and context as were the items in the Whitehill-Takezawa questionnaire. The "self" and "best friend" ratings were combined in a profile of self-perceptions, and the ratings of "typical members" of a contrasting ethnic group were combined in a profile that represented the way one group perceived the other.

A combined grouping compared Caucasians and non-Caucasians. We will mention a few of the findings from this comparison and show how these might affect communication with or between the groups.

The image of self-rating showed that, with respect to Caucasians, non-Caucasians saw themselves as more religious, sincere, and friendly. But only 29 percent of the non-Caucasians and 35 percent of the Caucasians considered the "religious" category to be important. Over 90 percent of both groups rated sincerity and friendliness as important traits.

With respect to non-Caucasians, Caucasian male undergraduates saw themselves as drinking more often, being more sexy, and working harder. However, the traits of drinking often and being sexy were considered unimportant by both groups. Both Caucasians and non-Caucasians rated being hard working as an important characteristic, 90 and 93 percent, respectively.

When non-Caucasians rated their "best friends" it became apparent that they idealized them. When the non-Caucasian best friend rating was compared to the Caucasian image of the best friend, the non-Caucasian friend was rated higher in being a good friend, polite, friendly, self-confident, a "good guy," good-looking, sincere, athletic, and easy to understand. These are positive traits and except for being good-looking and athletic, all are considered important by the non-Caucasians. In contrast, when the Caucasians rated their best friends, these excelled the non-Caucasian best friends in only two traits, drinking more often and being more religious, neither of which was considered to be important.

To obtain images of contrasting ethnic groups, the non-Caucasians were asked to rate the "typical Caucasian" and the Caucasians were asked to rate a "typical male student of Japanese origin." Caucasians saw the typical Japanese as hard-working, ambitious, polite, and sincere, with all of these receiving a predominantly "important" rating. The non-Caucasians viewed the typical Caucasian male student as talkative, drinking frequently, self-confident, open-minded, good-looking, and conceited. Drinking often and being good-looking were considered unimportant by the non-Caucasians, and over 50 percent rated the remaining traits as important. The trait ascribed to the Caucasians by the non-Caucasians that was rated most important was being open-minded.

Self-perception and perceptions of contrasting ethnic groups as illustrated by the Hawaii study can be related to specific behaviors and can be used to predict responses to messages. Within a culture the same technique can be applied to homogeneous groups whose members interact. In Minneapolis, Minnesota self and contrasting group images were assessed.[16] Four groups were involved: design engineers, production engineers, quality control engineers, and draftsmen. Each group perceived itself differently than any of the other groups perceived it. To improve communication among members of the different groups, all were given information of their self-image and what the others perceived them to be. The result seemed to be that outsiders began to talk to in-group people more realistically, adjusting to the traits they believed themselves to have rather than to characterisics projected upon them.

[16] H. Crawford, "Study of Ethnic Groups in an Industrial Setting," unpublished paper, University of Minnesota, 1967.

DESCRIPTIONS OF PATTERNS OF THINKING AND MODES OF SOCIAL DISCOURSE. People in different cultures set about solving problems in quite different ways. "Being objective" and collecting the facts in the case first, then suspending judgment until the facts are understood, are Western phenomena. Eastern and Middle Eastern peoples assign little importance to evaluation of evidence and the use of logic. Thinking is shaped by the belief that man has free will and controls his destiny, or the belief that man is incapable of modifying the future, that all events are predestined and beyond his influence.

A fatalistic outlook perhaps accounts for an almost total absence of cause-to-effect reasoning in the Arab world. The North American talking with a Lebanese fellow worker in Beirut without thinking about it will base his suggestion for revision of a manufacturing operation on causal relationships. He will expect the Middle Easterner to appreciate the probable change in productivity caused by the recommended procedure. But the Lebanese co-worker will find this extremely difficult to do. The North American might be considerably more persuasive by simply asserting, vigorously, that the new way is better. Strong positive suggestion is a more effective persuasion than is cogent analysis in the Middle East.

Researchers in intercultural communication are confronting the necessity to be systematic and relatively comprehensive in their studies of patterns of thinking and modes of social discourse. As information about subcultures within particular cultures accumulates, methods of relating these to display critical similarities and differences will be developed. To indicate the direction of coming efforts at such integration, we cite as an example the *cognitive matrix*.

Bryant Wedge and Edmund Glenn combined two continua of procedures observable in problem solving and discourse to form a rectangular space in which a culture can be assigned a position. Its location is determined by two variables, and when several cultures are positioned in the matrix, certain similarities and differences become obvious. Table 9–1 shows their matrix, positioning selected national cultures, published in 1968.[17]

Most of the terms on horizontal and vertical axes in table 9–1 will be meaningful to the reader, with the possible exception of two. "Universalism" is a way of thinking in which "global, idealistic theory determines to a very high degree the perception of any kind of evidence."[18] "Association" is a process that links happenings, ideas, and interpretations

---

[17] B. Wedge, "Communication Analysis and Comprehensive Diplomacy" in A. S. Hoffman, ed., *International Communication and the New Diplomacy* (Bloomington, Ind.: Indiana University Press, 1968), p. 41.

[18] Ibid.; p. 40.

Table 9–1

	ASSOCIATION	INTUITION	RATIONALIZING	RATIONAL	ABSTRACT
UNIVERSALISM	Brazil				
DEDUCTION					U.S.S.R.
RELATIONALISM			France		
INDUCTION					
CASE-PARTICULARISM	Dominican Republic				U.S.A.

because they have occurred together, without relationship other than coincidence. Western logic terms this "reasoning from sign."

Wedge explains how a culture or subculture can be assigned a location in the matrix:

> The identification of the most common or modal pattern of thinking and social discourse among a given population is based on the analysis of the styles of argument and presentation which are normally used in attempting to teach or convince others. Such observations may be made in the classroom, in dialogue, and by analysis of written documents.[19]

It would be difficult to identify an area of knowledge more vital to intercultural communication than patterns of thinking and modes of social discourse. Cultures, subcultures, and sub-subcultures will be described with steadily increasing detail and validity as researchers pool their findings. Tools like the Wedge-Glenn cognitive matrix will display pertinent information to the professionals in communication analysis and to international communicators. Research results will be applied in day-to-day intercultural communication to reduce distortion and increase understanding.

Applying results of research to intercultural persuasion

Although results of research as exemplified by the studies cited above would seem to have obvious applications, two prerequisite conditions must be met before information can be used effectively. The North American who would become influential in another culture must understand his own culture with some objectivity. He must accept the relativity of mores and folkways, including his own. Second, he must

[19] Ibid., p. 42.

anticipate and resist a universal tendency to assume that his manners, morals, and methods are best. Until these insights are firmly grasped, his efforts at adaptation will probably be superficial and unconvincing.

Objectifying the premises that shape behavior in our culture and appreciating their arbitrariness and relativity are aided by familiarity with perceptions other peoples have of us. A valuable by-product of travel is the discovery that most of the world's people stereotype us in ways we are reluctant to accept. The contrast between our self-image and the image other peoples project upon us is pertinently summarized as follows:

> An American is a man with energy and drive, Americans say: he is strong and self-confident, yet friendly and straightforward in manner. Alien eyes perceive these same traits. Yet the composite American described by peoples of other cultures is awkward, well meaning, embarrassingly friendly, and, most irritating of all of them, perpetually impatient and possessed of an annoying sense of superiority.[20]

Certainly, perceptions of Americans as a group vary widely, although the stereotype in the preceding quotation generally holds true around the world. After confronting these and other value judgments about Americans, a next step is to become specific about behavior patterns related to the judgments. Here the typical American needs to change his concept of behavioral guidelines from a *category* to a *continuum*, a process that furthers his ability to recognize cultural imperatives as variables. Tables 9–2, 9–3, and 9–4 show three such continua of "appropriate behavior."[21]

To resist the insidious impulse to assume his ways are best, and hence, should be exported, the American can consciously avoid referring to his homeland for guidance and turn to the premises of the other culture in seeking a solution for a problem in that culture. James Lee terms this tendency to look inward the application of a "Self-Reference Criterion."

Table 9–2
Time to Personalize (before doing business)

5 SECONDS		1 DAY		3 WEEKS	
New York	South Dakota	Lebanon	Upper Volta	Hong Kong	Japan

[20] H. Cleveland, G. Mangrove, and J. C. Adams, *The Overseas Americans* (New York: McGraw-Hill & Co., 1960), p. vi.

[21] W. S. Howell, "The Study of Intercultural Communication in Liberal Education," *Pacific Speech Quarterly* 2:4 (May, 1968): 7, 8.

Table 9–3
Being "On Time"

ON THE MINUTE	15 MIN. LATE	30 MIN. LATE	45 MIN. LATE	ONE HOUR LATE	MAY NEVER COME
Germany Switzerland Scandinavia	U.S.	French Switzerland	Italian Switzerland	Brazil	Java Colombia

He advocates the following "SRC-free" approach for businessmen operating in a strange culture:

Step 1. Define the business problem or goal in terms of the American cultural traits, habits or norms.

Step 2. Define the business problem or goal in terms of the foreign cultural traits, habits and norms. Make no value judgments.

Step 3. Isolate the SRC influence in the problem and examine it carefully to see how it complicates the problem.

Step 4. Redefine the problem without the SRC influence and solve for the optimum business goal situation.[22]

Applying an adaptation of the "SRC-free" formula to a problem of intercultural persuasion would at least bring cultural influences into awareness. Depending on the information the visitor has about the foreign community and his sensitivity to the local situation, he will be able to convey messages of increased persuasiveness.

In the late twentieth century several varieties of intercultural persuasion engage United States citizens. Domestically, minority groups are busily persuading what they consider to be social justice, and majorities are persuading minorities in the direction of peaceful cooperation.

Table 9–4
Relationship between Age and Authority

VERY LITTLE		SOME		A HIGH CORRELATION
U.S. West Coast	N.Y.	U.S. Mid-West	Africa India	The Orient

---

[22] J. A. Lee, "Cultural Analysis in Overseas Operation," *Harvard Business Review* 44: 2 (March/April 1966): 110.

Abroad, three major areas of intercultural persuasion are diplomacy, military assistance, and aid to developing countries. The three areas have benefited from research in intercultural communication, although application of research results is found to be most advanced in aid to developing countries. A few examples will show results possible from these applications.

American diplomats are often puzzled because a signature to a treaty seems to be honored by diplomats from some countries in all circumstances but is binding to other diplomats only under certain conditions. In particular, commitments by Russians, orally and on paper, have caused misunderstanding. Probably United States diplomats fail to understand the Russian promise. One of the authors traveled in the Soviet Union with several other professors and noticed that the interpreter, a graduate of Moscow University Law School, would often promise to do something requested by a member of the group, then do nothing about it. When the interpreter was asked to explain this behavior the reply indicated that it would be impolite to reject a professor's request. The Russian way, he explained is to always say "yes." Since many requests are impulsive and unrealistic, both parties dismiss them on second thought, and face is saved. If the professor has a reasonable request and it is important to him he will come back and ask it again. After approximately the third attempt, the interpreter said he would begin to consider taking some action.

Evidence from other analyses of patterns of discourse in the USSR support the interpreter's explanation. It would seem unwise for a diplomat representing the United States in a conference to attach great significance to the Russian representative's first tentative monosyllable of affirmation. Further, Russians tolerate displays of emotion that we would label "tantrum behavior," explaining that it is healthy and helpful to express one's self freely and openly. When Premier Khrushchev, visiting the United States, showed his displeasure by taking off his shoe and pounding the table at the United Nations, Americans may have distorted the meaning of the act by interpreting it in the framework of our culture rather than his.

Military advisors from the United States are increasingly using research results in their persuasion overseas. The following is a concrete example of the application of information about values and perceptions of a culture to military communication.

> In each cultural pattern, experiences are organized by means of certain concepts. Western European and U.S. cultures, for instance, employ a subject-predicate relationship, clearly separating the agent both from his actions and the context in which they occur. Then cultural

focal points allow for the development of separate abstractions such as the individual and his feelings, and various kinds of activities in which he may engage.

Practically speaking, in the case of the military profession, the American can readily separate tactical and logistical problems and consider each problem by itself. An even more fundamental distinction can be made between military and political or social problems in a war like that being fought in Viet Nam.

The Chinese, however, do not have clear parallels for such abstractions. They do not recognize the subject-predicate relationship, and do not clearly distinguish between the individual and his thoughts and feelings, the individual and his actions, and the context in which these occur. The Chinese mind is concrete and he is situation-centered to a degree unbelievable to a Westerner. He does not derive laws and principles that presumably govern events in the way that the Westerner does. In the writings of Mao Tse-tung we read that the laws of war are different according to the character of the war, its time, its place, and the nation.[23]

Military advisors abroad are in continuous, task-oriented interpersonal communication with host nationals. What they can accomplish is almost totally dependent on their ability to win the willing cooperation of the people they are attempting to guide. The persuasion they plan and execute must be in the framework of the strange culture. Information like Stewart well-stated distinctions between Chinese and Western conceptualizations of the individual and his task is essential if the ends of persuasion are to be achieved.

Perhaps the most dramatic examples of using or failing to use knowledge about other people and their ways of living in intercultural persuasion are found in programs of aid to developing countries. The Agency for International Development (AID) and the Peace Corps are United States agencies that have sponsored extensive, global efforts to supply know-how, guidance, and material goods to nations wishing to accelerate economic, health, and social progress. Typically, natives of the United States enter the underdeveloped nation and work for periods of years with natives to secure acceptance of innovations. Because these programs are associated with universities, their expertise has been interdisciplinary. Anthropology, sociology, social psychology, psychology, linguistics, speech, journalism, foreign languages, and many other academic fields of study have contributed information about cultures and modes of communication. Field experiences of workers have been

---

[23] E. C. Stewart, "American Advisors Overseas," *Military Review* 45:2 (February, 1965): 8.

studied, some data collection has been "built into" the dissemination of innovation, and returning workers have been used to train their replacements so that their firsthand learning from experience will not be wasted. As a result, representatives of the United States in development programs overseas are probably the most effective intercultural persuaders.

It is exciting and informative to read about the success and failure of well-intentioned Americans trying to innovate in a strange culture. When a local population feels no need for the improvement the agency wishes to introduce, the need for locally adapted persuasion occurs. From 1937 to 1948 a campaign was waged in northern Nigeria among the Hausa people to eliminate sleeping sickness by controlling the tsetse fly.[24] The means of control was cutting brush along the streams. Compulsion was used, the brush was cut, sleeping sickness was eliminated. But because the people believed sleeping sickness to be caused by spirits, they saw no connection between stream clearance and improved health. Hence, after ten years, all the village headmen testified that they would stop the brush cutting if the threat of punishment were removed. Though desired results were achieved there was no permanence to the change because felt needs of the people were not involved. Persuasion based on motivations of those being persuaded was not accomplished.

Community development in India challenges ingenuity of Western innovators because of the complexity and strangeness of values and beliefs. An outbreak of smallpox in a village of Kalahaedi district of Orissa State brought in a Western vaccinator who was unable to make the people understand what vaccination was and the need for it.[25] The villagers assigned a name to the medical aid, "The one who makes the babies cry." Meanwhile the local priest had prescribed the sacrifice of a goat followed by a feast to appease the Goddess Thalerani who was angry. Later the medical aid and a social worker, recognizing the power of local leadership, approached the priest to request his help in securing cooperation of the people in vaccinating their children against smallpox. As a result, the priest called the villagers together, worked himself into a frenzy to again contact the Goddess, and announced that she would save only children "vaccinated with a magic herb." The vaccination proceeded smoothly, as the priest proved to be an excellent channel to the people. He endorsed hygiene practices in his religious services and

[24] H. Miner "Culture Change Under Pressure: A Hausa Case" in A. H. Niehoff, ed., A Casebook of Social Change (Chicago: Aldine Publishing Co., 1966), pp. 109–17.

[25] E. P. Link and S. Mehta, "A New Goddess for an Old," A Casebook of Social Change, pp. 219–24.

soon was, in effect, a member of the health team. Here persuasion was successful because local authorities and lines of communication were respected and used. Any attempt to bypass the existing network of social control would have guaranteed failure.

In 1965 in Northeast Thailand aid programs for community development were overlaid with a special urgency because Communist cadres from Laos were operating in the same area. To learn how to communicate effectively with the villagers, USOM (United States Special Operations Mission to Thailand) imported research teams from the United States. Written messages were rejected for communication because of under 40 percent literacy. Pictures (slides, motion pictures, posters) were ineffective because the target audience had not seen pictorial representation of things and people and were unable to interpret this medium. Simplified stick figures were tried as a simple representational device. These also failed.

Finally, the investigators noticed that every Thai peasant in a rice paddy had a transistor radio plugged into his ear. What were they listening to? The favorite program was a man-woman team on a local station who played native instruments, sang, and told stories, many of which were pornographic. A listening survey revealed that over 90 percent of adults in Northeast Thai villages listened to this one program every day. The channel of communication the researchers were seeking was immediately obvious. USOM hired the two popular performers to weave desired messages into their daily programs.[26]

It seems obvious that the problems of communicating with people outside our environment are culture-based. Differing values, contrasting sets of expectations and unlike perceptions of the nature of human interaction cause misunderstanding. These are cultural differences. If no one had to converse with anyone who was born and lived to a teen age at a spot more than five miles distant, communication problems would be fewer. We should establish a high priority for culture-based studies of interpersonal communication; then we can learn to apply the findings to the improvement of communication among the varied citizens of our world.

Conclusion

All cultures, and national cultures in particular, have a vested interest in persuasion as a means of preserving and propagating their beliefs

[26] From an interview with Dr. Orlin Schoville, USOM official in Bangkok, in April, 1965.

and values. Military means of advancing a life style have become too costly to be practical. Competing political ideologies necessarily rely on formulating their offerings as attractively as possible to appeal to an uncommitted audience. Arensberg and Niehoff summarize the implications of this state of affairs to the West, and to the United States:

> No American or any other Westerner, whether a government official, a private businessman, or a missionary, can enforce his presence or impose his ideas on the people he is working with if they don't want him there. National sovereignty is the rule now, which means that *change must be accepted voluntarily by the host people.*[27]

The mode of life we prefer can compete in the world market *only* if it is advanced by effective persuasion. The people who represent us need more than knowledge in their technical specializations. In addition, they must understand the process of persuasion and be skilled in its execution. These are conscious talents, not arrived at intuitively. Arensberg and Niehoff summarize:

> It is our belief that the insights for cross-cultural interaction must be lifted above the level of intuitive judgment. The brain surgeon must use his best judgment for each individual operation, but this judgment is based on thorough prior knowledge of the nature of the human body, the characteristics of infection, the uses of various drugs, and all the other aspects of medicine which make him an M.D. We believe that the social engineer, the government technician, the foundation representative, the missionary and the businessman, should also have all the knowledge that is available about the nature of human society and culture before he begins to administer new ideas, which constitute the medicine of social change.[28]

The future of a free society may well depend on the study and practice of intra-cultural and intercultural persuasion.

[27] C. M. Arensberg, and A. H. Niehoff, *Introducing Social Change* (Chicago, Ill.: Aldine Publishing Co., 1964), p. 3.

[28] Ibid., p. 6.

10

The ethical dimension of persuasion

Introduction

In a political campaign one candidate sends "volunteers" to work in his rival's office. They manage to obstruct progress of the rival's efforts and act as spies in providing detailed information to the other side.

Uncle Ferd on a popular children's television program tells his audience, "Ask mommy to buy Toasted Tootsies for your breakfast. Tell her it is the best tasting cereal with a prize in every package. Uncle Ferd wants you to eat Toasted Tootsies every day, so you can grow up big and strong. Don't eat any other cereals. Scream for Toasted Tootsies!" Whereupon the children in the studio scream, and wave their packages of Toasted Tootsies.

A wife makes a special request of her husband that he attend a Parent Teachers Association meeting which is to discuss a problem related to difficulties their son Stephen is having in fourth grade. The husband says, "I'll make a deal. I'll go if I can have two nights out in the next two weeks, no questions asked. OK?"

A father offers to buy his son a motorcycle if he will stop dating his current girl friend. Permanently.

The above hypothetical examples of attempts to influence may or may not seem improper to a reader. At least some of us experience distaste, revulsion, resentment, anger, or mild to strong disapproval when we encounter efforts to persuade that resemble these instances. Often without understanding our own response to persuasion we feel that something is wrong. We are intuitively making ethical judgments, rejecting persuasion because it falls short of our standards of fairness, decency, honesty, or openness.

Feeling our way to moral judgments of actions of others and of ourselves is helpful and necessary but unreliable. A systematic and conscious process of assessing the ethical quality of persuasive attempts would be better. The present chapter discusses several approaches to the thoughtful criticism of ethics of persuasion. Our goal is to equip the reader with a variety of criteria and methods of applying them, to be used when he finds them helpful in making ethical decisions about persuasion.

A philosophical base for an ethics of persuasion

Before we can proceed to the details of structuring a system of ethics for persuasion we must postulate a relationship between morality and rhetoric. When we have justified linking these concepts in theory we will examine other philosophical implications and the pragmatic application of our ethical system.

Morality, culture, and persuasion

In 1963 Wallace called attention to the intimate but frequently ignored relationship of ethics and rhetoric: "First, rhetorical theory must deal with the substance of discourse as well as with structure and style. Second, the basic materials of discourse are (1) ethical and moral values and (2) information relative to these."[1] Later in this article Wallace elaborated on those "ethical and moral values" by showing that moral imperatives are derived from whatever institutions and concepts are important to a society. Propositions asserted to be of value to individuals or groups are advanced most effectively by "good reasons," supporting material in harmony with cultural values. Wallace says, "One can scarcely declare that something is desirable without showing its relevance to values. . . . One could do worse than characterize rhetoric as the art of finding and effectively presenting good reasons."[2]

The sources of morality in rhetoric (or persuasion) are then to be sought in the values of a society, and the ethical dimension of persuasive discourse looms large indeed. Changes of cultural values imply modified ethical standards, and perpetuation of central, long-lasting values implies semi-universal standards—for a particular cultural unit.

The conceptualization of morals and values as basic to rhetoric was extended by Burgess: "While rhetoric derives its unique strategic dimension from itself, its moral dimension ultimately derives from culture, considered as a system of moral demands. The mediator between the two is moral purpose that strategic purpose simply serves."[3]

The key to an ethical system is found in the stipulated definition of culture as a system of moral demands. All persuasion has moral purpose by virtue of its existence within a culture, and its response to the demands of that culture becomes a measure of its ethical quality.

Viewing persuasion as an attempt to meet the moral demands of its culture (to deal with desirability) and the strategic demands of a situation (to deal with the possible) settles an old dispute as to whether

---

[1] Karl R. Wallace, "The Substance of Rhetoric: Good Reasons," *Quarterly Journal of Speech* 49 (October, 1963): 240.

[2] Ibid., p. 248.

[3] Parke G. Burgess, "The Rhetoric of Moral Conflict: Two Critical Dimensions," *Quarterly Journal of Speech* 56 (April, 1970): 126.

persuasion is moral, immoral, or amoral. It is none of these, says Burgess, it is *metamoral*: "Lying literally 'beyond' the moral yet without negating its influence in rhetoric, a metamoral perspective would most invite analysis of the rhetoric of moral conflict, whether generated by traditionalists, by radicals, or, indeed, by reactionaries."[4]

In culture X at time Y and in situation Z, the persuader makes his moral and strategic choices. If his recommendation is in harmony with cultural values in his audience, and if his means of advancing the recommendation are acceptable, again in terms of the moral demands in the community, his choices accumulate morality and can be judged ethical. The strategies are judged by more tangible consequences. If the proposition is accepted by the audience as possible and desirable, then the strategies are successful, that is, they have merit.

To serve as the key organizing principle for an ethics of persuasion, the concept *moral demands* requires further analysis. There are three identifiable levels of moral demands in any culture: (1) sets of expectations, (2) assumptions, and (3) values.

Sets of expectations, which were discussed in chapter 9, are patterns of verbal and nonverbal behavior routinely appropriate to specific situations in a culture. For example, in New York it is expected that two executives will begin to discuss a proposed transaction almost immediately after meeting. In Tokyo it is expected that business will be discussed only after a prolonged period, often several weeks, of socializing and getting acquainted. Meeting the demands imposed by sets of expectations is a moral imperative and violating them is to some degree unethical.

Assumptions in a culture are *not* situational, as are sets of expectations. Stewart makes this important distinction:

> Cultural assumptions may be defined as abstract, organized and
> general concepts which pervade a person's outlook and behavior. . . .
> For example, the middle-class American usually thinks of himself
> as an individual, the world as inanimate, success as his goal, impersonal
> cooperation with others as desirable, and *doing* as his preferred activity.[5]

The people in a culture take for granted that assumptions such as those cited by Stewart are universally believed and understood. Typically, the discovery that members of another culture or subculture live by quite different assumptions comes as a surprise. The Micronesian who

4 Ibid., p. 124.

5 Edward C. Stewart, *American Cultural Patterns: A Cross-Cultural Perspective* (Pittsburg, Pa.: Regional Council for International Education, 1971), pp. 10, 11.

knows only communal belongings cannot respect a Westerner's private property rights. The North American who sharply separates work and play finds it difficult to understand that his Latin American associate makes no such distinction.

Assumptions are not readily identified or described by either the member of a culture or by his visitor because their influence is exerted out-of-awareness. Although the general principles that shape appropriate behavior are seldom articulated, these unspoken premises of a culture are no less effective than those which are talked about. The norm of behavior that is out-of-awareness is probably a more potent producer of rigid conformity than is the rule that is subjected to discussion and criticism.

Assessing assumptions in a particular culture necessitates first bringing them into conscious awareness. This can be done by locating a uniform pattern of appropriate behavior and constructing the premises that must have been followed to produce it. For example, in America we can observe that, in general, those who come earliest to any of a variety of functions or activities are waited on before the latecomers. We can conclude that Americans believe the assumption that it is proper in many different contexts to live by the principle "first come, first served."

Quite obviously, persuasion that goes contrary to basic assumptions violates the morality of its culture. If a persuader were to advocate behavior that requires giving preferential treatment to latecomers and ignoring those who have waited patiently, he would defy a normative moral demand of twentieth century America, hence he would deserve ethical criticism.

Values are those premises defining appropriate general behavior which are *within the awareness* of a cultural group. People talk about them, codes of ethics display them, and conforming to them becomes both a duty and a source of pride. Values come from revered documents like a national constitution, from agencies such as churches, schools, and public service organizations, and most importantly, from the historical antecedents of a cultural unit. When we try to explain our way of life, we attempt to summarize the current system of values that predominates in the culture with which we most identify. When we talk about differences among cultural or ethnic groups, we typically compare and contrast their patterns of values.

Obviously, values play a particularly important role in contributing to the moral demands of a culture. Achievement is a high-ranking American value, while in many other cultures it is of little importance. In fact, in most of the world's cultures achievement is not an assumption or a factor in shaping sets of expectations. Cooperation and "fair play" are respected

American values. Belief in representative government, that it is important to be liked, that progress is necessary and desirable are other American convictions that enjoy uniformly high-value status.

Extending the list of American values suggests the complexity of ethical considerations in persuasion. Americans believe in equality, freedom of choice, the unique value of the individual, and his responsibility for his own fate. They know the value of work for its own sake, the importance of getting things done "on time," the importance of quantifying and comparing consequences of individual and group performance, and the importance of winning in whatever competition one may engage. Success can best be measured, they believe, by wealth and personal possessions. Americans recognize the desirability of holding religious convictions and of actively supporting with money and participation some unit of some organized religion. They have faith in majority rule, systematic problem solving and decision making, and prefer doing rather than becoming. It is important to have a large number of friendships, though none need be intimate or long-lasting. These and other values form the basis of many social motives in America as was discussed in chapter 5.

When Wallace and Burgess refer to "ethical and moral values" we believe that they include all demands in a culture that are generated by its complex sets of expectations, assumptions, and values. The perpetuation of a culture, including an orderly evolution of its expectation-assumption-value system, is the ultimate moral imperative in that society. Thus whatever contributes to a culture's perpetuation and orderly growth *is* ethical.

Moral contribution to a culture needs further explanation. An ethically adequate persuasion is more than just compatible with its culture. Moral persuasion has positive *social utility*. Socially useful communication increases the *survival potential* of a community. This kind of persuasion carefully assesses the short-range and long-range consequences of the communicative act, including the benefits to and negative effects on the group and on particular individuals. Socially useful persuasion, then, should benefit most of the people involved in long- or short-term consequences, with minimum harm to individuals. "Benefits" and "harm" are defined in terms of the culture's ongoing value system, and thus can be described as *cultural-specific*. What is useful in one culture may well be detrimental in another.

The above philosophical view of factors contributing to ethical decisions we would label a *metamoral perspective*. By "metamoral" we mean that it goes beyond formulas and rules to first principles and in itself constitutes a theory of culture-based morality. It can be applied to the process of persuasion in whatever form it takes, wherever it may occur.

We recognize that a case can be made for universal ethical standards and that our position denies this possibility. We believe, however, that the variability of applied ethical standards around the world cries to be understood. The quest for one or more fixed moral rules seems unimportant by comparison.

Pragmatism, idealism, and persuasion

Much more energy has been expended in perfecting notions of what human behavior *should* be, in a moral sense, than in assessing what current morality *is*. Reformers dangle utopian goals before an audience of sinners but offer little help in the self-analysis that is necessary for an individual to plan his step-by-step progress toward one of those ideals.

The authors believe that idealism can modify behavior effectively only when combined with pragmatics. We contend that the sensible route to a more ethical persuasion is to first inventory the strengths and shortcomings of present practices, then to decide what should be changed to facilitate progress toward a desired behavior. The pragmatic approach permits specific adjustment to situations and people, and the idealistic elements provide directional guidance. Combining pragmatism with idealism enables the change agent to cope with human problems realistically.

Changes in ethical practices come slowly and in tiny steps, with probable periods of regression. An ideal is seldom if ever attained. The pragmatic view is that progress in a desired direction is all that can be expected or hoped for at a given time.

When applied to the study of ethics, pragmatism and idealism yield two separate yet supplementary procedures which we categorize as *descriptive* and *prescriptive* methods. How they differ in purpose and implementation and how each is necessary to the constructive application of the other is our next concern.

DESCRIPTIVE ETHICS. One way to examine the morality of any behavior is to attempt to answer the question: "What ethical principles must have contributed to the making of decisions in this situation?" Instead of concentrating on what *should* be done we attempt to ascertain what *was* done. From information about particular decision making, we can identify the moral demands that were met. An analysis of a number of representative decisions in a category of behavior, for example the selling of encyclopedias, reveals the ethical criteria functioning in that body of persuasion. This method illustrates the descriptive ethics approach.

We should concern ourselves about present standards because an understanding of the nature of the status quo is helpful in deciding how to improve. Any planned change moves from somewhere to somewhere else. Without knowing your starting point, you cannot know the length of your journey or the direction to take. Modification in applied ethics is a "patching" procedure—the glaring deficiencies should be treated first.

Another reason for using descriptive ethics is that similar operations in the same culture often have sharply differing ethical norms. Persuasion in political campaigning has lower ethical standards than does persuasion in the United States Senate. Practices accepted in the selling of used cars in the United States, if used by a salesman of new refrigerators, would be sufficiently unethical to ensure his loss of employment. Differences such as these will go unrecognized and unappreciated unless ethics of particular persuasive endeavors are examined descriptively.

We believe that the pragmatics of ethics have been neglected and that this omission can be corrected only by devoting much more time and effort to descriptive studies. Only in this way can a society draw its "ethics profile" to display, in the words of Wallace, "the desirable, the obligatory, and the admirable or praiseworthy, and their opposites."[6]

PRESCRIPTIVE ETHICS.   The ethical advice that predominates in all cultures *prescribes* what conduct is desirable. Although the medical prescription is adjusted to specific symptoms, prescribed morality purports to be universal.

Moral rules (prescriptions) are ideals of behavior that express a culture. How are they formulated? Thoughtful scholars reflect on the potentials of humanity, the purposes of God and man, the organizing principles of their society, their own prejudices and vested interests; then they compose the "should" and "ought" statements which, if they were acted on, would supposedly be good for everybody.

There are several practical problems in applying moral rules. Of course, the scholars may have goofed, and what they claim to be good for everybody may actually be good for only a few. The high level of abstraction in the phrasing of ethical prescriptions makes it difficult and frustrating for the man in the street who attempts to benefit from their wisdom. "Honesty is the best policy" seems clear as long as no situations are encountered in which being honest has disadvantages. But when a layman needs moral guidance most, when a tiny white lie would see him safely through a crisis, it becomes obvious that the maxim lacks precision. Does it mean that honesty *is* the best policy always, usually, or sometimes? And "policy" is confusing. A policy is something that seems to permit exceptions, but how many? Treating the statement as an

6 Wallace, "The Substance of Rhetoric," p. 244.

absolute makes no sense either. Everyone knows of famous and praise-worthy people who saved a life or their country by timely misrepresentation of facts. When you come to a difficult fork in the road, turning to a moral rule for guidance leaves much to be desired. You may solve your problem, but seldom by literal application of the rule. Your frustration may leave you quite willing to accept the rationalization that is most attractive to you at the time.

On the other hand, granting that much adaptation, reinterpretation, and redefinition are necessary to modify prescriptive advice into something useful in the specific instance, moral rules are important because they express the essence of a culture. For example, the importance and uniqueness of the individual person is central to American society, and this value yields many items of prescriptive advice. One sweeping generalization is represented by Nilsen as a summation of the concept of "good" in this culture: "Whatever develops, enlarges, enhances human personalities is good; whatever restricts, degrades or injures human personalities is bad."[7] Nilsen suggests that using this concept of the good as a basis for ethical judgments commits one "to a teleological or utilitarian theory of ethics." The present authors would add that such a commitment is in harmony with many values of contemporary America.

To illustrate the intimate relationship of "essence of the culture" concepts and moral prescriptions we will cite a somewhat parallel and contrasting instance in Japan. In Japanese society the concept of "good" for the individual person is "saving face," an inadequate translation of the notion that a person's image, self-respect, and reputation are more important than his other attributes.

Kleinjahns relates the experience of an American architect who contributed to the design of a science building for International Christian University in Tokyo. The workability of some of his designs was in doubt, and the resolution of the problem is reported as follows by Kleinjahns: "Since one of the Japanese scientists on the faculty was going to New York, he was asked to see the architect and talk the thing over. When he came back he reported that he felt the university was obliged to use the architect's original scheme in order to save his face."[8]

We could reword the Japanese concept of individual good to parallel Nilsen's American-oriented statement: "Whatever safeguards and en-

[7] Thomas R. Nilsen, *Ethics of Speech Communication* (New York: Bobbs-Merrill, 1966), p. 9.

[8] Everett Kleinjahns, "Communicating with Asia" in Larry A. Samovar and Richard E. Porter, *Intercultural Communication: A Reader* (Belmont, Calif.: Wadsworth Publishing Co., 1972), p. 259.

hances a person's 'face' is good, whatever harms or injures a person's 'face' is bad." To complete the contrast we note that the use of this generalization as a basis for an ethical judgment commits the user to a nonutilitarian view in which the feelings of the individual outweigh all other considerations.

Compiling representative collections of prescriptive ethical statements is a good way to compare the value systems of cultures. Major similarities and differences become immediately apparent, and the implications for generalized behavioral standards can be inferred. The study of comparative prescriptive ethics may advance our understanding of intercultural communication.

But prescriptive ethics is most useful when combined with a descriptive approach. When current ethical practices of a particular category of persuasion in a culture are defined through description, prescriptions—that is, that culture's moral demands—supply goals and guidelines for change.

Popular American approaches to ethical problems in persuasion

This section of the present chapter is culture-bound. Because the majority of our readers will be Americans, and because space will not permit detailed examination of ethical systems around the globe, we are choosing to survey and summarize only American attempts to build a system of persuasive ethics. The following categories and examples are typical of criteria used by critics and practitioners of persuasion in the mid-twentieth century United States.

Forbidden words

The simplest way to improve the relative morality of an utterance is to eliminate words and phrases that are taboo. Polite social usage has resulted from a long history of word censorship by church, school, and other civilizing agencies. Euphemisms are one result of censoring certain explicit uses of language. Certainly persuasion that conforms carefully to a polite vocabulary would be ethically good in one concrete sense.

The practice of using certain symbols to produce a response of rejection has been labeled "name-calling." It was one of the seven propaganda devices specified by the Institute for Propaganda Analysis. The term has come to have such a negative sanction that to use the technique of name-calling in persuasion is in itself often considered unethical.

Not as clearly negative as name-calling, but a member of the same family, is the concept of "loaded words." There are many degrees of connotative meaning, but it is generally agreed that extreme "loading" or relying on the emotional impact of words rather than their referential meanings smacks of the unethical in persuasion.

Listing and avoiding forbidden symbols are aids to ethics, but this is only a fragment of our problem. Through subtle suggestion, an intelligent but unprincipled persuader can convey a message without using forbidden terms, name-calling, or heavily loaded words. Advertisers have seldom found the inability to use a particular phrase a severe handicap in conveying it to the public. Control of symbols amounts to little or no control over goals and methods of the modern persuader. The key to wise ethical decisions lies elsewhere.

Shameful deceptions

Because attempts to deceive the persuadee are numerous, it may be helpful to describe and classify some tricks of the trade. The Institute for Propaganda Analysis offers four ways to deceive: (1) "glittering generality," the unsupported sweeping statement; (2) "the plain folks device," the attempt to appear as an ordinary person to disarm the persuadee; (3) "card-stacking," the selective distortion of an issue by presenting it in an unfair, one-sided fashion; and (4) "bandwagon," the technique of inducing people to go along, not because of the merits of your proposition but because you apply the social pressure resulting from adoption of your recommendation by many other people. A fifth instance from the Institute for Propaganda Analysis is that of "transfer," which may or may not be ethical depending on the nature of the transfer of qualities from one example or context to another. Certainly using the American flag and patriotic songs to enhance a commercial's appeal by simply meshing them together could be a shameful deception.

A brand of deception that caught the fancy of the American public was the concealed persuasive effort, particularly that disguised as entertainment, information, or inspiration. A best-selling book titled *The Hidden Persuaders*[9] was published by Vance Packard in 1957. Packard alerted his readers to many varieties of influence they had not previously identified, and he attempted to so instruct them that they would be more able to detect and resist concealed persuasive messages.

Haiman picked up Vance Packard's idea and treated it in more scholarly fashion. His definition of this nefarious business of hidden persuasion and his reasoning leading to the conclusion that it is unethical appeared in a 1958 article:

---

[9] Vance Packard, *The Hidden Persuaders* (New York: David McKay Publishing Co., 1957).

Who is the hidden persuader and how does he differ from the ordinary advocate? He can best be defined by describing the common denominator of his techniques. Whether they be subliminal cues, mass hypnosis, constant repetition, loaded language, the subtle use of social pressures, or the appeal to irrelevant loves, hates and fears, they all seek the same kind of response from the listener or viewer. They attempt to make him buy, vote, or believe in a certain way by short-circuiting his conscious thought processes and planting suggestions or exerting pressures on the periphery of his consciousness which are intended to produce automatic, non-reflective behavior. The methods are similar to those of Pavlov's famous conditioned-reflex with dogs. Ring a bell and the dog salivates. No thought processes intervene here. Non-critical reflex action—this is the goal of the hidden persuader.[10]

While Haiman develops an impressive indictment of concealed persuasion, two circumstances deny the wisdom of applying this criterion. First, much obvious persuasion is in effect "hidden" because its consumers fail to recognize it as persuasion. Second, the out-of-awareness processing of data that is coming to be recognized as part of the critical thinking process makes it difficult and less meaningful to classify persuasion as concealed or revealed. The perceptual criterion is of little help here, for persuasion in a message may be apparent to one receiver and totally unperceived by another. In addition, a significant part of every persuasive interaction is embodied in context and personal relationships that are not commonly included as components in the act of persuasion. Nevertheless Haiman and Packard have a point worth remembering. Concealing your persuasion cannot be said to increase its ethical quality!

A simpler approach to the practice of unethical deception is to list specific acts that are normatively in conflict with the goals of American society. With the passing years such lists are becoming rarer and shorter. One of the few survivors is advanced by Minnick, who says:

> ... the following means of persuasion are generally agreed to be unethical:
> 1. Falsifying or fabricating evidence
> 2. Distorting evidence
> 3. Conscious use of specious reasoning
> 4. Deceiving the audience about the intent of the communication.[11]

[10] Franklyn S. Haiman, "Democratic Ethics and the Hidden Persuaders," *Quarterly Journal of Speech* 44 (December, 1958): 385.

[11] Wayne C. Minnick, *The Art of Persuasion*, 2nd ed., (Boston: Houghton Mifflin Co., 1968), p. 285.

The reader will note that the unethical practices listed by Minnick are stated from the point of view of the persuader, and represent his intent, that is, his conscious choices of evidence and reasoning. In this same frame he later advances a fifth criterion: "An ethical advocate is obliged to reject propositions which, when tested by his best thinking, prove to have a low truth-probability."[12]

This last standard lacks utility because low probabilities are better than none, and often, because of the unavailability of better evidence, should be used. The first four are generally sound, but there are many exceptions as Minnick would undoubtedly agree. Most of the time the advice to avoid these specified deceptions is good counsel, but careless application of these suggestions as absolutes, to test the ethical soundness of all instances of persuasion, is absurd. Just as telling the literal truth often amounts to extreme and unnecessary cruelty, belief that certain practices are bad per se can lead to damaging and even unethical results.

The cult of reason

Writers dealing with the ethical problems of persuasion have tended to dwell on the so-called psychological techniques of influencing people. What is not as generally recognized is the smaller but almost equally evangelical counter-movement we call the cult of reason. Advocates of this view believe that the hard core of solutions to ethical (and many other) problems of persuasion is to be found in a rigorous interpretation of the maxim, "stick to the facts." According to the advocates of this approach, if we as persuaders limit our evidence to what we know for sure, and our rhetoric to reasoning according to strict logical forms, we will become ethical. The zeal of the person dedicated to reason is often as irrational as are many of the targets of his criticism.

Honesty, including revealed intent, is paramount to the cult of reason. Concealed purpose is considered to be inherently unethical. Secondary characteristics of the cult of reason include the elimination of emotional appeals, emotive language, and all communication that tends to stimulate the secretion of adrenalin rather than reflective thought. This approach assumes that the persuadee is capable of setting aside his prejudices and focusing his intellect on an issue, and it tries to provide every incentive for him to do just that. There are obvious values in being factual and logical, but much human conduct is nonlogical. Choices are made frequently on bases other than those of evidence and reason, which, though involved, are not deciding factors.

12 Ibid., p. 286.

The cult of reason evangelist fails to recognize the need for supplementing his scientific method with known behavioral tendencies derived from psychology, sociology, philosophy, and other studies dealing with nonlogical conduct. A realistic middle ground would be to increase the emphasis on facts and logic but to rely on them only where they are clearly pertinent. For example, don't expect logical analysis to change religious convictions.

Since at least a great many decisions made by people are more nonlogical than logical, the voluntary self-limitation of the persuader to the tools of facts and reason may purify his ethics but do little for his effectiveness (which is also a matter of ethics, since he may not have the moral right to be ineffective in a crisis). Quite possibly he may misrepresent the facts of his case through attempting to reason logically about matters of nonlogical motivation.

The deception of such pseudologic in persuasion, while not a part of the cult of reason, has prospered because of the prestige won by reasoned discourse. The speaker says, "Now let's be logical and look at the record," then presents a complicated pattern that confuses his audience. He later draws a conclusion with appropriate "therefores" and "because of's" which he asserts to be logically inevitable. This intentional trickery is only a small step from the persuasion of a person attempting to reason about nonlogical matters with too little information to satisfy the requirements of reason. He has his conclusion to begin with, and the temptation is great to claim for it a purely logical development. Intentional and unintentional pseudologic grow out of extreme reliance on evidence and its logically patterned manipulation. Increasing the reasoned discourse content of a communication has some bearing on its ethical qualities, but the relationship is not close. Other factors that we can term nonlogical are of at least equal importance.

Ethics of the "end that justifies the means"

A popular indictment of ethics in persuasion is found in the statement that "some unprincipled rascal is letting the end justify the means." In other words, the desirability of the goal is so great that the persuader considers the use of shady tactics to be necessary and therefore ethical. A universal implication is that the end should not be used to justify the means.

Yet great students of human behavior, for example, Aristotle and John Dewey, have told us with devastating and simple proofs that the purpose of persuasion can be a sound justification of the techniques used to reach it. If the end does not justify the means, what can? Obviously total rejection of the principle that one should study his desired objective in judging the ethics of his method is absurd. Studied in context, the end can serve as a most excellent and meaningful check on the ethical legitimacy of the means.

Evaluating means of persuasion in terms of their goal is a first step in establishing an ethical base. This has gained an unsavory reputation probably because of partial and selfish estimation of end results. The end includes immediate and long-term effects, from the persuader's viewpoint and from the point of view of all other people whose lives will be touched directly or indirectly by the persuasion. If we justify means solely by personal, immediate benefits, ignoring such items as injury to others, we are misapplying the perfectly good procedure of examining the end to determine (partially) the ethical quality of the means.

We say partially, because this good principle is far from the complete story. Highly moral ends sometimes encourage immoral means; an extreme example is the willingness of some reformers to resort to physical force, torture, and execution to achieve their goal. Methods themselves must meet many ethical standards (for example, humanitarian and social). The zealous proponent of a good cause must continually review his methods to be sure that he is not slipping into practices he himself would condemn when used for a "lesser" purpose. Because of the intimate relationship between means and ends, borderline methods detract from moral worth of the goal. Inducing people to give to the Community Chest by publishing names of contributors and amounts given would cheapen the reputation of this praiseworthy agency.

To illustrate the nature of the ends-means relationship in persuasion we remind the reader that a persuader starts with his conclusion, and the means grow out of the predetermined end. Since his strategies serve a chosen purpose, it is desirable that a moral judgment of his persuasion evaluate strategy in terms of purpose and purpose in the context of strategy, as well as the extent to which the entire interaction is consistent with the demands of his culture.

Ethics of "what you can get away with"

Although unsavory, this theory of the ethics of persuasion probably has more popular support than ends-means justification. A laissez-faire capitalist tradition has left us with a small, durable core of this philosophy. Two powerful negative forces control ethics of the persuader operating on the "what you can get away with" principle: (a) social sanctions (including boycotts) and (b) the law.

Rough, tough, and Machiavellian, this school of ethics has the great advantage of simplicity. Considerations of forbidden words, deceptions, rationality, and worthy ends go out the window. Our persuader has only to worry about staying out of jail and avoiding ostracism and retaliation. All known tools for controlling people lie close at hand. Let the buyer beware—if you get hurt it is your own fault and you will (possibly) be more careful next time.

Mass communications increase the potential danger of this philosophy. For example, some giant corporation or combination of business interests could conceivably obtain a virtual monopoly of these channels for a particular kind of advertising. The natural exclusion of competition would leave us dependent on the ethics of the advertiser. "What they could get away with" would increase, possibly to the point of real damage if unrestrained by their own voluntary limitation of profits.

With its vindictive overtones of "getting even with the world," the principle of "what you can get away with" is probably the least defensible base for an ethics of persuasion. Yet we must recognize that it contributes direct and powerful controls; we have all become more ethical persuaders because of the long list of things we know we "cannot get away with!"

The doctrine of responsibility

Throughout the five preceding approaches to the ethical problems of persuasion in America a persistent theme has been stated or assumed. In each of the categories a person (or persons) has had the responsibility of applying the criteria. Assuming responsibility for the act of influence and its consequences has become in itself a recommended prescription, not only for the persuader but also for the persuadee. In this section we will examine that doctrine and its implications.

Persuasion has as its purpose modifying thought and action of people. When persuasion succeeds, lives are changed. Since there is always the possibility that persuasion may be successful, the persuader as instigator of change should plan his responsibility for it. To assume such a responsibility intelligently requires thoughtful assessment of short- and long-term consequences to groups and to individuals. Failure to do so may be the result of a conscious decision not to be responsible. More often it is caused by careless neglect. In the latter instance, the persuader is so self-centered that concerns other than his own do not enter his mind. Unintentional oversight or deliberate irresponsibility are equally unethical.

If a persuader is to plan the ethics of his persuasion and do this effectively he must have a functioning system of ethical standards and methods. We do not presume to recommend any particular code of ethics for a persuader, but we will argue that he has the responsibility of developing a code that is adequate for his person and purposes, and of applying this code to all the acts of persuasion he initiates.

Thus far the doctrine of responsibility has been developed in a one-way, sender-receiver frame of reference, placing all responsibility for ethical quality on the source. A moment's reflection will convince the reader that this interpretation is neither sensible nor fair. Throughout this book we have stressed that persuasion is interactive, that both persuader and persuadee contribute to ongoing events and ultimate results. Further, one of the major reasons for studying persuasion is to become a more discriminating and perceptive consumer. These propositions suggest that responses of the persuadee may be more or less ethical as may be the messages and methods of the persuader.

Andersen recognizes the double bind in ethics of persuasion when he suggests that while the persuader has the responsibility not to try to deceive, the persuadee has the obligation not to be deceivable. The source should use good evidence and sound reasoning, and the receiver should be critical and rational. Andersen dramatizes this dualistic approach to ethical pragmatics by his "200 percent responsibility theory." Briefly, he argues that it makes sense for both the persuader and the persuadee to assume 100 percent responsibility for keeping the transaction ethical. In this way neither passes the buck to the other, and nothing is taken for granted. The persuader considers himself responsible if the persuadee is deceived into agreement, and if the persuadee is fooled he knows it is his own fault.

Andersen summarizes his 200 percent theory:

> It seems logically contradictory to regard the source as having 100 percent responsibility for his persuasion efforts and the effects of those efforts, and simultaneously view the receiver as having 100 percent responsibility for the effects of the persuasion effort. However, this seems a desirable condition.
>
> Source and receiver are two different individuals. They operate with different perceptions, with minutely or markedly different value systems. Just as a conclusion that is supported by more than one piece of evidence and more than one independent line of reasoning has greater probability of being valid, so a persusaion effect that results from two relatively separate independent assessments would likely turn out to be a more beneficial one to the receiver and to the society at large and in many senses to the source.
>
> Further, if either source or receiver defaults on his responsibility, the other active participant presumably continues to shoulder sufficient responsibility to provide some protection for both. If we cannot trust

others, we can at least trust ourselves whether as persuader or persuadee.[13]

Our survey of some approaches to ethical problems of persuasion provides much helpful but fragmentary advice. These suggestions must be interpreted as comments on central tendencies. The better rules apply to the majority of one type of persuasion, but no rule covers every specific case, and the frequent necessity to adapt advice to concrete circumstances leads us to formulate a topic sentence for this chapter: *ethics of persuasion is a function of context.* This topic sentence applies to all cultures and brings us back from America to our multi-cultural approach to the ethical dimension of persuasion. To return to cultural diversity we will mention that in Western cultures responsibility centers on the individual while in the East it is shared, with the group bearing any ultimate responsibility.

Inducing an emotional condition for purposes of persuasion

A speaker is addressing a crowd assembled to protest the military draft. The setting is a parking lot outside a government building wherein draft records are stored. The speaker's purpose is to convince the crowd to break into the building and destroy the records. He knows that calm reason cannot persuade these persons to commit a criminal act. So he attempts to incite the crowd to violence by arousing their anger. He recites atrocities, the bombing of hospitals, the napalming of children, the conversion of peaceful youth into ruthless murderers, and implies that only the draft makes these horrors possible. He is impassioned and eloquent, and successful in his persuasion.

While many writers have commented on the moral problems that attend the use of suggestion and deliberate concealment in persuasion, few have confronted the ethical issues raised by the intentional provoking of an upset emotional condition to further the purposes of the persuader. We believe that arousing intense emotion is a fairly common technique in certain categories of persuasion in all cultures. Further, the emotional condition robs the persuadee of his abilities to respond as he would while calm. Consequently, we should examine the ethical implications of using intense emotion as a means of persuasion. A detailed treatment of the nature of emotions and their role in persuasion is found in chapter 5.

---

[13] Kenneth E. Andersen, *Persuasion Theory and Practice* (Boston: Allyn and Bacon, 1971), p. 326.

The emotional condition

To decide whether using intense emotion to persuade is un-ethical, we must first ascertain what being upset in this manner does to people. Since the emotions used most around the world to control be-havior are anger and fear, we can examine the effects of being very angry or afraid on persons in a persuasive interaction. Experiencing either of these emotions intensely creates the psycho-physiological state psychologists term "the emotional condition."

The emotional condition brings about profound physiological changes within the human body. Heartbeat and blood pressure change, breathing patterns are altered, and endocrine secretions are modified. Most im-portantly, the production of adrenalin is increased. As consequence of both physical and psychological stresses three symptoms of the emotional condition appear. Because these symptoms are important to persuasive communication we will discuss each briefly.

SYMPTOMS OF THE EMOTIONAL CONDITION.   *Shock* is loss of rationality. A popular notion is that a person in shock is rigid and uncon-scious. This may well be the case as in the medical use of the term to designate a sudden, drastic collapse of the nervous system. But the shock important to communication is the loss of ability to think clearly. The more pronounced the emotional condition, the more intensely anger or fear is experienced, the greater the shock effect and the less able the person is to think critically.

Diffusion is a physical symptom of the emotional condition. The upset person loses precision in his physical movements. Fine control in finger dexterity, for example, is reduced. Further, excessive physical responses occur, as when the angry man shouts, paces the floor, and waves his arms.

Transference is a psychological symptom. All persons and objects in the environment of the emotional individual may be treated as though they were causes of the emotion. The emotion spills over and colors all actions and interactions of the upset person. The man who has been reprimanded for something he did not do goes home after work and orders the children out of the house, shouts at his wife, and kicks the dog. None of these actions are related to the cause of his emotion in any way, but he treats them as if they were. He transfers his anger to his environment.

BEHAVIORAL CONSEQUENCES OF THE EMOTIONAL CONDITION IN PERSUASIVE INTERACTIONS.   Some effects of upset emotion on interper-sonal communication that are direct results of shock, diffusion, and trans-ference are:

1. The emotional person is less predictable than when he is his normal self. He is impulsive, nonrational, physically uncontrolled.

2. The emotional person feels compelled to make critical decisions when he is least able to think clearly.

3. Emotion tends to feed upon itself, creating a spiral effect.

4. Emotion takes time to build and time to decay, in part because of physical changes involved.

5. Emotion is self-centered, hence energy devoted to being emotional is not available for doing useful work.

6. People tend to respond to emotion with emotion.

7. Interactions involving people who are emotionally upset are likely to get out of control.

We can summarize the behavioral consequences of the upset state by saying that when emotional, man resembles the impulse-dominated creature more than he does the symbol-using intelligent human being.

The ethical issue

Let us postulate two situations in which Americans tend to rely on the arousal of intense emotion to persuade. The first is an interpersonal relationship involving a supervisor and his employee. The employee has been careless at work, so the supervisor decides to scare him by threatening to fire him.

The second example is the previously described speaker-audience situation in which the leader of a protest movement is trying to persuade his listeners to break into a government building. He attempts to incite sufficient anger to make *some* vigorous action imperative and to prevent thoughtful contemplation of long-term consequences of the recommended impulsive act.

We feel that such uses of intense emotion to attain a persuasive goal are ethically undesirable. We cannot label them "unethical" per se, because we recognize that particular circumstances in a given instance may make necessary and ethical the use of a procedure that is clearly unwholesome in most similar situations.

Because the communicator who uses intense emotion to attain his ends relies on shock, diffusion, and transference, and because these symptoms of the emotional condition reduce the control persuadees have over their responses, we suggest that the responsible persuader will view this method as ethically suspect. At the very least, when he is tempted to use anger or fear as a tool he should force himself to justify that choice quite meticulously.

Social utility as a guide to ethical persuasion

We have repeatedly referred to the effects of persuasion on the people involved because this pragmatic check on ethics seems sensible to us. It is multi-cultural in that it is responsive to the values of the community in which a persuasive act occurs. We will now consolidate this "effects approach" in a concept we term "social utility" and recommend it as a guideline to help the persuader and persuadee improve their ethics.

When we try to take the "long view" or to estimate effects of our actions on other people, we are applying an ethical standard of great importance. Will the social group concerned benefit? Is there a revealed or concealed penalty to be paid? Could injury to one or a few individuals outweigh the group gains? Such questions must be answered in measuring the social utility of an act of persuasion.

Social utility can be defined as usefulness to the people affected. But in order to say what we mean by "useful" in this context, we must first define the group and develop a general understanding of its members' common objectives, and then estimate the ways in which our contemplated action (utterance) will help or hinder their attainment. A conscientious effort to understand (1) the group members and their common interests, (2) ways our persuasion may help or hurt the group, and (3) favorable and adverse effects on individuals will yield a rough estimate of probable social utility.

Because persuasion is, essentially, rearranging the lives of other people, we believe that the persuader's sincere effort to abide by some social utility principles is the first, and perhaps most important, step toward being ethical.

No universal formulas exist, no firm recommendations are made. But every persuader will be more ethical if he gives thoughtful consideration to factors of social utility as perceived by his community.

Conclusion

Much has been written and spoken concerning the ethical quality of acts of persuasion. The preoccupation of scholars with what we term the "ethical dimension" of influence seems to be increasing. Judgments of right and wrong, decency and indecency, appropriateness and inappropriateness of persuasive attempts seem necessary and inevitable.

In the present chapter we have attempted to satisfy five criteria we consider vital tests of any system of ethics which purports to be useful to ongoing persuasive communication in the modern world. We present those criteria and their rationales and invite our reader to evaluate our concepts and recommendations against these and other standards he finds appropriate.

ᴧ Our first criterion: Any satisfactory system of ethics in persuasion must be multi-cultural. We recognize that most writings about ethics are narrowly culture-bound, and we suggest that failure to develop a trans-cultural ethics of communication has limited the usefulness of this schol-arly productivity more than any other single factor. Further, writers in the past have tended to be projective. They wrote about the ethics of their in-groups as though they were dealing with universal problems. To avoid being provincial in writing for Spaceship Earth, we require that any system of ethics for persuasion be applicable at the very least to all communities on this planet.

ᴧ second criterion: Ethical standards must recognize the active role of perception in persuasive communication. When persuasion is con-ceptualized as interaction, ethical responsibilities are shared by persuader and persuadee. What the receiver does with the message he receives can contribute as much to the ethical quality of a communication as the intent and strategies of the sender.

Our third criterion for an ethics of persuasion: It must be both pragmatic and idealistic. While we recognize the function of the un-attainable ideal, we know that a substantial gap often separates an identified standard and current practices. To be sufficient, an ethical methodology must be analytical, that is, useful in diagnosing ethical deficiencies, and equally helpful in supplying directives to design reme-dial measures. In other words, an adequate system of ethics for persuasion must be both *descriptive* and *prescriptive*.

The fourth criterion: An ethical system for persuasion must recognize and adjust to the infinitely variable differences between verbalization and related behaviors. The credibility gap separating our actions from our words and our prescriptions has been too little examined. Where does the truth lie, in one of the two levels of fantasy, or in the verifiable activity? While the reader speculates about the answer to this question we reiterate: our system of ethics must allow for the human capacity to say one thing and do something else.

Our fifth criterion: A system of ethics for persuasion recognizes rela-tivity in the application of ethical principles. People who agree that truth should always be told reserve the right to lie under certain circum-stances, for example, to save the life of an innocent man who is menaced by a mob. Pareto shows that court decisions often depend more on whims, circumstances, and sentiments than on the written and official law.[14] When there is concensus on an ethical principle in a society, the application of the principle produces a normative tendency toward uniformity in conduct, but there are also many variations, both slight and extreme, from the accepted principle. In this regard it may be said: *ethics of persuasion is a function of context.*

Of the many concepts entering into our treatment of ethics we should like to stress the following ideas:

• Moral demands of a culture are the source of idealistic and pragmatic criteria of ethics in that community. These can be derived from examination of sets of expectations, assumptions, and values in that society.

• The prevalent ethics of persuasion in a culture can be described, listed, and criticized as were American approaches in this chapter.

• The arousal of intense emotion for purposes of persuasion merits criticism on ethical grounds.

• The concept of social utility can be applied in all cultures as part of a system of ethics for persuasive discourse.

[14] Vilfredo Pareto, *The Mind and Society* (New York: Harcourt Brace, 1935).

III

Implementing
the persuasive process

A number of factors play significant roles in the success or failure of the persuasive attempt in specific situations. This section discusses the most important of these factors.

Chapter 11 deals with the concept of ethos and assesses the significance of the credibility of the message source. Chapter 12 considers the important problems of attention and perception. Chapters 13 and 14 discuss the nonverbal personal interactions and nonverbal contextual elements, which can be very important influences in a persuasive situation. Finally, chapter 15 surveys the ways in which persuasion may be applied to extended commercial and social action campaigns.

11

The role of credibility in persuasion

Introduction

"What you are speaks so loudly I cannot hear what you say," said Emerson. "No man can be as great as he looks," said a member of an audience listening to the great orator, Daniel Webster. "He seems like a good man, but how can he be reliable when he is affiliated with that political party?" muses the partisan voter. And all of us have heard repeatedly, "How can I believe a guy like that?" Such statements point to a fundamental fact in human communication: the receiver of a message finds it virtually impossible at the outset to disassociate the message from what he thinks and feels about its source. In fact, one might well consider the source as a significant part of the message.

Ever since the rhetorical treatises of the ancient Greeks, it has been postulated that the more credible the source of a message, the greater the likelihood that the message will be believed. We tend to believe a credible source. Advertisers encourage us to buy only *name brand* products, to use the toothpaste that has the dental association's seal of approval, and to buy the insurance policy put out by a company that is as solid as the Rock of Gibraltar. The salesman is told to sell himself first. The young junior executive is admonished to wear the right clothes and look like he is destined to be successful. The political advisor emphasizes that the average voter considers himself more a judge of personalities than of issues. It was the confidence in the character of Kate Smith that helped her sell an astonishing 39 million dollars worth of World War II war bonds in an 18-hour radio marathon.

As we explore this source of influence, the reader should keep in mind that the receiver evaluates the source or speaker. What the speaker thinks of himself may be comforting, indeed, but what the audience thinks of his credibility provides the basis for their judgments and subsequent responses. Here, of course, is another reason for an audience-centered approach to the study of persuasion.

The speaker may or may not be the source of his message. In the case of a diplomat carrying out his government's wishes or a salesman reciting his employer's pitch for a product, the speaker is merely the encoder of another person's message. Nevertheless, the persuader will be evaluated in terms of the total impact he makes on the receiver; the mouthpiece of the message and its source merge into one persuasive image.

Classical theories of ethos

Aristotle supplies a definition of the role of ethos in persuasive speaking:

> The character [*ethos*] of the speaker is a cause of persuasion when
> the speech is so uttered as to make him worthy of belief; for as a
> rule we trust men of probity more, and more quickly about things in
> general, while on points outside the realm of exact knowledge,
> where opinion is divided, we trust them absolutely. This trust, however,
> should be created by the speech itself, and not left to depend upon
> an antecedent impression that the speaker is this or that kind of man.
> It is not true, as some writers on the art maintain, that the probity
> of the speaker contributes nothing to his persuasiveness; on the contrary,

we might almost affirm that his character [*ethos*] is the most potent of all means to persuasion.[1]

Reputation is thus conceded to be important, but Aristotle stresses that the conduct of the speaker and the speech itself can do much to communicate the "probity" of the speaker to the audience. He recommends calculated action on the part of the speaker to build his prestige and warns the speaker not to rely solely on a previously established virtuous record.

Quintilian agrees with Aristotle in substance, asserting that public speaking demands first of all that the speaker possess, "or be thought to possess," praiseworthy virtues. To be thought a bad man, he notes, is a severe handicap, for such a person will not be given credit for speaking sincerely. In elaborating on characteristics of speaking useful to the building of ethos, he contends that in order to move the feelings of others the speaker himself must be moved. Although he considers use of humor an asset, he fears that excessive joking damages dignity. Quintilian, more than Aristotle, stresses the desirability of a speaker's *being* sincere in order to *appear* sincere. Also, he seems to assign greater weight to establishment of the speaker's character *before* his speaking appearance.

Writers dealing with ethos usually specify its components. Aristotle says that the sources of personal credibility are three—sagacity, high character, and good will. Classical writers also advise the means to establish and enhance a speaker's ethos. Aristotle recommends the use of "virtuous maxims" because they give the impression of virtuous character to the speaker. Cicero advises the speaker to select speech content carefully with an eye to building ethos; by praising particular virtues, the speaker leads the audience to assume that he possesses them. Cicero warns against overdoing the effort to build ethos, for it may become too apparent or result in "pleading your own cause instead of that of your client." Quintilian calls attention to the positive ethos-building effect of humility and of representing oneself as weak and inferior. Conversely, ethos may be destroyed, says Quintilian, by a speaker's appearance of being "insolent, malignant, overbearing, or reproachful."

Other early writers on rhetoric frequently discussed elements of ethos in persuasive speaking. In the sixteenth century Thomas Wilson advised the advocate to call attention modestly to his qualifications and accomplishments, particularly to his good deeds, and especially to those affecting his audience. John Ward, writing in the seventeenth century, defined the

---

[1] Lane Cooper, trans., *The Rhetoric of Aristotle* (New York: Appleton-Century-Crofts, 1932), pp. 8–9.

four qualities of an orator as "wisdom, integrity, benevolence, and modesty," all of which we would consider as contributing to ethos. Some years later George Campbell provided a list of factors designed to increase and decrease sympathy for the speaker in an audience. On the positive side he mentioned "connective circumstances," including consanguinity, acquaintance, common citizenship, common religion, and, greatest of all, common interest. A lively and expressive delivery is useful in strengthening the bond of sympathy between speaker and audience. Campbell phrased a warning concerning the listeners' prejudices in respect to the speaker's ethos.

> Sympathy in the hearers to the speaker may be lessened several ways, chiefly by these two: by a low opinion of his intellectual abilities and by a bad opinion of his morals. The latter is the more prejudicial of the two. . . .
> As to personal prejudices in general, I shall conclude with two remarks. The first is, the more gross the hearers are so much the more susceptible they are of such prejudices. Nothing exposes the mind more to all their baneful influences than ignorance and rudeness; the rabble chiefly consider who speaks, men of sense and education, what is spoken.[2]

Writing in the early nineteenth century, Campbell emphasized, as did Gilbert Austin, the role of delivery in communicating ethos to the audience. Austin somewhat cynically contended that since the majority of one's listeners are incapable of reaction to the matter of the speech, as separate from the manner of the speaker, delivery considerations become supremely important. If the speaker's manner outweighs what he says, then delivery becomes a means of conveying to the audience the impression of the speaker's personal worth—the item that amounts to the principal power of his persuasion. A large share of the effectiveness of delivery is found in bodily action, said Austin, and he supplied detailed advice on the kinds and uses of gestures.

Contemporary approaches to the study of credibility

In recent years many scholars have become interested in conducting experimental investigations in the area classically called *ethos*. Because these studies have come not only from the field of speech and communi-

---

[2] Lester Thonssen, *Selected Readings in Rhetoric and Public Speaking* (New York: The H. W. Wilson Company, 1942), p. 241.

cations but also from the fields of psychology, social psychology, sociology, education, business, and journalism, their frames of reference, terminology, and purposes differ. Some do not employ rhetorical terminology and are not interested in the effects of ethos in the manner considered by the student of public address or interpersonal communication. Instead of the term *ethos*, the terms *credibility*, *prestige*, and *image* appear more frequently. And concern is not limited to the public speaking situation but also includes written and nonverbal communications. But whatever the approach, the interest, or jargon, the contemporary probes into this concept have provided us with new insights into the varied divisions of this complex topic. In spite of the many recent researches and the increasing sophistication of research methods, we need still more study before completely reliable conclusions can be drawn regarding the operation of this source of influence.

In view of the numerous studies extant, this chapter will not be an attempt to review all the researches but will instead give representative samples of research support in several areas of the topic. The student who wishes to pursue the researches more completely is encouraged to start his review by reading the summary of research findings by Andersen and Clevenger.[3]

The identification of credibility as a general persuasive variable

Without experimental evidence, the ancients contended that the more credible the source (the higher the speaker's ethos) the greater the likelihood that the message will be believed and accepted. In an early study (1949), Haiman recorded a speech on national compulsory health insurance and presented it to three different audiences. One audience was told that the speaker was Dr. Thomas Parron, Surgeon-General of the United States. The second audience was told the speaker was Eugene Dennis, Secretary of the Communist Party of America; and the third audience was led to believe the speaker was an anonymous university sophomore. The results of the study showed a significantly greater number of students shifted from neutral and unfavorable positions in the direction of the speaker's proposal when they believed the speaker to be Dr. Parron.[4] In a similar study, Hovland and Weiss found that high credibility sources were perceived by the receivers as being

---

[3] See the summary of research on ethos by Kenneth Andersen and Theodore Clevenger, Jr., "A Summary of Experimental Research in Ethos," *Speech Monographs* 30 (June, 1963): 59–78.

[4] Franklyn S. Haiman, "The Effects of Ethos in Public Speaking," *Speech Monographs* 16 (1949): 192.

more "fair" and "justified" in their conclusions than were the sources of low credibility. The amount of attitude change in the direction desired was three and a half times greater in favor of the high credibility sources. It might be added, however, that this amount of change decreased over a period of one month, and the subjects receiving the message assigned to a low credibility source moved toward accepting the attitude change suggested by the message. The experimenters called this change over time the "sleeper effect," an effect which may be explained by the dis-association which occurs in time between source and message.[5]

Other experimental evidence supports the persuasive influence of credibility. Because credibility results from a complex set of perceptions or values assigned by the receiver, a closer look at some of its specific components is necessary. We now turn to examine the factors that establish credibility.

Factors related to credibility

In reporting researches on the factors involved in credibility, Hovland, Janis, and Kelley state that "the research evidence indicates that the reactions to a communication are significantly affected by cues as to the communicator's intentions, expertness, and trustworthiness. The very same presentation tends to be judged more favorably when made by a communicator of high credibility than by one of low credibility. Furthermore, in the case of two of the three studies on credibility, the immediate acceptance of the recommended opinion was greater when presented by a highly credible communicator."[6] The experimenters point out that *trustworthiness* and *expertness* are the main components of credibility, that it was impossible to disentangle their effects as far as the experimental results were concerned, but that both are important variables. As for the communicator's *intentions*, they point out that it is possible that a receiver of a message may believe "that a communicator is capable of transmitting valid statements, but still be inclined to reject the communication if he suspects the communicator is motivated to make non-valid assertions. It seems necessary, therefore, to make a distinction between 1) the extent to which a communicator is perceived to be a source of valid assertions (his 'expertness') and 2) the degree of confidence in the communicator's intent to communicate the assertions he considers most

---

[5] Carl I. Hovland and Walter Weiss, "The Influence of Source Credibility on Communication Effectiveness," *Public Opinion Quarterly* 16 (1961): 635–50.

[6] Carl I. Hovland, Irving L. Janis, and Harold H. Kelley, *Communication and Persuasion* (New Haven: Yale University Press, 1953), p. 35.

valid (his 'trustworthiness')."[7] Whether trustworthiness is a general value that may remain relatively constant over more than one subject or a value that will vary according to the topic under discussion is not definitely established.

In a carefully executed study, Berlo, Lemert, and Mertz identified factors of credibility which they termed the *safety*, the *qualification*, and the *dynamism* factors.[8] The "safety" factor appears to be akin to that of trustworthiness discussed above. Thus the speaker may be perceived as a friendly, gentle, fair, ethical, and hospitable person, one who possesses those qualities in which one can *safely* place confidence. The "qualification" factor is roughly equivalent to the "expertness" factor reported by Hovland and associates. That is, the speaker is considered to be competent, well-trained in the subject matter being discussed, and highly experienced. The "dynamism" factor was not as well established as were the safety and qualification factors. Dynamism, to the researchers, characterizes a source who is frank, aggressive, forceful, bold, emphatic, and energetic. Winston Churchill has been thought to have presented these qualities effectively, whereas such men as Calvin Coolidge and Robert Taft were thought to lack them.

The relation of similarity and dissimilarity to credibility

A different approach may be used to determine the sources of credibility as perceived by the message receiver. Granting whatever personal qualities a persuader may have, one may ask if perceived similarities (age, sex, status, race) between persuader and receiver has a useful effect on the receiver. Also, one may ask if dissimilarities (such as in status or prestige) between the persuader and receiver can produce persuasiveness when the speaker holds the higher status or prestige position.

SIMILARITY AND CREDIBILITY. Traditions, habits, customs, mores, and values of a society become useful to the self-interests of those participating in that society or culture. A speaker reflecting the attitudinal and behavioral patterns the receiver possesses and respects will thus probably be more credible. The speaker of approximately the same age as the receiver, or in the same economic bracket, the same cultural background, the same race, religion, or vocation will likely though not

[7] Ibid., p. 21.

[8] David K. Berlo, James B. Lemert, and Robert J. Mertz, "Dimensions for Evaluating the Acceptability of Message Sources," unpublished paper, Michigan State University, 1966.

necessarily be perceived as more familiar and sympathetic with the receiver's condition of life.

Speakers on controversial topics such as genetic control, abortions, busing, and United States military involvement abroad find it extremely difficult to muster enough credibility to even be heard by those of *different* attitudes on the subjects, but they are very popular with and earn large fees from speaking to those with *similar* attitudes. The experimental research in this area is meager, but when added to the case studies and general experience, it seems warranted to conclude that a persuader's influence can be increased when he is perceived by the receiver as similar in one or more significant ways to the receiver. We would suggest that *attitude similarity* relative to the topic under discussion is more important than similarity of age, sex, status, education, or race.

DISSIMILARITY AND CREDIBILITY: THE ROLE OF STATUS AND PRESTIGE.　When the source of the message and its receiver are quite dissimilar, that is, when the persuader has the greater *status* or *prestige*, how is the persuasive situation affected? The studies by Haiman and by Hovland and Weiss demonstrated that the speaker of a higher status in reference to the topic was more effective in changing attitudes. Lorge investigated the effect of prestige (reputation) in the acceptability of passages that were attributed to various sources.[9] For example, using the passage "I hold that a little rebellion, now and then, is a good thing, and as necessary in the political world as storms are in the physical," the subjects agreed with the statement when it was attributed to Jefferson, but they disagreed with it when they were told it was written by Lenin. Other researches tend to add confirmation to the point that sources of greater status or prestige influence the receivers of their messages.

In studying this point we should keep in mind that status or prestige are relative points; it is the comparative relationship between the speaker's and the receiver's status or role that is important. If the receiver perceives the speaker's prestige as greater than his own, he is more likely to be influenced. Likewise we should point out that suggestibility to prestige does not correlate well with intelligence, subject matter competence, education, age, sex, or speech training. One's initial attitude toward the topic under discussion appears definitely related to suggestibility to prestige.

DISSIMILARITY AND CREDIBILITY: THE ROLE OF SEX.　Although the feminist movement in the United States has made much progress in obtaining equal opportunities for women, the debate on the equality of

---

[9] I. Lorge, "Prestige Suggestion and Attitudes," *Journal of Social Psychology* 7 (1936): 386–402.

the sexes continues. The question of the comparative persuasive skills of males and females has also arisen. Should a company hire a male or female salesperson? Does a female lawyer have as much chance of winning an acquittal as a male lawyer? The researcher asks, if other factors are equal, how does the credibility of women compare to that of men?

We have only limited evidence regarding the comparative credibility of men and women in persuasive situations, but some evidence suggests that male chauvinism still lurks within an audience's perceptions of a communicator. Goldberg found that, when the nature of the work was held constant, females evaluated the professional work of males (as indicated by titles of articles in scholarly journals) more highly than that of females.[10] Miller and McReynolds tested the following hypothesis: "even if all other source qualifications and the message content are held constant, receivers will rate a male communicator as more competent than a female communicator."[11] The experimenters divided the subjects by sex so that it could be determined whether the hypothesized effect would vary significantly between sexes. Attitude change measures were obtained to assess the relative persuasiveness of the message when attributed to a female and to a male communicator of a written message favoring an expanded ABM missile system. In each case the source was identified as a Ph.D. in nuclear physics, a director of a radiology laboratory, and as a scientific advisor to the National Security Council.

The results were as predicted, and competence ratings were higher for the male source. It was interesting to note that although the competence ratings of the male and female communicator did not differ significantly, the female subjects (receivers) rated the male source as more competent at a significant level. The researchers gave the following as possible explanations of their findings: (1) "perhaps women, while resentful of the male chauvinistic tenor of our society, are conditioned to respond consistent with the very sex roles they deplore," and (2) that it may be the area of expertise used (nuclear physics) is a discipline "typically perceived as a 'man's' field."[12] However, in the Goldberg study, female subjects rated the males higher in competence in the fields of school teaching and dietetics, fields that to some extent have been considered "feminine" fields.

More research is needed regarding the ethos of the sexes in varying

[10] Philip Goldberg, "Are Women Prejudiced Against Women?" *Transaction* 6 (1968): 28.

[11] Gerald R. Miller and Michael McReynolds, "Male Chauvinism and Source Competence: A Research Note," *Speech Monographs* 40 (June, 1973): 154–55.

[12] Ibid., p. 155.

persuasive situations before we can make confident conclusions. We can now say only that there appears to be a tendency for both males and females to assign greater competence or expertness to males.

Source credibility and the process view of persuasion

We introduced the process view of persuasion by suggesting that persuasive communication is a dynamic constellation of many variables operating between the communicator and the receiver. Although mindful of the end-products of persuasion, we have been concerned with the process itself; the anatomy of the persuasive process must be understood before we can analyze the results of persuasion or the causes of breakdowns in persuasion. In the following sections, we examine source credibility from this process point of view.

Ethos—a varying quantity during message presentation

For the persuader to think that his high ethos will remain unchanged during his message presentation would be a great mistake, indeed. This assumption is as faulty as thinking that high attention at the beginning of a message will continue to remain high throughout the message. Although we know that a persuader's credibility varies during a message, we have little objective evidence to support the point. Much of the research in the various dimensions of persuasion is of the pretest-posttest design; it is much more difficult to study the dynamic processes that occur *during* the message.

In a pioneering study, Brooks and Scheidel attempted to study the evaluative responses of an audience to a speech as the speech progressed.[13] A tape-recorded twenty-five-minute speech by Malcolm Little (Malcolm X), a spokesman for the Black Muslims, was presented to a predominantly white college audience. The tape was edited by splicing into the tape seven thirty-second silent periods in which the subjects made evaluations. Evaluations were also made at the conclusion of the speech. The silent periods were placed at what were considered "natural" divisions of the speech in order to disturb the continuity of the speech as little as possible. Control groups heard the uninterrupted speech. The results from the pretest and posttest data for both the experimental and the control groups indicated that there was an increase in the speaker's

---

[13] Robert D. Brooks and Thomas M. Scheidel, "Speech as Process: A Case Study," *Speech Monographs* 35 (March, 1968): 1–7.

ethos during the speech. However, a look at the profile data from the evaluations written during the silent periods on the tape indicated that after a great rise in the speaker's ethos early in the speech there followed a general *decline* during the remainder of the speech.

This method of study, though needing some refinements, demonstrated the manner in which a variable (ethos) actually operates during the on-going persuasive process. It can indicate where shifts in ethos occurred and how these shifts are related to content and delivery patterns.

Although more research is needed, it seems safe to say that a speaker's perceived credibility varies constantly during the message and, therefore, it behooves a persuader to assess his actions and try to determine how to maintain or increase his credibility during the delivery of his message.

The opinion leader

Thus far we have discussed the general factor of credibility largely in relation to the original *source* of the message. We must keep in mind, however, that despite the high credibility source, a receiver may not accept or reject a proposal until the idea or product message is filtered through the reactions of an *opinion leader*. Thus a farmer may not decide to use an insecticide until his prosperous neighbor recommends it. A doctor may be influenced to adopt a new drug after he learns a respected colleague uses it. And our final judgments of the President's speech are colored by the panel of television commentators who discussed the message immediately after its presentation. The opinion leader serves as a gatekeeper controlling the decision-making materials. He may serve not only as a transmission line of information but also as a model for opinion or attitude formation.

This intervention of the opinion leader in the flow of information from source to ultimate receiver has been called the *two-step flow theory* of communication. In a significant pioneering study, Katz and Lazarsfeld studied the effects of messages on attitude and behavioral change when carried by the mass media.[14] In examining the effects of a message carried by one of the media, they found minimal immediate effects. However, a delayed posttesting of the subjects showed a significant increase in attitude shift. The researchers accounted for the change by suggesting that the receivers changed their attitudes *after* discussing the topic with others in whom they had confidence. Other research has tended to confirm that the personal influence of those regarded highly in relation to the subject

---

[14] Elihu Katz and Paul F. Lazarsfeld, *Personal Influence: The Part Played by People in the Flow of Mass Communications* (New York: The Free Press, 1955).

area involved (the opinion leader) plays an important role in persuasion. The effects of persons who intervene between media and persuadees are discussed further in chapter 15.

What characteristics do such individuals have and what are their functions? Opinion leaders usually operate among peers; they have no heightened status. Some may even be unaware of their leadership status among those with whom they associate. Berelson, Lazarsfeld, and McPhee point out that the opinion leader probably serves as a *model* for the members of his group, and therefore his opinions are sought in the subject area in which he serves as a model; he usually has a slightly higher social status and tends to be regarded as well-informed because he pays greater attention to the mass media.[15] Katz and Lazarsfeld suggest that opinion leaders seem to have no single unique qualities, but that they have such common traits as: (1) a strong interest in the subject area; (2) a position regarded as endowing them with special competence; (3) accessibility and gregariousness; and (4) having contact with information from outside their immediate group.[16] In his study of the diffusion of innovations, Rogers notes the role of opinion leaders in decision making and believes that they differ somewhat from their followers in personality and in role, that such leaders (as sources of information) tend to use technically accurate and cosmopolite sources, and that in at least some areas of influence, they have a higher social status and are more innovative.[17]

Although the role of the opinion leader is quite well established, it is highly complex, and all of its components may not yet be known. We would profit from further study concerning this complex area of personal influence.

Source credibility and the adoption process

On some occasions, particularly when the subject involves a significant new idea or product, persuasion cannot be completed in a single exposure to a message. This diffusion process is a multi-step flow that may involve a number of opinion leaders operating at various stages of the process leading to final adoption of a proposal. The "adoption

[15] Bernard R. Berelson, Paul F. Lazarsfeld, and William N. McPhee, *Voting: A Study of Opinion Formation During a Presidential Campaign* (Chicago: University of Chicago Press, 1954).

[16] For a detailed discussion of these traits see Elihu Katz and Paul F. Lazarsfeld, *Personal Influence: The Part Played by People in the Flow of Mass Communications.*

[17] Everett M. Rogers, *Diffusion of Innovations* (New York: The Free Press, 1962), pp. 237–47.

process," as it has come to be called, is a very useful concept to those interested in how people come to accept new ideas or products. A pioneer investigator, Everett Rogers, describes the adoption process as that mental activity a person engages in as he progresses from his awareness of the innovation to final acceptance of it.[18]

This process also involves an adoption period—that is, the time needed to progress through the various stages. A single speech might be sufficient to persuade the receiver to adopt an innovation, but in matters of considerable significance, the adoption period may require repeated exposures to messages over a period of hours, days, weeks, months, and even years. Rogers suggests that the following five stages are part of the adoption process.[19]

1. THE AWARENESS STAGE. In this stage the individual is exposed to the idea. Although he lacks complete information, he is not yet motivated to seek additional information. Usually the information at this level comes from printed or broadcast sources rather than from a public speaker or a personal source.

2. THE INTEREST STAGE. Here the individual becomes interested and allows himself to be exposed to further information. The mass media may continue to be the persuasive vehicles here, but now interpersonal sources of information begin to play a role. The individual talks to opinion leaders and early adopters of the idea. The public speaker can operate at this stage to stimulate greater interest in the idea.

3. THE EVALUATION STAGE. During this stage the receiver begins to assess the relevance of the idea to his life, to determine whether he can accept the idea. Personal communication becomes increasingly important. Conversations and group discussions may be held, and the advice of specialists is sought. Public persuasive speeches are frequently used here, but these are not as effective as the word of opinion leaders selected from one's peers.

4. THE TRIAL STAGE. Of course not all new ideas or products lend themselves to trial. One cannot try out his vote for a candidate; a vote is final. Nonetheless, many new ideas, services, and products do lend themselves to trial. In these cases commercial change agents are very important, for the receiver is disposed to use the idea on a probationary

---

18 Ibid., p. 76.

19 Everett M. Rogers with F. Floyd Shoemaker, *Communication of Innovations,* 2nd ed. (New York: The Free Press, 1971), pp. 100–101. In this revised volume, Professor Rogers also introduces the "innovation-decision process" which is broader in scope than the adoption process. Although our purposes in this chapter are served by the adoption process, we urge the reader to study this new paradigm.

basis. Interpersonal communication with respected peers (opinion leaders) is also very common practice during this stage.

5. THE ADOPTION STAGE. If the trial experience was satisfying and if reassurances are forthcoming from opinion leaders and satisfied adopters, the individual usually will decide to adopt the innovation. Reassurances after the adoption decision tend to come from the mass media. Speeches stressing that adoption is a wise decision are also used.

In such *extended systems* of persuasion the credibility of the sources of the informative and persuasive materials used in each of the stages is of considerable importance in the ultimate acceptance (or rejection) of the innovation.

Limiting reliance on credibility during persuasion

Although we have contended that the credibility of the source of the message is generally a key to persuasiveness, it may occasionally be wise for the persuader to reduce reliance on his credibility. When considering beliefs, loyalties, and responsibilities of great personal or social concern, the receiver of the message may be more convinced by a direct exposure to the issue than by an indirect reliance on the source's credibility. One student found he could strengthen his persuasion by taking his classmates on a tour of a city ghetto where they could experience directly the needs of the inhabitants instead of relying solely on his credibility as a reporter of the ghetto situation. Back in the classroom, the student successfully completed his persuasion by discussing the direct experiences of his classmates' tour.

Thus at times neither the prior ethos of the persuader nor the favorable ethos that may be created during the message is adequate to establish a genuinely helpful credibility. There are occasions, also, where the source credibility is sufficient to help produce some attitudinal and/or behavioral change, but where the use of some direct experiencing by the receivers would result in still greater change. It is believed that international student exchanges, cultural exchanges, and other people-to-people programs are more effective in producing attitude change than those relying solely on rhetorical means. The open-house technique of churches, corporations, rehabilitation centers, and schools has the potential of gaining more public support than the straight public address or advertisement. Demonstrations on how a new farm implement, car, kitchen appliance works can be a very useful part of a persuasive message. In effect the persuader is saying, "Don't take my word for it. Try it. Experience it yourself."

The use of slides, films, pictures, and television coverage also permits the receiver to sense other people, events, and places more directly, even

though these media are still a representation of the real th:
cases this experiencing becomes so real that the receiver fail
the credibility of the producer of the visual aid.

Of course, all of these methods relying less on the credibility of the
persuader assume, first, that there is sufficient prior persuasion to assure
the presence of the intended receiver at such events and, secondly, that
the direct experiencing segment of the message is followed by those
rhetorical means that will direct the receiver to the desired goal.

A credibility checklist for the theorist and practitioner

It should be helpful to provide a checklist to bring together the chief
points and their implications as put forth in this chapter. A mounting
store of knowledge useful to the persuader is now available, and it is
hoped that those materials will be studied carefully and pondered as to
their application in attempts to persuade.

1. Research findings show that ethos, or the esteem granted the
source of a message, plays some part in the total persuasiveness of the
message. In general, the higher the credibility of the source the greater
the persuasiveness of the message.

2. The credibility evaluation of a source of communication is assigned by the receiver of the message. This perceived image normally
results from prior knowledge of or experience with the source, the content
of the message, the conduct of the persuader during and sometimes
after the message, and the ultimate goal sought.

3. Although a high credibility source is more effective in changing
attitudes than a low credibility source, the changes tend to disappear in
time. Reenforcement of original credibility by additional exposures can
help reestablish the high credibility of the source.

4. The influence of the speaker usually is underway before he utters
the first word of his message. It would be a mistake, therefore, to assume
that a persuasive communication begins when the formal part of the
message begins.

5. Although the research is at times contradictory, it appears that
credibility can be helped before the formal presentation of a message by
an introducer who has favorable ethos and whose speech of introduction
is carefully prepared in terms of those credibility factors which are
important to the particular audience considering a particular topic on a
particular occasion.

6. Trustworthiness, expertness, and dynamism stand out as the chief
components of credibility.

7. Similarity between the persuader and the persuadee in terms of culture, race, tradition, customs, and values apparently can be a helpful source of influence. Similarity of attitude toward the topic is likely to be the most important influence.

8. The status and prestige of the communicator can be an effective aid to credibility. It should be remembered that status or prestige is the result of a comparative relationship between the role of the persuader and that of the receiver.

9. Research indicates that expert opinion may be about as influential as majority opinion in producing attitude change.

10. There is some evidence that such non-content stimuli as dress, voice, and physical appearance apparently affect the receiver's attitude toward the speaker. However, these factors may not be related to persuasiveness on a given occasion.

11. Evidence suggests that, other factors held constant, males tend to be assigned greater credibility than females by both males and females.

12. The factors involved in credibility tend to vary in evaluation by the receiver during the presentation of the message. An initially high credibility quotient cannot be expected to remain so throughout the message without rhetorical means of sustaining it.

13. Opinion leaders often play an important part in the ultimate acceptance or rejection of a proposal. The opinion leader plays a gate-keeper role between the original source of a message and the receiver.

14. In the mind of the receiver, proposals seeking the adoption of a new idea, service, or product tend to go through the stages of awareness, interest, evaluation, trial, and, finally, adoption. This adoption process usually involves more than one source of persuasion. The impersonal sources (radio, television, newspaper advertisements) are most useful in the awareness stage, while the more personal sources (friends, opinion leaders) are important during the evaluative stage. A persuader must keep in mind that each stage has its own unique credibility problems.

15. On some occasions the process of persuasion is best served by limiting reliance on the credibility of the message source and using more direct participation by the receiver.

Conclusion

We have attempted to consider here those aspects of credibility that have supporting evidence and that we regard as important to the student of persuasion. We have not explored all germane factors, of course, because the available literature is very extensive; the serious practitioner in persuasion can learn much about the problems of credibility and their possible solutions by studying the research in the field. But many areas of this complex topic remain unexplored. Populations other than students need to be used as subjects. And the interactions among source, topic, receivers, occasion, and setting also require further exploration. Here again, much virgin territory awaits the interested scholar of the persuasive process.

12

Attention and perception in persuasion

The role of attention and perception in persuasive discourse

"He didn't get the message!" We've heard the expression many times. Clearly a breakdown has occurred in the communication process. Our observations of the world about us depend on the proper function and direction of our sense organs and the whole perceptual process that gives meaning to what we observe. Without attention communication cannot exist and nothing is perceived. Because the persuader desires to influence the perceptions of the recipient of his message, he must concern himself fundamentally with the psychology of attention and perception. And, lest a distraught speaker seek to shift the blame, let it be clear that there is no such thing as an inattentive audience, for the human organism is attending constantly, selectively during its waking hours. It may be, of course, that the audience is not attending to the speaker but to a more interesting and vital source. What we attend to and what we perceive determines to a great extent what we are and what we shall be.

The nature of attention

Attention is often wrongly considered as a power of the mind which can be turned on and off. Thus we may say that a person "turned his attention" away from the highway momentarily and ran into the ditch, or that we "focus our attention" on our work, or we may hear the unresourceful speaker command his audience to "give me your attention." We would suggest that in treating attention and perception, we should be concerned only with behavior that can be defined with some precision. .

Psychologists tend to differ in their approaches to attention. Some earlier writers (Tichener, 1921) treated attention as a characteristic of experience. Dashiell (1928) and others discussed attention in its relationship to the concept of temporary set of the receptive mechanisms of the body. Because of its mentalistic implications, traditional behaviorists tended to avoid the term attention. More recent psychological theory and research tucks the term attention in with discussions of perception and/or motivation. It stresses that the nature of attention is best understood by focusing on those internal, motivational factors within the individual that prompt him to choose or select certain stimulations. This contrasts with the emphasis some theorists place on those external or environmental factors having the natural capacity to command attention because of their physical attributes—for example, size, shape, or intensity. Many writers in the field of public address have emphasized the role of these stimulus characteristics and have neglected the relation of perception and motivation in attention.

It is our belief that we should not ignore the stimulus characteristics that in themselves have capacities to elicit attention, but that more stress should be placed on attention as a "set" that can organize the perceptual field and thus help determine motivational patterns.

We can respond only to a very small fraction of the numerous potential stimuli in the world about us. Our senses limit our responses considerably. Some objects are too large or too small, some energies too fast or too refined for our senses to detect. We cannot tactually sense extremely light pressures, nor can we see certain colors in the spectrum. These and other physiological limitations keep us from responding to a good share of the energies and objects in our environment. Additional selection through attention and perception enables us to further limit those stimuli to which our senses are capable of responding, to which we choose to respond, and to which we can provide meaning.

Definition of attention

Attention may be regarded as a set, or posture, by which we select out of our environment those stimuli that are related to our interests and needs. This set is usually viewed as having three interrelated aspects that are part of a single, complex act: (1) an adjustment of the body and its sense organs; (2) a clear and vivid consciousness; and (3) a set toward action.[1] These three elements of attention suggest that there is first an adjustment of the sense organs to permit the maximum reception of a given stimulus. The reader is aware of the adjustments he may make in an attempt to hear a sound clearly. You may close your eyes, cup your hand over an ear, adjust your total posture to facilitate reception—that is, to shut out competing stimuli. The preoccupied person is doing just this; he seems oblivious to all distractions.

This set also suggests that at any given moment other stimuli of equal or greater intensity are kept in the fringes of our attention, that is to

---

[1] F. L. Ruch, *Psychology and Life*, 7th ed. (Glenview, Ill.: Scott, Foresman and Company, 1967), p. 295.

say, within our perceptual field. If you as a speech correctionist are looking for certain deviations in the production of a given vowel, you may regard these as major sound difficulties, when, actually, you are attending to a sound of very low intensity, quite inconspicuous to the layman. Thus the focus of your attention stipulates the threshold of stimulation. In short, the adjustment of the sense organs, linked with your momentary interests, produces a specific clarity in your consciousness regarding the source of stimulation.

This set approach to attention suggests too a certain orientation that can facilitate the direction, motivation, or readiness to respond in a specific manner. The football team lined up against its opponents prepares its set as the quarterback begins barking the signals. His final "h-hut" will demonstrate just how response ready the team is.

The duration and span of attention

Because of the mobile, selective nature of the attention-perception process and the numerous stimuli (both internal and external) that are available for reception, we cannot attend continuously to a given stimulus. Attention comes in spurts; it is an exploratory rather than a static condition. Ruch points out that in observing the eyes of a person who is looking at a picture "you will see that they dart here and there, pausing but a short time in any one position. This is typical attentive exploration. The individual's attentive adjustment is not stable and fixed, but shifts constantly from one aspect of a situation to another."[2] A number of experiments demonstrate that the duration of attention is very brief indeed, usually a matter of a few seconds. How long we can attend to something depends on the degree of attention that is needed and the conditions of the attention situation. A desk cluttered with unrelated materials and walls filled with vacation pictures are not optimal study conditions. The degree of attention necessary to study and the many distractions in competition will likely result in very brief attention to the subject.

If the duration of attention is brief, what can be said of the span of attention—the number of things that can be attended to at one time? A general answer would be that a person's span of attention contains as many things as a person can organize into a meaningful pattern. In experiments using a type of tachistoscope (an instrument in which the subject's head rests against a hood as he looks into a darkened box where a pinhole in the box permits the subject to fix his attention on cards containing the materials to be observed) the subjects were found to be

[2] Ibid., p. 298.

able to report correctly (at least 50 percent of the time) from 6.2 to 11.3 dots in a tenth of a second exposure. When letters were used instead of dots, the thresholds fell in a range from 5.9 to 7.9 letters. The thresholds ranged from 3.2 to 4.3 when geometric forms were used.[3] One may deduce that the more complex the task involved, the fewer the elements that could be observed during the exposure time, an exposure brief enough to prevent eye movement and a shifting of attention. Thus the pure act of attention in a laboratory situation can embrace a very limited number of objects at a given moment. When the subject is asked to attend to much more complex objects or ideas, it can be readily seen that the thresholds will be reduced still more. We can learn to read several words or musical notes at a glance. Studies show that subjects can attend to approximately four or five objects visually and five to eight auditorily. As the number of objects increases, the quality and intensity of the focus of attention is reduced, and the awareness of the stimuli is not definite or clear.[4]

These facts are of utmost importance to the persuader as he plans the points of his message and their vocal and visual presentation.

Attention and the nature of an external stimulus

We said earlier that attention is influenced by the nature of the stimulus in our external environment as well as by those personal, internal factors of the person for whom a persuasive message is intended. Let us first identify the external stimulus in a more specific way.

SIZE.   When other factors remain relatively constant, something large is more effective in gaining attention than something small. The large, full-page advertisement, the large building, the large visual aid is favored over the smaller one. But largeness may be weakened in its attention value when it is in competion with a stimulus that has a more striking use of color, that is associated more vitally with the receiver's interests, or when it must compete with other large objects.

INTENSITY.   Intensity of sound, color, light, odor, and pressure usually competes successfully against similar stimulations of less intensity. To speak more loudly will usually gain the attention (for a brief period) of the otherwise preoccupied person. Of course, continued shouting at an already attending audience may well distract the listener from the subject matter of the message.

[3] A. D. Glanville and K. M. Dallenbach, "The Range of Attention," *American Journal of Psychology* 64 (1929): 207–36.

[4] D. W. Chapman and H. E. Brown, "The Reciprocity Between Clearness and Range of Attention," *Journal of General Psychology* 13 (1935): 357–66.

MOVEMENT.   Changing, moving stimuli are more readily sensed than static, unchanging objects. Since attention is mobile and exploratory, it is to be expected that variations in stimuli tend to be given priority. Once gained, attention can only be maintained by varying the stimulus patterns. A monotonous stimulus leads to certain inattention. The speaker's use of voice and body, as well as his substantive materials, must demonstrate animation, alertness, and variety if he is to maintain attention.

REPETITION.   Closely allied with the principle of movement or change is the matter of repetition. Repetition is simply variations in time of the same idea, event, or object. Even a repeated weak stimulus may be as useful as a strong one given only once. An interrupted tone from an alarm clock frequently is more efficient in waking us up. A sign flashing lights intermittently gains attention more than a continuous light. Repetition of a central theme plays an important role in attention to forms of archtecture and music. A speaker's repetition of key ideas or phrases, the radio or television commercial's repetition of the main appeals or slogans, and the reoccurring poster on a billboard are examples of effective means. Repetition tends to continue to be effective until the very repetition takes on a monotonous quality.

VIVIDNESS.   A final quality that may cause one stimulus to stand out from competing stimuli is vividness—vividness of contrast, of color, or of contour. The vividness of a green tree in a grove of trees with browning leaves produces by its contrast unusual attention value; the vividly colored dress attracts more attention than the one of rather drab color; and the outline of a well-defined mountain range gains our attention more than does a rather gently rolling, commonplace contour. The rhetoric of the speaker should provide the ideational and emotional elements of his message with such vividness that they stand out sharply in our consciousness; then we attend readily.

The personal-social conditions of attention

We turn now to those personal, internal factors that play an important part in what and how much we attend. They explain to a great extent why individuals differ greatly in their responses to identical external stimuli.

ORGANIC CONDITION.   A strong biological need at the time of competing external stimuli usually becomes the strongest stimulus. As research demonstrates, if you are thirsty or hungry, any stimulus related to water or food is likely to be given priority. A fatigued condition will likely cause you to respond to a stimulus associated with rest rather than to any other stimulus. The sirloin steak dinner before the sales talk and a comfortable setting for the talk serve a more basic purpose than mere social custom.

PERSONAL INTERESTS AND PURPOSES. People vary greatly in their responses to the same stimulus for a second reason—interests or purposes. A group of students walking through the university arboretum will react variously. A student in landscape gardening will attend to some provocative planting formations, the geology major to an interesting rock outcropping nearby, the plant pathologist to a rare disease of one of the trees, and the lover may see only a beautiful place to stroll on his next date. A classic example involves students studying the human brain. During the course of a discussion of the fissures and convolutions of the brain as given from a picture, a large chart containing not the fissure and convolutions but a picture in which a number of infants framed in a contour resembling the cerebral hemispheres was substituted. Only after several minutes did any student realize what his interests led him to perceive.

Behind our interests and purposes lie rewards which can cause us to select stimuli that serve them. If you wish attention, know the interests—momentary and enduring—of the persuadee, and speak to them.

EMOTIONAL STATES. Emotional states produce moods that affect the direction of attention. Moods of affection can cause us to note items in the behavior of the loved one which go unnoticed by others. A hostile mood frequently selects for attention some minute shade of meaning in another's remarks that would not otherwise be noticed. Emotional states are often elusive but can play a very significant role in determining attention.

SOCIAL SUGGESTION. The group with which we identify can influence our selection of stimuli for attention. You may attend to certain news stories because you do not want to seem uninformed at the meetings of your sorority or the bull sessions in your fraternity; you may study quite late, so that you can demonstrate considerable preparation for the class of your favorite professor; or you may follow the suggestion planted by the fellow ahead of you as he removes his hat upon entering the elevator where ladies are present. In short, social stimuli control attention to the degree to which we have learned to react to the behavior of others. It should be clear to the persuader that he must become very sensitive to the social stimuli that are significant to the persuadee.

The kinds of attention

Because of the varying attributes of potential stimuli and the varying internal conditions of the respondent, not all acts of attention are of precisely the same nature. Some external stimuli by their very nature, demand that the sense organs respond to them—for example, loud sounds, and unusual odors. There are other stimuli to which we respond only as a result of effort; and still others to which we attend in a more effortless and motivated manner. These kinds of attention may be called involuntary, voluntary, and nonvoluntary.

INVOLUNTARY ATTENTION. We have to attend to unusual changes in our environment, be they loud sounds, intense colors, great size, bright lights, or repetitions. The nature of the stimulus is such that our sensory equipment of necessity will respond.

VOLUNTARY ATTENTION. In some situations, the nature of the external stimulus or of our internal interests and motivations is not sufficient to command attention readily; we force ourselves to attend because of social pressures, authority, or some desired but remote reward. Reading a textbook may take a special disciplining of the senses to maintain attention. The problem in voluntary attention is to keep distractions out or to a minimum in order to achieve some required goal. Some speakers are so boring, so uninteresting or lacking in arousing our motivations that we have to force ourselves to attend. A speaker who requires this form of attention is failing. The advertiser who operates on this level has failed.

NONVOLUNTARY ATTENTION. When the source of a message or the message itself arouses our interests, when stimuli are found to be linked vitally with our desires, a listener or reader finds it easy to attend. He becomes wrapped up in a subject which, at the outset, may have required a voluntary response. The effective speaker (or writer) is able to shift our initial voluntary attention to this highly desirable nonvoluntary attention where communication has its best chance to succeed.

The nature of perception

Definition of perception

Earlier in this chapter we made some general observations regarding the companion nature of attention and perception. We briefly separate them here for pedagogical reasons only. Because perception involves more than mere sensations, it deserves some separate treatment, even though some of the factors that help influence perception are akin to those aiding attention. We must keep in mind that to an infant without the experience to perceive—that is, to bring past experience into some specific and organized responses to stimulation—the world he senses is just a buzzing confusion. It is necessary to select, phrase, and present the idea so that the consumer of the message can readily organize the data into a meaningful, useful perception. This potential consumer of the message must be thoroughly analyzed. One cannot hope to persuade a person whose perceptions of an incoming message cannot be quite accurately predicted.

Let us assume that the sense organs tuning in a stimulus are functioning properly and thus can provide the brain with a reasonably accurate record of the event. By using the sensory data from stimulation and the learning that experience provides, the perceptual process then attaches some meaning to the stimulation. It aids in maintaining a certain continuity and stability in our environment. Perception has been defined as "a process whereby sensory cues and relevant past experience are organized to give us the most structured, meaningful picture possible under the circumstances."[5] The manner in which a consumer of a persuasive message receives the sensory data (attention) and then organizes these data into some meaningful pattern (perception) for himself will determine in considerable measure his response. In this process one cannot assume that because the stimulus is received accurately, the perception is an exact replica of that intended by the sender. The receiver may take only a part of the stimulus, distort some of it, exaggerate other parts, add elements, or make still other changes to create for himself a meaningful, structured interpretation of the message. Thus in human communication accurate transmission of thought from speaker to receiver is the exception and not the rule.

External factors that influence perception

PROXIMITY.   The physical nearness of one object to another tends to facilitate perception, to place the object or idea into a more meaningful framework. Linking known objects, ideas, and people with an unknown tends to help bring useful meaning to them. The speaker can do this by references to elements in the immediate speaking situation—its audience, environment, and so on.

THE FAMILIAR.   If the persuader can link his thought or suggested course of action to similar ideas or courses of action now accepted by the audience, he can facilitate the perceptual process, for we tend to perceive similar elements as actually belonging together. Thus the receiver of the message is helped in structuring his perceptual data into a meaningful whole. The completely unfamiliar is impossible to fit into a meaningful frame of reference and thus fails to achieve the desired response.

THE CLOSURE PRINCIPLE.   In our disposition to fit objects and ideas into a meaningful and whole or stable pattern, we may even supply elements not present in the original stimulus to help create this mean-

---

[5] F. L. Ruch, *Psychology and Life*, p. 300.

ingful whole. Thus the mere suggestion of an idea may be sufficient to cause an audience to complete it for you. A well-phrased question or periodic sentence will create considerable suspense because it yearns for an answer, a completeness. The use of the enthymeme in argumentative discourse will cause us to supply the missing premise. This principle has great value for the persuader, be he an advertiser, preacher, politician, or salesman.

CONTEXT.   Since we tend to perceive things as a *whole*, we assign meaning to some part of the whole through contextual clues. We decide whether it is a cloudy or bright day by checking points of surrounding illumination. If the general contextual materials of a message are marked by unusual order, clarity, and vividness, the perceiver is helped markedly in making sense out of one poorly explained idea. If the overall environment of a persuasive communication offers a clear context as to its purpose, the receiver of the message can more accurately perceive the intent of one vague concept.

The personal-social influences of perception

PERSONAL EXPERIENCE.   Perception relies on one's experience. Any stimulus we receive, therefore, is given meaning only in the light of our experiences. So it can be said that we *see things not as they are but as we are*. Every incoming message is interpreted in terms of our informational, cultural, linguistic, and social experiences; we distill from the message only those aspects that fit into our familiar world. It is at this point that much communication goes awry, for to know the persuadee's past experiences accurately and in depth presents an almost insurmountable barrier, certainly one that a hasty audience analysis cannot overcome, but one with which we constantly must strive to cope. The person who does the best job of this—other things being equal—will likely be the most effective persuader.

MOTIVATIONAL FACTORS.   Closely linked with our experience is the role of motivation in perception. What motivates a listener at a given time influences to a considerable degree what he attends to and perceives at that moment. In one of the best-controlled studies related to this point, Gilchrist and Nesberg found that college students who were deprived of food for a period of twenty hours tended to perceive slides of T-bone steak, fried chicken, and so forth as being brighter than the pictures of non–food related objects.[6] As the subjects' hunger progressed, they evaluated the food pictures as brighter and brighter. Thirsty subjects evaluated pictures of ice water, orange juice, and other liquids brighter

---

[6] J. C. Gilchrist and L. S. Nesberg, "Need and Perceptual Change in Need-Related Objects," *Journal of Experimental Psychology* 44 (1952), pp. 369–76.

as their thirst increased. When the subjects were given a drink of water there was a significant drop in the brightness adjustment of the thirst-related pictures and only a very minor decrease in the adjustment in the others.

Evidence suggests that some people employ a *perceptual defense* in dealing with fear and other negative motivations, and thus they tend to avoid unpleasantness. We tend to shut out painful situations from our perceptual field or modify our perceptions to avoid psychological pain.

In conclusion, it seems safe to say that the motives of the message receiver influence what message stimulus he perceives and how he perceives it. Here, again, we see that a strictly message-oriented rhetoric or system of criticism can be very inaccurate, misleading, and incomplete. The receiver's motivational system must be understood.

The persuader's perception of the persuadee's attention and perceptual behavior

Any treatment of the nature and uses of the factors of attention and perception would be incomplete if the persuader is not very aware of his own participation in the complex social act of persuasive communication; he is the receiver of the persuadee's feedback (oral and visual) and as such he is attending to and perceiving messages of utmost importance to him as he continues to present his own message. He must receive and interpret those cues with as much accuracy as possible. Let us examine several basic problems he confronts in this regard, starting with the least difficult.

• A persuader usually has least trouble with those primary movements a persuadee may make in adjusting his sense organs to the speaker. He may lean forward and turn one ear, showing he has difficulty in hearing but is interested enough to try to receive the message more clearly. His eyes may suggest whether he is attending your visual code. His general posture may indicate a focus and interest or disinterest. Studies show that the organism becomes more active in attending; the circulatory and respiratory systems tend to increase their normal function. These internal changes are difficult to detect by a speaker; the external manifestations of the attentive or inattentive person may be observed readily in small face-to-face situations, less readily in a large audience situation. The problem here is, first, to be able to observe whatever signs are available and, second, and much more difficult, to interpret these signs accurately. Many speakers assume that people demonstrate attentiveness in the same manner. This erroneous notion disregards the role of habits that become associated with the attention process. The student may be in the habit of studying with the radio or hi-fi on, his legs propped up on a nearby chair, and his head listing to starboard. An unexpected glance at his posture by the professor may cause him to conclude "that chap isn't attending to his assignment," because the student isn't fitting the traditional pattern associated with serious study. But many movements not actually essential to attention (secondary movements) may become associated with attending; these secondary movements may well be misunderstood by a communicator who is attempting to decide whether his receiver is attending to him.

• Now let us consider the student who is looking directly at the professor, his eyes fixed on the lecturer, his physical attitudes seemingly demonstrating a keen interest in what is being said. Assuming this and wanting to be reassured of his successful lecture, the professor at the close of the address asks this student a question on the subject of the lecture, confident that the student will supply an apt and ready response. The student, however, seems quite startled at being questioned and, after a brief delay to collect his wits, asks the professor to repeat the question. Here, although the outward signs seemed to spell attentiveness, they were actually simulated.

• A third and still more complex problem comes when the persuader attempts to assess the visual and oral cues he thinks provide insight into the emotional and ideational responses of the receiver. The same physical-social information may be interpreted in different ways. The whispering of audience members may be interpreted as indifference to or distress caused by the speaker's message or as involvement that must be shared at once. A laugh at the use of humor may be interpreted as outright appreciation or as a mere courteous expression when the laughter seems somewhat reserved.

The study of facial expressions (as well as physiognomy and physique) has been a concern of most laymen and a few experts in their quest for insights into personality, emotions, and intentions. Most physiognomic theories of personality have limited acceptance. The human face, however, has become an important index on revealing and concealing states of emotion, desires, and purposes. In certain cultures the outgoing person is said to wear his feelings on his face; the "poker face" attempts to conceal. Studies tend to show that judges can place test photographs of faces rather consistently into broad classifications. However, when one is dealing not with static or even motion pictures but with living, dynamic facial expressions in direct social intercourse, the matter becomes much more complex and judgments less reliable. Actually very little is known with certainty about studying such facial expressions. Appropriate units of analysis must be established. What are the words and grammar of our visual language? This point is considered more fully in our treatment of the emotions in chapter 5 and in our discussion of nonverbal interactions in chapter 13.

The person dealing in persuasive communication (or in any form of communication) must thus become a very astute observer of the receiver's responses, but he must be very cautious in his perceptual appraisals of the nature and implications of these responses. Research in perception has centered largely on physical objects and events; the area of social perception in communication is still in its infancy and offers a most necessary and challenging field of study.[7]

Conclusion

All attempts at persuasive communication start with the rhetorical creation of stimuli that energize our senses through the use of posture, gestures, words, sentences, visual aids, and so on. What we attend to and how we perceive and react to these sensations depend on the interaction of many factors in the nature of the stimuli presented, the circumstances surrounding the interaction, and the conditions within ourselves. The successful persuader must be a serious student of attention and perception if he hopes to gain and maintain the persuadee's attention and to guarantee the proper perception of his message as he proceeds with the work of changing attitudes and modifying behaviors.

Normally, the persuader seeks merely to know enough about the receiver of his message to predict with some accuracy how his message will be perceived. On occasion, however, perceptions are deliberately controlled or misperceptions created. Sometimes a leader may be intent on the creation of a mob and ultimate riot by deftly moving a group of socially conscious but naive idealists from a concerned discussion group to a more active demonstration group and, finally, into the rioting mob; he may move the group so gradually into his desired behavior that its members will not *perceive* the change. A group intent on taking over the political power of a community may prepare its steps so secretly that the duly elected officials do not *perceive* the danger because of the lack of events on which judgments could be based.

In sum, attention and perception are companion processes which play a primary role in the process of persuasion. The perceptual problems involved in the many aspects of the persuasion process are, as we have discussed, both numerous and complex.

[7] J. E. Hochberg, *Perception* (Englewood Cliffs, N.J.: Prentice-Hall, 1964), pp. 100–13.

13

Nonverbal persuasion: personal interaction

Introduction

Persuasion viewed as interaction involves much more than words exchanged, that is, the linguistic content of messages. Neil Postman has used the label *media ecology* to encompass a broadened perspective of the study of communication. He includes in a unit of communication all of its surroundings. "Communication," he says, "is environment."[1]

Obviously, the student of persuasion could not hope to identify all variables that influence a persuasive interaction, given Postman's global frame of reference. An objective capable of practical attainment might be the location and description of major variables that contribute significantly to an outcome. The utility of Postman's wide open approach would seem to be to free the student from excessive preoccupation with

[1] Neil Postman, in Keynote Address at the 9th Annual Speech Communication Summer Conference, Palmer House Hotel, Chicago, Illinois, 12 July 1973.

traditional and familiar variables and encourage a wide-ranging search for items of influence unique to the individual instance.

Since environmental influences, including personal behaviors of participants, are predominantly other than language, the term *nonverbal* has become accepted as a designate for all other-than-linguistic elements in communication. Usefulness of the category has been reduced through its having served as a dumping ground. Every aspect of the environment from weather to acoustics has been included in nonverbal elements of communication as have appearance and personal mannerisms of speakers.

While we recognize the great complexity of factors "beyond words" in human interactions, we will attempt an arbitrary simplification by separating personal interactive behaviors from the context in which these occur. We admit that the separation is completely artificial, but it seems advantageous to focus first on one aspect, then the other, stressing their interdependence. Hence this chapter will consider nonverbal personal behaviors of the participants in persuasion, and the following chapter will deal with contextual elements.

With our reader alerted to the emphasis on persuasive considerations other than language in this and the following chapter, let us turn to a sampling of the various nonverbal factors that may profoundly affect the outcome of an act of persuasion.

A close friend comments on your giving the wrong answer to a simple question by saying, "You *are* a stupid dolt." His tone of voice, head shaking, and facial expression convert this brutal judgment to a gentle chide, given with warmth and affection.

In a persuasive dyad the interaction has proceeded smoothly, with your partner in the dialogue accepting your suggestions and supplementing them with his own. Then things begin to go wrong. You sense an increasing reluctance, even though his agreement in words continues. You notice a hesitation preceding his responses and a prolongation of the words of affirmation, particularly an extended "Yeeeesss." You conclude that he has shifted from the role of agreer to that of doubter.

A salesman is approaching the moment of truth in his attempt to sell you a large life insurance policy. He asserts that your welfare is the only consideration in his mind and that he is not permitting any personal gain for himself to enter in. You reach for the pen as if to sign the contract, then appear to change your mind and settle back in your chair to deliberate further. You note the tension in the salesman's face and body, and a tremor in his voice as he answers your questions. You decide he was trying to "play it cool" but was very much concerned that he might not get his commission. This seems deceptive to you, so you decide not to buy.

You have requested advice on a personal problem from a counselor you do not know. As you approach his door you are filled with doubts and insecurity. You resolve not to be influenced and to receive any advice with a highly critical skepticism. As you enter the counselor's office he comes to the door, shakes hands, greets you with warmth. He has you sit beside him in a comfortable chair, rather than across his desk. He clears away all papers, and tells his secretary to take all messages and prevent any interruption. His attention to you is obviously undivided, and his understanding is made clear by continuously reactive facial expressions and by appropriate nods and side-to-side shaking of his head. You find it easy to speak openly of delicate matters. At a point of some emotional tension he leans forward and pats you gently on the knee in a way that tells you "I understand." When you leave, he walks to the door with you, his arm around your shoulders, and you part with a second friendly handshake. As you board the elevator you are thinking how difficult it would be not to trust this man, and that you are already planning to follow his advice without the critical examination you had resolved to conduct.

In each of these hypothetical persuasive interactions, we have placed our reader in the position of making a perfectly understandable decision on the basis of nonverbal interactions rather than on substance of the message. Our task in learning about the forms and functions of such nonverbal communication is clear. We wish to better understand what it is, how it works, and how to use it in our own efforts to persuade.

The material that follows is new and often not based on the extensive behavioral science research which made the statements about human relationships given earlier in this book relatively secure. Much is still speculative, and admittedly many of the concepts and ideas included here are not destined to be long-lived and productive. Your authors are in the predicament of the professor of marketing who told his class, "Half of what I tell you is baloney. The catch is, I don't know which half! Learn it all!"

Following this professorial example we are including some possibly productive concepts that need further development. We believe that it is wiser to anticipate what *may* happen, but is not certain, than to be unpleasantly surprised.

Further, we intend to dispense some mechanical advice about the management of nonverbal elements in persuasion that could not be classified as scholarly by even our most "practical" reader. We do so only because persuasion often ends disastrously when these elementary bits of information are not known or applied.

Functions of nonverbal interpersonal behaviors in persuasion

In chapter 9 we discussed categories of nonverbal communication important to persuasion within and across cultures, using a "modes approach." There we labeled different forms of nonverbal communication which could be identified by their "shape," independent of function or purpose. Kinesics, proxemics, haptics, paralanguage, and nervantics were treated as major components of a nonverbal code, as nouns, verbs, adjectives, and adverbs are useful parts of the English language.

For intercultural applications this nonverbal grammar approach had advantages, and we will refer to the above classification system from time to time in the discussion that follows. For a deeper penetration into nonverbal patterns in intracultural persuasion, however, we have found a functions approach to be more rewarding—that is, we define nonverbal categories by a particular purpose or function. This classification system is readily applicable to such purposeful uses of rhetoric as persuasion, and is open-ended, so that as new purposes served by nonverbal behaviors are discovered, categories can be added. Because our overall treatment of persuasion has followed a task-oriented, get-the-job-done schematic, the reader will find that consideration of the nonverbal dimension of persuasion in terms of empirical contributions to the process fits in nicely.

Substituting nonverbal behaviors for linguistic constructs

Nonverbal behaviors that are the equivalents of units of language and that are used instead of languages are termed "emblems" by Ekman and Friesen. Their definition clarifies the nature of this category of nonverbal communication.

> *Emblems* are those nonverbal acts (a) which have a direct verbal translation usually consisting of a word or two, or a phrase, (b) for which this precise meaning is known by most or all members of a group, class, subculture or culture, (c) which are most often deliberately used with the conscious intent to send a particular message to the other person(s), (d) for which the person(s) who sees the emblem usually not only knows the emblem's message, but also knows that it was deliberately sent to him, and (e) for which the sender usually takes responsibility for having made that communication. A further touchstone of an emblem is whether it can be replaced by a word

or two, its message verbalized, without substantially modifying the conversation.[2]

North America equips its residents with a substantial vocabulary of emblems. In context, a shrug of the shoulder or a lifting of eyebrows accompanied by a side-to-side head shake says "I don't know" as clearly as words, and with the option of a wide range of shading and emphasis not available to the person who chooses to limit himself to verbalization. Hand signals directing the driver of an automobile to park in a tight space seem to be more direct communication than verbalizing "A little to the left," "No, that's too much," "Come about ten inches further," and "Stop."

The reader can readily extend our list of nonverbal behaviors which can, on occasion, replace words, phrases, or sentences. Choosing to "say it nonverbally" may have many advantages, such as saving time, adding precision, gaining and holding attention, and contributing redundancy to the verbal message in a memorable way. The student of persuasion should become sensitive to the use of emblems and assess their effects in the persuasion of others and in his own efforts to persuade.

Amplifying or emphasizing linguistic structures

When a speaker talks slower and louder, frowns, and shakes his fist in the air, he usually adds emphasis rather than content to what he is saying. There may be linguistic equivalents for these behaviors, but they are usually ambiguous or vague. He may be saying nonverbally "This is important" or "Pay attention" or "I'm upset" or "I'm just trying to be heard in a noisy room" or any of a dozen other messages. Since there is no standard, accepted word equivalent for behaviors such as these examples, we note simply that nonverbal vocal and physical variants in this category amplify or emphasize what is being said and are interpreted according to the situation and the experiences of the particular auditor.

This category resembles the Ekman and Friesen class termed "illustrators." Again, their definition/description is helpful in determining the boundaries of this function of nonverbal interpersonal communication.

Illustrators are those acts which are intimately related on a moment-to-moment basis with speech, with phrasing, content, voice contour,

[2] P. Ekman and W. V. Friesen, "Hand Movements," *The Journal of Communication* 22:4 (December, 1972): 357.

loudness, etc. Illustrators usually augment what is being said verbally, but they may contradict the verbalization or be used as a substitute for a word. Illustrators are similar to emblems in that they are used with awareness and intentionality, although the use of illustrators is usually in peripheral, not focal awareness. Illustrators differ from emblems in a number of ways. Many of the illustrators do not have as precise a verbal definition as the emblems, and for some illustrators there is actually no obvious or agreed upon verbal translation of the act.[3]

People tend to use relatively more illustrators when they are anxious to communicate, when they feel that they are being misunderstood, when they are in a state of physical well-being, when they are emotional, and when they are responding to another person who uses illustrators extensively and vigorously. When a person is depressed, tired, ill, intimidated, feels insecure or inferior, his use of illustrators is curtailed.

The reader will note that the first two functions of nonverbal interpersonal behaviors we have discussed, those (1) substituting for or (2) emphasizing language units, make use mainly of kinesics and to a lesser degree, of paralanguage and proxemics. Haptics and nervantics are used on occasion, as when touch serves as an emblem or a trembling hand changes the meaning of an illustrator. Our point is that any function of nonverbal persuasion *can* be served by any one, any combination, or all of the modes of nonverbal communicative interaction.

Controlling the flow of interaction

An easily identified function of nonverbal behaviors in interpersonal communication is to speed up, slow down, or stop the interaction. Ekman and Friesen label these behaviors "regulators." The regulation of a formal or informal conversation can be accomplished by literal and obvious signs that are difficult to ignore or by subtle and indirect means of control that operate largely out-of-awareness.

Behaviors that function as unmistakably as a traffic semaphore include persistent head nodding or shaking, turning away, leaning forward or approaching, maintaining or breaking eye contact, physical withdrawal, repeated mm-hmm's, hand raised with palm toward speaker in a "that's enough" gesture, facial expressions of interest or puzzlement, increase in or reduction of fidget behavior, and obvious preoccupation with a competing source of stimuli.

Subtle but powerful nonverbal regulators include active or passive facial and bodily response, doodling, signs of boredom such as drumming fingers on a table or looking out a window, hesitation in responding

[3] Ibid., pp. 358, 359.

verbally or nonverbally, lively response with increasing physical animation, frowning or smiling, slumping in one's chair, a gradual decrease in responsiveness, and a tendency for eyelids to lower, then to snap open, showing the onset of drowsiness and the necessity for the persuadee to force attention.

The competent persuader develops a high sensitivity to nonverbal regulators in dyads, and in small and large audience situations. He learns that by exhibiting regulators that speed up and intensify the interaction he can, through empathy, produce similar behaviors in his audience. When he identifies signs of a slowdown in communication, he changes what he is doing to arrest deterioration before significant damage is done.

An important proxemic factor enters into control of the regulatory function of nonverbal interaction. As distance between persons increases, regulators operate less effectively. Dyadic distances are ordinarily small enough that handling this factor is no problem. But when one speaker is interacting with a grouped audience, it becomes an important, sometimes critical, element.

A simple formula represents the major problem of using nonverbal communication with grouped, somewhat remote auditors: $R = 1/D$. R represents the physical response of persons, and the formula can be translated into this statement: the amount of overt response a person gives to a speaker is inversely proportional to the distance between that person and the speaker. Since the speaker gets his cues for feedback from overt responses, it becomes important for him to be as close to his listeners as a situation permits.

A related reason why regulators and other elements of nonverbal communication function more effectively in close proximity is that the persons in the communication transaction can see and hear each other better. Considering the interactive nature of human communication it is seldom if ever desirable to choose a greater rather than a minimum physical separation of the persons engaged in communication.

Regulators operate, in the main, out-of-awareness. In dyadic communication a continuous flow of voiced and action responses make possible the feedback which controls the entire process. If one member of a dyad stops his regulatory nonverbal behavior artificially, the interaction immediately falters and soon grinds to a halt. To lesser degree the same phenomenon can be observed when a grouped audience stops responding.

Expressing feelings, emotions, and attitudes

Much important nonverbal communication is accomplished by vocal and body movement signals which let others know how the person signaling feels about what is going on. Like illustrators, these expressive elements influence meanings of linguistic structures, but unlike illustrators their main burden of information concerns the mental state of the sender rather than the content of the message.

Most expressive nonverbal behavior in interpersonal communication is out-of-awareness. It would be difficult for a participant in a dyadic interaction to tell himself, "Now I'll register anger by frowning" or "Perhaps I should smile to show I'm receptive to this proposal" or "Guess I'll let my mouth hang open in astonishment." Planning and consciously executing expressive responses is probably impossible except for a professional actor, and even the skilled actor relies mainly on automated behaviors that come intuitively from his concept of the character he is playing.

Goffman distinguishes purposeful from unintended cues by labeling such signs as either "given" or "given off."

> The first involves verbal symbols or their substitutes which he uses admittedly and solely to convey the information. . . . The second involves a wide range of action that others can treat as symptomatic of the actor, the expectation being that the action was performed for reasons other than the information conveyed in this way.[4]

What distinguishes "given" from "given off" communication behavior in a most basic sense is *intent*. If the person emitting the stimuli attempts thereby to produce certain consequences in a receiver, the signs he makes are "given." If he makes no effort to anticipate the consequences of his behavior in the other person, then his expressive actions are truly out-of-awareness, or "given off." Given and given off meaningful cues in an interaction may be blended in all possible proportions, but as involvement of the participants increases, given signals yield to a predominance of communicative elements that are "given off."

Appropriate expressions of feelings, emotions, and attitudes are quite rigidly controlled by cultural norms. As a consequence, sets of expectations in particular situations dictate both given and given off behaviors and their interpretation by perceiving persons. The effects of cultural standardization of expressive communication are summarized by Goffman.

> Although an individual can stop talking he cannot stop communicating through body idiom; he must say either the right thing or the wrong thing. He cannot say nothing. Paradoxically, the way in which he can give the least amount of information about himself—although this

---

[4] Erving Goffman, *Presentation of Self in Everyday Life* (Garden City, N.Y.: Doubleday Anchor Books, 1959), p. 2.

is still appreciable—is to fit in and act as persons of his kind are expected to act. (The fact that information about self can be held back in this way is one motive for maintaining the proprieties.) Finally, it should be noted that while no one in a society is likely to be in a position to employ the whole expressive idiom, or even a major part of it, nevertheless everyone will possess some knowledge of the same vocabulary of body symbols. Indeed, the understanding of a common body idiom is one reason for calling an aggregate of individuals a society.[5]

The reader will recall that in chapter 9 the mode of nonverbal communication termed "nervantics" (fidget behavior) was shown to vary from culture to culture. Fidgeting, while beyond the disciplinary powers of the person who fidgets, is restricted effectively by his society. It is predominantly "given off." Certainly there are times when persons "act nervous" to produce predetermined consequences, but usually other means of generating desired responses are more direct and reliable.

Social pressures to conform to prevailing sets of expectations modify expressive acts more than is the case with emblems, illustrators, and regulators. Ekman and Friesen refer to "display rules," the conventional restrictions in a social situation that dictate the expression of feelings, emotions, and attitudes.

> We believe that there are well-established social norms about which display rule is appropriate for each affect when experienced by individuals of varying status, role, sex, age, physiognomy, etc. These display rule norms take into account not only the characteristics of the displayer, but also those of any other persons present when the display is evoked, and of the social context.[6]

Ekman and Friesen identify five kinds of display rules that structure expressive behavior in interpersonal communication. The "natural" expression may be *amplified,* or *de-intensified,* depending on the situation and persons present. A third display rule is to *neutralize* the expression, to pretend that no feeling, emotion, or attitude is present. The expression may be *blended* by showing the affect momentarily, mixing it in with other conventional expressions, as when distaste for an off-color joke is hinted at by a quick grimace and immediate reversion to a pleasant, smiling expression. *Masking* is hiding the affect by substituting the external symptoms of another, as a person may enact a casual, confident role in moments of great insecurity.

[5] Erving Goffman, *Behavior in Public Places* (New York: The Free Press, 1963), p. 35.

[6] P. Ekman and W. V. Friesen, "The Repertoire of Nonverbal Behavior: Categories, Origins, Usage and Coding," *Semiotica* 1 (1969): 75.

The reader will find it rewarding to formulate the display rules that govern expressive behaviors in dyads and the multi-person interactions in which he participates. He will find that the permissible and appropriate ways of displaying feelings, emotions, and attitudes *in context* are indeed defined and restricted with a severity that justifies referring to these conventions as "rules." As Goffman and others have noted, insane asylums are populated to a significant degree with persons who failed to conform to display rules of their society. Sensing the difference between proper and improper expressive behaviors in familiar situations has always been accepted as the hallmark of sanity.

Controlling tensions of source and/or receivers

In purposeful interpersonal acts of communication such as persuasion, the control of tension is a significant function of nonverbal behaviors. Before examining this function we must first explain the nature of the kinds of tension that develop in spoken interaction, their effects on the communication process, and the difference between the tensions that facilitate communication and the tensions that impede it.

To help in understanding constructive and destructive tensions, we will postulate a difference between feelings and emotions. Emotions are associated with greater physical change (endocrine secretion, blood pressure, heartbeat, breathing) and persist longer than do feelings. Typical feeling-states are euphoria, enthusiasm, nostalgia, reverence, and anticipation. Basic emotions are love, rage and fear.

When a person is in a definite emotional condition he loses some of his ability to think clearly, he tends toward excessive physical activity, and he transfers his emotion to surrounding people and objects. As a consequence his behavior in communication contrasts with his interaction patterns when he is calm.

Feelings such as excitement and even exhilaration do not impair thinking, reduce physical control, or produce transference. In fact, positive feelings such as enthusiasm often enhance mental and physical task-oriented efforts. Positive feelings we thus consider to be constructive tensions, and emotions of significant intensity we view as tensions destructive to purposeful interpersonal communication.[7]

Where do emotion and feeling tensions originate? In the mind of the tense person, obviously. His interpretations (perceptions) of the situation cause him to be angry, exhilarated, fearful, and so on. The concern of

---

[7] For a detailed treatment of feelings and emotions and their effects on interpersonal communication see Ernest Bormann, W. S. Howell, R. G. Nichols, and G. L. Shapiro, *Interpersonal Communication in the Modern Organization* (Englewood Cliffs, N.J.: Prentice-Hall, 1969), pp. 242–48.

both persuader and persuadee is to be continuously aware of their own and the other's emotions and feelings and to have techniques to maximize facilitative tensions and minimize destructive tensions.

First, let us consider the problem of a communicator controlling his own tensions. Let us say that he feels apprehensive and notes that his body is stiff and taut as he begins an interaction. Nervantic behavior, fidgeting, is nature's way of giving off excess energy, but the side effects of conspicuous jitters in communication cancel out the benefits. Strong positive autosuggestion, telling himself to relax, is often helpful. Animated speaking, using vigorous movement and gestures, works well in lowering unpleasant tension. Best of all is the direction of the attention of the speaker to responses of his audience. When the source is concentrating on collecting evidence of how his message is being received he is not thinking about himself, and this other-directed concern is almost magical in its ability to neutralize bothersome tensions.

Now, let us discuss the predicament of the communicator who realizes that he is in the grip of a rather intense emotional condition. Perhaps he is very angry because of events unrelated to his present task of communication. Since he has insight into his emotion, he knows that he cannot trust his judgment, that his speaking mechanism will not function with its usual agility and precision, and that his anger is likely to show itself most inappropriately during the interaction. Armed with insight he may attempt to keep his emotion from interfering with his communication task. He is unlikely to be happy about this decision later, however, because his impaired critical faculties limit his ability to "be objective" about his condition. Since an emotional state like rage or pronounced fear persists for many hours at the very least, he will not expect his anger to burn itself out quickly. A wise decision might be to postpone or otherwise avoid any critical interpersonal communication until an emotional condition has run its course and has subsided.

How can the persuader control tensions in the other person? He will use predominantly nonverbal means of communication. It is possible to emit soothing words and phrases, but when a speaker says "Keep relaxed" while his musculature vibrates with tension, his nonverbal message typically obliterates any dissonant linguistic content.

The basic mechanism of interpersonal tension control is *empathy*. To better understand how empathy functions as a tension regulator in human interaction we will stipulate a physiological definition: Empathy is the tendency to replicate physically what we see and hear.[8] When a person feels close to a speaker he experiences a flow of muscle tensions

---

[8] The physiological approach to empathy in communication and its implications are discussed in William Howell and E. G. Bormann, *Presentational Speaking in Business and the Professions* (New York: Harper and Row, 1971), pp. 221, 284–86.

that imitate on a much reduced scale the movements and bodily tone of the speaker. The sensations from his own muscle tensions and movements contribute to the listener's involvement. Out-of-awareness, the receiver "acts out" the role of the source—through physical imitation—and as a result he comes to share the feelings and attitudes of the speaker.

The first application of empathy to tension control in others is a negative admonition: Don't exhibit postures or movements or facial expressions which, if imitated by the receiver, would make him uncomfortable. Recall occasions on which you were in an audience being addressed by a speaker in the throes of stage fright. His voice shook, his hands trembled, his knees knocked together, and you suffered such discomfort that you said to yourself, "If only he would stop speaking and sit down!" When empathic reactions cause unpleasant responses, attention is diverted from the message to the cause of pain felt by the receiver. Thus, the intended communication is quite thoroughly blocked.

A second means of effecting tension control is for the speaker to exemplify whatever physical postures and movements he wishes to elicit from his listeners. As he approaches a vital point in his message, he talks louder and more deliberately, leans forward, moves toward his audience, tenses his body, and uses stronger gestures and more pronounced head movements and increased facial expression. Persons receiving these stimuli will empathize, and as a result of assuming the bodily characteristics of complete attention and high interest, will probably comprehend better and remember longer what is spoken. If a speaker wishes his audience to relax and take a break, he can step back, relax, smile, and talk with minimum tension in his voice.

To summarize briefly, tensions of persons interacting in persuasion are influenced by empathy. Destructive or constructive tensions are produced through replication of each other's behavior. A participant with the requisite insight and skill can purposefully influence the tensions of others through nonverbal means of interpersonal communication.

Quantifiable modalities of nonverbal interpersonal persuasion

Thus far in our discussion of elements other than language that are influential in person-to-person persuasion, we have not confronted the problem of quantification. Is it helpful to measure these variables of interaction and represent their functioning with a series of numbers? In studying the language of persuasion we count words per minute, the number of repetitions of an idea or a phrase, the occurrence of "loaded" words, the numbers of simple, complex, and compound sentences, sentence length, etc. What can be done to similarly describe significant nonverbal behaviors statistically? Obviously, time and distance can be measured, as can angular relationships such as directness or avoidance in eye contact. Quantifying these three dimensions of nonverbal communication behaviors has begun, with the result that we are no longer limited to noting the presence or absence of a phenomenon but are increasingly able to say *how much* of it is needed to produce certain results.

Our stress on *interaction* suggests that measurement of nonverbal communicative acts should not take place in isolation; any act carries meaning only as it relates to something else, and it should be scrutinized in terms of that relationship. In other words, the questions of significance of the behavior can be answered only with information about its consequences and/or correlates. Ekman and Friesen define "five indicative methods for the analysis of nonverbal behavior" that are truly categories of interaction.[9] Each relates at least two variables in a way that contributes to understanding the function of a unit of communication.

The first "indicative measure" they note is the rate of nonverbal behavior related to the characteristics of the sender. Certain personality traits may be associated with rapid or slow sequences of nonverbal elements in conversation, for example, as the cautious person may be both verbally and nonverbally deliberate.

A second indicative method relates rate measures of nonverbal behaviors to selected elements in the context or situation. The presence of a supervisor may dramatically increase an employee's use of head movements and hand gestures, for example.

"A third indicative method analyzes rate measures of nonverbal behavior in relation to the other interactant's characteristics or behavior. For example, eyecover acts might occur most frequently when the other interactant is an older male, or expresses disapproval, or shifts his gaze to the sender's face, etc.[10]

A fourth way of examining a nonverbal behavior is to relate it to other nonverbal acts that are concurrent or that precede or follow it. A hand gesture of rejection may accompany a side-to-side shaking of the head, for example, or after a person has been offered a trophy there may be a significant pause before he reaches out to grasp it.

Finally, the linguistic elements in a message may be related to nonverbal behaviors of the person sending or receiving it. The speaker

[9] P. Ekman and W. V. Friesen, "Nonverbal Behavior in Psychotherapy" in J. Schlien, ed., *Research in Psychotherapy* (Washington, D.C.: American Psychological Association, 1968), pp. 196, 197.

[10] Ibid.

delivering an accusation to his opponent may point, or possibly shake his fist, while the accused may stare at the ceiling and affect disinterest by smiling smugly.

In any of the five relationships, quantification of the elements involved is meaningful. The more precise the measurements of time, distance, and directness, the more understandable and predictable these nonverbal interactions become.

To quantify nonverbal behaviors a standard unit, the *act*, is necessary. Ekman and Friesen explain the nature of this unit:

> The beginning of an act is determined as the point at which the part of the body under scrutiny begins to move from the still body *position*; the end is the point at which the movement ends, either by return to the same or to a different position, or by the addition of another distinctive act. Acts which look alike, established through paired comparison procedures, are given the same classification label. Positions, when a body area or areas are still, are similarly classified in terms of visual appearance. An example of a hand act is the eyecover, where one hand is brought up to one eye, covers it, and then returns to the preceding position, or to another still position.[11]

Two variables in nonverbal interaction in person-to-person communication seem to be more susceptible to quantification than others, namely, visual interaction behaviors, and the management of time. Since these are of obvious importance we will limit our discussion to them, at the same time recognizing that they are arbitrarily selected from a very long list of nonverbal items that need to be and ultimately will be quantified.

Visual interaction behaviors

The manner in which eyes are used by participants in interpersonal communication has been the subject of considerable study. We will review a sampling of findings in several categories of relationships that have been investigated. Our purposes are to acquaint the reader with the many possibilities for using visual interaction to enhance persuasion and to encourage him to assess the role of eye contact and avoidance in all person-to-person persuasive interaction.

Duncan offers a useful five-way classification of variables related to patterned visual behaviors in person-to-person talking:

> Researchers taking the psychological approach have studied the effects on visual interaction of such variables as (a) sex of interactants,

[11] Ibid., p. 194.

(b) speaking versus listening, (c) affective quality of the interaction, (d) personality characteristics of the interactants, and (e) distance between interactants.[12]

A survey summary of some results of studies in Duncan's five areas will suggest to the reader a wealth of applications to persuasion. There is general agreement that females use more eye contact than males and that when the interaction becomes more warm and intimate, women tend to look at their interacting partners more, while men look less. When the nature of the interaction becomes hostile, both men and women tend to look at each other less, but females maintain more eye contact than do males.

There is approximately twice as much eye contact while listening as there is in the act of speaking, for both males and females. Females are more uncomfortable than are males when conditions restrict visual interaction, or make it impossible to see interactants. When visual contact is restricted, males increase their verbal participation. Subjects of all ages are very sensitive to being watched, whether or not they are engaged in task behavior.

Argyle and Ingham explored the influence of distance separating members of a dyad. They studied four variables in visual interaction, with these major findings:

> These two experiments show that distance has a clear effect on the amount of individual gaze, mutual gaze, length of mutual glance, and length of glance. The effect is large, for example mutual gaze is 21.7% at 2 feet, 42.6% at 10 feet. The relationship is curvilinear for gaze, approaching an asymptote at about 65–70% of gaze, though this shape is most marked for opposite sex pairs. The increase of EC with distance is almost entirely due to the increased amount of individual gaze; there is a small change in the synchronizing of gaze with distance, in that mutual gaze is avoided at closer distances. Most of the effect of distance is on looking while listening, though for MF pairs looking while talking is also affected.[13]

When members of a dyad were separated by a one-way glass partition, the person who could see the other but could not be seen increased his looking significantly. Argyle and Ingham interpret this to mean that the possibility of "mutual gaze" reduces eye contact. They further report

[12] Starkey Duncan, Jr., "Nonverbal Communication," *Psychological Bulletin* 72: 2 (August, 1969): 129.

[13] Michael Argyle and Roger Ingham "Gaze, Mutual Gaze and Proximity," *Semiotica* 6 (1972): 47.

that male-female pairs looked less than did male-male or female-female pairs, and that in male-female combinations the females are more inhibited by the possibility of eye contact than are the males.[14]

Patterns of nonverbal interaction are coordinated with linguistic elements in complex ways that can be analyzed. Speech, while people are looking at each other, is faster and more fluent. As one member approaches the termination of his verbalization, he looks at the other, and as the second person begins to talk, he tends to look away. When a speaker hesitates and searches for words he looks away, a behavior that contrasts with his looking toward his interactant before and during the pause that follows the termination of a verbal unit.

Visual interaction behaviors appear to be systematic and amenable to description and quantification. We anticipate rapid progress in accumulating useful information concerning this central variable in interpersonal nonverbal communication.

The management of time

The ebb and flow of language in person-to-person persuasion as well as specific meanings assigned to words and phrases are influenced profoundly by *timing*. The effective speaker increases the impact of his central point by placing it at the climax of a series of carefully timed elements, and the humorist knows better than most of us the importance of split-second timing in releasing his "punch line." We speak of eloquent pauses and of the significance of markedly slowing down or speeding up one's rate of speaking. These and other considerations in the time-spoken language relationship are both quantifiable and subject to conscious control by the skilled communicator.

Of the many possible ways in which the timing of spoken interaction can be described we discuss but two, hesitation phenomena and the interaction chronograph. The first is treated to expand our understanding of the effects of various types of pauses in differing circumstances, and the second is to acquaint our readers with a device that is uniquely well-suited to the study of timing patterns in spoken exchanges.

Hesitation Phenomena. Duncan defines this category of nonverbal communication and suggests the major kinds of investigations that have been done:

> Hesitation phenomena include various types of pauses and other nonfluencies, such as stutters and repetitions. These phenomena have attracted the attention, both of psychologists interested in behavioral

[14] Ibid., p. 48.

manifestations of affective states and of psycholinguists interested in the cognitive processes of speech encoding. There has been more extensive investigation of hesitations than of any other class of paralinguistic behaviors.[15]

Pauses vary in length, in their type (whether they are silent or phonated, repetitive, false starts, or slips of the tongue), and in their location. Filled pauses are associated with imprecise and inefficient use of language, and unfilled pauses tend to accompany more carefully constructed and efficiently worded language units. In therapy, filled pauses occurred more frequently in sessions which both patient and therapist considered to be relatively unproductive. Generally, filled pauses are detrimental to purposeful communicative interaction, while unfilled pauses may be helpful.

Listeners tend to ignore unfilled pauses in expected places. At the end of a clause with either a rising or falling inflection, a substantial pause is appropriate, hence unnoticed. At a "sustained termination," the end of a unit of language with no change in pitch, a shorter pause is expected, while a longer delay is conspicuous.

In an extended interaction, periods of hesitancy and abundant nonfluencies usually alternate with fluent periods. Apparently the state of the moment-to-moment interpersonal relationship, the fluctuating "quality of dyadic interaction," causes wide swings from easy and spontaneous exchange to forced and labored taking turns in talking. One should not expect a productive person-to-person communication to proceed rapidly, steadily, and smoothly.

To generalize about the constructive use of hesitations in task-oriented speaking: avoid filled pauses, use a variety of silent hesitations at the ends of thought units, and accept these hesitations as preferable to wide variations in fluency during any extended communication episode.

THE INTERACTION CHRONOGRAPH.   When people interact in purposeful communication, a record of who talks for how long, how much silence separates contributions, who interrupts whom how often, who persists until others yield the floor to him, and as the event continues, what trends develop in these variables can carry a great deal of information about the interaction although we might not even know the topic discussed. A device that discards content but makes highly reliable and complete records of these items is the interaction chronograph.

Two forms of the device are used. One is operated by a trained observer, who views a communicating dyad through a one-way glass. Oscillating circuits produce a magnetic tape recording of two signals.

[15] Starkey Duncan, Jr., "Nonverbal Communication," p. 127.

When A is communicating, button 1 is depressed, when B communicates, button 2 is pushed, when A and B are both talking, both buttons are held down. The second form dispenses with the observer-operator by using two voice operated relays, with separate microphones for A and B.

Form one of the chronograph produces a record that shows how a participant usually begins communicating nonverbally before vocalization begins and continues with his communication for substantial periods after his vocalization stops. Form two records only onset, duration, and termination of vocalization. Because the initiation of communication is more often than not nonverbal, as is its ending, the observer record would seem to yield a more faithful representation of stimulus-response patterns than would any voice-operated device.

In addition to putting on record how long each person communicates each time he talks, the chronograph record distinguishes among twelve possible interaction sequences.[16] (see figure 13–1)

Chapple has used the interaction chronograph to provide information about an individual's communication behavior while interacting with a trained interviewer who provides at first normal lively conversation, then two kinds of stress (that of being interrupted and that of the interviewer not responding), and finally a recovery period when the interviewer becomes once again a responsive, lively conversationalist. Computer analysis of the chronograph tapes provides much information about the behavior of the individual tested. Chapple lists the following traits as revealed by the chronograph records of stress interviews: level of activity, listening ability, dominance, initiative, quickness, flexibility, persistence, hesitancy, and overeagerness. He also identifies various patterns of reactions to stress that are characteristic of particular persons.[17]

A severe limitation on the use of the chronograph stress test to ascertain the traits of communicators is the necessity to keep the purpose and method of the interview secret from the person being tested. If the testee understood the rationale of the testing procedure, he could easily simulate whatever behaviors he wished to record.

It seems to the present writers that the potential contribution of the interaction chronograph lies in advancing our understanding of patterns of interaction rather than in classifying personality traits of individuals. For example, one of the authors made chronograph records of Monday morning conferences between sales managers and salesmen in different cultures around the world. He found that in the unproductive conferences

[16] Eliot D. Chapple, "Quantitative Analysis of Complex Organizational Systems," *Human Organization* 21: 2 (Summer, 1962): 70.

[17] E. D. Chapple and L. R. Sayles, *The Measure of Management* (New York: The Macmillan Company, 1961), pp. 138–41.

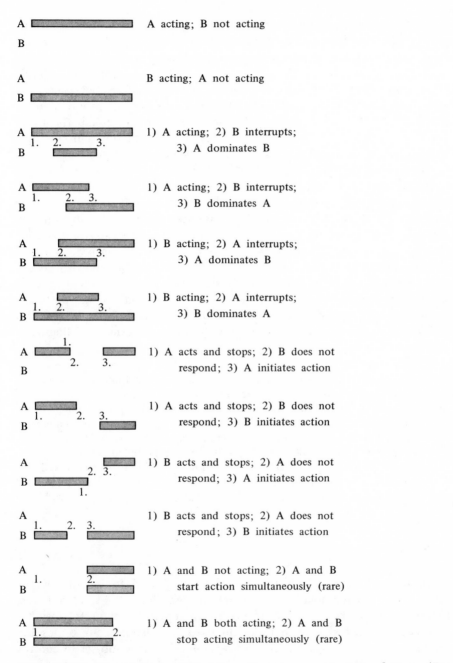

Figure 13–1. The twelve possible interaction sequences in pair relations. (Reproduced by permission of the Society for Applied Anthropology from *Human Organization* 21:2, 1962.)

the sales manager and salesman took turns speaking, there were uniform pauses between utterances, and contributions tended to be about the same length. In contrast, the more productive conferences became increasingly irregular, with a few very long pauses, but much simultaneous speaking. In several of the best conferences, where both salesman and sales manager were thinking together and making progress, both participants were speaking at the same time as much as half the time, with no confusion or misunderstanding. The interaction chronograph will be helpful in the study of simultaneous sending and receiving, which to the present time has received little attention.

When the interaction pattern of a particular application of persuasion, such as selling a new car, is thoroughly understood, it may be possible to teach the salesman to so structure his interview that it approximates a productive arrangement of time sequences. No one can say that the "feel" of a successful interaction pattern is less persuasive than the cognitive content of the language used! Our preoccupation with verbal elements has prevented adequate consideration of time factors as well as of other nonverbal elements. And time has the advantage of being easily recorded, quantifiable, and unambiguous. Chapple highlights the comparative complexity of working with time patterns and linguistic elements:

> In everyday life, we recognize that what people actually do is what counts and tell our children that "actions speak louder than words." Yet, research effort has concentrated on finding out what is going on inside the person through the use of ink blots, pictures, questionnaires, or the full-fledged treatment on the psychoanalyst's couch. What is learned from the resulting word patterns is highly difficult even for the experts to interpret. Too often their findings remind one of the sacred oracle at Delphi repeating the message of the gods in words so tangential to meaning that only the fact can prove the soothsayer right.[18]

Conclusion

Since nonverbal communication can be interpreted to include everything in the environment of an interaction, some limitations are required if the student of persuasion is to acquire a repertoire of useful insights and skills in this area. The rationale used in selecting our topics for discussion includes these criteria: we examined factors subject to control by the persuader; we recognized the interdependence of verbal and

[18] Ibid., pp. 114–15.

nonverbal elements; we treated nonverbal communication events as a continuous flow of interactions; we distinguished interactive behaviors from contextual surroundings; and we emphasized the *functions* of the nonverbal components of persuasion rather than their origins, coding, or modes.

We have identified and discussed five distinct but not mutually exclusive functions of nonverbal interpersonal communication. Quantification is a means of increasing our understanding of nonverbal factors in persuasive interaction; it can be applied to three modalities: visual interaction phenomena, hesitations, and overall time patterns in the dyad. The study of these readily quantifiable elements promises to yield insights valuable to person-to-person persuaders. In addition, the interaction chronograph has proved to be a useful device for identifying intricate patterns of timing that can be associated with linguistic content and behavioral consequences.

It is hoped that the reader now better understands what nonverbal person-to-person communication is, how it works, and how to use it in his own efforts to persuade.

14

Nonverbal persuasion: context

Introduction

While the previous chapter dealt with physical behaviors of people in communicative interaction, this chapter is concerned with the environment in which that interaction occurs. We will look at the *scene,* the circumstances, objects, and people that accompany and influence an act of persuasion. Again, we will attempt to emphasize elements the persuader can control so that we avoid to some extent the pitfalls of trying to list environmental influences comprehensively.

Among circumstances of a nonverbal nature we must include a speaker's credibility or ethos, his reputation as it is perceived by persuadees. Much of the influence of credibility is both situational and nonverbal, but because chapter 11 covered extensively this important role of credibility in the process of persuasion, it will be referred to only peripherally in this chapter.

The power of both related and unrelated events to influence persuasion is undeniable yet often goes unrecognized. A sales campaign to aggressively promote the sale of Cadillacs may be made impotent by an energy crisis that limits the supply of gasoline. The efforts of Arab and Jewish members of a model community to work together may be destroyed by news of an airplane hijacking and murder of hostages by Palestinian terrorists. The effectiveness of student participation in governing a university may be measurably increased by an undefeated football team. A political candidate who is a potential loser may become a winner after a member of his opponent's political party is convicted of embezzlement. Placing a man on the moon probably increased the persuasive power of appeals for support of many varieties of scientific research, most of which were unrelated to the conquest of space.

Objects modify the act of persuasion as well. The suitor proposing marriage may be aided or thwarted in his appeal by the size of the diamond in the proffered engagement ring. An uncomfortable crowding of seats with restricted leg room may create a climate unreceptive to persuasion. Pleasant, tasteful surroundings and a properly functioning public address system may well have as much effect in persuasion as the content of a speaker's message. Appropriate dress enhances interaction, dissonance in dress makes high quality of interaction unlikely. Often objects distract and divide one's attention. When a stray dog mounts the platform and curls up at the feet of the speaker, audience perception of his message deteriorates beyond the point of no return. The knowledgeable speaker takes time out to deal with the puppy problem before resuming his persuasive presentation.

Finally, people in the environment often influence ongoing persuasion significantly. Distractions from inappropriate intrusion are most obvious. An appraisal interview is marred when someone accidentally opens the wrong door. The supervisor and his employee fail to gain rapport because the extraneous interference has disrupted their conversation. A teacher's harsh reprimand of a student's habitual tardiness changes abruptly to gentle chiding and constructive admonitions when the superintendent enters.

Certainly events, people, and surroundings shape the act of persuasion and contribute to its outcomes. The reader will recall the model of the process of persuasive communication discussed in chapter 1. The *scene* we are discussing may be envisioned as an encapsulation of that model. Steps and elements in the model all exist without direct connection to the scene, yet every component and each relationship is affected by that enclosure.

We reiterate that materials on nonverbal interpersonal communication are new and tentative, and the study of elements in the nonverbal context is similarly undeveloped. Again, we ask the reader to recognize a need for the less-than-scholarly, somewhat mechanical advice on managing critical factors in the environment of persuasion.

Personal space in the context of persuasion

Proxemics was defined in chapter 9, as the use of space and the physical relationships of people to implement interpersonal communication. We noted that appropriate distances, arrangements, and bodily attitudes tend to be firmly fixed in the environment of a particular culture.

Personal space is an element of proxemics. It is the territory occupied by an individual with boundaries established by his sense of "proper" distance between himself and others; in a specific situation each person is surrounded by a "bubble" of space that he treats as though it belonged to him. If interacting individuals invade it, he is made uncomfortable, and if his respondent is further away than the wall of his bubble, he moves toward the other person until the conversational distance is the radius of his territory, that is, his partner in communication is at the boundary of his bubble.

While personal space is determined mainly by culture, the range of variations among cultures is limited by vision and hearing and influenced by olfaction, thermal receptors, and the capabilities of the human voice. Edward T. Hall in 1966 produced a fascinating synthesis of physiological and cultural variables entering into the establishing of personal space under differing situations in the northeastern United States. Hall's summation of these elements (see figure 14–1) shows better than any other resource the interaction of the senses and cultural norms.

As the headings on Hall's chart suggest, he identifies four zones of personal space, that is, distinct and different interpersonal distances for four categories of communicative interaction. Because participants in persuasion *need* to have their expectations of personal space met, we are adopting his convenient classification of personal space in our treatment of nonverbal contextual elements. The impact of including this concept of personal space in the study of behavior in persuasion is significant. Hall suggests how the discovery of this proxemic patterning develops a new perspective in human communication:

> Until recently man's space requirements were thought of in terms
> of the actual amount of air displaced by his body. The fact that man has

CHART SHOWING INTERPLAY OF THE DISTANT AND IMMEDIATE RECEPTORS
IN PROXEMIC PERCEPTION

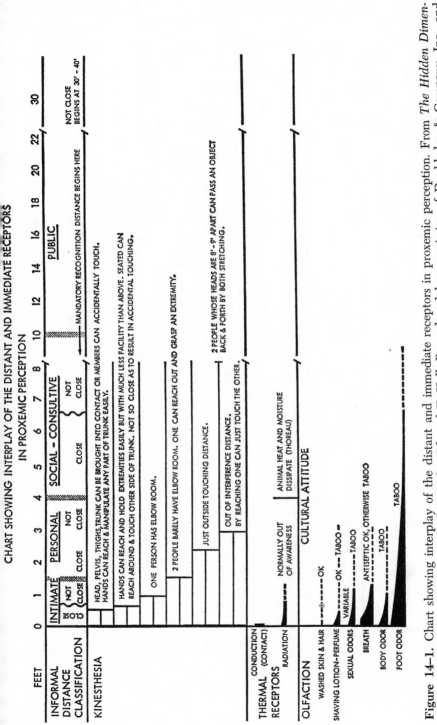

Figure 14-1. Chart showing interplay of the distant and immediate receptors in proxemic perception. From *The Hidden Dimension* by Edward T. Hall. Copyright © 1966 by Edward T. Hall. Reproduced by permission of Doubleday & Company, Inc., and the author's agent, Lurton Blassingame.

305

FEET: 0 · 1 · 2 · 3 · 4 · 5 · 6 · 7 · 8 · 10 · 12 · 14 · 16 · 18 · 20 · 22 · 30

VISION

DETAIL VISION (VIS ∠ OF FOVEA 1°)
- 0: VISION BLURRED / DISTORTED
- 1: ENLARGED DETAILS OF IRIS, EYEBALL, PORES OF FACE, FINEST HAIRS
- 2–3: DETAIL OF FACE SEEN AT NORMAL SIZE: EYES, NOSE, SKIN, TEETH CONDITION, EYELASHES, HAIR ON BACK OF NECK
- 4–5: SMALLEST BLOOD VESSELS IN EYE LOST. SEE WEAR ON CLOTHING HEAD HAIR SEEN CLEARLY.
- 7–8: FINE LINES OF FACE FADE DEEP LINES STAND OUT SLIGHT EYE WINK LIP MOVEMENT SEEN CLEARLY
- 12–14: ENTIRE CENTRAL FACE INCLUDED
- 16–18: SHARP FEATURES DISSOLVE, EYE COLOR NOT DISCERNIBLE, SMALL-SCOWL VISIBLE HEAD BOBBING MORE PRONOUNCED
- 20–30: SNELLEN'S STANDARD FOR DISTANT VISION EMPLOYING ANGLE OF 1 MIN, GUILD OPTICIANS OF AMERICA EYE CHART A PERSON WITH 20-40 VISION HAS TROUBLE SEEING EYES & EXPRESSION AROUND EYES THOUGH EYE BLINK IS VISIBLE.

CLEAR VISION (VIS ∠ AT MACULA 12° HOR, 3° VERT)
- 1: 25" x 3" ON EYE NOSTRILS OR MOUTH
- 2: 3.75" x .94" UPPER OR LOWER FACE
- 3: 6.25" x 1.60" UPPER OR LOWER FACE
- 5: 10" x 2.5" UPPER OR LOWER FACE OR SHOULDERS
- 7–8: 20" x 5" 1 OR 2 FACES
- 12–14: 31" x 7.5 FACES OF TWO PEOPLE
- 18: 4'2" x 16" TORSOS OF TWO PEOPLE
- 30: 6'3" x 1'7" TORSOS OF 4 OR 5 PEOPLE

60° SCANNING
- 1: 1/3 OF FACE EYE EAR OR MOUTH AREA FACE DISTORTED
- 2: NOSE PROJECTS WHOLE FACE SEEN UNDISTORTED
- 3: UPPER FACE CAN'T COUNT FINGERS
- 5: UPPER BODY & GESTURES
- 7–8: WHOLE SEATED BODY VISIBLE PEOPLE OFTEN KEEP FEET WITHIN OTHER PERSON'S 60° ANGLE OF VIEW
- 16–18: WHOLE BODY HAS SPACE AROUND IT, POSTURAL COMMUNICATION BEGINS TO ASSUME IMPORTANCE

PERIPHERAL VISION
- 1: HEAD AGAINST BACKGROUND
- 2: HEAD & SHOULDERS
- 3: WHOLE BODY MOVEMENT IN HANDS, FINGERS VISIBLE
- 5: WHOLE BODY
- 8: OTHER PEOPLE SEEN IF PRESENT
- 16–18: OTHER PEOPLE BECOME IMPORTANT IN PERIPHERAL VISION

HEAD SIZE
- 1: FILLS VISUAL FIELD FAR OVER LIFE SIZE
- 2: OVER NORMAL
- 3–4: NORMAL SIZE
- NOTE: PERCEIVED HEAD SIZE VARIES EVEN WITH SAME SUBJECTS AND DISTANCE
- 7–8: NORMAL TO BEGINNING TO SHRINK
- 14–16: VERY SMALL

ADDITIONAL NOTES
- 1: SENSATION OF BEING CROSS-EYED
- 10–12: PEOPLE & OBJECTS SEEN AS ROUND UP TO 12'-15'
- 16–18: ACCOMMODATIVE CONVERGENCE ENDS AFTER 15' PEOPLE & OBJECTS BEGIN TO FLATTEN OUT

TASKS IN SUBMARINES
- 1–2: 67% OF TASKS IN THIS RANGE
- 3: 23% FALL IN THIS RANGE
- 8: DIMMICH, F.L. & FARNSWORTH, D. VISUAL ACUITY TASKS IN A SUBMARINE, NEW LONDON, 1951

ARTIST'S OBSERVATIONS cf GROSSER
- 1–2: VERY PERSONAL DISTANCE
- 3: ARTIST OR MODEL HAS TO DOMINATE
- 5: A PORTRAIT, A PICTURE PAINTED AT 4-8' OF A PERSON WHO IS NOT PAID TO "SIT"
- 8: TOO FAR FOR A CONVERSATION
- 10–12: BODY IS 1/3 SIZE
- 18–30: FULL LENGTH STATE PORTRAITS. HUMAN BODY SEEN AS A WHOLE, COMPREHENDED AT A GLANCE, WARMTH AND IDENTIFICATION CEASE

ORAL   AURAL
- 0: GROANS GRUNTS
- 1: SOFT VOICE WHISPER INTIMATE STYLE
- 3–4: CONVENTIONAL MODIFIED VOICE CASUAL OR CONSULTIVE STYLE
- 8–10: LOUD VOICE WHEN TALKING TO A GROUP, MUST RAISE VOICE TO GET ATTENTION FORMAL STYLE
- 18–30: FULL PUBLIC SPEAKING VOICE FROZEN STYLE

NOTE: THE BOUNDARIES ASSOCIATED WITH THE TRANSITION FROM ONE VOICE LEVEL TO THE NEXT HAVE NOT BEEN PRECISELY DETERMINED

Figure 14.1 (cont.). From *The Hidden Dimension* by Edward T. Hall. Copyright © 1966 by Edward T. Hall. Reproduced by permission of Doubleday & Company, Inc., and the author's agent, Lurton Blassingame.

around him as extensions of his personality the zones described earlier has generally been overlooked. Differences in the zones—in fact their very existence—became apparent only when Americans began interacting with foreigners who organize their senses differently so that what was intimate in one culture might be personal or even public in another. Thus for the first time the American became aware of his own spatial envelopes, which he had previously taken for granted.[1]

Intimate distance

Intimate distance ranges from zero to about eighteen inches. Zero distance—touching—Hall characterizes as "the distance of love-making and wrestling, comforting and protecting." With Americans, communicating while bodies are in contact is ordinarily appropriate only in circumstances of privacy.

The far phase of intimate distance, six to eighteen inches, as noted in the above chart, is accompanied by distortions of vision and communication through olfaction and thermal receptors. While many cultures use this distance for general communication and appreciate breath and body odors, Americans reject public interaction that brings people this close together. When crowded conditions force Americans to use intimate distance, they avoid eye contact and seem to pretend that others have not invaded their private, personal space.

Personal distance

Close personal distance is estimated by Hall to be one and a half to two and a half feet, while the far phase extends to four feet. Close personal distance used in public in the United States informs observers that the persons conversing have a close relationship. An engaged couple, a man and wife, a parent and child, and possibly siblings would find use of close personal distance comfortable.

Far personal distance is appropriate for close friends, associates of long standing, informal dining, and other interactions while seated, particularly in crowded or noisy surroundings. While most business negotiations are conducted at greater distance, there is a trend toward informality, even intimacy, that brings some transactions into the far phase of personal distance.

[1] Edward T. Hall, *The Hidden Dimension* (Garden City, N.Y.: Doubleday and Company, 1966), p. 121.

Social distance

Most interpersonal communication in social and work situations is conducted at social distance, with a close phase of four to seven feet, and a far phase of seven to twelve feet.

While persons in the United States are engaged in a common task they tend to use close social distance. The four- to seven-foot range is a zone of compulsory involvement. It is not possible to stop communicating and go about other business. People in the close social distance feel obliged to center attention on the other person or persons and maintain interaction.

The far phase of social distance permits disengagement at will, and easy reestablishment of communication. Use of a loud voice and eye contact to maintain or initiate interaction is conventional. The unique feature of far social distance in America is that it permits people to drop in or out of involvement with others and thus permits some privacy in a populated space.

Public distance

In the United States communication becomes definitely more formal at public distance, which is any interpersonal interval over twelve feet; the maximum limit is imposed by audibility of the human voice. When a public address system is used, maximum public distance may become so great that visual communication through body language is negligible. As distance between communicators increases beyond the twelve foot threshold, both linguistic composition and speaking manner become more decorous and ritualistic. Many Americans have a conversational style quite different from their public speaking style; when the boundary between social distance and public distance is crossed, Americans usually assume a public speaking style.

In the close phase of public distance, twelve to twenty-five feet, we find the arena of most speaker-to-small-group persuasion. The speaker delivers a presentation; he does not participate in a conversation. An audience is created, and while free interaction between members of the audience and the persuader may occur, there is no doubt in any participant's mind that the occasion is a public speech and that it should conform to stereotyped public performance expectations.

Beyond twenty-five feet, in the far phase of public distance, both verbal and nonverbal interaction drop sharply. Only gross physical reactions can be perceived at these greater distances, and vocal nuances are replaced by exaggerated and standardized cues of vocal emphasis.

Speech is slowed, enunciation is overly precise, an active speaker/passive listener norm tends to develop. With large audiences the communication event resembles a group listening to a radio loudspeaker more than the shared interactive experience characteristic of persuasion at personal and social distances.

Awareness of Hall's four zones of distance in interpersonal communication is useful to the persuader and to the student of persuasion. Attempting to use a public distance style of communication at a social or personal distance could be a costly mistake. An eager persuader might carelessly intrude upon the privacy of a persuadee by talking at a close personal distance while the persuadee considers close or even far social distance appropriate. The thoughtful participant can experiment with distance judiciously, and by adjusting to the nonverbal responses of his respondent, discover the interval at which his conversational partner is most comfortable.

Close communication, of course, has many advantages; subtle cues are perceived, more senses are used, and more flexible interaction is possible. Consequently, the closest distance that is comfortable to the persons communicating should be chosen. Using public distance when social distance is acceptable or social distance when personal distance is appropriate could create a handicap impossible to overcome.

The above suggestions are random generalizations applying the theory of personal space to ongoing persuasion. The reader can extend applications of Hall's proxemic patterns to suit his own interests and needs.

Nonverbal elements in the setting for persuasion

Considerations of personal space describe a perceptual dimension of an interactional world; *setting*, on the other hand, refers to the physical world surrounding an interaction. Its importance to persuasion is suggested by Bennett and Bennett's succinct statement about the function of the setting: "All social interaction is affected by the physical container in which it occurs."[2]

Bennett and Bennett supply six categories of elements that together constitute the setting of social interaction:

1. The *container*—the fixed external enclosure of human interaction.
2. The *props*—physical objects which adhere to persons in the enclosure or to the enclosure itself, including dress and furnishings.

---

[2] David J. Bennett and Judith D. Bennett, "Making the Scene" in Gregory P. Stone and Harvey A. Farberman, eds., *Social Psychology Through Symbolic Interaction* (Waltham, Mass.: Ginn and Co., 1970), p. 190.

3. The *actors*—persons involved in, peripheral to, or spectators to the transactions carried on in the enclosure.

4. The *modifiers*—elements of light, color, odor, temperature and humidity which serve to affect the emotional tone or mood of the interaction.

5. *Duration*—the objective time in measurable units (minutes, hours, etc.) during which the interaction occurs, as well as the anticipated time the interaction will require.

6. *Progression*—the order of events which precede and follow, or are expected to follow, the interaction and have some bearing upon it.[3]

The Bennett and Bennett categories cover the vital elements of the setting more comprehensively than do other classification systems. Still, the necessary separation of elements for the purpose of defining them artificially isolates one element from the rest. Bennett and Bennett recognize the interdependence of their carefully defined elements, and, to put them together again, present a paradigm to assist the reader in assessing effects of the setting on social interaction (see table 14–1).

The paradigm helps us apply the elements to ongoing interactions by integrating container, props, and participants, and by specifying roles played by modifiers, duration, and progression. We will continue application of the Bennett and Bennett concept of the setting to a range of persuasive interactions. To accomplish this we will consider the components of the setting separately, but attempt to preserve their interrelationships.

Effects of the container on persuasive interaction

The Bennett and Bennett paradigm suggests several container variables important to an act of persuasion. Location could be indoors or outdoors. Outdoors, the used space could be definitely bounded (as in a natural amphitheatre) or relatively unbounded, as in a park or on a sidewalk or in a field. Indoors, the enclosed space varies in size and shape, and single or multiple spaces may be used. Modifiers, props, and actors are more subject to control inside than they are outside.

Perhaps most important of the container characteristics, indoors or out, is the size and shape of the enclosure. A purposeful interaction such as an act of persuasion is facilitated by encapsulation within a container of optimum volume and shape suited to the nature of the interaction. Too much or too little space is damaging, and the shape of the space may be a severe handicap if it is improper for a particular communication.

---

[3] Ibid., p. 192.

Table 14-1. The Setting

BASIC PHYSICAL CONTAINER AS IT MIGHT AFFECT SOCIAL INTERACTION	NUMBER AND ARRANGEMENT OF PROPS AND PERSONS IN THE ENCOUNTER
1. Natural, man-made, or both.	1. Physical objects which are not part of the space, but are in it and are taken into account in the interaction, e.g., furniture, automobiles, etc.
2. Interior, exterior, or both.	2. Number of people who act as participants and their measurable spatial relation to each other.
3. Meaningful size in relation to type of interaction (too large? too small? not culturally significant?).	3. Number of people who act as spectators and their spatial relation to the other participants and to each other.
4. Single or multiple spaces.	4. Number of people who are neither participants nor observers, but who occupy the same significant area and who, by being present, affect interaction.
5. Connected or disconnected.	
6. Relative proximity (measured in real time, subjective time, means of locomotion).	
7. Salient features, scale, size, multiple levels, etc.	

Modifiers

LIGHT	SOUND	COLOR	TEXTURE	ODOR	RELATIVE TEMPERATURE AND HUMIDITY
Source(s)	Volume	Hues	Location	Source(s)	
Intensity	Pitch	Location	Mixture	Mixture	
Direction	Intensity	Mixture		Permanence	
Color	Duration	Chromatic			
	Source	intensities			
	Direction				

Duration

Objective time span measured against conventional and/or subjective expectations.

Progression

The actual sequence of events implied by the scene and considered significant by those persons encountering one another on the scene.

Reprinted by permission of the publisher from: SOCIAL PSYCHOLOGY THROUGH SYMBOLIC INTERACTION, edited by Gregory P. Stone and Harvey A. Farberman, copyright 1970 by Ginn and Company, published by Xerox College Publishing.

In an overly large room participants in conversation seem drawn apart by excess space. Interviews, for example, are much more satisfactorily conducted in a plain six-by-eight-foot room than across the end of a large table in a sumptuously furnished board room designed for meetings of twenty executives. Rooms that are too small make people uneasy by invading one's personal space. Optimum size of a room, however, is often smaller than one would guess because some crowding, as long as it does not produce discomfort, lowers the appropriate interpersonal distance of communication, reduces formality, and is conducive to abundant feedback. A well-filled room contributes to group cohesiveness, which in turn leads to uniform response and nurtures common feelings and convictions.

Room shape is conventionally square or rectangular, and its proportions dictate the arrangement of persons. In a long narrow room a public speaker confronts a dilemma. Talking from one end reduces contact with remote listeners and gives him the impossible assignment of adapting to two or three zones of personal space. Speaking from the middle of the room makes the central segment of his audience a primary group and relegates those at the ends of the room to the status of observers. The effort of maintaining eye contact with remote persons in this situation is disturbing and difficult for both speaker and audience.

For most public speaker-audience situations the optimum floor shape for an enclosure is a square or a rectangle close to being a square. High ceilings have much the same dampening effect on interaction as overly large rooms. Norms of ceiling height are established by room floor area and architectural precedent in different locations. A lower-than-average height of ceiling has the same positive effect on speaker-audience interaction as does a well-filled room, and hence is preferable to a higher-than-average ceiling.

Occasionally it is necessary to use multiple spaces to accommodate an audience. The speaker, for example, talks to a present audience while persons in other rooms listen to loudspeakers. The speaker in this circumstance is well-advised to develop as much interaction with his present audience as possible, and not, in a mistaken effort to be fair, attempt to give present and remote groups equal attention. The only adaptation to the remote group that is practical is to explain for their benefit events in the main arena that would not be conveyed adequately by an eavesdropping operation.

For presentations and other persuasive forms involving more than fifteen or twenty people, particularly when demonstration equipment, films, etc., are used, a wedge-shaped room is advantageous, with message sources at the narrow end of the wedge. The elevation of seats relatively remote from the speaker makes the wedge shape still more effective for audiences larger than thirty or forty people.

Rooms that resemble half a bowl are rare but functional. The speaker is located at "bowl bottom" and seats are arranged up the sides of the semi-bowl. Distance from speaker to each member of his audience is thus held relatively constant. There are no remote auditors, eye contact and audibility are easily maintained, and the illusion of three dimensionality contributes to audience cohesiveness. Although less than one quarter of such a sphere is populated, persons in the bowl mentally complete the sphere and feel enclosed by it. Apparently this sensation of being wrapped up with others in a ball generates a feeling of togetherness.

Outdoors, definitely bounded space such as a patio, amphitheater, or an area enclosed by urban buildings functions to affect interpersonal communication much as do room size and shape. The ceiling is usually unlimited, and walls are irregular, with one or two walls often physically absent.

When no near objects enclose an outdoor arena of communication, a container nonetheless operates to affect interaction. It is large, possibly extending to the horizon. It contains props and persons, most of them unrelated to the communication and uncontrolled by the communicators. Climatic modifiers, wind, sun, rain, snow, heat, and cold, exert powerful influence. He who would entrust a critical incident of persuasion to the elements in an out-of-doors setting is either foolhardy or possessed of superior means of weather prediction.

We have called attention to an assortment of ways in which the container of persuasive communication can affect the ongoing interaction. In no way have we purported to be comprehensive. Our purpose is to alert the reader to influences of which he may have been unaware and encourage him to explore further effects of enclosures on the process of persuasion.

The role of props in persuasion

"Props," as we use the term, includes only physical objects that adhere to persons in the enclosure or to the enclosure itself. Some items classified as props are furniture, decorations, lighting fixtures, audiovisual equipment, clothing, and all the gadgetry of personal adornment and display.

Two kinds of props can be distinguished by their function in a persuasive interaction. The *integrated* prop is used by participants in the communication purposefully to accomplish their ends. The *incidental* prop, although it may affect persuasion profoundly, is not an intended part of the communicator's persuasive plan.

Use of a prop is *revealed* when the persuadee perceives it as being used in the persuasion and *concealed* when its use for persuasive purposes is not detected. Intent to conceal or reveal the use of a prop undoubtedly correlates with perception of or failure to perceive its use.

Integrated props are *revealed* and *concealed*. When a Fuller Brush salesman gives a housewife a free brush, he is using a revealed prop. When he draws his chair close to hers and asks her to lean back, relax, and sniff the perfume, his use of props is at least intended to be concealed. Audio-visual aids such as films and demonstrations are revealed, but carefully modulated and coordinated background music is concealed. Any purposeful use of props falls on a continuum from revealed to concealed, and many integrated props are both partially concealed and partially revealed.

Taking a customer to lunch is so well understood to be a persuasive device that the food and drink are usually revealed props. Music and decor in the carefully selected restaurant, as well as the services of a pretty and attentive waitress are concealed. Automobiles on the showroom floor are revealed props but the clusters of gaily colored balloons that cover the ceiling and the colored spotlights that set apart the featured "Bargain Car for Today" are concealed.

The range of integrated props used in persuasion is limited only by the inventive talents of the persuader. Using objects to supplement other means of persuasion is a major tool of social influence.

Incidental props have received little attention because they are of infinite variety, difficult to categorize and control. Usually they are treated as part of the container. However, we treat the enclosure as space, and to us, objects in that space are basically different in their influence on interaction from the boundaries of the space itself.

Unless it serves a particular purpose in an act of persuasion all *clothing* can be classified as incidental. Clothing props that would be classed as integrated might be costumes to be merchandized in a boutique fashion show. Typical furnishings of a conference room, office, or auditorium are incidental props. These furnishings may facilitate or hinder interpersonal communication. Generally unobtrusive and pleasant furnishings are preferred because any feature in a room that stands out and demands attention has some negative effect. A garish color scheme, uncomfortable chairs, hard wall surfaces that generate annoying reverberations, a drab and colorless environment, excessive neatness or excessive clutter, obstacles separating interacting persons such as desks, tables, or pillars may inhibit persuasion. Out-of-doors distractions caused by incidental items are even more numerous, and we will ask the reader to recall how automobiles, aircraft, bicycles, and numerous other man-made devices routinely complicate open air communication.

Too little attention is given to incidental props and how they influence persuasion. Our tendency is to accept what is available and use it, rather than to expend effort in rearranging it to create a more congenial situation. One of the authors only recently discovered that even furniture in a banquet hall can be moved. He was to deliver an after-dinner speech, and found himself at one end of a long, narrow ballroom. There was a short speakers' table seating eight persons across the end of the room, and from its center extended a line of banquet tables placed end to end, forming in effect a single table four feet wide and possibly a hundred feet long. If the audience continued to occupy their banquet seating as was obviously intended, the speaker would find himself addressing one of the narrowest and longest audiences in the history of public speaking.

He noted unused space in the ballroom beyond the lengthy table and decided that drastic steps were necessary. After being introduced he began his speech by saying, "This is not a pleasant speaking arrangement for any of us. Not only are many of you far away, but in order to see me you will all have to look sideways, and you will develop stiff necks. So, will you please push your chairs back from the tables, then push the tables to the rear of the room, and then bring your chairs up close to the speaker's table and make your own seating arrangement."

The group went to work with a will. In less than five minutes banquet tables were out of the way and a neat semicircular audience was created close to the speaker. Natural leaders emerged and directed the placement of chairs, making a center aisle, with boundary aisles to the right and left. Persons in the audience obviously enjoyed the opportunity to move about participating in a new experience, and many seemed to appreciate the opportunity to unobtrusively visit the bathroom. When the speaker began his talk he found that his audience was cohesive, warmed up, and ready to go. They had contributed to the occasion and became a responsive part of it. Speaker and audience had become a team eager to interact and make the most of the occasion.

Another dimension of our failure to manage constructively the props that influence persuasion is the low level priority we assign to communication in layout and design. Seldom do we plan and furnish a room *primarily* for certain types of interpersonal communication. It would make abundant sense to request architects and interior decorators to be sure that every detail in a room is decided by its effect on the interpersonal interaction that will take place in that space. A few training rooms in modern business organizations have been constructed and furnished according to this principle, and communicating in their environment is pleasant and easy.

Where large numbers of people are involved, by far the most important prop is the public address system. With intelligent use of modern electronic devices, each person in an audience of any size or arrangement can hear accurately and with comfort everything the speaker says. Because public address systems are often inadequate and inefficiently applied, we now turn our attention to making optimum use of this essential prop.

Amplifiers, the part of public address systems that strengthens and distributes the signals to remote loudspeakers, are often too weak. Power ratings of amplifiers should be well in excess of maximum demands made on them. An amplifier that is working at full capacity or is overloaded distorts the reproduced sound. Squeals and echoes can be minimized by careful adjustment of tone and volume controls on the amplifier. A properly adjusted amplifier produces sound that reinforces the speaker's voice rather than replacing it. Sound should be distributed unobtrusively so that all persons in the audience tend to forget that they are listening to a loudspeaker and perceive the speaker as speaking to them directly. The illusion of direct interpersonal communication obviously contributes to interaction and increased effectiveness.

Loudspeakers tend to be used in insufficient number and to be placed so that sound is unevenly distributed over the area occupied by the audience. Many small loudspeakers are better than a few large ones to distribute and reinforce the sound uniformly and unobtrusively. It is not necessary to have the loudspeakers near the speaker to accomplish the illusion of reinforcement. In most enclosures, installing a relatively large number of loudspeakers strategically spaced in the ceiling is the best solution to the problem of public address sound distribution. Ceiling loudspeakers do not call attention to themselves, and sound coming gently from above seems to envelop an audience in a cocoon that binds them to the remote speaker.

Microphones inhibit the speaker by restricting his movement. If the microphone is attached to the speaker's stand, he is anchored to one spot behind that piece of furniture for the duration of his speech. If it is on a floor stand, he is similarly tied down. A floor stand also makes it extremely difficult for an animated speaker to maintain a constant distance from the microphone. As a result, his voice alternately booms and fades away in his listeners' ears.

The solution to these microphone problems is to attach microphone to speaker. The lavalier microphone, hung around the speaker's neck, is the best such device. A microphone thus suspended is about six inches under the speaker's chin, which happens to be the best possible place for picking up his voice. Puffs of air from plosive sounds or breathing cannot reach the microphone. The mike is so close to the source of sound that other noises are made comparatively weak, and distractions are minimized. With a long cord and a little care in managing it, a speaker can move freely with a constant and uniform delivery of his voice to remote auditors. His interaction with his audience improves also, for the microphone is no longer a physical barrier between himself and his audience.

Possibly the ultimate refinement in public address application of the microphone is the "cordless mike," which needs no wire connection to the amplifier. This lavalier device contains a tiny frequency modulated broadcasting station. An FM receiver at the amplifier picks up the signal and decodes it into audio frequency impulses. With the cordless microphone the speaker is emancipated from most restrictions inherent in use of the public address system.

Our somewhat extended discussion of props and their influence on persuasive interaction reflects our conviction that the role of props is insufficiently understood and their thoughtful management neglected. We trust that our readers agree that props are often critical to persuasion, in fact are among the more important nonverbal contextual elements, and deserve meticulous implementation.

People as context in persuasion

In the previous chapter we observed that subjects of all ages are sensitive to being watched. This universal human characteristic makes it possible for any person known by participants to be in the environment to influence an ongoing interaction. People who are visible and close have more effect than do remote or invisible bystanders, but even the suspected presence of an unknown eavesdropper, as in the case of a telephone conversation that might be "bugged," will modify an interpersonal transaction.

The people we classify as "context" are (1) those who act as observers or spectators and (2) those who simply happen to be present but whose presence is unrelated to the interaction they influence. We exclude participants, although we recognize that during intervals of non-participation they may function temporarily as observers.

How do observers modify an interpersonal interaction? Mainly, they interact with participants in a process Scheflen terms "monitoring."[4] "Monitors" are behaviors which prevent deviancy by feeding back censoring responses to a communicator. A participant advances an unorthodox point of view, notes the raised eyebrows and startled look of an observer, and retracts or softens his statement. The power of monitoring

---

[4] Albert E. Scheflen, *Body Language and the Social Order* (Englewood Cliffs, N.J.: Prentice-Hall, 1972), pp. 104–21.

is cumulative: the larger the number of spectators the greater the pressure on participants to limit themselves to stereotyped exchanges. Often spectators are permitted to witness a critical persuasive event that will decide a public policy without recognizing that their nonverbal monitoring may turn off novel approaches to the central problem.

Monitoring operates largely out-of-awareness through frowns, cocking the head to one side, a sly smile, a shoulder shrug, looking away, moving away physically, and many other subtle indices of disapproval. Scheflen notes overt censure as well, citing obvious motions such as shaking the head from side to side, extending the arm toward the participant with palm out in a "stop" gesture, and shaking the index finger at the participant.

Spectator-participant interaction may occasionally reinforce and thus encourage deviant behavior, but not often. Observers contribute stability, which requires suppression of the unusual and unpredictable. As Scheflen puts it, "Ordinarily a transaction occurs in a highly stable environment. Not only is the place highly organized but the people and groupings tend to be stable as well."[5]

We will mention a sampling of situations in contemporary America in which monitoring by observers influences persuasive interaction. A sales manager is accompanying one of his sales representatives on a call, not to participate, but to observe the salesperson in action. A man is selecting a sports coat in a clothing store while his wife witnesses the selection process. The president of a university is justifying the decision to abandon intercollegiate football in a press conference with his public relations officer present as an observer. The head of the union in a corporation is discussing next year's contract with management, witnessed by a panel of five members of the union. A legislative interim committee is conducting a hearing on conditions in a state prison with prisoners' relatives, prison staff, and news media represented among the spectators. Our reader will have no difficulty in adding to this list cases from his experience where spectator influence weighed heavily in determining the outcome of persuasive communication.

Persons present in the role of disinterested bystanders also influence an interaction, but in less specific ways and to a lesser degree than do observers. Human beings claim attention by their mere presence in a way that inanimate objects cannot. Consequently, participants in an interaction are somewhat distracted by coincidental people, and communication suffers.

People who keep quiet, pretend to ignore the interaction, and try to blend into the surroundings are least disturbing. Usually bystanders are

5 Ibid., p. 123.

involved in a separate activity, however, and their pattern of interaction interferes with other interaction. Sound and movement are physical distractions, but much more disturbing to the communication is psychological involvements with extraneous individuals or groups. When participants in one activity can see or hear participants in another, the temptation to speculate about what the other people are doing is irresistible. Human curiosity guarantees that people in the environment of an interaction will receive much attention from persons who are participants.

The experience of one corporation points out the influence upon persuasion of other people's presence. A corporation moved into new quarters and in an effort to increase communication among various units, private offices for middle managers were abolished. Instead of small enclosures with doors, desks in a large space were partially isolated by low, movable partitions. When a manager conferred with an associate or visitor and both were seated they could not see or be seen by others, although the sounds of surrounding interactions was difficult to ignore. When standing, persons in one space could look over the partitions into several other "personal spaces."

Communication was indeed increased in the new arrangement, but opinion was sharply divided as to whether the added communication helped or hindered in getting work done. In particular, interviews with customers were adversely affected. Whether anyone on the other side of a partition was listening or not, the manager and his customer assumed, often out of awareness, that such was the case. A strong monitoring effect resulted, and interviews were uncomfortably inhibited. Top management of the corporation now seems to be ready to switch back to private offices at considerable expense to remove incidental persons from the context of persuasive communication.

Modifiers, duration, and progression as elements in the context of persuasion

When container, props, and persons impinge upon participants in an interaction, they produce subjective responses by the audience. If we isolate physical conditions that contribute negative or positive transfer and thereby cause discomfort or pleasant receptivity, we have identified the modifiers that are at work. In table 14–1, Bennett and Bennett suggest a comprehensive list of modifiers: light, sound, color, texture, odor, and relative temperature and humidity. These variables are determined by the functioning interrelationship of enclosure, props, and people.

Modifiers are useful because each is measurable and each can be related to a subjective response. Thus, a persuader can decide what mood he wishes the persuadee to experience and design modifiers to facilitate that mood. During the interaction each of the modifiers can and should be frequently assessed. When a modifier, often temperature or sound, gets out of kilter, corrective measures should be immediately taken. More than any other element in the context, modifiers can be controlled. Failing to build an atmosphere favorable to an act of persuasion through good management of all modifiers is in most instances a result of carelessness.

Duration focuses attention on the overall time frame in which an interaction occurs. Our expectations about how long certain kinds of interactions should last are just as rigid as our expectations about other social behavior. Further, while the conviction that scheduled events should begin and end on time is almost universal in the United States, this is not the case in many other cultures.

Negative transfer from late beginnings and from interactions that extend far beyond the announced or anticipated closing time needs no elaboration. Resentment from wasting time waiting without an explanation, or being trapped overtime because of bad planning of others can reach a fearsome intensity. Punctuality prevents this particular destructive response.

We are generally aware of punctuality in openings and endings, but our expectations of the appropriate duration of various categories of interaction are at least partially out of awareness. As Bennett and Bennett summarize the significance of this expectation:

> We enter a situation with a learned expectation of its duration and are prepared to participate for that length of time. If that expectation is not met, our definition of the situation will be altered, and our ability to sustain the appropriate mood of the encounter will be seriously tested. . . . In the unitary linear treatment of time which characterizes "in the American Way of Life" time units, in discrete segments and in highly conventionalized sequences, are a salient feature of the way we give form and meaning to the sensational chaos of experience.[6]

The overworked physician who examines a patient, diagnoses his ailment, prescribes a drug, and hurries the patient out of the office in five minutes probably produces an angry patient who may retaliate by not filling the prescription. The patient may require a duration of at least fifteen minutes of apparently careful deliberation about symptoms and collection of related data to feel satisfied about the interaction.

A skilled salesperson knows how to discover the duration of a dress or suit selection for a particular customer and how to avoid shortening or extending it. A job interview stretched by the interviewer to a half hour

[6] Bennett and Bennett, "Making the Scene," p. 194.

or forty-five minutes tends to become an interrogation in the perception of the interviewee. After luncheon talks in academic or business communities in America should be of twenty to thirty minutes duration. If under twenty minutes, many in the audience will agree "it wasn't *really* a speech," and if much over thirty minutes, the speaker will be accused of being "longwinded" and "lacking terminal facilities."

Adapting to conventional duration for different categories of persuasive events is ordinarily rewarding to the persuader. Like starting and stopping on time, conforming to sets of expectations of duration of an interaction is easy and prevents unnecessary, possibly punishing, dissonance.

Progression involves timing as does duration, but progression is a matter of sequence of events rather than elapsed time. If events do not conform to our scheme, we have real difficulty adjusting to a novel arrangement. Perhaps the greatest argument for careful, logical organization of a presentation is that such a pattern meets the audience's expectations of progression. When such expectations are obviously met, satisfaction results. Talking about pleasant and inconsequential matters *before* discussing serious business is an accepted sequence. Obviously, persuasion must always take into account, and adapt to, what has happened before. Similarly, post-persuasion events are important considerations of the persuader. Anticipation of an expected happening colors audience response to persuasion, and later events may validate or invalidate outcomes of a previous persuasive communication.

All persuasion to influence future belief or action rests upon certain assumptions about that future. If those assumptions match the per-persuadee's beliefs, he will tend to accept persuasion consistent with those assumptions. If the salesman says inflation is out of control, and the prospect believes that he is the victim of runaway inflation, the probabilities of a sale are increased.

Unanticipated events can of course cancel out the benefits of the best planned and apparently successful persuasion. In 1973 ski resort owners mounted an impressive campaign to convince skiers to come to their remote lodges. Droves of ski enthusiasts were persuaded. Later they reversed those decisions when an unanticipated gasoline shortage made it difficult or impossible to travel to the resorts.

Conclusion

The nonverbal context of persuasion is shaped by a vast number of objects, events, and people. The present circumstances as well as the participants' idealized notions of what *should* be also influence the nonverbal context. Contextual elements important to persuasion may be divided into two categories: (1) those dealing with the interpersonal distances separating participating individuals, and (2) those of the environment surrounding the interacting persons.

We have noted four zones of interpersonal space and explored their applications to different types of persuasive interaction. Elements of the setting are: container or enclosure, props, persons, modifiers, duration, and progression. When information about personal space and the setting are combined with knowledge of nonverbal behavior codes, more complete understanding results regarding the baffling complexities of the complicated human interaction we term "persuasion."

We recognize that the study of nonverbal elements in communication is in its infancy. However, a significant beginning has been made. We agree with Harrison and Knapp when they say:

> Research on nonverbal communication appears to be moving into scientific maturity, with a shift from loose models to well-articulated theory, a move from anecdote to empirical research, and a swing from casual observation to sophisticated technologies and rigorous methodologies. Looking to the future, we anticipate even better theoretical formulations, a diffusion of research technology and methodology, a quickening pace of empirical research, and an ever increasing application of findings to man's practical communication problems.[7]

[7] Randall P. Harrison and Mark L. Knapp, "Toward an Understanding of Nonverbal Communication Systems," *The Journal of Communication* 22: 4 (December, 1972): 350.

15

Persuasion in campaigns

Introduction

Throughout this book we have emphasized that an incident of persuasion is a series of related events arbitrarily isolated from the continuous flow of communication in which we live. Many persuasive acts are part of a larger and persisting effort. Often these efforts are ongoing, long-lasting, complex systems of persuasion that ebb and flow with environmental changes and successes and failures. Some are cyclical, such as the political persuasion associated with periodic elections. All can be classified as propaganda or large-scale persuasion, as defined and explained in chapter 1.

In this chapter we examine extensive attempts to persuade great numbers of people, phenomena we term "campaigns." The mass media are used extensively in the "patterns of advocacy and reaction"[1] that develop in campaigns, many sources of messages are involved, and the level of coordination among diverse elements of people and media justify the label "systematic." Advances in technology have made possible ever more potent strategies of influencing human thought and action. Because the tools that assist the persuader in communicating effectively with great numbers of persuadees are rapidly expanding in quality and quantity, we can expect that persuasive campaigns of all sorts will become increasingly more prevalent.

What kinds of campaigns concern us? Larson classifies campaigns as *politically-oriented, product-oriented* and *cause-oriented*.[2] Because we find it difficult to separate the political and cause orientations, we will consider here two types of systems classified by function, *commercial* and *social action* campaigns. *Commercial* campaigns seek to merchandize goods and/or services for profit. In the United States, private rather than governmental agencies are predominantly involved. *Social action* campaigns seek to stabilize or modify patterns of living for groups of people for reasons other than private profit. A program of social action such as building a new school may result in some persons making large amounts of money, but the primary mission of that social action is not their personal gain.

We will resist the temptation to speculate about the relative importance of commercial and social action campaigns in the contemporary civilized world. Both are omnipresent and powerful. In many ways they are comparable because their strategy and tactics are similar. Rather than attempt to treat both in detail we have chosen to examine commercial campaigns somewhat comprehensively, because more reliable information about marketing is available than can be found to document social action campaigns.[3] A section following that treating commercial cam-

[1] James R. Andrews, "The Passionate Negation: The Chartist Movement in Rhetorical Perspective," *The Quarterly Journal of Speech* 59: 2 (April, 1973): 197.

[2] Charles U. Larson, *Persuasion: Reception and Responsibility* (Belmont, Calif.: Wadsworth Publishing Co., 1973), p. 165.

[3] For an overview of commercial campaigns that will acquaint the reader with major modern trends, we recommend Edward C. Bursk and John F. Chapman, eds., *Modern Marketing Strategy* (New York: The New American Library of World Literature, 1964).

paigns will show how campaigns for social action resemble and differ from the commercial variety.

Persuasive campaigns in modern times are seldom devised and executed by those who support them financially. Whether for social action or private profit, the overwhelming majority of campaigns is *professionally mediated*, that is, hired experts make critical decisions and assume responsibility for specific content, persons, and media that are used. Persuading through a third party, whether in the case of Miles Standish retaining John Alden to propose to Priscilla on his behalf, or the Republican Party hiring an advertising agency to manage its presidential campaign, has always introduced complexity and some loss of control over the subsequent interactions. Many of the perplexing problems associated with persuasion in campaigns are rooted in less than perfect communication between source and mediating agency.

Another general comment about modern campaigns is that they all tend to be very expensive. Access to radio, television, and print media requires that the persuader buy air time or space in a publication, and the effective use of telephone, billboards, soundtrucks, leaflets, lawn signs, and brochures demands substantial financing as well. In a free-enterprise, democratic society that relies on competitive persuasion as a means of decision making, restricting the use of the more powerful channels of communication to the affluent poses a serious problem. In chapter 2 we noted that the persuadee has difficulty in separating the message from its carrier. It thus follows that the more expensive the medium that conveys a message, the greater is the credibility conferred by its use. Available money seems to be the factor that, more than any other, limits the effectiveness of extensive persuasive campaigns.

A rationale for understanding the effects of persuasion in campaigns

Many treatments of persuasion in campaigns are based on the assumption that any significant consequences involve attitude reinforcement or change.[4] These do not exclude behavioral change, for attitude modification is thought to be necessary for action to be modified. A second way in which mass media can influence choice of persuadees is markedly different from changing attitudes. The mechanism involved in this alternate type of persuasion is *shifting perceptions*.

[4] Three attitude-based treatments of persuasion via mass media can be found in Erwin P. Bettinghaus, *Persuasive Communication* (New York: Holt, Rinehart and Winston, 1968), chapter 11; Charles U. Larson, *Persuasion: Reception and Responsibility*, chapters 7, 8; Otto Lerbinger, *Designs for Persuasive Communication* (Englewood Cliffs, N.J.: Prentice-Hall, 1972), chapters 4, 18.

The transmission of a message via mass media is not always directly to a primary receiver. Frequently intervening persons relay the message and often contribute substantially to the shaping of its effects. The role of interpersonal communication as a supplement to mass media in campaigns becomes part of a rationale for the study of large-scale, ongoing persuasion.

Two contrasting methods of persuasion via the mass media

Let us assume a national political campaign is underway. It is two weeks before election. The contending candidates have committed the remaining contents of their campaign chests, plus the money they are able to borrow, to the purchase of radio and television time. The mediating agencies in charge of spending their money have advised them to concentrate on short "spots" ranging from thirty seconds to one or two minutes. With the aid of professional actors, directors, and producers, these short tapes are prepared and broadcast.

Two kinds of persuadees view or listen to the spots. One category is that of the *involved*, those people vitally interested in issues and candidates, and the other category is populated with those who are *uninvolved*, with little or no interest in politics. But the uninvolved voter's whim counts the same as the involved citizen's labored decision in the voting booth, and the uninvolved voters may well outnumber those who are involved.

The committed audience is little affected by the barrage of radio and television political spots while the uninvolved receivers are capable of being profoundly influenced. The involved voter selectively attends only to the messages of the candidate he favors while the casual and non-political person will turn to whatever catches his fancy. Dan Nimmo explains this fundamental difference between the responses of the involved and the uninvolved:

> The highly involved individual contrasts opposing views with his own and resists any persuasive effort to change; the less-committed person, however, assimilates alternative positions into his own point of view and accepts any one of a broad range of options as suitable behavior, without changing the attitude with which he has a low degree of involvement. . . .
>
> Following this reasoning, then, the purpose of persuasion is not to change the attitudes of the committed, but to shift the perceptions of voters with low involvement.[5]

[5] Dan Nimmo, *The Political Persuaders* (Englewood Cliffs, N.J.: Prentice-Hall, 1970), pp. 180, 181.

The motivation of the uninvolved person to watch a political telecast can be better understood if we divest him of serious purpose; he is looking for entertainment rather than instruction. From this vantage point, as Stephenson notes, "at its best mass communication allows people to become absorbed in subjective play."[6] Through play responses, decisions on casual matters may be heavily influenced.

To see how this comes about, the nature of play should be understood:

> Playing is pretending, a stepping outside the world of duty and responsibility. Play is an interlude in the day. It is not ordinary or real. It is voluntary and not a task or moral duty. It is in some sense disinterested, providing a temporary satisfaction. Though attended to with seriousness, it is not really important. . . .
>
> Mass communication in its play aspects may be the way a society develops its culture—the way it dreams, has its myths, and develops its loyalties; what it does in inculcating work may be quite a different matter. What kind of a culture is it, for example, that thinks only of learning, production, and work?[7]

Stephenson terms the process of influencing a person through providing opportunities for play *convergent selection,* in contrast to social control through the attempt to change basic attitudes. Most advertising tries to bring about convergent selection, according to Stephenson. The fascination of reading or viewing the news is also play-motivated, he contends, since it stimulates fantasies, and news of crime and punishment may provide us with a sense of superiority, of winning the game others have lost.

Stephenson summarizes his play theory to explain influences of mass media:

> Our theory more generally therefore is to the effect that mass communication, where it concerns entertainment, is characteristically a matter of communication-pleasure. It brings no material gain and serves no "work" functions, but it does induce certain elements of self-enchantment.[8]

Effectiveness of Stephenson's convergent selection is totally dependent on the perpetuation of pleasure. If the message is taken seriously and made to be important to the receiver, the process is no longer play, and the perception loses its power.

[6] William Stephenson, *The Play Theory of Mass Communication* (Chicago: The University of Chicago Press, 1967), p. 1.

[7] Ibid., pp. 46, 48.

[8] Ibid., p. 59.

We prefer Nimmo's term "shifting perceptions" to Stephenson's "convergent selection" to designate the process by which an uninvolved person is influenced through play experiences provided by the mass media. The two labels seem to be identical semantically, but shifting perceptions suggests the nature of the effect on the persuadee more literally and vividly than does convergent selection.

To summarize, mass media messages can either persuade committed persons through attitude change or influence the uninvolved through shifting of their perceptions. In an extensive campaign few committed persons will be reached or changed through media messages because those people will not expose themselves to dissonant themes and will resist the messages that do reach them. The uninvolved will listen to a message of any persuasion. Their capacity to accept any viewpoint or proposition without fighting it renders them persuasible. If the message provided by a medium induces the receiver to play with it for his own pleasure, the consequences in terms of votes, purchases, and the support of social action may be substantial. Mediating agencies devising campaigns might do well to abandon their concentration on changing attitudes and devote their resources to the shifting of perceptions.

Formerly, when the prime objective of social action propaganda was thought to be the changing of attitudes of involved and interested persons, conveying of highly selected, issue-related information was assigned a high priority. With the discovery that being reasonable and factual didn't do the job, and that committed persons were not influenced by media persuasion, the old methods were challenged. In 1972 Swanson identified the need to revise theories of influence through the mass media as a major problem confronting students of communication. He summarized:

> Argumentative strength and logical validity seem to be equally
> dangerous standards for judging the strategies and messages of the new
> politics. This is true most obviously because many elements of strategy
> are independent of the content of campaign messages.[9]

Swanson identifies what doesn't work but does not recommend a substitute. We believe that careful exploration of ways in which the theory of play can be applied to the shifting of perceptions of the uncommitted by using the media promises to increase the effectiveness of persuasion in campaigns.

[9] David L. Swanson, "The New Politics Meets the Old Rhetoric: New Directions in Campaign Communication Research," *The Quarterly Journal of Speech* 58: 1 (February, 1972): 38.

How interposed persons modify media persuasion

When students of persuasion first attempted to analyze the effects of mass media communication a simple model served their purposes. It was the hypodermic needle model, so called because a message was injected directly into the nervous system of the receiver by the medium. The receiving organism then modified itself to assimilate the message. No intervening variables were recognized. The process was one-way, direct, and simple: sending–receiving–response.

The delightful simplicity of the hypodermic model was destroyed by a famous bit of research, the Erie County (Ohio) study of the presidential election of 1940.[10] In spite of comprehensive media coverage and much mass persuasion, the study revealed a negligible effect on voting behavior. Voting decisions resulted from interpersonal interaction rather than from reading newspapers or listening to the radio. Further, the interpersonal influence came from *opinion leaders*, persons whose ideas commanded respect. Because much of the information used by the opinion leader came from radio or print sources, the role of intervening persons was somewhat clarified. Messages were received by opinion leaders as they monitored the media and relayed fairly accurately and with added interpretation to others in work and social groups. Apparently *talking about* information caused it to have considerably more impact than acquiring it through reading or by radio or television.

The two-step flow model was devised to incorporate the persons who bridged the gap between the media and the secondary audience. Here the hypodermic model was extended but not fundamentally revised. The flow was now *sending–opinion leader–relaying–receiving–response*, but the flow was still unidirectional, and the final receiver played a passive role. The major contribution of the two-step flow concept was the integration of the two major ingredients of a persuasive campaign, dissemination of materials by mass media and interpersonal interactions based on those materials.

Much more person-to-person communication was involved than the two-step flow model could account for, however. Often double and triple relaying of messages took place, and the persons performing important relay functions were often *not* opinion leaders. Some opinion leaders were passive and some were active, a circumstance that did not fit into the two-step flow plan. Students of the diffusion process, examining the introduction and promotion of innovations in developing

---

[10] Paul Lazarsfeld et al., *The People's Choice* (New York: Duell, Sloan, and Pearce; Meredith Press, 1944).

countries, subjected the theories of hypodermic and two-step flow models to rigorous field testing. While their research confirmed the importance of the opinion leader role, it demonstrated the inadequacy of all predominantly one-way models and rejected any hypothesis that media-originated social action could be explained in a fixed number of steps.

In any campaign opinion leaders obtain much of their material and many of their ideas from sources other than the mass media. Travel, conversations with visitors, discussions with followers, and personal experiences in the field may lead to the generation of new concepts that are later circulated. A surprising amount of testing and revision of disseminated materials comes not only from interaction of persuadees and opinion leaders but from discussions among persuadees. The myth of passive reception leading to action at any level of the diffusion process was thoroughly debunked. When social change takes place, the persons involved accomplish it through give-and-take interaction rather than sending and receiving.

Commercial campaigns

In this section we will discuss the characteristics and complexities of commercial campaigns. To help us accomplish this task systematically, we will apply the model of the process of persuasive communication presented in chapter 1.

Functions and problems of the source in marketing goods and services

The model specifies that primary tasks of the source in any persuasive communication are to: formulate the persuasive recommendation, analyze receivers, and prepare messages. These apply directly to that persuasion we term "marketing," but commercial considerations necessitate specific strategies that differ from procedures used in simpler interpersonal instances of persuasion. We will examine these influences in turn.

FORMULATING THE PERSUASIVE RECOMMENDATION IN A COMMERCIAL CAMPAIGN. The persuasive recommendation in a commercial promotion is a product, product line, or package of services designed to fit the needs of certain customers and is priced competitively. Through extensive market research, great amounts of time, energy, and money are expended to develop the specifications of the items to be sold. Likely customers are identified. Data are collected from controlled samples of prospects regarding their need or desire for the items and their reactions to proposed pricing; often the products or services are actually marketed in a representative community. Such a trial run provides an opportunity to estimate how many customers will buy the new item initially and also computes repeat purchasing and interviews customers to discover their reactions to items purchased.

When a company is satisfied that the products or services to be merchandized can be sold in sufficient volume and at a price that will probably produce a profit, all data from market research are used to make items attractive to customers resembling those studied. The persuasive recommendation is thus a compromise between the requirements of production (including cost and quality control) and modifications that will meet the needs and whims of the consumers. For example, a new color television receiver model will have as large a screen as its intended market can afford, a cabinet as plain or ornate as the tastes of the market prefer, and automatic controls and optional features to the extent that probable buyers favor gimmicks and gadgets.

The persuasive proposition or recommendation in a commercial campaign is thus adjusted to the preferences and requirements of receivers before the major marketing effort begins. Other kinds of persuasion seldom complete such extensive audience analysis or use findings as thoroughly in revising their persuasive propositions.

ANALYSIS OF THE RECEIVER. At the onset of a commercial campaign analysis of potential buyers is combined with the finalizing of the sales package or proposition. But information about customers has many uses, and there can never be enough of it. From the market research that provides a foundation for launching the campaign comes much information useful to message preparation and channel selection. As the marketing effort begins, more information about potential and actual customers accumulates. Salespeople and retail outlets report reasons for not buying or for preferring the competition, for example.

Word-of-mouth exchange of information among customers is found to aid or hinder sales. Complaints and expressions of satisfaction come unsolicited to distributors or to the source itself. Sales curves showing increase of buying in certain localities and decrease in others provide material for analysis. Frequently, market research programs are continued throughout a sales campaign because systematic collection and interpretation of information about buyer behavior is a perpetual need of marketing managers.

The continuous process of revising the image of the customer to make it more accurate and keep it up to date is accomplished through feedback from customer response. We noted in chapter 1 that in any complex persuasive interaction there are many cycles of the model. An effective novelty in advertising may become stale. Customer response reveals this loss of effectiveness, the reaction is fed back to the "analysis of the receiver" stage, and a new characteristic of the customer is added to his previous description, "no longer responsive to ad #22." Later another company introduces a competing item that has greater customer appeal. Analysis of the customer shows that the original item has become his second choice. Then a series of television spots conquers the competition, and the customer returns to his first preference.

Whenever the customer and his responses are reevaluated, changes in message preparation and use of channels may result. Product modification is also a possibility, in which case analysis of the receiver feeds back to the "formulating the proposition" stage. The important point is that in any campaign, unexpected responses of receivers cause revision of key elements through feedback, and every revision initiates a new cycle of the model.

PREPARING MESSAGES FOR THE MARKETING CAMPAIGN. At the stage of developing particular messages to implement merchandizing, most companies call in a mediating agency and rely on its expertise. Message preparation involves producing themes suited to the hypothesized audience and implementing those themes in messages compatible with channels selected. With several media to coordinate, it is usually more practical and efficient to hire an advertising or marketing agency to design the message system than to create within the source company agencies with necessary varied and specialized resources.

Before the message can be prepared the details of the persuasive proposition (the item to be sold) must be examined, and all information about prospects (receivers) must be carefully interpreted. The people who will create the messages must look ahead to available and suitable channels and decide how much to rely on each channel. When the optimum volume of communication to be attempted on each selected channel is agreed on, preparation of actual marketing messages can begin.

Under the direction of a coordinator the mediating agency assigns preparation of messages for different channels to appropriate specialists. Major categories of specialization are newspaper and magazine advertising, radio and television commercials, billboards and signs, direct mail advertising, and person-to-person selling. Wherever possible messages in different media interlock; that is, they supplement and complement each other, hopefully with cumulative effect.

As a selling campaign progresses, the activity of message preparation is heavily influenced by continuous feedback. Responses of buyers and nonbuyers lead to message modification ranging from repeating successful units of persuasion ad infinitum to totally eliminating substantial categories of the sales effort. The persons who develop messages are highly sensitive to current events. Often an event of high interest can be woven into a sales pitch with transfer of interest from the event to the product. In 1973, the Watergate hearings were exploited by many United States advertisers, as was the energy crisis. Much advertising for large and heavy automobiles, scheduled for late 1973 and 1974 release, had to be scrapped because of unanticipated gasoline and other fuel shortages. With rigorous gasoline rationing on the horizon, an advertisement based on the luxurious features of a limousine would discredit the sponsor. Economy and efficiency themes multiplied in the selling of heating, lighting, and transportation. Bicycles, small foreign-built cars, and locking caps for gasoline tanks met new needs that produced abundant and specialized sales messages. Message preparation in marketing is truly a contingent and unpredictable enterprise.

The most variable messages in the sales campaign are those of person-to-person selling. Because of the ever-changing context of things, events, and people, the skilled salespeople learn to evaluate feedback almost instantaneously. They trust their intuition and improvise freely, creating new messages on the spot. The able salesperson attempts to deviate from any predetermined pitch. He or she becomes a valuable source of information concerning changes in persons and circumstances that are important to the marketing of a product. Any message preparation center that fails to collect information frequently from its sales force is neglecting its most effective insurance against catastrophe.

Effects of the vehicle that carries the commercial message

We noted earlier the apparent correlation between expense involved in using a channel and the prestige it confers on the message it transmits. Consequently, the nature, cost, and sales volume of an item influences the choice of channel used to sell it. Color television spots at prime time are now the most costly messages. Expensive articles such as automobiles, television receivers, and major household appliances are widely advertised on TV, but so are high-volume, low-priced items that compete keenly among brands, such as cosmetics, shaving cream, panty hose, and soft drinks. In addition to status, the color television commercial combines sight and sound dramatically, assaulting the visual and auditory senses with lifelike situations that generate far more empathy than can a printed paragraph or a still picture.

Since television reaches nearly everyboody in America, it cannot be regarded as a demographically selective channel. Print media, however, can be chosen to reach particular groups of potential customers. *Playboy*, *Penthouse*, and *Oui* might be appropriate channels to convey advertising messages to affluent members of the avant garde, liberal, swinging population but inappropriate as a means of reaching church going and conservative persons. *Saturday Review/World* and *Scientific America* are read by middle- and upper-class intellectuals while *Woman's Day* and *Redbook* are selective in reaching a feminine, middle-aged, and middle- or lower-class audience. *Sports Illustrated* appeals to sports-minded people of all ages and classes. Many other examples could be cited, but these are sufficient to show that the selection of a magazine to carry certain advertising is one method of reaching carefully defined groups of possible buyers.

Still more selective as a channel is direct-mail advertising. Lists of names and addresses are available—for a price—that permit an advertiser to put his message in the private mailboxes of the precise group he wishes to contact. Such controlled and personalized exposure would seem to be highly effective, but in fact the volume of direct-mail solicitation has reduced its impact. Several envelopes well stuffed with commercial messages reach the citizen's mailbox every day, overloading his input capacity and causing him to treat them all as alike and trivial.

Billboard and sign advertising, like direct mail, boomerang when used to excess. A tasteful billboard well away from the highway, limited to a frequency of one per mile, might be highly effective as a selling device. In contrast, crowded, stacked, and garish clusters of billboards that prevent the motorist from viewing the countryside may well produce resentment and loss of effect.

More than any of the other channels, the personal salesperson comes to be identified with the source of the items he sells. To the prospect, he functions as both source and channel. With repeated contacts the customer tends to behave more and more as though the salesrepresentative *is* the company he or she represents. A few long-lasting and striking television or magazine advertisements achieve this degree of identification, but successful salespeople accomplish it routinely.

The advantage salespeople have over other channels is their ability to exploit interaction. More than any other method of marketing they can ascertain and adapt to the individual customer's particular preferences and needs.

The strategy of the skilled salesperson is to treat interaction with the customer as a joint venture, creating a team approach to a common problem. His tactics include bringing useful information to the customer, demonstrating understanding of the customer's problem in question, and showing high motivation toward helping the customer find the best solution. If salesperson and prospect come to a team relationship, it is important that the salesperson be objective to the point of recommending a competing product when his own is not as good. The notion that salesmanship involves deception dies hard, but the success of a sales force whose basic premise is that service to the customer is their highest priority is gradually undermining the "oily trickster" salesman stereotype.

Much of the success of a commercial campaign depends on the co-ordination of all channels so that they reinforce each other. Themes can tie together messages in different media. The "young-folks-on-a-picnic" series in promotion of a soft drink can be implemented by television, radio, billboards, and printed advertisements, and salespeople can refer to any one or several of these examples in person-to-person selling. Deciding what a channel can do best and how messages on different channels can be interrelated are key decisions in a marketing effort.

The reception of messages in a commercial campaign

The process by which a sales message ultimately triggers a customer's reaction occurs in three distinct stages: decoding, activation of the receiver's motivational system, and covert or overt response.

THE DECODING OF SALES MESSAGES. Television has increased the ability of the general buying public to decode sales messages. Now those in the lower economic brackets know about vacations in the Caribbean, luxuries available in exclusive shops on Fifth Avenue, and the latest fashions of the jet set. But more important, persons formerly isolated and provincial now have a cosmopolitan outlook. Before television, residents of rural Nebraska had little information about life in San Francisco or New York City. Now they have such abundant information that the rural Nebraskan often feels quite at home when he first sets foot on Times Square.

As a result of this tremendous dissemination of information across class, ethnic, and geographical boundaries, the public is able to decode a great range of messages in context. Vicariously the viewer or reader transports himself to the locale of almost any commercial. His fantasy may resemble actuality only slightly, but this interferes little with decoding. He treats his vision as though it were true and interprets messages with confidence.

The astute builder of sales messages understands that decoding will be consistent with what receivers believe to be true rather than with literal reality. He knows that television and other media have made possible the chaining out of fantasies and rhetorical visions that supply meaning for his signals and symbols. To accomplish its purpose his persuasion must be compatible with accepted fantasy. As noted in chapter 8, the ultimate reality useful in predicting response is the perception of receivers rather than the world of objects and events.

ACTIVATION OF THE MOTIVATIONAL SYSTEM OF THE RECEIVER. Let us assume that the meaning intended by the writer of a sales message has been perceived by a possible buyer. What, if anything, is done about it is determined by the impact of that perception on the receiver's system of motivation.

A person's interests active and potential, constitute his structure of motives. To be more concrete we can list major components of motivation as habits, interests, needs, desires, values, and goals. If the perceived meaning directly impinges upon one or more of these elements, the receiver's motive structure is activated.

Most commercial messages perceived by potential buyers do *not* activate their motivational systems. Probably the most important function of a motive system is to protect its owner from being disturbed by messages in which he has no interest. Only if a meaning promises something desirable to a receiver does it achieve furthur consideration.

Once a motive is activated by a meaning that survived its initial screening, two products of the impact of the message emerge: (1) the decision as to whether the receiver will expend energy pursuing the option recommended by the message, and (2) if energy is to be expended, a tentative decision on how much energy will be devoted to this end, over how long a time. Thus, casual and momentary responses or substantial and long-lasting efforts may result from activation of a motivational system by a sales message.

We would emphasize that any significant response to a persuasive communication can come about only through the activation of the receiver's motivations. Without the contribution of energy released by one or more motives the decoded message dies. When the receiver decides that the recommended action is irrelevant to his needs, further consideration is rejected as a waste of time and energy.

POSSIBLE RESPONSES WHEN MOTIVES ARE ACTIVATED BY A SALES MESSAGE.   The motivated decision to explore further the possibilities recommended by a sales message leads to three levels of possible response: cognition, either attitude change or the shifting of perceptions, and overt action.[11]

The most elementary response to decoded information is *cognition,* "the acquisition of knowledge, the discovery of insights, and the extension of awareness."[12] If a response is limited to cognition no perceptions important to a buying decision are modified, no attitudes that relate to present or later purchase are changed, and no action results. The receiver has become interested in his reception process to the extent of adding some information to his store of knowledge, nothing more.

[11] Ernest G. Bormann, William Howell, Ralph Nichols, and George Shapiro, *Interpersonal Communication in the Modern Organization* (Englewood Cliffs, N.J.: Prentice-Hall, 1969), p. 29. This reference will clarify the relationships of cognition, attitude change, and action as responses of receivers, but the present authors add the element of shifting perceptions to make this theoretical conceptualization more comprehensive and useful.

[12] Ibid., p. 29.

But cognition may lead to either *shifted perceptions* or *attitude change*. If the acquired information involves the receiver in play activity, the fun he has with the message may transfer to the items to be sold, and he will perceive them as desirable *to him*; his perception of a possible purchase has thus *shifted*.

However, should the new information impinge upon a definite conviction, a well-established tendency to reject or accept the product, then a change in attitude toward greater rejection or acceptance may come about. For example, a customer who has been a satisfied user of Gillette razors and blades for a dozen years may find himself making a careful comparison of Schick's new shaving system and either weakening his favorable attitude toward Gillette products, or quite possibly strengthening it. This *attitude change* takes time and is serious business, in contrast to the casual and whimsical shifting of perceptions.

It is important to stress that shifted perceptions and changed attitudes do not necessarily lead to action. We define *action* in the context of commercial persuasion as making a purchase that would not have been made without the message, or desisting from making a purchase that would otherwise have been made. In a commercial campaign many shifts of perceptions or changes of attitude may accumulate before the aggregate becomes sufficient to modify overt behavior. The advertiser knows that daily "booster shots" of persuasion produce cumulative effects in persuadees. Many tiny shifts in perception and gradual changes in attitude over time ultimately influence buying decisions.

To summarize the ways in which a potential customer responds to a decoded sales message, we call attention to a definite sequence of response. Cognition is prerequisite to the shifting of perceptions or changing of attitudes. To say it differently, unless the customer learns something he did not know before, he has no material to cause perception shift or attitude change.

Similarly, overt action will not result unless perceptions have shifted or attitudes have changed. Through habit the same old perceptions and attitudes produce the same old behaviors. From the point of view of the commercial persuader, his task is not only to produce significant cognition in a customer but to carry it through to shifted perceptions or changes in attitudes and then to precipitate the ultimate consequence, an action in the form of the recommended purchase.

Our treatment of commercial campaigns has followed our model of the process of persuasive communication. Through use of the model we were able to emphasize source, channel, and receiver considerations in turn, yet deal with many other variables and show important interrelationships. One element of the model cannot be neatly located at one sequential spot in the process. That element is *feedback*. Because it operates continuously in a campaign and affects all other stages and elements, it cannot be isolated.

The reader will recall the frequent mentions of feedback and its effects on the planning and implementation of the commercial campaign as we described them. Our final observation might be that continuous feedback is the element in the campaign that enables it to adapt to change, to learn from its own experience, to survive.

Social action campaigns

Campaigns of social action come in greater variety and, on the whole, are less systematic than are commercial campaigns. Often a variety of sources contribute to the persuasive effort with little coordination, as in the crusade against the smoking of cigarettes or the drive to promote the early detection of cancer. Another category of social action campaign is sponsored by an organization financed by popular subscription. The American Civil Liberties Union performs a watchdog function in identifying and opposing threats to constitutionally guaranteed liberties. Similarly, Ralph Nader has developed a substantial public relations organization with the objective of protecting the American consumer from exploitation.

Every movement, civil, military, or religious, that wishes to increase its influence conducts a campaign of persuasion. The extent of a social action campaign may be limited to a community or its scope may embrace states and nations. Indeed, some are worldwide, as is the ongoing effort to secure support for the United Nations. Some are in sharp competition and are waged extensively and expensively. An example is the Cold War, the efforts of the Soviet Union and the United States to win the allegiance of the uncommitted peoples of the world.

Social action campaigns contribute more to the barrage of persuasion we experience than most of us realize. Just as the Soviet citizen comes to accept as routine daily blasts in the media against the United States, we tolerate innumerable pleading requests for support from worthy causes and respond to them minimally.

However, some campaigns *do* bring about social change. Although many diverse and unconnected sources have contributed to the Women's Liberation Movement and its thrust has been in many directions, a core of common ground has persisted that justifies classifying this social phenomenon as a "movement" and its complicated network of communications as a "campaign." Women's Lib has helped to bring about increased opportunities for women in business and education through its vigorous campaigns.

How social action campaigns
resemble and differ from commercial campaigns

Selling a product and merchandizing a social innovation have much in common. The same steps in the process of persuasion must be accomplished by use of the same channels of communication. To compare these different kinds of campaigns we will look at source, channel, and receiver characteristics.

We have mentioned that the sources in a social action campaign are often diversified. Consequently the campaign itself is less precisely coordinated than is a commercial campaign. The formulation of the persuasive proposition is less influenced by analysis of intended receivers of the message; in fact, social action persuasion tends to neglect the process of studying receivers and adapting to their interests. Whereas the commercial campaign collects data that establishes a probability of success, the social action persuaders tend to advance "what ought to be" rather than "what we know will sell."

Social action movements usually cannot afford to hire expensive mediating agencies, so much audience analysis and message preparation are amateurish in execution. Volunteers staff the typical social action organization. They do not usually understand the complexities of campaigning, and their collection and use of feedback data are sporadic. However, the social action campaign confronts the same problems of formulating the persuasive proposition, analyzing receivers, and building messages as does the commercial campaign, and the same strategies and tactics are needed to solve these problems satisfactorily. In both instances the hiring of professional mediating agencies is the key element that increases persuasive effectiveness.

Limited financial resources are even more damaging to the social action campaign in channel selection and in making use of the media. High cost limits possible air time and newspaper space. A double bind traps the impoverished crusader, for he may be tempted to buy space or time and do his own program or layout. But amateurism in a newspaper advertisement or on a television program can be highly damaging. Hence, the decision to spend money for a mass medium carries with it the added obligation to spend more money for expertise to design and implement its use. As a result, social action causes use mass media less extensively, less systematically, and less effectively than do commercial campaigns.

The sharp distinctions that set apart social action and commercial campaigns are found in receiver reception and response. Decoding is similar in both, but the activation of the motivational systems of receivers

provides contrast. The impulse to purchase a product or service is ordinarily rooted in a self-serving or affiliative motivation, while the motive
activated by a social action appeal is usually not self-centered. With the
exception of a few health-oriented social action campaigns (for example,
"stop smoking") most social changes advocated are to benefit other
persons more than the receiver.

When selfish motivations such as physical well-being, safety, social
approval, and self-esteem are inappropriate, the range of motivation for
appeal in social action is limited to interests in processes and people
for their own sake. Duty motivations such as the obligations of citizenship, pride in community, church, and country, concern over the welfare
of one's fellow men and other *altruistic* habits and motives are the object
of appeal. The fact that social action campaigns must rely on predominantly altruistic impulses for their effects results in social action propaganda showing much less variety and creativity than are found in
commercial campaigns. Ways in which one can request persons to give
money to supply food to a starving child in an underdeveloped country
are limited and, consequently, such appeals tend to be repetitive.

Responses of receivers in social action persuasion range from simple
cognition, or the acquiring of specified information, through changes
in attitudes and perception, to overt action, as in the commercial campaign. While a purchase is the ultimate intended outcome of the com-
mercially motivated effort, the social action campaign strives for money,
time, personal committments, or votes. Both commercial and social action
persuasion lead to a high proportion of shifted perceptions rather than
changed attitudes. Whimsical decisions predominate, which are soon
forgotten and have little carry-over to other situations. Lasting dedication
to a cause is not a common consequence of social action campaigning.
Other forces must combine to shape an intense and durable conversion.
When an evangelist in a crusade welcomes many new converts to the
altar, he knows that a large proportion of the penitent sinners will falter
and require reconversion, again and yet again.

Political campaigns in the United States

From the birth of the representative system of government in
the United States, political campaigns have preceded every election. If
a voter is to choose among issues and candidates rationally, he must
possess relevant information. Since he lacks both the motivation and the
means to acquire this information, it must be brought to him. The
principle method of enlightening voters and thereby enabling them to
exercise their judgment at the polls is the political campaign.

In early America, person-to-person conversation and informal discussions disseminated and processed political information. With the growth of geographical area, population increase, and the burgeoning uses of mass media, the problems confronting candidates and political organizations have multiplied. Political campaigns have become gigantic arenas of competing persuasions. Because of the possibility that the side with the largest volume of messages will win, every contending faction and candidate expends all human and financial resources to mount the most impressive campaign possible.

In spite of these massive efforts and costs, the motto of the professional mediating agencies in charge is, necessarily, "We do precision guesswork." So many variables are involved in the making of voting decisions that no one knows whether any campaign ever influenced an election. *But—* the possibility exists that one *might!* Consequently, gargantuan campaigns continue to be waged because the possibility cannot be disregarded. We can confidently predict that all-out political campaigning will continue as it has in the past, without proof that results in any way justify its human and monetary cost.

TRENDS IN POLITICAL CAMPAIGNING. We can identify several trends in political campaigning in the second half of the twentieth century that promise to influence campaigns of the future. The most striking and obvious is growth: political campaigns are becoming longer and more extensive.

While concentrated campaigning in national politics in the United States begins some five weeks before the party convention, planning for the campaign is continuous. The day after an election aggressive action is underway to prepare for the next election. Expenditures are another measure of the extent of campaigns. In the presidential election of 1960, $24,000,000 was spent by the two major parties. In 1964 this figure had risen to $37,500,000, and in 1968, Republicans and Democrats invested $100,000,000 in campaigning for the presidency. The presidential campaign in 1972 cost substantially more. White refers to this trend as pollution of the political process by money.[13] The only possibility of stemming the commercialization of campaigns seems to be legislation by Congress to limit campaign spending and, possibly, appropriate public funds to finance at least a portion of the cost of running for office.

A second trend in contemporary political campaigning is the increasing importance of the style and image of the candidate as a decisive factor in the campaign. Formerly, the contending parties were clearly differentiated on issues. The Democrats represented one approach to governance, the Republicans another, and a preference for party policy

[13] Theodore H. White, *The Making of the President 1972* (New York: Atheneum Publishers, 1973), p. xx.

frequently outweighed any responses to the person of the candidate. Now party position is unclear, Democrats and Republicans span the continuum from liberal to conservative, and the overall approaches of the two parties to the management of America are almost indistinguishable.

All the media, particularly television, focus attention on the private life and personality of the candidate. The voter, confused in his attempts to identify clear-cut issues that correspond to party lines, understandably turns to his perceptions of the character of the candidate as a basis for his choice. These perceptions are the products of second-hand experiences, that is, they are shaped by what writers choose to write and by what television directors, producers, and newscasters choose to put on the tube. Further, the ability of a candidate to appear at ease and competent on television gives him or her a great advantage over an able rival who appears awkward on camera. Largely through the media the style and image of a candidate as perceived by the public often represent fantasies and rhetorical visions rather than an accurate facsimile of that person in real life.

A third trend is rapidly increasing professionalization. The direction of this trend is summarized by Nimmo:

> Professional campaign management is a diversified industry involving individuals and firms, general personnel and technical specialists. Not all management personnel perform the same functions; indeed, some aspects of the industry are so specialized that a candidate may have to contract for the services of several individuals and agencies in order to obtain the variety of expertise necessary. For example, in waging an unsuccessful campaign for the U.S. Senate from Texas in 1966 against Republican John Tower, former Attorney General Waggoner Carr drew upon the services of a public relations man, an advertising agency, a person with responsibility to build local organizations, a finance chairman, a central office director, a campaign chairman, a pollster, press secretaries, and a staff of speech-writers. Such fragmented contracting is often unavoidable, but a number of firms now supply a full range of services.[14]

Since 1966 great strides have been made toward improving polling procedures, coordinating media and person-to-person appeals, and in using modern marketing techniques to sell candidates and programs. We might summarize this third trend by stating that the business of political campaigning is coming to resemble the commercial campaign. The possibility that the best financed candidate will usually, if not always, win an election is no longer remote.

[14] Dan Nimmo, *The Political Persuaders*, p. 38.

TELEVISION AND POLITICAL CAMPAIGNS. Because the impact of television on political campaigning is greater than that of the other media, we will consider its effects on the political process in this separate section. We will summarize the positive effects, the detrimental influences, and some suggested solutions for political problems posed by this potent medium.

Television brings politics to the people more comprehensively than ever before. It replaces the indoor or outdoor rally with livingroom contact. By using the fun theory and attempting to shift perceptions rather than change attitudes, it reaches disinterested persons and undecided voters better than other methods. It is speedy. A candidate can become known to large numbers of voters quickly. It produces more response than do other media. Because of its pervasive characteristics it makes possible shorter campaigns. Rubin recommends that total length of actual soliciting of votes in a national election be limited to six weeks of television exposure.[15]

Use of television increases confrontation of candidates, advances discussion of problems, and results in more fully developed issues. Both educational and commercial networks and stations do abundant background telecasting, supplying context helpful to the voter in interpreting other messages. Finally, television is impartial. The "fairness doctrine" of the Federal Communications Commission attempts to bring about equal time allotments to established political organizations, and to some extent this compensates for unequal financial resources.

Chief among the detrimental influences of television is the advantage enjoyed by the candidate with the most money. Closely related is the advantage it gives larger political parties over small political parties. Its use in local elections is limited because of expense, inadequate production facilities in local stations, and the networks claiming the telecasting time of local outlets.

Television is a "personality medium." A handsome face, a glib manner of speaking, and an attractive family divert attention from a candidate's fitness for office. TV tends to stress the human interest angle rather than to present all possible points of view. Many capable candidates are driven away from candidacy by the threatened invasion of their privacy by television. They prefer not to devote their time and energy to "mastering the art of TV." They understand that exposure on television builds a stereotyped and oversimplified version of their characters and the lives they lead.

News reporting on television concentrates on issues that build au-

15 Bernard Rubin, *Political Television* (Belmont, Calif.: Wadsworth Publishing Co., 1967), pp. 192, 193.

diences and often neglects unknown, new, and little-supported candidates. It influences elections by reporting results before the polls close. It distorts campaigning by highlighting key primaries (for example New Hampshire) with the result that their influence is increased far beyond the numbers of votes involved. And television has changed the nature of the national political convention, which is now directed to the national viewing audience rather than managed to select efficiently the best candidates to represent the party. Hidden advocacy is always a possibility in television coverage of an event, as in the selection of shots to be telecast from a political convention. Finally, television news is not generally suited for depth discussion of issues. Candidates and other spokesmen typically find themselves obliged to enunciate positions on complex issues in from fifteen to thirty seconds.

Solutions to the problems suggested by these detrimental influences become a top priority when we realize that television and politics have become inseparable. In Rubin's words, "for tens of millions of Americans, the television view *is* the campaign."[16] Certainly the following recommendations will not correct injustice and restore rationality to elections, but they might be significant improvements.

1. Legislation to limit campaign expenditures and provide financial aid to impecunious candidates may correct to some extent the present advantages of affluence.

2. Government regulation of the content of politically sponsored programs could safeguard against unethical and vicious practices.

3. Stations and networks might provide sustaining time, equitably allocated.

4. The networks, instead of competing in the coverage of conventions and other key political events, might cooperate in pooled coverage.

5. Legislation might limit the length of campaigns to four to six weeks, with no "head start" permitted.

6. Regulation will probably be necessary to ensure that no one candidate or party can, in effect, monopolize the television medium.

If our highly valued system of governing the United States through the process of competing persuasions is to continue to be effective, use of television in the political process must be improved. We urge our readers to give the matter their serious consideration.

---

[16] Ibid., p. 135.

Conclusion

In a world of rapidly growing communication it is inevitable that persuasion will increasingly occur in complex and extensive systems that affect great numbers of people over huge distances. We have identified these extended instances of persuasion as *campaigns*, which can be divided into two groups, those serving commercial ends and those for purposes of social action.

The means by which individual decision making is influenced by campaigns are the shifting of perceptions and attitude change. These methods represent contrasting strategies and techniques in the use of mass media. The mushrooming cost of political campaigns and the ever-increasing influence of television are important areas of concern to all students of persuasion.

This onrush of technological innovation can be expected to continue, and the role of campaigns in global persuasion is certain to increase. Both student and practitioner of persuasion, therefore, must seek an understanding of this complex human interaction.

Author Index

Subject Index